Anonymous

A cloud of witnesses for the royal prerogatives of Jesus Christ

1680

Anonymous

A cloud of witnesses for the royal prerogatives of Jesus Christ
1680

ISBN/EAN: 9783337270315

Printed in Europe, USA, Canada, Australia, Japan

Cover: Foto ©Lupo / pixelio.de

More available books at **www.hansebooks.com**

A

CLOUD of WITNESSES,
FOR THE
Royal Prerogatives
OF
JESUS CHRIST:
OR, THE LAST
SPEECHES and TESTIMONIES
Of thofe who have Suffered for the
TRUTH in SCOTLAND,
Since the Year 1680.

Together with
An APPENDIX, containing the *Queensferry* Paper;
Torwood Excommunication; a Relation concerning
Mr. RICHARD CAMERON, Mr. DONALD CARGIL,
and HENRY HALL; and an Account of thofe who
were killed without Procefs of Law, and banifhed to
foreign Lands: With a fhort View of fome of the
oppreffive Exactions.

Rev. vii. 14. *Thefe are they which came out of great tribulation, and have wafhed their robes, and made them white in the blood of the Lamb.*

The Ninth Edition, corrected, and enlarged with the Teftimonies of *John Nisbet* younger, *John Nisbet* of Hardhill, *Robert Miller, Thomas Harknefs*, &c. A Letter of *John Semple's*, and of *Archibald Stewart's*. The Paper found upon *Mr. Cameron* at *Airfmofs*, and an Acroftick upon his Name. The Teftimony of *John Finlay*, in *Kilmarnock*. The Epitaphs upon the Grave Stones of *Mr. Samuel Rutherford*, *Mr. John Welwood*, and the noble Patriots who fell at *Pentland*, &c.

GLASGOW:
Printed by WILLIAM BELL and Company.
For J. GILMOUR and SON, J. TAIT, Glafgow,
J. REID in Lanark. MDCCLXIX.

THE
PREFACE
TO THE
READER.

Chriſtian Reader,

THE glorious frame and contrivance of religion, revealed by the ever bleſſed JEHOVAH, in the face or perſon of Jeſus Chriſt, for the recovery of loſt mankind into a ſtate of favour and reconcilement with himſelf, is ſo excellently ordered in the councils of infinite wiſdom, and exactly adjuſted to the real delight, contentment and happineſs of the rational world; that it might juſtly be wondered, why ſo many men in all ages, otherwiſe of good intellectuals, have not only had a ſecret diſguſt thereat themſelves, but laboured to rob others of the comfort and benefit of it, and make the world a chaos of confuſion by perſecutions raiſed againſt it; had not the Holy Spirit in the Scriptures laid open the hidden ſprings of this malice and enmity, which exerts itſelf in ſo many of the children of men. We are told in theſe divinely inſpired writings, that the firſt ſource of this oppoſition that the true religion meets with in the world, flows originally from Satan, that inveterate enemy of God's glory, and man's happineſs; who having himſelf left his original ſtate of obedience to, and enjoyment of God his Creator, hath no other alleviament of his inevitable miſeries, but to draw the race of mankind into the like ruin, which is the only ſatisfaction that malicious ſpirit is capable of. This reſtleſs adverſary perceiving, that thro' the grace and love of God manifeſted in Chriſt, a great number of theſe whom he thought he had ſecured to his ſlavery, are redeemed, and called by the goſpel out of that intolerable ſervitude, into a glorious liberty, and ſecured by faith to ſalvation; la-

A 2

bours by two great engines of open force, and secret fraud, to keep them in, or regain them to his obedience : hence the sacred Scriptures describe him, both as a dragon for cruelty, and a serpent for subtilty. But because he either cannot, or thinks not fit to do this visibly in person ; therefore he does it more invisibly, and so more successfully by his agents, in whom he works : who, because of their unreasonable unbelief, are called, children of impersuasion. These he acts and animates, as it were so many machines, to endeavour by crafty seduction, or violent persecution, to draw, or drive the followers of the Lamb, from their subjection, obedience and loyalty to *the Captain of their salvation*, that he may drown them, in perdition and destruction. This is the latent origin of all persecution ; the mint where all the other more visible causes of the bloody violence the people of God meet withal, are struck and framed. This is the grand design to which they tend, to root out the obedience of faith out of the world, and deprive the Son of God of his rightful dominion over his subjects, whom he hath chosen, redeemed and sanctified for himself.

As this holds true of all the persecutions raised against the church and truths of God, whether in the persons of Jews or Christians, by whatever hands, Pagan or Antichristian, so 'tis eminently verified of the persecutions of the Church of Scotland, prosecuted by a profane wicked generation of malignant prelatists, during the reigns of the late King Charles II. and James VII. For as the other persecutions were all levelled against some point of truth, or other, wherein the obedience of faith was concerned, respecting either the existence and worship of the true God, or the person, natures or offices of Jesus Christ, &c. so this persecution was directly bended against that office and authority of Jesus Christ, whereupon his formal claim to the obedience of his church is founded, viz. *his headship over his church*. This was the peculiar depositum concredited to the church of Christ in Scotland, and her distinguishing dignity to have the royal supremacy of the king of Zion to defend against the kings of the earth, who not content with the princely authority of ruling the persons of their subjects, according to the laws of God and the realm, would needs usurp a blasphemous sacrilegious prerogative of ruling the church and consciences of men in room of the mediator, by what laws and sta-

The Preface to the Reader.

tutes they pleafed, and found moſt ſubſervient to their luſts, for advancement of Popery and arbitrary government.

Jeſus Chriſt, *the only begotten of the Father*, having received the church of Scotland, as one of the utmoſt iſles of the earth for his poſſeſſion, by ſolemn grant from Jehovah, was pleaſed, as to call her from the deplorable ſtate of Pagan, and reform her from the ruinous condition of Antichriſtian darkneſs; ſo to dignify her in a peculiar manner, to contend and ſuffer for that truth, *That he is king and lawgiver to his church*, having power to inſtitute her form of government, to give her laws, officers and cenſures, whereby ſhe ſhould be governed, and hath not left it ambulatory and uncertain, what government he will have in force for the ordering of his houſe, but hath expreſly determined in his word every neceſſary part thereof, and hath not put any power into the hands of any mortal, whether Pope, Prelate, Prince or Potentate, as a vicarious head in his perſonal abſence, whereby they may alter the form of government at their pleaſure, and make what kind of officers, canons and cenſures they pleaſe; but all the power that this king hath left in his church, concerning her government, is purely and properly miniſterial, under the direction and regulation of his ſovereign pleaſure, revealed in his written word.

This, this is the moſt radiant pearl in the church of Scotland's garland; that ſhe hath been honoured valiantly to ſtand up for the headſhip and royal prerogative of her king and huſband, Jeſus Chriſt, in all the periods of her reformation. For no ſooner had ſhe thrown off the yoke of the Pope's pretended juriſdiction and authority, but preſently, while ſhe was labouring by means of theſe cenſures, that Chriſt had inſtitute, to root out the damnable hereſies which that enemy had ſown, all on a ſudden king James VI. naturally ambitious, and inſtigate by intereſted and projecting counſellors, attempts a rape upon her chaſtity and loyalty to her huſband and Lord; and by his royal order ſtops her freedom of ſitting, voting and acting in her ſupreme courts, impriſons ſome of her moſt zealous and faithful miniſters, calls them before his council, indicts them of treaſon and leeſe majeſty, for their making uſe of the freedom Chriſt hath given them; and after their declining his and his council's uſurped authority in ſpiritual matters, and ſo witneſſing a good confession for the royal dignity of their Master, banish them their native country *. Upon the same bottom of a pretended royal jurisdiction over the church, he attempted, and in a great measure effected, the establishment of Popish hierarchy, and Romish ceremonies, by setting up prelates, and bringing in the Perth Articles, flattering some, and over-awing others of the ministers into a compliance therewith; persecuting the zealous and faithful contenders for Christ's headship, and the government of his divine institution, with vexatious prosecutions before high-commission courts, suspensions from their office, wardings, confinements, &c. And in like manner Charles I. following his father's example and instructions, endeavoured, upon pretence of the same prerogative, to improve upon what his father had begun, and complete the church's slavery by obtruding upon her a liturgy and canons, formed *a la mode d'Angleterre*, collected out of the Romish Mass-book, and canon law; which put the faithful sons of the church of Scotland to much wrestling and contending, partly by humble and submissive, yet zealous and faithful addresses, supplications, remonstrances and representations; partly by more bold and daring protestations and associations for mutual defence, even till they were forced to take arms for defence of religion, and the liberties of their country. Which contendings for Christ's royal authority, and his church's liberties, at length, by the blessing of God, issued in a glorious work of reformation, thro' Britain and Ireland, wherein the churches of Christ in these lands, not only received their former beautiful order, shining purity, and precious liberty, but also had several degrees of new attainments, in purity and uniformity in religion, added thereunto.

But the church's sun of prosperity is soon at the tropick: scarce was that spring-time well begun to blossom and bud, when behold a world of malignant vapours, arising out of the earth, clouded all her sky again, and turned her spring to a deplorable winter. Various heresies in England, growing Popery in Ireland, public resolutions for advancing malignants to places of power and trust in Scotland, like so many inundations breaking in upon the church of Christ, laid all her pleasant things waste. And no sooner was Charles II. advanced to the

* See *Calderwood*'s Hist. from p. 491, to p. 536, and downward.

exercife of the royal authority, but, drowning the fenfe of all facred obligations with a glut of fenfual pleafures, he authorized a malignant crew of ftatefemen to perfecute and deftroy the people of God, for their adherence to the covenants, which himfelf had entered into as the fundamental ftipulation of government, and to that reformation which he had fworn to maintain and practife: and for their bearing witnefs againft the grand principle and foundation upon which he built his power of overthrowing religion, and fetting up a new frame thereof in Britain, namely the blafphemous headfhip of ecclefiaftical fupremacy.

Hence it is evident to a demonftration, that the grand ftate of the quarrel, upon which the martyrs laid down their lives during the late tyrannical reigns, was really one and the fame with that for which the zealous and faithful minifters fuffered fuch hardfhips in the time of King James VI. and afterwards. This being the precife foundation upon which all the other acts and oaths were built, which the enemies made a handle of, to involve honeft people into the crime of treafon and rebellion againft the ftate, as it was then determined by their iniquitous laws. For as it was ftill the principal queftion put to them, *Own ye the King's authority?* and the chief article of their indictment, if they either anfwered in the negative or kept filence; fo it is evident, that by this queftion they really meant, not his civil authority only, but alfo his pretended claim to fupreme headfhip over the church. For no fooner had he authorized a parliament to meet at Edinburgh, under the infpection of that malignant wretch, John Earl of Middleton, anno 1661, but that generation of enemies to the work of God, intending the utter ruin thereof, fet up this Dagon of the royal prerogative, not only with refpect to things civil, as in the choice of his officers of ftate, councellors and judges, *Act fecond;* in the calling and diffolving of parliaments, and making laws, *Act third;* in the militia, and making peace and war, *Act fifth,* which were great invafions upon the national liberties of the fubjects; but alfo in things facred, in the making of leagues, and the conventions of the fubjects, *Act fixth;* wherein all the former work of reformation is condemned, and the Covenants made for its defence are declared treafonable and rebellious actions againft the royal prerogative: And in confequence hereof, it is declared, *Act seventh*, " That the League and Covenant is not obligatory upon this kingdom, nor doth infer any obligation on the subjects thereof, to meddle or interpose in any thing concerning the religion and government of the churches of England and Ireland; and all the subjects are discharged to renew the same, as they will answer at their highest peril." And in the oath of allegiance and acknowlegement of his majesty's royal prerogative, statute by the eleventh act of said parliament, all persons of whatsoever trust, post, office or employment, are obliged to swear, " That they acknowledge the king only supreme governor of this kingdom, over all persons, and in all causes. And that they do with all humble duty acknowledge his majesty's royal prerogative, in all the particulars, and in the manner aforementioned.

And to make the matter clearer, what they meant by the king's authority, in the preamble of the first act of the second session of the same first parliament, they assert, " That the ordering and disposal of the external government and policy of his church, doth properly belong unto his majesty, as an inherent right of the crown, by virtue of his royal prerogative and supremacy in causes ecclesiastical." And upon this bottom, he, with advice and consent of the estates of parliament, sets up the Episcopal form of church-government, the jurisdiction of bishops and archbishops over the inferior clergy, with their concomitant of patronages; and " Rescinds, casses and annuls all acts of parliament, by which the sole and only power and jurisdiction within this church, doth stand in the church, and in the general, provincial and presbyterial assemblies, and kirk sessions; and all acts of parliament or council, which may be interpreted to have given any church power, jurisdiction or government to the office bearers of the church, their respective meetings, other than that which acknowlegeth a dependance upon, and subordination to, the sovereign power of the king as supreme." And in pursuance hereof, in the second act of the foresaid second session, intituled, Act for preservation of his majesty's person, authority and government, he doth, with advice of his estates of parliament, declare, " That the assembly kept at Glasgow in the year 1638, was in itself (after the same was by his majesty discharged under the pain of treason) an unlawful and seditious

The Preface to the Reader. 9

meeting: And that all thefe gatherings, convocations, petitions, proteftations, and erecting and keeping council tables, that were ufed in the beginning, and for carrying on the late troubles, (thus they call the work of reformation) were unlawful and feditious; and that thefe oaths, whereof the one was commonly called The National Covenant, and the other A Solemn League and Covenant, were and are in themfelves unlawful oaths; and therefore declares their obligation void and null, and refcinds all acts or conftitutions, ecclefiaftical or civil, approving them." Nor does it fuffice them to refcind thefe Covenants, and other proceedings for carrying on the work of reformation, as contrary to his royal prerogative of ecclefiaftic fupremacy; and to inhibit all perfons to fpeak, write or act any thing in defence of the fame, and againft the fame prerogative; but likewife in the fifth act of the forefaid feffion, all perfons in any place, office or truft, are obliged to fwear all the particulars contained in the forefaid acts, in that moft impious oath, commonly called, The Declaration. And again in the fourth act of the third feffion of the forefaid parliament, intituled, Act for eftablifhment and conftitution of a national fynod, it is declared, " That the ordering and difpofal of the external government of the church, and the nomination of the perfons, by whofe advice matters relating to the fame are to be fettled, doth belong to his majefty, as an inherent right of the crown, by virtue of his prerogative royal, and fupreme authority in caufes ecclefiaftical." And in the firft act of the fecond parliament, holden by that apoftate, John earl of Lauderdale, intituled, Act afferting his majefty's fupremacy over all perfons, and in all caufes ecclefiaftical, commonly called, The Act Explanatory, it is exprefly declared, " That his majefty hath the fupreme authority and fupremacy over all perfons, and in all caufes ecclefiaftical within this kingdom; and that by virtue thereof, the ordering and difpofal of the external government and policy of the church, doth properly belong to his majefty and his fucceffors, as an Inherent Right to the crown: and that his majefty and his fucceffors may fettle, enact and emit fuch conftitutions, acts and orders, concerning the adminiftration of the external government of the church, and the perfons employed in the fame, and concerning all ecclefiaftic meetings, and matters to be proposed and determined therein, as they in their royal wisdom shall think fit."

From all which acts it plainly appears, that the true sense of that authority, which they would have their private thoughts about was really, as the martyrs understood it, his ecclesiastic supremacy, and that no less than a recognition hereof would serve their turn: and tho' some of the martyrs offered a distinction between the two, professing to own his civil authority abstract from the ecclesiastical, (as, for instance, Mr. John Dick) yet they were not absolved, because they would not own his authority in grofs. And besides, their including the supremacy over church matters, into the formal notion of the king's authority, they could be pleased with no less from any that they called before them, than an owning the whole acts and laws, and entire exercise and administration of things in church and state, which was an implicite condemning of all the preceeding reformation, and consenting to the persecution and murder of the saints, who stood up for its defence.

It is true indeed, these things were so impious and abominable, that had they been proposed without mask, they would presently begot an horror in the mind of any, who was not entirely lost to all conscience and goodness; and therefore these children of the old serpent had so much of their father, that they made it their work to hide these horrid hooks with some specious baits, that they might the more easily entice simple people into that snare they had laid for them: and hence, knowing how much it is the effect of true religion to make men loyal, and that the Presbyterians were of all others the readiest to yield all lawful subjection to their rightful princes, they still made use of the specious title of authority as a blind to hide the ecclesiastical supremacy, and bloody exercise of their government, from these they laboured to ensnare. They saw the supremacy they intended to fix in the king, was such a *monstrum horrendum, informe, ingens, Heccate atque Erebo ortum*, that without some vail of this nature, no man would be so mad as to embrace it. But when this would not do, but that still its ill-favoured face appears thro' the vizard; and all good men saw, that that authority which sought no other way to maintain itself, but by blood and rapine, was really degenerated into tyranny, then they pretended to come

The Preface to the Reader.

some steps lower, and said, That they required no more at the hands of the people in order to difmifs them, but that they would at their defire pray for the king, in their prefcribed form of words, viz. God fave the king; or that they would drink the king's good health. Thofe were by them reprefented to be fo minute and eafy things, and by a great many profeffors looked upon as fo trivial and indifferent, that they were in the fair way either to enfnare, or with more opportunity to expofe fuch as refufed to the contempt of indifferent fpectators, as being fuch fcrupulous fools, and brain-fick perfons, as were tranfported with an extravagant wild zeal without knowledge, who had rather have a hand in their own death, than do fo fmall and indifferent a thing in order to prevent it. And hence not the perfecutors only, but even a great many who profeffed prefbyterian principles, ftood not to call them murderers, inftead of martyrs.

But all this notwithftanding, it is certain they had nothing elfe before them, but to bring people to a tame fubmiffion and flavifh compliance with the whole courfe of their Chrift-dethroning, and land-enflaving conftitutions and adminiftrations; for they intended the fame thing by urging people to fay, God fave the king, as by the Oath of Allegiance, Declaration, or Teft; namely, an acknowledgment of their authority, wherewith they had vefted him in the forementioned articles, and others of like nature. Lefs than this could never ferve their defign, which was ftill the fame, whatever alterations might appear to be in their way of profecuting it: for either thefe things were fo infignificant and indifferent as they gave them out to be, and as others conceived of them, or they were not; if we fay the former, then what monfters of mankind were thefe perfecutors, who purfued poor innocent people to death, and inflicted fuch cruel tortures upon them for trifles and things of indifferency. This is what themfelves (I fuppofe) would never admit, to be reckoned a degree further loft to humanity than a Nero or Caligula, fo as to torment and deftroy men for fport: nay, they ftill pretended, that all thefe perfecutions were made upon weighty and juft caufes. If then we fay the latter, namely, That they were not fo very inconfiderable things as fome conceived, wherein could the moment and weight of them confift, but in this, That they were in owning of the authority, as it was contained in the laws? And what else was the scope of the most openly impious oaths, tests, and bonds, but this? And besides, when any yielded this much, they were still urged further, till they had debauched them out of all conscience and integrity, as much as themselves.

The rest of the questions put to them, and made causes of their indictment, were all but so many branches from this root, and rivulets from this spring. The chief was that about defensive arms, which their laws had declared rebellion; which all the martyrs, without the least jar or discord, did stedfastly maintain, as being a thing so very consonant, not only to the positive commands of God in his word, but also to the very law of nature stamped on the heart, and to the laws and practices of all kingdoms; and undertaken upon so necessary grounds, as the defence of the gospel, and the lives of the innocent, in consequence of their covenant engagements; which, however these wicked persecutors had declared void and null, and the adhering to them capital, yet all such as had any love to God, and zeal for his cause, believed to be perpetually obligatory upon them and the nation, and therefore adhered to them with a stedfastness, and courage invincible, against the most bloody opposition. And it is observeable, that whatever any of the martyrs had not so much light in as others, or differed from others anent, or was silent when interrogate upon it, yet they all agreed perfectly, and were clear abundantly in owning, and bold, harmonious, and couragious in asserting the lawfulness, and avouching the obligatory force of the Covenants. National covenants were the means that God had constantly from the beginning of the reformation made use of, and blessed, to cement and strengthen his people in Scotland, in their adherence to the truth; of these his church was as a strong city and incorporation, prosecuting all the same common cause of religion and liberty, so by that common bond, the injury offered to any one of her members, was taken as done to all. And beside the express commands of the word, this was a blessed tye and engagement, to every one in their place and station, to stand up for the purity of the doctrine, simplicity of the worship, beauty and order of the government and discipline of Christ's house, and his royal supremacy over the same. And hence malignant and disaffected persons perceiving that there was

The Preface to the Reader.

nothing fo conducive to the advancement and prefervation of national reformation, as thefe mutual bonds and facred covenants, fet themfelves chiefly to deftroy thefe; and in an ignominious manner burnt them; declared them treafonable and feditious, made the owning of them criminal, and perfecuted fuch as adhered to them : And on the other hand, God was pleafed mightily to animate his fuffering faints, both with light and zeal, in the defence of them, againft all the efforts of hellifh violence.

Wherefore, when this alone was not like to effectuate their defigns, thefe perfecutors betook themfelves to another ftratagem, and fell upon more mild, but more fuccefsful meafures, of giving out indemnities and indulgencies, fo reftricted and limited, as the accepters fhould be gained to a peaceable compliance with, and fubmiffion to their impious laws; aud taken off from their zeal in maintaining the work of reformation, and divided from their covenanted brethren : By this means they weakened the remnant that had not complied with Prelacy, fet them at variance one againft another, allured the one to fit quietly ftill, till they had made an end of their brethren ; and, in fhort, rent and almoft quite ruined the poor Prefbyterian church of Scotland. And hence, as the fuffering remnant, which was by far the fmaller part, were much oppofed and reproached by thefe minifters and profeffors, who accepted of thefe pretended favours, fo it became a neceffary head of teftimony, to witnefs againft the Indulgence and acceptance thereof, or finful connivance thereat. The particular difquifition of this affair is not confiftent with the narrow limits of a preface. Wherefore the reader may fee, for his fatisfaction therein, *The Hiftory of the Indulgence, Informatory Vindication, Hind let loofe,* &c.

Afterwards when the perfecution became fore and violent againft the remnant that refufed thefe deceitful baits, and ftood to their covenanted religion and liberty, and that both by the open violence of the enemies, and falfe flanders and calumnies of pretended friends, they were obliged to emit feveral declarations of their principles, and to defend themfelves from thefe unjuft flanders and calumnies: which declarations, fo foon as the perfecutors got into their hands, thinking they had got a good handle therein, for taking away the lives of all fuch as fhould adhere to them, in regard that therein they had more explicitely and fully caſt off the authority of the tyrant Charles II. and ſpecified the reaſons why they could not own his authority, they never failed on all occaſions, to make that a part of their examinations, Own ye the Sanquhar declaration, the papers found at the Queensferry? &c. and many were indicted upon their adherence to theſe declarations, and other papers. I conceive it is not neceſſary to ſwell this preface with a particular defence of theſe declarations, that being ſo well done by themſelves in the Informatory Vindication, which the reader may have recourſe to: And as to the paper found upon Mr. Hall of Haugh-head, when he was murdered at Queensferry, the reader ſhall ſee it, with a ſhort relation concerning that worthy gentleman's death, in the appendix to this book.

Another queſtion commonly put to ſufferers was, Whether they owned the excommunication at the Torwood? Which they did with much freedom, as a neceſſary duty and lawfully performed, ſo far as that broken ſtate of the church would permit, and upon moſt weighty and ſufficient grounds. The form and order of which excommunication is alſo added by way of appendix to this book.

But their fineſt topick, wherein they inſulted and gloried moſt, was the death of James Sharp archbiſhop of St. Andrews, which they reckoned a cruel murder, and therefore hoped, that if the ſufferers ſhould approve of the ſame, they would have a colour to deſtroy them, as men of aſſaſſinating and bloody principles, deſerving to be exterminate out of any well governed common-wealth; and therefore it was ſtill one of their queſtions, Was the biſhop's death murder: To which queſtion ſome anſwered directly, That it was a juſt and lawful execution of God's law upon him, for his perjurious treachery, and bloody cruelty; others were ſilent, or refuſed to anſwer any thing directly to the point, as conceiving that it being no deed of theirs, they were not obliged by any law divine or human, to give their judgment thereupon, eſpecially when they could not exactly know the circumſtances of the matter of fact, and ſaw that the queſtion was propoſed with a deſign to enſnare them, or take away their life: yet was their very ſilence or refuſal to give their opinion, made a cauſe of their indictment, and

The Preface to the Reader. 15

ground of their sentence, and some were put to torture to make them give their sentiments anent it. If any would be further satisfied on this head, let him see *Hind let loose*, head VI. p. 633.

But however these murderers of the servants and people of God, made use of such questions as these to entangle them, yet still the grand state of the quarrel was, "Whether Christ alone, or king Charles, should be owned as head and lawgiver to the church? And, Whether the divine form of government and discipline, which Christ had institute, should continue in her, or if an usurper should have leave to mould it as he pleased, and conform it to the pompous dress of the Romish whore?"

And hence it is also evident that the state of the sufferings before the engagement at Bothwel, was really one and the same with that which was after it, as to the main, though things came to be clearer after it, concerning the civil authority, when by that and many other instances, it was made evident, that the pretended rulers were setting themselves directly to ruin the whole interests of the subjects, as well civil as sacred; and that it was in vain to be any longer in suspense, waiting for a satisfactory redress of grievances, or opportunity to represent the same. So that the charge of rebellion laid against them, not only by our episcopal passive-obedience men, but also by the indulged, and such as tread their steps, is a most groundless imputation; for king Charles had violate all the conditions of government, and manifestly degenerate into a tyrant, long before they rejected his authority, and had refused all claim to the subjects allegiance, upon account of the contract which he entered into at his coronation, and had no pretence to authority but hereditary right and bloody force, with the consent of such profligate noblemen and gentlemen as sat in these packed and pretended parliaments, which could never, in law or reason, oblige the honest and faithful subjects of the kingdom to comply with these tyrannical courses, and submit to him, who had as really forfeited his right to be king of Britain, as did his brother afterwards by his abdication.

But it is no new thing for the followers of Christ to meet with this charge of rebellion, if a Jezebel wants a Naboth's vineyard, and he stands up for his property, she will not want sons of Belial to bear witness, That he

B 2

blasphemed God and the king. Do the adversaries of Judah and Benjamin intend to stop the building of Jerusalem, they'll not want a Rehum the chancellor, and Shimshai the scribe, to write, " That this city is a rebellious city, and hurtful unto kings and provinces, and that they have moved sedition within the same of old time." Would Haman have all the Jews destroyed, because Mordecai will not honour him, this is the charge he lays against them, as most likely to effectuate his purpose, " That their laws are diverse from all people, neither keep they the king's laws." Have the presidents a purpose to be rid of Daniel, this is the engine, " That Daniel, who is of the children of the captivity of Judah, regardeth not thee, O King! nor the decree that thou hast signed." Is a Tertullus to employ his eloquence against Paul, here's the artifice, " We have found this man a pestilent fellow, and a mover of sedition among the Jews." Were the Romans desirous to have the Christians exterminated out of the empire, what shift took they! why, truly, this was it, " The Christians are rebellious and seditious; they wont swear by the life of Cæsar, nor adore his image; and therefore *Christianos ad leones*." If we look through the whole ecclesiastic history, we shall scarce find a persecution raised, but this is an article of the charge. But it is no paradox, " The servant is not greater than his Lord;" even Christ himself was accused and condemned as an enemy to Cæsar, and a mover of sedition. But I shall not enter into this argument; the sufferers for Christ in Scotland have been frequently vindicated from the charge of rebellion, by more learned pens, and yet still we have a generation of absurd men, who will not fail to renew it; nor can the strength of argument silence them, while they have brow enough to return railing in the room of reason.

 The reader having thus briefly seen the causes, upon which they laid down their lives; it were necessary to proceed to a short delineation, both of the cruelty of the persecutors inflicting, and of the courage, patience and chearfulness of the martyrs, suffering these severities; but as for the former, what tongue can express, what pen can describe the barbarous cruelty, and hellish rage of the sons of wickedness? One might write a volume upon their cruelties, and after all fall far short of drawing them to the life, or giving any just idea of them, they were so

The Preface to the Reader.

extremely inhumane and brutish. At first, they began with noblemen, gentlemen and ministers, who had been eminent for the cause of God; beheading some, and placing their heads upon the ports of Edinburgh, in token of the highest contempt, banishing others, ejecting all from their charges, but such as would subject to Prelacy, and the blasphemous supremacy; and vitiating all the springs and seminaries of learning: Next, they fell to compel the common people to hear curates, by vast and exorbitant fines, extorted by troops of soldiers, plundering, quartering, beating, wounding, binding men like beasts, chasing them away from their houses, compelling them, though sick, to go to church, consuming and wasting their provision with dogs, and promiscuously abusing, as well those that conformed, as them that refused: and if any testified their resentment at these vermin of ignorant and scandalous curates, or refused to give them their titles, they were imprisoned, scourged, stigmatized, and banished to Barbadoes, or other foreign parts. Any that were hearing their own ministers in private houses, were seized, dragged to prisons, and close kept there in great hardship, and that of every age and sex.

These were their tender mercies, and but the beginnings of sorrow: for after the defeat at Pentland-hills, beside what were killed upon the spot, such as surrendered upon quarter and solemn parole to have their life, were, contrary to the law of nature and nations, treacherously and bloodily murdered, to the number of forty; one of them, a much reverenced young minister, had his leg squeezed to pieces in the boots, and was afterwards hanged, tho' he was not in the fight, but had only a sword about him.

Soldiers were ordered to take free quarters in the country, to examine men by tortures, to compel women and children to discover their husbands and fathers, by threatening death, wounding, stripping, torturing by fire matches, &c. crouding into prisons so thick, that they could scarce stand together, in cold, hunger, and nakedness; and all this, because they would not, or could not discover who were at that expedition.- Likewise many ensnaring bonds, oaths and tests were framed, and imposed with rigour and horrid severity; people obliged to have passes declaring they had taken them, or to swear before common soldiers, under pain of being presently shot dead. Severe laws were made against ministers, that came to Edinburgh for shelter, they and their wives were searched for, by public search, crouded into prisons, sent to foreign plantations to be sold as slaves. Dragoons were sent to pursue people that attended field preachings, to search them out in mosses, moors, mountains and dens of the earth. Savage hosts of Highlanders were sent down to depopulate the western shires, to the number of ten or eleven thousand, who acted most outrageous barbarities, even almost to the laying some countries desolate.

After the overthrow of the Lord's people at Bothwel, they doubled these severities, issued out more soldiers, imposed cess, localities, and other new exactions; forced people to swear *superinquirendis*, and delate upon oath all that went to field preachings, set up extraordinary circuit courts, enlarged their Porteous rolls, pressed bonds of compearance to keep the peace, to attend the church, refrain from field meetings, &c. examining country people upon several questions which they had no occasion to understand, as concerning the death of King Charles I. and the archbishop of St. Andrews, and condemning them to death for not answering; quartering some alive, cropping their ears, cutting off the hands of some, and then hanging them, cutting their bodies in pieces after they were dead, and fixing them upon poles in chains, and upon steeples and ports of cities, beating drums at their executions, that they might not be heard speak, detaining others long in prison, loaden with chains and fetters of iron, and exposed to greater tortures than death itself, and after all sent to be sold as slaves, to empty the prisons, exercising all these bloody deaths and cruelties upon poor country people, which had no influence to do hurt to their government, though they had been willing; yea, upon women of tender age, whom they hanged and drowned, for refusing their oaths and bonds, and resetting the Lord's suffering people.

It would be endless to enumerate all their barbarities, exercised upon particular persons, only for a swatch, take these inflicted on that excellent gentleman David Hackston of Rathillet. He was taken out from the place of judgment to his execution, and his body, which was already wounded, was tortured while he was alive, by the cutting off both his hands, which was done upon a

The Preface to the Reader.

high fcaffold prepared for the purpofe; thereafter being drawn up by a pulley to the top of the high gallows, by the rope which was about his neck, and fuffered to fall down a very confiderable way upon the lower fcaffold three times, with his whole weight; then he was fixed at the top of the gallows, and the executioner with a big knife cutting open his breaft, pulled out his heart, while he was yet alive, as appeared both by the body's contracting itfelf, when it was pulled out, and by the violent motion of the heart when it dropt upon the fcaffold, which the executioner taking up upon the knife, fhewed it to the people upon the feveral corners of the ftage, crying, *Here is the heart of a traitor*, and then threw it in a fire prepared for the purpofe upon the ftage, together alfo with his other inwards and noble parts; and having quartered his body, fixed his head and hands on a port at Edinburgh, and the other quarters at Leith, Coupar of Fife, and other places: Such was the fize and proportion of their perfecutions, while yet they pretended to bring them to the knowledge of affizes and colour of law.

But being now weary with thefe perfecutions, according to the tenor of their own laws; The counfellors to rid themfelves of this trouble, gave out an edict for killing them, wherever they might be found, immediately upon the fpot, unlefs they would take the oaths, and fhew their pafs, which they behoved to fwear, that it was not forged; and if they found any arms or ammunition upon them of any fort: By means of which edict, many were fuddenly furprized and fhot dead, by the brutifh and mercilefs foldiers, who were either peaceably living at home, following their lawful employments, or wandering in mountains, to hide themfelves from their bloody enemies, not being allowed time to recommend their fouls to God; and the country was engaged by oath to raife the hue and cry againft them, in order to deliver them up to the hands of thefe burriors. The chief contrivers and framers of this horrid murdering edict, were the earl of Perth chancellor, duke of Queenfberry, marquis of Athol, and particularly the vifcount of Tarbet, now earl of Cromarty, who invented this murdering device, wherein yet he carried fo cunningly, that he procured the act of the difpatch to the king with fuch fuddennefs, that he found a way to fhift his own fubfcribing it; and though he wants power now to practife fuch bloody mifchief, yet it is evident, he has not repented thereof, but is, as yet a contriver of the prefent encroachments made upon the eftablifhed church, by the late mifchievous acts of parliament.

But I muft not launch any further into the relation of thefe cruelties, the true hiftory of which would commence into a volume. I own indeed, that a fuller narration of thefe things, with pertinent obfervations thereupon, would have been proper enough for the intended work; but hoping, that the Lord may yet raife up fome of better abilities for fuch an undertaking, to fet thefe fufferings in a true light, and give an impartial recital thereof; this fhort hint, together with fome account of thefe cold blood murderers, in the appendix, may fuffice at prefent.

Let us next view a little, with fome attention and concern, with what undaunted courage, holy refolution, and greatnefs of mind; with what unfhaken ftedfaftnefs and conftancy thofe worthy fufferers underwent all thefe bloody feverities. Thofe difciples of Jefus had been fo trained up in his fchool, and learned the great Chriftian doctrines of bearing the crofs, mortifying the flefh, and contemning the world; they had been fo throughly inftructed by the great Mafter of affemblies, who teaches to profit, *and leads the blind in a way they know not,* to difcern the precioufnefs of truth, and excellency of the knowledge of Chrift, that they were made willing, yea, chearfully willing to forego riches, honours, pleafures, liberty, and life itfelf, when they came in competition with a fteady adherence to the truth, and honour of their lovely Lord. Love to Jefus Chrift was the great fpring which fet all the wheels of their affections in motion, to do and fuffer for him, whatever he called them to. Every one of them could fay to their perfecutors, what Chryfoftom faid to the emprefs Eudoxia, who fent him a threatning meffage, *Nil nifi peccatum timeo,* I fear nothing but fin. They faw fo much of the evil of fin, and beauty of holinefs, that they would rather undergo the fevereft of fuffering than ftain their confciences with the leaft fin, or lofe the fmalleft filing of this fine gold of truth. Many of the things for which they fuffered, were reckoned fmall by the indifferent world, but to them they appeared in their juft magnitude. Tertullian in his book,

The Preface to the Reader.

de corona militis, tells us, That when a certain Chriſtian ſoldier, in the emperor's army, refuſed to wear a crown of bays upon his head, as all the reſt of the ſoldiers did, upon a day ſacred to one of the heathen idols, he was not only mocked at by the infidels for his nicety, but even by many of the Chriſtians, conceiving it a folly that this one man, for ſuch a ſmall and indifferent thing, ſhould endanger both himſelf and other Chriſtians; but Tertullian defends him, and ſays, " This ſoldier was more God's ſoldier, and more conſtant than the reſt of his brethren, who preſumed they might ſerve two lords, and for avoiding perſecution, comply with the Heathens in their ſuperſtitious rites." And when ſome Chriſtians, who, like our indulged people, would rather comply, than endure the hazard, objected, " Where is it written in all the word of God, that we ſhould not wear bays upon our heads?" Tertullian anſwers, " Where is it written that we may do it? We muſt look into the ſcriptures, to ſee what we may do; and not think it enough, that the ſcripture doth not forbid directly this, or that very particular." They knew, with the ſame Tertullian, in the forecited book, " That the ſtate of Chriſtianity doth not admit the excuſe of neceſſity; There is no neceſſity of ſinning to them, to whom it is only neceſſary not to ſin." And hence they would not ſo much as ſeem to call in queſtion any of the truths of Chriſt: when the enemies would have given them time to deliberate and adviſe anent them, they were ſo confirmed in the preſent truth, that they anſwered their adverſaries, as Cyprian once did his, *In materia tam juſta non eſt deliberandum,* in ſo juſt a cauſe there needs no deliberation. When they were urged with the example of other Preſbyterians, miniſters and profeſſors, who had complied and were far wiſer and better than they; this did not ſhake them, but rather heighten their zeal. As Chryſoſtom tells us, theſe two holy martyrs, Juventius and Maximus, when they were urged by their perſecutors with this argument, Do not ye ſee others of your rank do this? anſwered, For this very reaſon we will manfully ſtand and offer ourſelves as a ſacrifice for the breach that they have made. So the ſad defections of their brethren made them the more emulous to witneſs for Chriſt, when ſo many Demas like had forſaken him, having loved this preſent world.

These martyrs had such large discoveries of Christ's love, especially under the cross, that their hardest trials were accounted light. As Stephen the proto-martyr got the fullest views of Christ, while before the council, so these had most lively sights of him under the sharpest sufferings; and hence they could not find in their heart to deny so kind a master. As Polycarp that holy minister of Christ, at Smyrna, answered the proconsul, bidding him defy Christ, and he would be discharged, " Fourscore and six years, says he, have I been his servant, yet all this time he hath not so much as once beat me, how then may I speak evil of my king and sovereign, who hath thus preserved me?" They were under a lively sense of their vows and obligations to Christ, personal and national, and therefore durst not, could not deny his name, nor break his bonds, and cast away his cords, as the wicked hath done; they were of the resolute disposition of Victorianus, who being solicited by the emperor to turn Arian, told him, " You may try all extremities, torture me, expose me to wild beasts, burn me to ashes, I had rather suffer any thing, than falsify my promise made to Christ my Saviour in baptism." And as Christ had been very kind to them, so they trusted much to him, and depended on him for strengthning influence, being very sensible of their own weakness; and they durst promise much on Christ's head; they could say as Vincentius to the tyrant Darius, " Rage and do the utmost, that the spirit of malignity can set you on work to do: You shall see God's Spirit strengthen the tormented more than the devil can do the tormentors." And as Zuinglius to the Bishop of Constance, " Truth is a thing invincible, and cannot be resisted."

As they were well instructed in the necessity, so in the usefulness and benefit of the cross; they knew, that as the church and nation had deserved to be chastened and punished of God, so it was far more eligible to be chastened by sore adversities, inflicted by a loving father, than by severe impunities of an incensed and just judge. They knew that the grief they suffered, was medicinal, not penal; the correction of a father, not the indignation of an enemy: and that they needed such merciful files and furnaces of adversity, to scour off the rust they had contracted in prosperity. Nay, they were not only content to undergo these fatherly corrections, but accounted it a

The Preface to the Reader.

singular kindness and condescension, that what they deserved should be their punishment, was made their glory, crown and honour; that they who had merited to be scattered into corners, and have their remembrance made to cease from among men, for their lightly prizing the precious and glorious gospel, should be gathered into such a cloud of witnesses; and have their remembrance made everlasting, as honoured martyrs for Christ, and the defence of the gospel; that when they had provoked God, by their sinful lusting after a malignant to be their king, they should be dignified, to contend for the kingly prerogatives of such a glorious and good sovereign, as the King of kings. And as they had a good understanding in the doctrine of the cross, so likewise in the promise of the crown, that is upon the back of the cross; they had their eyes at the recompence of reward, and therefore endured, because by faith they saw him who is invisible. It was their looking unto Jesus, who endured the contradiction of sinners against himself, that made them bear all these reproaches, slanders, scoffs and jeers of enemies and professed friends, with such invincible patience.

Thou hast here, Christian Reader, the dying speeches of some of these noble heroes; and as the speeches of dying men are remarkable, the speeches of dying Christians more remarkable, how remarkable must the speeches of dying witnesses for Christ be? It is reasonably expected, that dying men, much more dying Christians, and most of all, dying martyrs, should speak best at last. They are immediately to give in their last account, they are disinterested from all the worldly views, that use to darken our understandings, and byass our affections, while living in health and prosperity; they are upon the borders of eternity; and as the motions of nature are the stronger the nearer they are to the center, so saints are most lively and heavenly, when nearest heaven: martyrs have a special promise, "That it shall be given them in that hour what they shall speak." The last speeches of Christ's dying witnesses have extorted, even from Heathens, acknowledgments to the honour of God; *Vere magnus est Deus Christianorum*, Truly great is the Christians God: They have been made the means of conversion to many thousands of sinners: as Justin Martyr testifies of himself, that the dying words of Christians, made him fall in love with the life of Christianity.

I own, they are not bedecked with the embellishments of oratory and fine language: who can expect that from people of so mean education? But they are full of the language of heaven, which is many degrees more forcible than all our artificial rhetoric. One will find several mistakes in grammar, no doubt in them; but they were never intended for the reflections of critics, but for the instruction of Christians; and their plain rude discourses may, thro' God's blessings, do more good to the latter, than the most elaborate composures can do to the former. They may serve both as a comfort and encouragement to sufferers, and as an instruction and example to saints. Herein, as in a glass, we may both see our blemishes, wherein we come short of them, and learn to dress ourselves with the like christian ornaments of zeal, holiness, stedfastness, meekness, patience, humility and other graces.

But alas! How can the best of us read these testimonies, without blushing, for our low attainments and small proficiency in the school of Christ? How unlike are we to them, how zealous were they for the honour of Christ? How lukewarm are we, of whatever profession or denomination? How burning was their love to him, his truths, ordinances and people? How cold is ours? How self denied and crucified to the world were they? How selfish and worldly are we? How willing were they to part with all for Christ; and what an honour did they esteem it to suffer for him, to be chained, whipped, haltered, staked, imprisoned, banished, wounded, killed for him? How unwilling are we to part with a very little for him; much less to endure such hardships, and account them our glory? Alas! are we not ashamed of what they accounted their ornament, and accounting that our glory, which they looked upon as a disgrace? How easy was it for them to chuse the greatest sufferings rather than the least sin? How hard is it for us not to chuse the greatest sin, before the least suffering? Oh that their christian virtues could upbraid us out of our lethargy of supine security? That their humility, meekness and patience could shame us out of our pride, haughtiness and impatience: They were sympathizing Christians, active for the glory of God and good

The Preface to the Reader.

of fouls, diligent to have their evidences for heaven clear, and having obtained affurance of God's love to their perfons, and approbation of their caufe, they went chearfully on in their way, fearlefs of men, *who can only kill the body*, and ready to die the moſt violent death at God's call: But oh! how little fellow-feeling is there now among Chriſtians? But inſtead thereof, bitternefs, emulation, wrath, envy, contentions and divifions. How little concern for the work and caufe of Chriſt? How dark are the moſt part, both as to their fpiritual ſtate, and their proper and pertinent duty? And how much is the fear of man prevailing above zeal for the glory of God?

I know, it is objected by fome, that they much wanted that virtue which is the greateſt ornament of Chriſtians, and trueſt character of martyrs, namely a forgiving difpofition; becaufe they lay their blood at the door of the principal contrivers and executors of their death, which the objectors fuppofe not to have been done by any of the former fufferers for Chriſt. But to this I oppone. 1ſt, Granting for argument's fake, that they had expreſt themfelves with fome more fervency on that head, than others formerly had done, and that this was a piece of their infirmity; it will not follow that we ſhould prefently admit the invidious inference, that therefore they were no martyrs for Chriſt: For as neither the many grofs failings of the Old Teſtament faints, nor the miſtakes of primitive Chriſtians, about the truths for which they fuffered, could deprive either of the honour of the faintſhip or martyrdom, fo neither ought any infirmity of theirs to be improven againſt them for that end. Solomon tells us, that *oppreſſion makes a wife man mad;* and they met with it in the higheſt degree, and that not from the hands of Pagans, Turks or Papiſts, but of thofe who had been their covenanted brethren by profeſſion; and when a holy felf-refigned David had much ado to bear reproaches from the hand of one, that had been his equal, guide and acquaintance, with whom he had formerly fweet fellowſhip; it was not to be wondred, if they were put upon fome vehemency of expreſſion by their fevere fufferings from fuch hands; and ſhould rather be favourably conſtructed of

———————*Si quid*
Intumuit pietas, ſi quid flagrantius actum eſt.

pentance, nor is the thing unprecedented; for befide the example of Jeremiah, who laid his innocent blood at the door of the princes, if they fhould take his life, there might be feveral more recent parallels adduced; it fhall fuffice to inftance one of our own nation, imprifoned for bearing witnefs to the fame truth, namely Mr. John Welfh, who in his letter to the Lady Fleeming, hath thefe exprefs words, "The guilt of our blood fhall ly upon bifhops, councellors and commiffioners, who have ftirred up our prince againft us; and fo upon the reft of our brethren, who either by filence approve, or by crying peace, peace, ftrengthen the arm of the wicked, that they cannot return; and in the mean time make the heart of the righteous fad. Next, upon all them that fat in council, and did not bear plain teftimony of Jefus Chrift and his truth, for which we fuffer: And next, upon thofe that fhould have come and made open teftimony of Chrift faithfully, although it had been to the hazard of their lives. Finally, all thefe that counfel, command, confent and allow, are guilty in the fight of God." Sure I am, this is as full as any thing they have on this head, and proves, that what they did, was confiftent with a chriftian and forgiving temper of fpirit.

And as they went off the ftage, both with magnanimity and meeknefs, fo it has been obferved concerning many of their perfecutors, that they departed this world with vifible fymptoms of God's wrath and judgments, efpecially with hell in their fouls, I mean, the horror of an awakened confcience, under the fenfe of God's indignation; than which there can be no greater torment in this life.

——*Siculi non invenere tyranni*
Tormentum majus——

Well, thefe martyrs are now in heaven, in Abraham's warm bofom, enjoying the crown laid up for them, confirmed in an unchangeable ftate of reft and bleffednefs; we are yet in the ftage of action and place of probation,

The Preface to the Reader.

we have our trials before us, let us imitate the *cloud of witnesses, and contend for the faith once delivered to the saints.* We know not what storms are abiding us. The Canaanite and the Perizzite are yet in the land. A restless Popish and Jacobite party, projecting a new revolution of affairs; as sanguinary and cruel yet as ever, and retaining as much of the old malignity and enmity against the covenanted work of reformation as ever, only waiting an opportunity to exert it, and many things in the present aspect of affairs portending, that they may be our scourge in the hand of our displeased Lord, for our misimproving mercies and deliverances, satisfying ourselves with our own things, not minding the things of Christ; chiefly for our undervaluing the offers of the blessed Son of God in the gospel, and visible breach of national obligations to be for him and his cause. Seeing then such clouds are gathering, and threatning a dismal tempest, let us arm ourselves with the same mind, to stand up for the truth upon all hazards, whether we be called of God to do, or to suffer, for the joint interest of true religion and national liberty, for these, like Hippocrates's twins, weep or laugh, live or die together. *Righteousness exalteth a nation,* saith the wise Solomon; and Theodosius the emperor owned, That the establishment of a christian state depends chiefly upon piety towards God. On the other hand, civil liberty is an excellent bulwark to religion, without which its purity cannot long be preserved: for, as the same emperor said, *Multa inter ecclesiam et rempublicam cognatio intercedere solet; ex se invicem pendent, et utraque prosperis alterius successibus incrementa sumit.* There is a great sibness betwixt the church and common-wealth: they depend the one upon the other, and either is advanced by the prosperity and success of the other.

'Tis to be feared, this time of ease and outward peace has so effeminated and softned our spirits, that we will find it hard to face a storm; we may complain with Eusebius, *Res nostræ nimia libertate in mollitiem et segnitiem divinitus difciplinam pax longa corruperat, jacentem fidem, et pene dixerim dormientem, cenfura cœleftis erexit.* Becaufe long peace had corrupted the divinely inftituted difcipline, therefore there needed heavenly chaftifement to awaken the faith of the church, which was lying low, and almoft faft afleep. All thefe dying witneffes, affure us of judgments abiding this church and nation, and our prefent condition feems to fay, that we are the people that are to meet with them; how much need then had we of the chriftian armour, the divine Panoplia, which made thefe Chriftians proof againft the fiery darts of Satan and the wicked: and of the holy fubmiffion which made them bear the indignation of the Lord patiently, becaufe they had finned againft him.

Having thus briefly uſhered thee in to the following ſheets, chriſtian and candid reader, I ſhall detain thee no longer from peruſing them, ſave only by the way to take notice of theſe few advertiſements.

1. It is not pretended, that here are all the fpeeches and teftimonies of thofe that fuffered in Scotland fince the year 1680. For many of them, which no doubt are extant, have not come into the hands of the publiſhers of this collection, and fome of them that were in their hands, did fo far coincide with other, in matter and phrafe, that they left them unpubliſhed, with fome remark upon them, to keep up the memory of thefe honourable fufferers; being defirous that the book ſhould not fwell to fuch a bulk, as might make it lefs ufeful to country people, who have not much money to buy, or leifure to read bulky volumes. And if encouragement be found in this attempt, there may more of them come to be publifhed afterwards. Only, this the collectors of thefe teftimonies can fay, that they have left out none, which were in their hands, that they conceived might be for the benefit of the public, upon any finifter view or account: And if any ſhall find any alteration in any of them from their own manufcripts (except it be in the grammar, wherein they took fome little freedom, where neceffity required it) they are to impute it to variety of copies, whereof they had feveral, and chofe that which they conceived the moft genuine.

2. As for the teftimonies of the baniſhed, they being much the fame, as to all material points, with thefe of

the dying witneſſes, they are omitted, and a liſt of their names added in the appendix.

3. The laſt ſpeeches of thoſe, who ſuffered on account of the Earl of Argyle's attempt, in the year 1685, are adviſedly pretermitted, both becauſe ſome of them are already publiſhed in a book intituled, The Weſtern Martyrology, and likewiſe becauſe it is the opinion of the encouragers of this work, that their teſtimony was not ſo directly concert, according to the true ſtate of the quarrel, for the covenanted intereſt of the church of Chriſt in Scotland, as it ought to have been; tho' they intend not hereby to rob them of the glory of martyrdom for the proteſtant religion. Nor can this be any prejudice to others, who may incline more fully to publiſh the tranſactions of the times.

May the God and Father of our Lord Jeſus Chriſt, who enabled his people to witneſs ſo good a confeſſion for his truth and cauſe, make theſe dying ſpeeches uſeful to animate all the lovers of the reformed religion, with the like chriſtian magnanimity and reſolution, to ſtand up for its defence, againſt a Popiſh, Prelatic, and Jacobitiſh faction, endeavouring its overthrow. May he unite us in the way of truth and duty, to ſtrive together for the valuable intereſts of our religion and liberty.

A dismal account of the form of burning the Solemn League *and* National Covenant *with God and one another, at* Linlithgow, May 29th, 1661, *being the birth-day of King* Charles *the* Second.

Divine service being ended, the streets were so filled with bonfires on every side, that it was not without hazard to go along them: the magistrates about four o'clock in the afternoon went to the Earl of Linlithgow's lodging, inviting his Lordship to honour them with his presence at the solemnity of the day; so he came with the magistrates, accompanied with many gentlemen to the market-place, where a table was covered with confections; then the curate met them and prayed, and sang a psalm, and so eating some of the confections, they threw the rest among the people. The fountain all the time running French and Spanish wine of divers colours, and continued running three or four hours. The Earl, the magistrates and gentlemen, did drink the king and queen's good health, and all royal healths, not forgetting his majesty's commissioner's health, Lord Middleton, and breaking several baskets full of glasses.

At the market-place, was erected an arch standing upon four pillars, on the other side whereof was placed a statue in form of an old Hag, having the Covenant in her hands, with this superscription, *A glorious Reformation:* on the other side was placed a statue in a Whigmuir's habit, having the Remonstrance in his hand, with this superscription, *No association with Malignants;* within the arch on the right hand was drawn a committee of estates, with this inscription, *An act for delivering up the King.* Upon the left hand was drawn the commission of the kirk, with this superscription, *A commission of the Kirk and committee of estates, and Act of the West-kirk of Edinburgh,* and upon the top of the arch stood the Devil as an angel of light, with this superscription, *Stand to the cause;* and on the top of the arch hung a table with this litany,

> From Covenanters with uplifted hands,
> From Remonstrators with associate bands,
> From such committees as govern'd this nation,
> From kirk commissions, and their protestation,
>   *Good Lord deliver us.*

On the pillar of the arch beneath the covenant were drawn kirk-ſtools, rocks, and reels; upon the pillar beneath the Remonſtrance were drawn brechams, cogs and ſpoons; on the back of the arch was drawn the picture of Rebellion in a religious habit, with turned up eyes, and with a fanatic geſture, and in its right hand holding *Lex Rex*, that infamous (rather famous) book, maintaining defenſive arms, and in the left hand holding that pitiful pamphlet, (rather excellent paper) *The cauſes of God's Wrath*, and about its waſte were all the acts of parliament, committees of eſtates, and acts of general aſſemblies and commiſſion of the kirk, their proteſtations and declarations during theſe twenty-two years rebellion, (ſo they called the time of Reformation), and above was this ſuperſcription. *Rebellion is as the ſin of witchcraft*. Then at the drinking of the king's health, fire was put to the frame, which gave many fine reports, and ſoon burnt all to aſhes: which being conſumed, there ſuddenly appeared a table ſupported by two angels, carrying this ſuperſcription,

Great Britain's monarch on this day was born,
 And to his kingdoms happily reſtor'd:
The queen's arriv'd, the mitre now is worn,
 Let us rejoice, this day is from the Lord.
Fly hence, all traitors who did mar our peace,
 Fly hence, ſchiſmatics who our church did rent,
Fly, covenanting, remonſtrating race;
 Let us rejoice that God this day hath ſent.

Then the magiſtrates accompanied the noble Earl to his palace, where the ſaid Earl had a bonfire very magnificent. Then the Earl and magiſtrates, and all the reſt, did drink the king and queen, and all royal healths. Then the magiſtrates made proceſſion, thro' the burgh, and ſaluted every man of account, and ſo they ſpent the day rejoicing in their labour.

AN ENCOMIUM

On the following

MARTYRS.

LO! here of faithful witneſſes a cloud,
For Chriſt their King reſiſting unto blood.
Lo! here upon their Piſgah top they ſtand;
Juſt on the confines of Emmanuel's land:
Leaving th' ungrateful world, longing to be
Poſſeſs'd of bleſſed immortality.
Lo! here they ſtand, accoſting cruel death
With Chriſtian braveneſs, to their lateſt breath:
The views they have of heav'n's eternal joys,
So far eclipſe all ſublunary toys,
Their ſouls are only charm'd with things above,
Exulting in their ſweet Redeemer's love.
Lo! here they ſtand, and will not quit the field,
They'll die upon the ſpot before they yield.
Lo! with what courage and brave reſolution
They bear the ſhock of bloody perſecution.
Hell's rage, Rome's fury, nor the ſcorn of thoſe
Pretending friendſhip, tho' the worſt of foes,
Could never ſhake their ſteady loyalty
To Zion's king, for whoſe ſupremacy
Over his church, thus boldly they contend,
And by his grace endure unto the end;
Refuſing e'er to make a baſe ſurrender
Of Chriſt's regalia to a vile pretender;
Who ſwoln with more than Luciferian pride
Could not in his own princely place abide;
But would uſurp the ſp'ritual pow'r and throne
By God JEHOVAH giv'n to Chriſt alone.
And having thus 'gainſt heav'n diſplay'd a banner,
The Covenant he ſwore in ſolemn manner,
He broke and burnt; divine and human laws,
Trod under foot; and to advance his cauſe,

Made bloody violence the only claim,
Whereby he wore the royal diadem.
Being ferv'd with beafts devoid of human fenfe;
Much more of honour and of confcience;
Who flew God's deareft faints in field and city,
'Gainft law and reafon, without fenfe and pity:
Whofe fharpeft fufferings could not affwage,
Nor death itfelf allay their hellifh rage.
As if their bodies dead felt fenfe of pains,
Cut all in parts, they hung them up in chains;
Heads, legs, and arms, they plac'd on ev'ry port
Of burghs, or other places of refort,
As ftanding trophies of their victory,
O'er divine truth, and human liberty.
Well, have they kill'd, and ta'en poffeffion too?
Is this the utmoft that their rage cou'd do?
Only to fend Chrift's loving fubjects home,
To their dear country; where they long to come:
What matter where their dufty parts do ly?
Interr'd in earth, or lifted up on high?
While as their fouls eternal anthems raife,
In fweet accents to their Redeemer's praife.
And will not Zion's King regain his crown?
Throwing fuch vain afpiring mortals down
Into that direful pit, from whence did flow
Thefe mifts of pride, which did enchant them fo.

    Come then, behold thefe noble witneffes
Adorn'd with holy zeal and faithfulnefs;
Who like a cloud, do us inviron round,
Viewing (as 'twere what way we'll ftand our ground),
Let's run our race with equal patience,
With eyes intent upon our recompenfe.

The LAST SPEECHES and TESTIMONIES of the Sufferers for the Truth in Scotland, since the Year 1680.

The Last Speech and Testimony of the Reverend Mr. DONALD CARGIL, *sometime minister of the gospel in the Barony parish of* Glasgow, *delivered by him in writing before his execution at the Cross of* Edinburgh, *July* 27. 1681.

THIS is the most joyful day that ever I saw in my pilgrimage on earth; my joy is now begun, which I see shall never be interrupted. I see both my interest, and his truth, and the sureness of the one, and the preciousness of the other. It is near thirty years since he made it sure; and since that time (tho' there has fallen out much sin) yet I was never out of an assurance of mine interest, nor long out of sight of his presence. He has dandled me, and kept me lively, and never left me behind; tho' I was oft times turning back. O he has shewed the wonderful preciousness of his grace, not only in the first receiving thereof, but in renewed and multiplied pardons! I have been a man of great sins, but he has been a God of great mercies. And now, thro' his mercies, I have a conscience as sound and quiet, as if I had never sinned. It is long since I could have ventured on eternity, thro' God's mercy and Christ's merits; but death remained somewhat terrible, and that is now taken away; and now death is no more to me, but to cast myself into my husband's arms, and to ly down with him. And however it be with me at the last, tho' I should be straitened by God, or interrupted by men, yet all is sure, and shall be well. I have followed holiness, I have taught truth, and I have been most in the main things; not that I thought the things concerning our times little, but that I thought none could do any thing to purpose in God's great and public matters, till they were right in their conditions. And O that all had taken this method; for then there had been fewer apostacies. The religion of the land, and zeal for the land's engagements, are coming to nothing, but a supine, loathsome and hateful formality; and there cannot be zeal, liveliness and rightness, where people meet with persecution, and want heart renovation. My soul trembles to think, how little of regeneration there is amongst the ministers and professors of Scotland. O the ministers of Scotland, how have they betrayed Christ's interest, and beguiled souls! *They have not entered in themselves, and them that were entering in they hindered.* They have sold the things of Christ, and liberties of his church, for a short and cursed quiet to themselves, which is now near an end: And they are more one, and at peace with God's enemies, after they have done all their mischiefs, than they were at first, when they had but put hand to them. And I much fear, that tho' there were not one minister on all the earth, he would make no more use of them; but there will be a dreadful judgment upon themselves, and a long curse upon their posterity.

As to our professors, my counsel to them is, that they would see well to their own regeneration, for the most part of them has that yet to do; and yet let never one think he is in the right exercise of true religion, that has not a zeal to God's public glory. There is a small remnant in Scotland, that my soul has had its greatest comfort on earth from. I wish your increase in holiness, number, love, religion, and righteousness: And wait you, and cease to contend with these men that are gone from us, for there is nothing that shall convince them, but judgment. Satisfy your consciences, and go forward; for the nearer you are to God, and the further from all others, whether stated enemies, or lukewarm ministers and professors, it shall be the better. My preaching has occasioned great persecution, but the want of it will, I fear, occasion worse. However, I have preached the truths of God to others; as it is written, *I believed, and so I preached;* and I have not an ill conscience in preaching truth whatever has followed: And this day I am to seal with my blood all the truths that ever I preached: And what is controverted of that which I have been professing, shall (ere long) be manifested by God's judgments in the consciences of men. I had a sweet calmness of spirit, and great submission as to my taking, the providence of God was so eminent in it; and I could not but think, that God judged it necessary for his glory, to bring me to such an end, seeing he loosed me from such a work. My soul would be exceedingly troubled anent the remnant, were it not that I think the time will be short. Wherefore hold fast, for this is the way that is now persecuted.

As to the cause of my suffering; the main is, *Not acknowledging the present authority, as it is established in the supremacy and explanatory act.* This is the magistracy that I have rejected, that was invested with Christ's power. And seeing that power taken from Christ, which is his glory, made the essential of the crown, I thought this was, as if I had seen one wearing my husband's garments, after he had killed him. And seeing it made the essential of the crown, there is no distinction we can make, that can free the conscience of the acknowledger, from being a partaker of this sacrilegious robbing of God. And it is but to cheat our consciences, to acknowledge the civil power; for it is not civil power only that is made of the essence of his crown: And seeing they are so express, we ought to be plain; for otherwise it is to deny our testimony, and consent to his robbery.

After he was come to the scaffold, standing with his back towards the ladder, he fixed his eyes upon the multitude, and desired their attention: And after singing a part of the cxviiith psalm, from the 16th ver. to the close, he looked up to the windows on both sides of the scaffold with a smiling countenance, requesting the people to compose themselves, and hear a few words that he had to say, which, said he, I shall direct to three sorts of folk, and shall endeavour to be brief. First, All you that are going on in persecuting the work and people of God, O beware, for the Lord's sake, and refrain from such courses, as you would escape wrath eternally, which will be a torment far beyond what we are to endure by the hands of cruel and bloody murderers. Upon this the drums were beaten, at which he smilingly said, Now ye see we have not liberty to speak, or at least to speak what we would; but God knoweth our hearts. But, O ye that are called ministers, and professors in the church of Scotland, who are wearied in waiting upon the Lord, and are turned out of his way, and run into a course of gross defection and backsliding; truly, for my part, I tremble to think what will become of you; for either you shall be punished with sore affliction, I mean, in your conscien-

Of Mr. Donald Cargil.

ces, becaufe of fin, or elfe you fhall be tormented eternally without remedy, which fhall be fhortly, if mercy prevent it not; which I pray God may be the mercy of all thefe to whom he has thoughts of peace. All ye that are the poor remnant, who fear finning more than fuffering, and are begging for his returning to Scotland to wear his own crown, and reign as king in Zion, in fpite of all that will oppofe him, whether devils or men: I fay to you that are thus waiting, Wait on, and ye fhall not be difappointed; for either your eyes fhall fee it, or elfe ye fhall die in the faith of it, that he fhall return, and *if you fuffer with him, you fhall also reign with him;* which reign will be glorious and eternal. I come now to tell you for what I am brought here to die, and to give you an account of my faith, which I fhall do as in the fight of the living God, before whom I am fhortly to ftand. *Firft,* I declare I am a Chriftian, a Proteftant, a Prefbyterian in my judgment, and whatever hath been faid of me, I die teftifying againft Popery, Prelacy, Eraftianifm, and all manner of defection from the truth of God, and againft all who make not the fcriptures, which are the word of God, their rule, that fo they may commend Chrift and his way to ftrangers, by a holy and gofpel converfation. The caufe for which I am fentenced to die here this day, is my difowning of authority in the unlawful exercife thereof, when they, inftead of ruling for God, are fighting againft him, and encroaching upon his prerogatives, by that woful fupremacy which my foul abhors, and which I have teftified againft fince I was apprehended; and now again I difown all fupremacy over the confciences of men, and liberties of Chrift's church. Whereupon the drums were again beaten, and he kept filence a little, and then faid, Of this fubject I fhall fay no more. Only I think the Lord's quarrel againft this land is, becaufe there has not been fo much heart-religion and foul-exercife among either minifters or profeffors, as there feemed to be, when the land owned Chrift and his truths: I wifh there were more true converfion, and then there would not be fo much backfliding; and for fear of fuffering, living at eafe, when there are fo few to contend for Chrift and his caufe.

Now, for my own cafe, I blefs the Lord, that for all that hath been faid of me, my confcience doth not condemn me: I do not fay I am free of fin, but I am at peace with God through a slain Mediator: and I believe that there is no salvation but only in Christ. And I abhor that superstitious way of worshipping of angels and saints, contrary unto the word of God: as also I abhor the leaning to self-righteousness, and Popish penances. I bless the Lord, that these thirty years, and more, I have been at peace with God, and was never shaken loose of it: and now I am as sure of my interest in Christ, and peace with God, as all within this Bible, and the Spirit of God, can make me; and I am no more terrified at death, nor afraid of hell, because of sin, than if I had never had sin; for all my sins are freely pardoned, and washen throughly away, thro' the precious blood and intercession of Jesus Christ. And I am fully persuaded, that this is his way for which I suffer, and that he will return gloriously to Scotland, but it will be terrifying to many; therefore I intreat you, be not discouraged at the way of Christ, and the cause for which I am to lay down my life, and step into eternity, where my soul shall be as full of him, as it can desire to be. And now this is the sweetest and most glorious day that ever my eyes did see. Now, I intreat you, study to know and believe the Scriptures, which are the truths of God; these I have preached, and do firmly believe them. O! prepare for judgments, for they shall be sore and sudden. Enemies are now enraged against the way and people of God, but ere long they shall be enraged one against another, to their own confusion. At this the drums were beaten a third time. And then being taken to the north-side of the scaffold, he stood a little, during the space that one of the rest was singing. And then being carried to the south-side of the scaffold, he prayed. Thence he was brought to the east-side of the scaffold; and then he said, I intreat you prepare presently for a stroke, for God will not sit with all the wrongs done to him, but will suddenly come and make inquisition for the blood that has been shed in Scotland. Then he was commanded to go up the ladder; and as he set his foot on it, he said, The Lord knows I go up this ladder with less fear and perturbation of mind, than ever I entered the pulpit to preach. And when he was up, he sat himself down, and said, Now, I am near to the getting of my crown, which shall be sure; for I bless the Lord, and desire all of you to blefs him, that he hath brought me here, and makes me triumph over devils, and men, and fin; they fhall wound me no more. I forgive all men the wrongs they have done to me, and pray the Lord may forgive all the wrongs that any of the elect have done againſt him. I pray that fufferers may be kept from fin, and helped to know their duty. Then having prayed a little within himſelf, he lifted up the napkin, and ſaid, Farewel all relations and friends in Chriſt; farewel acquaintances, and all earthly enjoyments; farewel reading and preaching, praying and believing, wanderings, reproaches and ſufferings. Welcome joy unfpeakable, and full of glory. Welcome Father, Son, and Holy Ghoſt; into thy hands I commit my ſpirit. Then he prayed a little, and the executioner turned him over praying.

[Becauſe this dying Teſtimony and laſt Speech are but ſhort, which was occafioned through want of time; and the perfecutors feverity, who took his larger teſtimony from him the day before he died; paper and ink being conveyed to him fecretly by a cord through the window the night before his death; it is thought proper to fubjoin theſe following letters of his, (they being all of public concern) to give a more full difcovery of the teſtimony which he held: and particularly, of his witneſſing againſt the errors, about that time, broached by the infamous John Gib; as the Letter written to the priſoners in the correction-houfe manifeſts.]

A Letter from Mr. DONALD CARGIL, *to Mr.* JAMES SKEEN, *who ſuffered Martyrdom at Edinburgh.*

Deareſt Friend,

THere is now nothing upon earth that I am fo concerned in (except the Lord's work) as in you and your fellows; that you may either be cleanly brought off, or honourably and rightly carried through. He is begun, in part, to anſwer me, tho' not in that which I moſt affected, yet in that which is beſt. My foul was refreſhed to fee any that had fo far overcome the fear and torture of death, and were fo far denied to the affections of the fleſh, as to give full liberty to the exoneration of conſcience in the face of theſe bloody tyrants and vile apoſtates. And yet theſe, by our divines, muſt be acknowledged as magistrates; which very heathens, endued with the light of nature, would abominate, and would think it inconsistent with reason to admit to, or continue in the magistracy, such perjured, bloody, dissolute and flagitious men, as to make a wolf the keeper and feeder of the flock. But every step of their dealing with God, with the land, and with yourself, and brethren, is a confirmation of your judgment anent them, and sufficient ground of your detestation, and rejection of them; and it is the sin of the land, and of every person in it, that they have not gone along with you, and these few in that action; but since they have not done that, they shall not now meet with the like honour, if ever they meet with it, till vengeance be poured out upon them; and they and their king shall either be keeped together in wrath, or divided in wrath, that they may be one anothers destruction. But go on valiant champion, you die not as a fool, tho' the apostate, unfaithful and lukewarm ministers and professors of this generation think and say so; they shall live traitors, and most of them die fools; I say, traitors, as some men live upon the reward of treachery, for their quiet and liberty; if it may be called a liberty, as it is redeemed with the betraying of the interest of Christ, and the blood of his people. But he himself hath sealed your sufferings, and their thus saying, condemns God, and his sealing, condemns them. But neither regard their voices, nor fear, for God will neither seal to folly nor iniquity; he then not only having sealed your sufferings, but your remission, go on to finish and perfect your testimony, not only against them, but against all that subject unto them, side with them, or are silent at them. And as for these men that will be our rulers, though they have nothing of worth or virtue in them: I am persuaded of this, that none can appear before them, and acknowledge them as they have now invested themselves (standing on a foundation of perjury, which is an act recissory of their admission to the government) with Christ's crown on their head, and a sceptre of iniquity, and a sword of persecution in their hand, but must deny Christ. And in effect, the whole land generally hath denied Christ, and desired a murderer. And as for that unsavoury salt, that lately appeared, acknowledged them, and was ashamed of this testimony, and in so doing, gave the first vote to your condemnation; and proclaimed a lawfulness to the rest of the assizers and murderers, to follow in their condemnations; God shall require this with his other doings at his hands; and I am somewhat afraid, if he be not suddenly made the subject of serious repentance, he shall be made the subject of great vengeance. But forgive and forget all these private injuries, and labour to go to eternity and death, with a heart destitute of private revenges, and filled with zeal to God's glory, and assign to him the quarrel against his enemies, to be followed out by himself in his own way, against the indignities done to God, and against the mocking perfidiousness, impieties and lukewarmness of this generation. And for yourself, whatever there has been either of sin or duty, remember the one, and forget the other: and betake yourself wholly to the mercy of God, and the merits of Christ; ye know in whom ye have believed, and the acceptableness of your believing, and the more fully you henceforth believe, the greater shall be his glory, and the greater your peace and safety. Farewel, dearest friend, never to see one another any more, till at the right-hand of Christ. Fear not, and the God of mercies grant a full gale and a fair entry into his kingdom, that may carry sweetly and swiftly over the bar, that you find not the rub of death. Grace, mercy, and peace be with you.

Yours in Christ, D. CARGIL.

A Letter to some Friends before he went abroad.

Dear Friends,

I Cannot but be grieved to go from my native land, and especially from that part of it, for whom and with whom I desired only to live: Yet the dreadful apprehensions I have of what is coming upon this land, may help to make me submissive to this providence, though more bitter: You will have snares for a little, and then a deluge of judgments. I do not speak this to affright any, much less to rejoice over them; as if I were taken, and they left; or were studying, by these thoughts, to alleviate my own lot of banishment; though I am afraid that none shall bless themselves long upon the account that they are left behind. But my design is, to have you making for snares and judgments, that ye may have both the greatest readiness and the greatest shelters, for both shall be in one. Clear accounts, and put off the old, for it is like that what is to come will be both sudden and surprizing, that it will not give you time for this. Beware of taking on new debt. I am afraid that these things that many are looking on as favours, are but come to bind men together in bundles for a fire. I am sure if these things be embraced, there shall not be long time given for using of them; and this last of their favours and snares is sent to men, to show that they are that which otherwise they will not confess themselves to be. Tell all, that the shelter and benefit of this shall neither be great nor long; but the snare of it shall be great and prejudicial. And for myself, I think, for the present he is calling me to another land. But how long shall be my abode, or what employment he has for me there I know not; for I cannot think he is taking me there to live and lurk only. I rest,

DONALD CARGIL.

A Letter to JOHN MALCOLM *and* ARCHIBALD ALISON, *Prisoners.*

Dear Friends,

DEATH in Christ, and for Christ is never much to be bemoaned, and less at this time than any other; when these that survive have nothing to live among but miseries, persecution, snares, sorrows and sinning; and where the only desirable sight, *viz.* Christ reigning in a free and flourishing church, is wanting, and the greatly grieving and offensive object to devout souls, *viz.* devils, and the worst of the wicked, reigning and raging, is still before our eyes; and though we had greater things to leave, and better times to live in, yet eternity does so far exceed and excel these things in their greatest perfection, that they who see and are sure (and we see indeed, being made sure) will never let a tear fall, or a sigh go at the farewel, but would rather make a slip to get death, nor to shun it, if both were not equally detestable to them upon the account of God's commandments, whom they neither dare, nor are willing to offend, even to obtain heaven itself. And there are none who are his, but they must see themselves infinitely advantaged in the exchange; and accordingly hasten, if sin, the flesh, and want of art surance did not withstand; and there is no doubt, but these must be weak and poor spirits, that are bewitched or enchanted, either with the fruitions or hopes of the world. And as earth has nothing to hold a resolute and reconciled soul, so heaven wants nothing to draw it; and to some to live here has been always wearisome, since their peace was made, Christ's sweetness known, and their own weakness and unusefulness experienced; but now it is become hatefully loathsome, since devils and the worst of men are become the head, and dreadful by their stupendious permissions, loosings and lengthnings in their reigning, and friends are become uncomfortable, because they will neither christianly bear and bide, nor rightly go forward to effectuate their own delivery. But for you, there is nothing at this time (if you yourselves be sure with God, which, I hope, either you are, or will be) which can make me bewail your death, though the cause of it doth both increase my affection to you, and indignation against these enemies. Yet for you, notwithstanding of the unjustness of the sentence, go not to eternity with indignation against them, upon your own account. Neither let the goodness of the cause ye suffer for, found your confidence in God, and your hope of well-being; for were the action never so good, and performed without the least failing, which is not incident to human infirmity, it could never be a cause of obtaining mercy, nor yet commend us to that grace from which we are to obtain it. There is nothing now which is yours, when you are pleading and petitioning for mercy, that must be remembered but your sins, for in effect, there is nothing else ours. Let your sins then be on your heart, as your sorrow, which we must bewail, before we be parted with them, as the captive her father, not because she was to leave him, but because she had been so long with him. And let these mercies of God, and merits of Christ, be before your eyes as your hopes, and your winning to these as the only rock upon which we can be saved; if there be any thing seen or looked to in ourselves but sin, we cannot expect remission and salvation allenarly thro' free grace, in which expectation only it can be obtained; neither can we earnestly beg, till we see ourselves destitute of all that procures favour, and full of all that merits and hastens vengeance and wrath. And besides, it heightens the price of that precious blood, by which only we can have redemption from sin and wrath; it being the only sufficient in itself, and only acceptable to the Father, and so it must be, being the blessed and gracious device and result of infinite wisdom, which makes the eternal God to be admired in his graciousness and holiness, having found out the way of his own payment, without our hurt, and which makes all return to their own desires, and there to rest in an eternal complacency; for this way returns to God his glory, to justice its satisfaction, to disquieted consciences of men, frighted and awakened with the sight of sin and wrath, ease, peace and assurance, and to the souls of men fellowship with God and hope of eternal salvation. Now, the righteousness of Christ being made sure to us, secures all this for us, and this both is believed and apprehenden by faith, it being the hand by which we grip this rock, and if it be true, it cannot but be strong, and we saved. Look well then to your faith, that it be a faith growing out of regeneration, and the new creature, and have Christ for its righteousness, hope and rejoicing, and be sealed by the spirit of God: and what this sealing is, when it comes it will abundantly show itself; and there can be no other full satisfaction to a soul than this. But seek till ye find, and whatever ye find for the present, let your last act be to lay and leave yourselves on the righteousness of his Son, expecting life thro' his name, according to the promise of the Father. Dear friends, your work is great, and time short; but this is a comfort, and the only comfort in your present condition, that you have a God infinite in mercy to deal with, who is ready at all times to forgive, but especially persons in your case, who have been jeoparding your lives upon the account of the gospel, whatever failings or infirmites in you, that action hath been accompanied with; for it is the action itself which is the duty of this whole covenanted kingdom, and not the failing, for which you are brought to suffering. Seek not then the favours of men, by making your duty your sin; but confess your failings to God, and look for his mercy thro' Jesus Christ, who has said, *Whosoever loseth his life for my sake, shall keep it unto eternal life*. And tho' it will profit a reprobate nothing to die after this manner, for nothing can be profitable without love, which only is, or can be, in a believer, yet it should be no disadvantage, but, in a manner, the beſt way of dying; for it would take ſome from his days that he might have lived, and ſo prevent many ſins that he would have committed, and ſo the ſin is leſſened that is the cauſe of eternal ſufferings.

And let not this diſcourage you, or lay you by, that the work is great, and the time ſhort, tho' this indeed ſhould mind you of your ſinful neglect, that were not better provided for ſuch a ſhort and peremptory ſummons, which you ſhould always have expected. It alſo ſhews the greatneſs of the ſin of theſe enemies, that not only take away unjuſtly your bodily life, but alſo ſhorten your time of preparation, and ſo do their utmoſt to deprive you of eternal life. Yet, I ſay, let not this either diſcourage, or lay you by, for God can perfect great works in a ſhort time, and one of the greateſt things that befal men, ſhall be effectuate in the twinkling of an eye, which is one of the ſhorteſt. I aſſure you, he put the thief on the croſs thro' all his deſires, convictions, converſion, juſtification, ſanctification, &c. in a ſhort time, and left nothing to bemoan, but that there did not remain time enough to glorify him on earth that had done all theſe things for him. Go on then, and let your intent be ſeriouſneſs; the greatneſs of your ſorrow, and the height of love, in a manner, make a compenſation for the ſhortneſs of time, and go on though ye yourſelves have gone ſhort way; for where theſe things are, one hour will perform more than thouſands where there were not, either ſuch enforcements or power; and be perſuaded in this, you have him as much and more haſtening than yourſelves; for you may know his motion by your own, they being both ſet forward by him. And dear friends, be not terrified at the manner of your death, which to me ſeems the eaſieſt of all, where you come to it without pain, and in perfect judgment, and go thro' ſo ſpeedily; before the pain be felt the glory is come: but pray for a greater meaſure of his preſence, which only can make a paſs through the hardeſt things cheerful and pleaſant. I bid you farewel, expecting, tho' our parting be ſad, our gathering ſhall be joyful again. Only your great advantage in the caſe you are in, is to credit him much, for that is his glory, and engages him to perform whatever ye have credited him with. No more, but avow boldly to give a full testimony for his truths, as you desire to be avowed of him. Grace, mercy and peace be with you.

DONALD CARGIL.

To the Prisoners in the Correction-house of Edinburgh.

Dear Friends,

I Think, ye cannot but know that I am both concerned and afflicted with your condition; and I would have written sooner, and more, if I had not feared that you might have been jealous (under your distempers) that I had been seducing you to follow me, and not God and truth. It has been my earnest and frequent prayer to God, (as he himself knows) to be led in all truths; and I judge, I have been in this graciously answered; but I desire none, if they themselves judge it not to be truth, to adhere to any thing that I have either preached, written, or done, to any hazard, much more to the loss of life. But I have been afflicted with your condition, and could not but be more, if God's great graciousness in this begun discovery, and your sincerity and singleness gave me not hope, that God's purpose is to turn this to the great mercy of his poor church, and yours, if ye marr it not; and yet the great sin and pillar of Satan that is in this snare, makes me tremble. It was God's mercy to you that gave such convictions, that made you, at least, some of you, once to part with these men; and it was undoubtedly your sin that you continued not so, but after convictions, did cast yourselves into new temptations; for convictions ought to be tenderly guided, lest the Spirit be grieved from whom they come; but this second discovery tho' it be with a sharper rebuke, as it makes God's mercy wonderful, so it shall render your perseverance in that course, sinful and utterly inexcusable; for God has broken the snare, and it will be your great sin, if you go not out with great haste, joy and thankfulness, when God's wonderful discovery has made such a way for your delivery; for God having now shown you, the ring-leaders and authors of these opinions to be persons of such abominations, calls you not only to deny credit to them, but also to make a serious search of their tenets, which will, I know, by his grace, bring you undoubtedly to see that these things are con-

of Mr. Donald Cargil. 47

God's glory and truth, that they fo much

lear friends, as I cannot be tender enough
in your zeal and finglenefs have been mif-
this did bewray a great fimplicity and un-
yet it did alfo betoken fome zeal and ten-
being beguiled, it was in things that were
fked with fome pretences to God's glory,
ormation. And on the other hand, I can-
enough abhorrence of thefe perfons, who
felves to be of fuch abominations, did give
to be of fuch familiarity with God, and of
iation, to make their delufions more paffing
uls. Let nothing make you think this is
natural enmity againft the power of god-
;refs in reformation, that is venting itfelf
o' I cannot win forward as I ought, yet I
o fee others go forward. And I am fure,
iis bed within you, a viper and a child.
ming himfelf into an angel of light, has
together, to make it paffing with fome,
:d of others, who are of tendernefs. But
e is, to kill the ferpent, and keep the child
d is calling you loudly to fevere the good
that the wit of Satan's fubtilty has mixed
to deliver yourfelves fpeedily, as a roe
of the hunter; and not only return, but
for your high provoking of God, in of-
l facrifices to his glory, and fewing your
i that new garment; in your making the
defpife that caufe and company, who are
d already, and difcouraging thofe who
, and going forward with joy in that which
iat now, neither have they heart nor hand
nor can they look out, till God recover
There is much in the whole of thofe, that
weight and overwhelm fome fpirits; but
g in all their cogitations about it, that
nfortable, unlefs it be, that he is cleared
and continuing to afflict us, becaufe there
ons among us. I fpeak this but of fome of
ed by us, tho' ignorantly; and we wifh
laft and great ftop that was to be remov-

ed before his coming to revenge himself and reign. I would not say, but by this also he shewed his tenderness, of preserving integrity of doctrine, and sound reformation, and his purpose not to suffer errors and heresies to prosper. This I told you, when I met with you, that there were some things ye were owning which were highly approved of God; such as an inward heart-love and zeal to God's glory, which I perceived to be in some of you, so far as it can be perceived, and setting up of that before you, as your end, in pursuing it always as your work, and a forgetting of all other things in regard of it, excepting only these things without which we cannot glorify him, (as a work-man that intends his work, must mind his tools) even our own salvation, and the salvation of all others, as if they were not things wherein he is greatly glorified, for his glory is in righteousness and mercy, and in and by these is the salvation of man infallibly advanced, and to these it is inseparably connected.

Next I would advise you, to set apart more, yea, much more of your time, for humiliation, fasting and prayer, in such an exigence, when the judgments of God appear to be so near, and so great, so that it be done without sin, for God cannot be glorified by sin; *For if my lie hath more abounded to his glory, why am I judged as a sinner?* I was against such who deny nature, and others, their right dues; for he that allows dues to others, allows them to be paid also: and we must be like prisoners, who are of great debt, and honest hearts, who know they cannot pay every one their full sums, yet are resolved to give every one some, and to the greatest most, and to the rest accordingly. And as there cannot be a total abstinence from meat, without self murder, so there cannot be a total denying others their dues, such as the benevolence of husband to wife, and a total abstaining from work, without a transgression of God's commandments and laws, which can never be a glorifying of him, which the more impartially they are keeped, the more he is glorified. Next, ways are allowed of him, that ye may make yourselves free, so much as in you lies, of all the public defections: Whatever may involve you in these, or contribute to their upholding, without either an overpowering force, or an indispensible necessity: For I may buy meat and drink, in *of Mr. Donald Cargil.*

neceffity, whatever ufe the feller may make of that money I give for my meat and drink. Next, he allows thefe particulars of reformation, fuch as change of the names of days, of weeks, of terms of the year, and fuch like, warranted by the word, and example of the Chriftians in fcripture, that have been neglected before in our reformation; fo that there be not too much religion placed in thefe things, and other things more weighty (which undoubtedly have more moral righteoufnefs in them) made little in regard of them: but in thefe good things Satan will quickly, if it be not already, over-drive you in your progrefs, and leave you only to hug a fpurious birth. But there are other things that ye maintained when I fpoke with you (and the viper has more fince appeared) as truths, and part of God's glory, that are utterly contrary to, and inconfiftent with the glory of God. As, *firft*, Laying afide of public preaching; fome of them faying no lefs, nor they had no miffing of it: fo that ye thought, *ye had reigned as kings without us, and would to God ye had reigned.* Your flourifhing fhould have delighted, tho' we had not been the inftruments and means thereof. But alas! this your liberty, that you fo much bragged of, would have lafted but a little while, and was among your other beguiles; and was nothing elfe but Satan ftirring you about to giddinefs, and raifing of fantaftic fumes to the tickling of the imagination; but leaving you altogether without renovation of heart, or progrefs in fanctification: fo that I cannot compare this your liberty to any thing elfe, but to an enchanted fabric, where the poor guefts, only placed in imagination, imagine themfelves to be in a pleafant place, and at a royal entertainment; but when God comes, and delufion vanifheth, they will find themfelves caft in fome remote wildernefs, and they left full of aftonifhment and fears.

I told you, while I was with you, that the devil was fowing tares among your thin wheat; but I was not long from you, exercifed in thoughts about you, but I faw clearly, there was forcery in the bufinefs: and now I tell you, I fear forcerers alfo. I know I have fpoken this againft mine own life, if they get the power they defire; but I am in a defiance of them, and I know alfo in a defence by him who hath preferved, and I know will preferve me, till my work be finifhed. But if your liberty that you talked of had been true, it would at least have stayed till it had brought you to other thoughts, other works, and other comforts; and it might have been easily discerned not a true liberty, but a temptation that led you from public preaching, the great ordinance of God's glory, and mens good; as the apostle has that word, *Forbidding us to preach to the Gentiles.* But especially to leave public ordinances at this time, when they are the only standards standing, which shows Satan's victory against Christ's kingdom in Scotland not to be complete.

Yet, dear friends, when you hear this, let not Satan cast you as far to the other side, (for it is rare to see the most devout souls altogether out from under his delusions and temptations) as to make you believe that it is impossible to attain unto any thing of certitude of truth, liberty, manifestations and communion with God, if that which seemed to be so firm, be delusions; but shall Satan have such power to make men believe lies, and shall not God go infinitely beyond him, in making men to see and believe truth? There were many that thought themselves at the height of assurance, when under the greatest temptations, as Psal. lxxiii. 13. *Verily I have cleansed my hands in vain.* And yet they have a greater certainty when they come to see, that there is no such unquietness of spirit under this, as they found in the former. And seeing it is so, rest not till ye attain that assurance of your own interest, and of his main truths, which is both above doubt and defect, that ye may be able to say, *Now we believe, and are sure.*

But in the next place, you will join with none in public worship, but these who have infallible signs of regeneration. This seems fair, but it is both false and foul; false because of its false foundation, *viz.* That the certainty of ones interest in Christ may be known by another; whereas the scripture says, *That none knows it, but he that has it:* Foul also, for this disdain has pride in it, and pride is always foul; and tho' there be a difference amongst men, and that we should have regard of repentance and brokenness of heart, yet these who have well sought and seen their own filthiness, will judge themselves the persons, of any, that should be thrust out of the assemblies of God's people ;' and that not only in regard of what they have been, but also in regard of what they daily are. Next, ye would have all to be prayed to eternal wrath, who have departed and made defection in this time: alas! we need not blow them away, the great part is going fast enough that way; but this, I am sure, is not to give God his glory, but to take from him, and limit him in his freedom and choice, in the greatness of his pardon. It is remarkable, that the angels in their *glory to God*, joined also with it, *good will to men*. Next, ye have rejected the Psalms, with many other things, by a paper come from some of you; and I cannot see upon what account, except it be, because it is man's work, in turning the Psalms out of prose into metre. Then you must reject all the other Scriptures, because the translation of them is of man's work; ye have not yet learned the original languages, ye must betake yourselves altogether to the spirit, and what a spirit will that be; that is not to be tried by the Scriptures! I told some of you, when I last saw you, that ye were too little led by the Scriptures, and too much by your own thoughts and suggestions, which indeed opens a wide door to delusion, and, alas! lays yourselves open to Satan's temptations.

As for the rest, of your denying all your former covenants and declarations; this cannot be from God, they containing nothing but lawful and necessary duties; and suppose they did not contain and include a complete reformation, yet they did not exclude it; so that still holding them, we might have passed on to more perfection, and they might be inviolable obligations with us. And next, Your cutting off all that were not of your mind, and delivering them up to devils, was not justice and religion, it being done neither in judgment nor righteousness, upon conviction of their crimes, but unbridled rage and fury. But these things I cannot fully speak to now: yet there is somewhat that I cannot pass; but must tell you, that I fear there shall remain some of the leaven within, that shall not only spoil an orthodox Protestant, but also a true, tender, and humble Christian, and give us nothing instead of it, but a blown bladder: For I am persuaded, if Satan should have the tutory but a while, he should bring it to this; for it has been his way with some, first to make them faint-like, and afterwards to settle them at atheism; like a cunning fisher, running a fish upon an angle, who at last casts it on dry ground. God is my witness, my my soul loves to see holiness, tenderness, and zeal, in such a generation, where there is nothing but untenderness, unconcernedness, and lukewarmness; and by his grace, I shall ever cherish it. I desire you then, in the bowels of Christ, to retain your zeal; but see well to this, that it be for his glory. Indeed, the more that you are zealous, and the further ye go forward, so that the word of God direct your course, ye are the more pleasing to God, and shall be the dearer to us. And persuade yourselves, that tho' I cannot equal or go before; yet it is the sincere desire of my heart to follow such. And my soul wishes you well, tho' it may be I cannot here point, nor lead you the way to well-being; yet this I must say, that if I could lead you the way that he has led me, I should let you see eternal life, without these things that I am desiring you to relinquish. Hold truth, glorify God, be zealous to have him glorified; but think not to desire the condemnation of any man, simply on that account, that they dare not come and continue where you are; or to put a bar by prayer between them and a return, is a glorifying of God: we glorify him in this kind, when, as he himself desires, we acquiesce in his sentence, when it is past, tho' we wrestle against it, before it be known to us.

I cannot bid you go forward in all, but I desire you to go forward in that which is surer and better. And dear friends, let not the world have that to say, that when ye are become right, ye are become the less zealous; only take the right object, and let your zeal grow. O let not your sufferings be stained with such wildness, and think it not strange that ye have not such liberty in your return as ye seemed to have before; if ye take the right way, and hold on, ye shall find it, in his time, greater and better, and surer. I shall only add, that there must be an express owning of his truths, whereof ye have been persuaded before now, which now are either denied or doubted, otherwise you will come to nothing of religion, or worse; this will either state your sufferings right, or be a mean to obtain a cleanly liberty from God in his due time. Grace, mercy and peace be with you. *Amen.*

DONALD CARGIL.

The dying Testimony and last Words of Mr. WALTER SMITH *Student of Theology, who suffered at the Cross of Edinburgh, July* 27. 1681.

Dear Friends, and Acquaintances,

AS I desire, while in the body, to sympathize somewhat with you in lamenting your various cases, and the case of the church, whereof we are the sons and daughters; so I must lay this request upon you, and leave it with you, that ye take some of your time, and set it apart particularly, to solace your souls, in blessing and magnifying your God and my God, for the lot he hath decreed and chosen out for poor unworthy me, from eternity, in time, and to eternity; in the immediate enjoyment of Father, Son, and Holy Ghost, one God, incomprehensible and unchangeable in his being, wisdom, power, holiness, justice, goodness, and truth; and that because he hath made me a man, and a Christian. And now I set to my seal to all his truths, revealed in his word; and particularly these: 1*st,* That he is one God, Father, Son, and Holy Ghost. But alas! who can think of him? who can hear of him, or write of him aright? O he is God! he is God! 2*dly,* That he made man perfect; and tho' we have destroyed and incapacitate ourselves to do any thing that is right, while out of Christ, yet we are under the obligation of the whole law, which is the perfect rule of righteousness. 3*dly,* That my Lord (yea thro' free grace, I can say, my Lord Jesus Christ) came to the world to save sinners: And tho' I cannot say that I have been the greatest of sinners, yet I can say, that he hath covered, pardoned, prevented and hid from the world, sins in me that have been heinous by many aggravations. 4*thly,* That *except a man be born again, he cannot enter into the kingdom of heaven.* My friends, this is the new birth, this is regeneration, that I am speaking of, to which the great part, even of professors, I fear, will be found strangers. 5*thly,* I set to my seal to the truth of that precious promise, Josh. i. 5. repeated Heb. xiii. 5. *For he hath said, I will never leave thee nor forsake thee;* together with all the other promises to that purpose: And I am sure, he hath carried me thro' divers conditions of life, many various and singular difficulties and damping discouragements. But omitting these things whereof the profane persecutors may as much boast as to the outward as any, he hath led me thro' the several steps of soul exercise, and the pangs of the new birth, into himself. This, this my friends, is the cognizance and distinguishing character of a saint indeed; and by this, and this only, *we pass from death to life*.

And as I adhere to the Confession of Faith and work of reformation, as I shall afterwards speak to; so particularly, I set to my seal to these truths in the eighteen chapter thereof, anent the assurance of grace and salvation. Alas! the ignorance of this generation is great. My dear friends, I leave this as my last advice to you, Make use of that book which contains the Confession of Faith, Catechisms, Sum of Saving Knowledge, Practical Use of Saving Knowledge, Directory for Worship, the Causes of God's Wrath, &c. And let none think this work below them, for the spiritual enlightening of the mind, which requires the literal with it, is the first work of the Spirit, after we first begin to come to ourselves, or rather to what we were in innocency, and ought to be by grace. But as to this, I do confidently refer you to Shepard's Sound Believer; which, in my poor apprehension, is the surest ye can meet with. And 6*thly*, I set to my seal to the covenant of grace, particularly that clause of it, Isa. lix. 21. *As for me, this is my covenant with them, saith the Lord, My spirit that is upon thee,* &c. And here I leave my testimony against all Atheists, speculative (if there be any such) and practical; and all mockers of godliness, all formalists and hypocrites, Quakers and Enthusiasts, who either pretend to the Spirit, neglecting the word, or lean upon the word, neglecting the teaching of the Spirit. And what shall I more say, but by what of truth I have in experience seen, I am bold to believe what I have not seen: his testimony is a ground sufficient, and there can be no deceit under it.

And now I am to die a martyr; and I am as fully persuaded of my interest in Christ, and that he hath countenanced me in that, for which I am to lay down my life, as I am of my being. And let the world and byassed professors say their pleasures, I am here in no delusion; I have the free and full exercise of reason and judgment; I am free of passion and prejudice, and, excepting that I am yet in the body, I am free of Satan's fire and fury:

of Mr. Walter Smith.

I have no bitterness nor malice at any living; so that what I am owning and dying for, I am solidly and firmly persuaded to be truth and duty, according to my mean capacity. And this is the main point this day in controversy, upon which I was peremptorily questioned, and desired positively to answer, yea, or nay, under the threatening of the boots, viz. Whether I owned the king's authority as presently established and exercised? which I did positively disown, and denied allegiance to him, as he is invested with that supremacy proper to Jesus Christ only. And who knoweth not that at first he was constitute and crowned a covenanted king, and the subjects sworn in allegiance to him, as such, by the Solemn League and Covenant? This was the authority wherewith he was cloathed, and the exercise of it was to be for God, religion, and the good of the subjects; and is not all this, as to God and his people, overturned and perverted! But, 2dly, The whole of this pleaded for authority at present, is established on the ruin of the land's engagements to God, and to one another. But I say no more as to this. Consider things seriously, and ponder them deeply; zeal for God is much gone: Look to it, and labour to recover it; your peace shall be in it, as to duty; tho' Christ's righteousness, I see, is the only sure foundation.

I leave my testimony against malignancy, ungodliness and profanity, and whatsoever is contrary to sound doctrine, professed and owned by the reformed anti-erastian Presbyterian party in Scotland, whereof I die a member and professor, being fully satisfied and content with my lot. And as to my apprehending, we were singularly delivered by providence into the adversaries hand, and, for what I could learn, were betrayed by none; nor were any accessory to our taking, more than we were ourselves: And particularly let none blame the Lady St. Johnskirk in this. I have no time to give you an account of the Lord's kindness and tenderness to us, in restraining the adversaries fury; for they began very brisk, by making us ly all night bound, and expresly refused to suffer us to worship God, or pray with one another, until we came to Linlithgow. But the Lord hasteneth to come; beware of going back, wait for him, be not anxious about what shall become of you, or the remnant; he is concerned, his intercession is sufficient:

Get him set up, and kept up in his own room in your souls, and other things will be the more easily kept in theirs. Be tender of all who have the root of the matter; but beware of compliance with any, whether ministers, or professors or adversaries. As to my judgment, insignificant as it is, I am necessitate to refer you to the draught of a paper, which I drew, at the desire of some societies in Clydsdale, intituled, *Some Steps of Defection*, &c. Beware of a spirit of bitterness, peremptoriness, and ignorant zeal, which hath been the ruin of some, and will be the ruin of more, if mercy prevent not. I was withdrawn from by some, as having given offence to them by my protesting against their way in particular, wherein, I am sure, as to the manner, they were wrong; and tho' they had been right, it was not a ground to have made such a separation from me, much less from those who joined with me: And if any division be longer kept up upon that account, they will find it a great iniquity, if rightly considered. I can get no more written, nor see I great need for it; for the testimonies of martyrs are not your rule. Farewel. *Sic subscribitur,*

From the tolbooth of Edinburgh, July 27, 1681.

WALTER SMITH.

BEing come to the scaffold, he accosted the multitude to this purpose: All ye beholders, who are come here upon various designs, I intreat you, be not mistaken anent the cause of my suffering this day; for however ye may be misinformed, yet it is of verity, that we are brought here upon the matters of our God; because we testified against the supremacy, and would not consent to the setting of Christ's crown upon the head of him who had by usurpation aspired thereto, contrary to his former engagements. Upon this they caused beat the drums, which obliged him a little to silence; but beckoning with his hand, he said I shall only say something to three particulars; And *first*, anent that which some are apt to believe, that we are against authority; but we detest that, and say, That we own all the lawful exercise of authority; and we hope there are none that are Christians will allow us to own the unlawful exercise, or rather tyranny of authority. At this the drums were again beat; and so he sung a part of the ciii. Psalm from the beginning, and prayed; which done, he turned his face to the crofs, and faid, I blefs the Lord, I am not furprifed, neither terrified with this death or the manner of it. I confefs the thoughts of death have been fometimes very terrible to me, when I have been reflecting upon my mif-fpending of precious time; yea, fometimes the ftrength of temptation, and my own weaknefs, have made me herein to raze the very foundation of my intereft; but my God builds fafter than he permits the devil and my falfe heart to caft down. I have had fome clouds even fince I came to prifon, but bleffed be God, thefe are all removed : for my God hath faid to my foul, *Be of good cheer, thy fins are forgiven thee.* And the faith of this makes me not to fear grim death; tho' it be called the king of terrors, yet it is not fo to me : for this that you think a cruel and fudden death, is but an inlet to life, which fhall be eternal. Let none be offended at Chrift and his way becaufe of fuffering, for I can perfuade you, there is more of Chrift's help, and fupporting grace and ftrength in a fuffering lot, than all that ever I heard of by the hearing of the ear : But now I am made to find it in my own experience, and I can fay, *He is altogether lovely.*

But a *fecond* thing that I promifed to fpeak to, is, That I deteft and abhor all Popery, Prelacy, Eraftianifm, and all other fteps of defection from the truths of God, and turning afide to the right and left hand. Alfo I teftify againft all errors, as Quakerifm, Arminianifm, &c. and all that is contrary to found doctrine, who walk not according to the Scriptures, and make not the word and Spirit of God their rule to walk by. I have lived, and now am ready to die, a Chriftian, a Proteftant, and a Prefbyterian in my judgment; therefore let none hereafter fay, that we walk not by the Scriptures; for once Britain and Ireland, and efpecially Scotland, were deeply fworn to maintain what now they difown; therefore beware of ftanding in the way of others, feeing ye will not go in yourfelves. *Thirdly,* I exhort all you that are the poor remnant, to be ferious in getting your intereft cleared; you that are in the dark with your cafe, take not flafhes for converfion : Study a holy converfation: be at more pains to know the Scriptures, and believe them; be ferious in prayer; flight not time; take Chrift in his own terms, and refolve to meet with trials, and that fhortly; flight not known duties; commit not known sins, whatever suffering ye may meet with for your cleaving to duty. Lippen to God, and you will not be disappointed. 'Construct well of him under all dispensations; weary not of suffering; ly not at ease in a day of Jacob's trouble. I have one word more to speak to all that are going on in persecuting the way and friends of Christ, and that is the very words of our Lord, Remember, *whatever you do to one of these little ones, you do it unto me*. I pray the Lord, that he may open the eyes of all the elect, who are yet strangers to regeneration; and also convince such of them as are fallen from their first love. Now, my friends, I have this to say in my own vindication, that, however I have been branded by some, and misconstructed by others, yet I can say in the sight of the Lord, before whom I am now to appear, that I am free of any public scandal; I say, I am free of drunkenness, I am free of whoredoms, thefts, or murder; therefore let none say, that we are murderers, or would kill any, but in self-defence, and in defence of the gospel. I truly forgive all men the wrongs they have done to me, as I desire to be forgiven of the Lord; but as for the wrongs done to a holy God, I leave these to him who is the avenger of blood; let him do to them as he may be glorified. Now I say no more, but pray that all who are in his way, may be kept from sinning under suffering; and that every one may prepare for a storm, which I do verily believe is not far off.

Then stooping down, he saluted some friends, and said, Farewel all relations and acquaintances; farewel all ye that are lovers of Christ and his righteous cause. And beckoning to the multitude, he said farewel also. And so he went up the ladder with the greatest discoveries of alacrity, and magnanimity; and seating himself upon it, he said, Now this death of mine I fear not, for my sins are freely pardoned; yea, and I will sin no more, for I am made thro' my God, to look hell, wrath, devils, and sin eternally out of countenance. Therefore farewel all created enjoyments, pleasures and delights; farewel sinning and suffering; farewel praying and believing; and welcome heaven and singing; welcome joy in the Holy Ghost; welcome Father, Son, and Holy Ghost, into thy hands I commit my spirit. When the executioner was about to unty his cravat, he thurst him away, and untied it himself; and, calling for his brother, threw *of Mr. James Boig.*

it down, saying, This is the last token you will get from me. After the napkin was drawn over his face, he uncovered it again, and said, I have one word more to say, and that is to all that have any love to God and his righteous cause, that they will set time apart, and sing a song of praise to the Lord, for what he has done to my soul; and my soul says, *To him be praise.* Then letting down the napkin, he prayed a little within himself, and the executioner doing his office, threw him over.

The last Testimony of Mr. JAMES BOIG *Student of Theology, who suffered at the Cross of Edinburgh, July* 27. 1681. *written in a Letter to his Brother.*

Dear Brother,

I Have not now time to write that which I would, but to satisfy your desire, and the desire of others who are concerned in the cause and work of God, that is now, at this time, trampled upon: I have given out mine indictment to a friend of yours, and now I shall give you an account of the enemies prosecution thereof against us. Mine indictment did run upon three heads; 1*st*, That I had disowned the king's authority. 2*dly*. That I said, the rising in arms at Bothwel-bridge was lawful, and upon the defence of truth. 3*dly*, That I owned the Sanquhar Declaration in the whole heads and articles thereof. And having again owned this before the justiciary and assizers, I held my peace, and spake no more; because I saw what was spoken by others was not regarded, either by our unjust judges or mocking auditors; all that our speaking did, was the exposing of us to the mockery of all present. But the reasons that were given in thus, for our defence in the first head were, That we could not own the authority, as now presently established, unless we should also own the supremacy, which the king hath usurped over the church. By our doing of this we should rob Christ of that which is his right, and give that to a man which is due to no mortal; the reason is, because the supremacy is declared, in their acts of parliament, to be essential to the crown; and that which is essential to any thing is the same with the thing itself; so that in owning their authority, we are of necessity obliged to justify them in their usurpation also. But there is another argument, which to me is valid, though I spoke it not their confent to the prefent acts and laws was never formally required of them, but that which is taken for their confent, is their fimple filence, when thefe acts were made and publifhed, and owning thefe parliaments as their reprefentatives; fo that I may clearly argue from this, that, even in their own fenfe, my owning of the prefent authority now eftablifhed as lawful, and the prefent magiftrates as my magiftrates, is a giving my confent to the prefent acts and laws, and fo confequently to the robbing of Chrift of that which is his right. As to the fecond, it being but one particular fact, deduced from that principle of the lawfulnefs of self-defence, and this principle being as pofitively afferted by all of us, I look upon the principle to be as exprefly fealed with our blood as that particular fact of rifing in arms at Bothwel-bridge is. As to the third, it being a deed confequential from the firft, I looked upon them both to ftand and fall together, and he that owneth the firft muft, of neceffity, own the laft alfo. And as to that of declaring of war, I did always look upon it to be one and the fame, tho' differently expreffed, with that contained in the paper found at the Ferry, and that the main defign of it was, to vindicate us before the world, in our repelling unjuft violence, and clearing us of thefe afperfions that were caft upon us, viz. The holding as a principle the lawfulnefs of private affaffinations, (which we difown) and murdering of all thofe who are not of the fame judgment with us. Thefe are the truths which we are to feal with our blood, to morrow in the afternoon, at the Crofs of Edinburgh. As to other particular actions, we declined to anfwer pofitively to them, as that of the bifhop's death; we told them, we could not be judges of other mens actions: As to the excommunication, becaufe we declined them, as not competent judges to cognofce upon an ecclefiaftic matter, they did not proceed upon it.

And now, dear brother, you may fee our quarrel clearly ftated to be the fame that Mr. James Guthrie laid down his head for; befide whofe, mine and my other two friends heads are to be set. There were many other things past in private betwixt me and Mr. William Paterson, sometime my regent, now council-clerk, with some others who strongly assaulted me with their snares; but now, I hope, I may say, that *my soul hath escaped like a bird out of the snare of the fowler.* And as to your second desire, of knowing how it went with my soul; many and strong have been the assaults of Satan since I came to prison; but glory to God, who hath not been wanting to me in giving me assistance, yea, many times unsought; and is yet continuing, and I hope, shall do to the end, to carry me above the fear of death, so that I am in as sweet a calm as if I were going to be married to one dearly beloved. Alas! my cold heart is not able to answer his burning love; but what is wanting in me, is, and shall be made up in a Saviour complete and well furnished in all things, appointed of the Father for this end, to bring his straying children to their own home, whereof (I think I may venture to say it) I am one, tho' fecklefs. Now, I have no time to enlarge, else I would give you a more particular account of God's goodness and dealing with me; but let this suffice, that I am once fairly on the way, and within the view of Immanuel's land, and in hopes to be received an inhabitant there within the space of twenty-six hours at most. Farewel all earthly comforts, farewel all worldly vanities, farewel all carnal desires. Welcome cross, welcome gallows, welcome Christ, welcome heaven and everlasting happiness, &c. I have no more spare time. Grace, mercy and peace be with you. Amen.

From Edinburgh tolbooth, } Sic subscribitur,
July 26. 1681. } JAMES BOIG.

The Testimony of that valiant and worthy Gentleman, DAVID HACKSTOUN *of Rathillet, who suffered at the Cross of Edinburgh, July* 30. 1680.

His Interrogations and Answers before the Privy Council, Saturday, July 24. 1680.

1. WHETHER or not had you any hand in the murdering of the late Bishop of St. Andrews? Answered, He was not obliged to answer that question, nor be his own accuser. 2. What he would declare as to the king's authority? Answered, That authority that

disowns the interest of God, and states itself in opposition to Jesus Christ, is no more to be owned; but so it is, the king's authority is now such, therefore it ought not to be owned. 3. Whether the killing of the archbishop of St. Andrews was murder, yea, or not? Answered, That he thought it no sin to dispatch a bloody monster. 4. If he owned the new covenant taken at the Queensferry, from Mr. Cargil one of their preachers? Answered, That he did own it in every particular thereof, and would fain see the man that in conscience and reason would debate the contrary. 5. If he were at liberty, and had the power to kill any of the king's council, and murder them as he did the bishop of St. Andrews, whether he would do it, yea, or not? Answered, That he had no spare time to answer such frivolous and childish questions.

The chancellor told him, that if he were not more ingenuous in his answers, he would presently be tortured. He answered, That is but a little addition to your former cruelties, and I have that comfort, that tho' you torture my wounded body, yet ye cannot reach my soul. The chancellor urged him with several other questions, which he refused to answer. But, said he, I would gladly speak a little if I could have liberty, which was allowed him. Then he said, Ye know that youth is a folly, and I acknowledge that in my younger years I was too much carried down with the spait of it; but that inexhaustible fountain of the goodness and grace of God, which is free and great, hath reclaimed me, and as a fire-brand hath plucked me out of the claws of Satan; and now I stand here before you as a prisoner of Jesus Christ, for adhering to his cause and interest, which hath been sealed with the blood of many worthies, who have suffered in these lands, and have witnessed to the truths of Christ these few years bygone; and I do own all the testimonies given by them, and desire to put in my mite among theirs, and am not only willing to seal it with my blood, but also with the sharpest tortures that you can imagine. Then being interrogate by the bishop of Edinburgh, what he would answer to that article of the Confession of Faith, That *difference of religion doth not make void the magistrate's right and authority?* He answered, He would not answer any perjured prelate: The bishop replied, He was in the wrong to him, because he never took the covenant, therefore he was not perjured, and fo deferved not that name. But fome of them afked him, how he would anfwer that queftion? He anfwered, That queftion was anfwered long ago by the Solemn League and Covenant, which binds us only to maintain and defend the king in the defence of the true religion; but now the king having ftated himfelf an enemy to religion, and all that will live religioufly, therefore it is high time to fhake off all obligation of allegiance to his authority. Thefe interrogations were all read to him in the face of the council, and he owned all. The next day that he was arraigned before the council, they afked if he had any more to fay? He anfwered, That which he had to fay was faid already in every particular thereof; and, faid he, I will not only feal it with my blood, but with all the tortures ye can imagine.

Follows the Extract of the proceedings of the Privy Council, Edinburgh, July 29. 1680.

IN prefence of the Lord's Jufticiary, Clerk and Commiffioners of Jufticiary, compeared David Hackftoun of Rathillet, and declines the King's Majefty's authority of the commiffioners of jufticiary as his judges, and abfolutely refufes to fign this declaration, as being before perfons who are not his judges. He refufes to anfwer concerning the murder of the late bifhop of St Andrews, and fays, the caufes of his declinement are, *Becaufe they have ufurped the fupremacy over the church, belonging alone to Jefus Chrift, and have eftablifhed idolatry, perjury, and other iniquities; and in profecuting their defign, in confirming themfelves in this ufurped right, have fhed much innocent blood.* Therefore the faid David, adhering to Chrift, his rights and kingly office over the church, declines them that are his open enemies and competitors for his crown and power, as competent judges; refufes, as formerly, to fign this his declaration, dated from his own mouth; whereupon his majefty's advocate takes inftruments, and requires the commiffioners of jufticiary to fign the fame in his prefence, as for him; and his majefty's advocate takes inftruments, that the faid David has declined his majefty's authority, and the authority of his commiffioners, and refufed to deny the murder of the late bifhop of St. Andrews, and requires Meffrs. John Vas, James Balfour, and the men of the court witneffes to the forefaid declaration. *Sic fubfcribitur,* Sir Robert Maitland,

James Foulis, David Balfour, David Falconer, Rodger Hodge.

Upon Friday, July 30 being again brought before the council, it was asked of him if he had any other thing to say? He answered, That which I have said I will seal it. Then they told him, they had something to say to him; and commanded him to sit down and receive his sentence; which willingly he did, but told them they were all bloody murderers, for all the power they had was derived from tyranny; and that these years bygone they have not only tyrannized over the church of God, but have also grinded the faces of the poor, so that oppressions, bloodshed, perjury, and many murders were to be found in their skirts. Upon which he was incontinent carried away to the scaffold, at the market Cross of Edinburgh, where he died with great torture inflicted upon his body, not being permitted to leave any testimony to the world, except what is comprehended in these missives directed to some of his christian acquaintances, from his prison in the tolbooth of Edinburgh; which are as follows.

The copy of a Letter written by DAVID HACKSTOUN *of Rathillet, to his Christian Friend N. Dated from the tolbooth of Edinburgh, July 26. 1680.*

Dear Acquaintance,

I Know, this late dispensation of providence will occasion much sadness to you, and other lovers of the Lord's truth, now in this day, when so few, by their practice, prove themselves to be zealous for God, or lovers of his truth; but instead of that growth in the graces of God's Spirit, and stedfastness which should be in Christians, have made defection from the truth, and are fallen from their first love, to the strengthening the hands of usurpers of the crown of Christ, in their unlawful encroachments on the privileges of the Son of God. Wherefore I intreat you, and all others, as you would not offend God, and provoke him to more anger, do not murmur, but bless and praise him, and submit to him in all humility; for if this be one of the steps of Zion's deliverance, and God's glory, why should not we praise him for every thing? If we had the manner of our delivery at our carving, we would spill it. He is the wisdom of the Father, who sits at the helm and orders all affairs.

The faith of this would filence all fuggeftions from Satan, our own hearts, and mifbelief. I defire you would charge all that have love or affection to me, not to be fad on my account, but rather to rejoice on my behalf, that God hath fo honoured me in all I have been tryfted with: For as he took me, when I was a flave to Satan and fin, and caft his love upon me, and plucked me as a brand out of the fire, and brought me into covenant with him, to promote and carry forward his work, without fear of what man can do unto me; and as he helped me to make the bargain with him upon good terms, which was a renouncing of my own ftrength, and a refolution to do all in his ftrength; fo now he hath been faithful in all things to me, and hath furnifhed me fufficiently for what he hath called me to, and hath paffed by my many grofs failings and breaches of my conditions to him, and hath done to me above what I could afk of him. O that I could commend him to all, and ftir up all to fear, admire, and praife him, and believe on him! But the lukewarmnefs and want of love to God, and indifferency in Chrift's matters, (which in his condefcendency to his church he hath referved as his declarative glory) and neutrality in thefe things are come to fo great a height among profeffors, that, I think, God is laying a ftumbling-block before them, one after another, that when they are fallen (whom he will have to fall) he may be glorified in his juftice, by bringing that ftroke of vengeance that feems to be hanging over thefe lands, becaufe of their fearful idolatry, perjury, bloodfhed, blafphemy, and other abominations, the whole land is, this day, guilty of. Think not ftrange that I fay, all are guilty; there are none free, nor fhall be reputed free in the fight of God, but mourners in Zion. Lord grant repentance, and a fpirit of mourning; brokennefs and contrition of fpirit is the only facrifice well-pleafing unto God; and I prove all guilty: Firft our reprefentatives, (and fo we in them) eftablifhed thefe fins, in our national decrees, which we have homologate in owning them ever after; and much more have we homologate there fins, in contributing, one way or other, to the ftrengthning of their hands againft God, as alas, but few be free of this, this day! O that preachers would preach repentance, and profeffors would exhort one another to mourn, in fecret, and together, becaufe of fin; and with their mourning would believe, for these are very consistent together. I find flesh and blood great enemies to faith, and friends, yea, fosterers of sinful fears. It is above nature to believe, especially when dispensations seem to contradict our faith: but if any had faith towards God concerning me, let not this brangle their faith, but rather strengthen; there is nothing can contradict what God hath determined; but over the belly of all opposition he will perfect his work in and by me, either to a remarkable delivery, or through-bearing, as he sees most for his own glory.

Wherefore let us submit to his will, and ly before the throne in behalf of Zion and her children; and O! that you yourself would, and desire others that are faithful, to hold up my case to Zion's God, that he would glorify himself in me, and let your prayers be in faith; *To him that believeth, all things are possible.* There are many feckless, misbelieving prayers, that prevail not with God because of unbelief. I know, these sufferings will be a great stumbling to many, otherwise gracious, but let it not be to you: I bless the Lord, it is not (as yet) so to me, but rather the power, yea, the love of God to me; for it was not altogether unexpected unto me: For (not to reflect upon any that have sealed that truth and cause, as we stated it, with their blood) I cannot deny, but it was over the belly of conscience, that I joined with some of our party; for some of them had not their garments clean of the late defections, and there was too much pride amongst us: Neither dare I allow that taking of satisfaction for practices which are the homologating of the public sins, which we did about half an hour before our break; which checked me exceedingly in the time. I think, real sorrow would make men like the prodigal, to think themselves not worthy to be employed in that work; real evidences of reconciliation with God should be seen before admission to such an employment. O that all would take warning, by my reproof, not to venture to follow any man over conscience! There were choice godly men among us, but one Achan will make Israel to fall. I fear the want of faith among us, first and last, and all alongst our late business: I know, many mouths will be opened against me because of what I did before this business, but I dare not but speak it, this is a stumbling block laid to drive them to more sin; and alas! that I did not more to purge us of every sin, especially known sin among us. These that abode within, and came not out with us, let them remember Meroz's curse; I am afraid, God think them not free of our blood, for not joining to our help.

And now, knowing ye will be anxious to know how it was then, and how it hath been since with me. First, We getting notice of a party out seeking us, sent two on Wednesday night late to know their motion, and lay on a muir-side all night; and Thursday about ten hours, we went to take some meat, and sent out other two, and desired them to consult with the first two, who had not come to us, but were lying down to sleep, who all four returned and told us, it was unnecessary to send any for intelligence, they having secured it. Whereupon, after we had gotten some meat, we came to a piece of grass, and lay down, and presently we were all alarmed that they were upon us; and so making ready, we saw them coming fast on; and that about three or four hours in the afternoon; and each one resolving to fight, I rode off to seek a strength for our advantage, and being desired by a country-man to go into such a place for the best strength, I went, and they followed; but coming to it, I found we could go no further; and so turning and drawing up quickly eight horse on the right hand with R. D. and fifteen on the left with me, being no more; the foot not being forty, and many of them ill armed, in the midst. I asked all, if they were willing to fight? who all said, Yes; especially 1. G. The enemy advanced fast, whom I took to be above one hundred and twelve, well armed and horsed; who sending first about twenty dragoons on foot to take the wind of us, which we seeing, sent a party on foot to meet them, and the rest of us advanced fast on the enemy, being a strong body of horse coming hard upon us, whereupon when we were joined, our horse fired first, and wounded and killed some of them, both horse and foot: our horse advanced to their faces, and we fired on each other; I being foremost, after receiving their fire, and finding the horse behind me broken, I then rode in amongst them, and went out at a side, without any wrong or wound; I was pursued by severals, with whom I fought a good space, sometimes they followed me, and sometimes I followed them, at length my horse bogged, and the foremost of theirs, which was David Ramsay one of my acquaintance: we both being on foot, fought it with small swords, without advantage to one another; but at length closing, I was stricken down with three on horse-back behind me; and receiving three sore wounds on the head, and so falling, he saved my life, which I submitted to. They searched me, and carried me to their rear, and laid me down, where I bled much; where were brought severals of their men sore wounded. They gave us all testimony of brave resolute men. What more of our men were killed, I did not see, nor know; but as they told me after, the field was theirs. I was brought toward Douglas. They used me civilly, and brought me drink out of a house by the way. At Douglas, Janet Cleland was kind to me, and brought a Surgeon to me, who did but little to my wounds, only stanched the blood.

Next morning I was brought to Lanerk, and brought before Dalziel, Lord Ross, and some others; who asked many questions at me, but I not satisfying them with answers, Dalziel did threaten to roast me; and carrying me to the tolbooth, caused me to be bound most barbarously, and cast me down, where I lay till Saturday morning, without any, except soldiers, admitted to speak to me, or look my wounds, or give me any ease whatsomever. And next morning they brought me and John Pollock, and other two of us, near two miles on foot, I being without shoes, where that party which had broken us at first, received us. They were commanded by Earlshall. We were horsed, civilly used by them on the way, and brought to Edinburgh about four in the afternoon, and carried about the north-side of the town to the foot of the Cannongate, where the town magistrates were, who received us; and setting me on a horse with my face backward, and the other three bound on a goad of iron, and Mr. Cameron's head carried on a halbert before me, and another head in a sack, which I knew not, on a lad's back; and so we were carried up the street to the parliament-closs, where I was taken down, and the rest loosed: All was done by the hangman. I was carried up to the council, and first put into a room alone, where the chancellor came, and asked if I knew him? I answered, Yes: He (after some protestations of love, to which I answered nothing) went his way; and then I was brought in before the council, where the chancellor read a ditty against me. First anent the bishop's murder; to which I answered, I was obliged by no law, either of God or man, to anfwer to it; and neither to accufe myfelf, nor reveal others by vindicating myfelf, or any other way. The advocate afked, Where I was the third day of May was a year? To whom I anfwered, I am not bound to keep a memorial where I am, or what I do every day. The chancellor afked, If I thought it murder? To which I anfwered, tho' I was not bound to anfwer fuch queftions, yet I would not call it fo, but rather fay, It was no murder. The advocate faid, Sir, you muft be a great liar, to fay you remember not where you was that day, it being fo remarkable a day. I replied, Sir, you muft be a far greater liar, to fay, I anfwered fuch a thing. Whereupon the chancellor replied, My lord advocate, he faid only, he was not bound to keep in memory every day's work.

The chancellor afked, If I adhered to Mr. Cargil's papers, which they called the New Covenant taken at the Ferry? I anfwered, I would know what any would fay againft them. He afked, if I owned the king's authority? I told, tho' I was not bound to anfwer fuch queftions, yet being permitted to fpeak, I would fay fomewhat to that. And firft, that there could be no lawful authority but what was of God; and that no authority, ftated in a direct oppofition to God, could be of God; and that I knew of no authority nor judicatory this day in thefe nations, but what were in a direct oppofition to God, and fo could neither be of God, nor lawful, and that their fruits were kything it, in that they were fetting bougerers, murderers, forcerers, and fuch others at liberty from juftice, and employing them in their fervice, and made it their whole work to opprefs, kill, and deftroy the Lord's people. The chancellor and all raged, and defired me to inftance one of fuch fo fet at liberty and employed. I anfwered to that, Tho' it were enough to inftance any fuch when I faw a judicatory to execute juftice, yet I would inftance one; and I inftanced a bougerer, liberated at the fheriff court of Fife, and afterwards employed in their fervice. At which the chancellor raged, and faid, I behoved to be a liar: But I offered to prove it. Bifhop Paterfon afked, if ever Pilate and that judicatory, who were direct enemies to Chrift, were difowned by him as judges? I anfwered, that I would anfwer no perjured prelate in the nation. He anſwered, that he could not be called perjured, becauſe he never took that ſacrilegious covenant. I anſwered, that God would own that covenant when none of them were to oppoſe it. They cried all, I was propheſying: I anſwered, I was not propheſying, but that I durſt not doubt, but God who had ſuch ſingular love to theſe lands, as to bring them into covenant in ſo peculiar a manner with him, would let it be ſeen that his faithfulneſs was engaged to carry it thro' in oppoſition to his enemies. Some aſked, what I anſwered to that article of the Confeſſion of Faith concerning the king? I anſwered, It was cleared in theſe two covenants. The advocate aſked, What I ſaid of that article of the covenant, wherein we are bound to maintain and defend the king? I deſired him to tell out the reſt of it, which was, in defence of religion, but not in the deſtruction of religion. The chancellor threatned me with boots, and other terrible things; and ſaid, I ſhould not have the benefit of a ſudden death. To which I anſwered, it would be but an addition to their cruelties uſed againſt God's people before, and that I was there a priſoner of Chriſt, owning his truths againſt his open enemies, and referred it to their own acts of parliament and council, to let their cruelty and oppoſition to God and his people be ſeen.

After this, they called for a ſurgeon, and removed me to another room; where he dreſſed my wounds. In which time, the chancellor came, and kindly aſked, If ever I ſaid to a ſhepherd on the Mounthill, that if I thought they would not put me to an ignominious death, I would refer myſelf to the chancellor? I ſaid, No. He ſaid, A ſhepherd came to him and ſaid ſo. I ſaid, that he, or any other who ſaid ſo to him were liars. I was aſked by ſome, concerning our ſtrength. To which I told, how few we were, and how ſurpriſed by ſuch a ſtrong party, and that knowing with what cruel orders they came againſt us, we were forced to fight. After dreſſing of my wounds, I was brought back to them, and theſe things being written, were read over to me; to which I adhered: and being aſked, If I would ſign them, I ſaid, Not. The chancellor ſaid, He would do it for me. Some one of them aſked, at the firſt time, concerning my being at ſome other buſineſs: To whom I anſwered, That tho' I was not obliged to anſwer ſuch queſtions, yet I adhered to all that had been done in be-

of David Hackſtoun of Rathillet. 71

half of that cauſe againſt its enemies. After which, I was ſent to the tolbooth, and have met ſince with all manner of kindneſs, and want for nothing. My wounds are duly dreſſed, which, I fear, may prove deadly, they being all in the head, the reſt of my body is ſafe.

In all theſe trials (I bleſs the Lord) I was ſtayed, unmoved, no alteration of countenance in the leaſt, nor impatience appeared. Some of them have come to me, and regreted that ſuch a man as I ſhould have been led away with Cameron. I anſwered, He was a faithful miniſter of Jeſus Chriſt, and as for me, I deſired to be one of theſe deſpicable ones whom Chriſt chooſed. They ſaid, It was a Quaker-like anſwer. I told it was the words of Chriſt and his apoſtles. Biſhop Paterſon's brother, unknown to me, had a long reaſoning with me, but, I think, not to truth's diſadvantage. He told me, that the whole council obſerved, that I gave them not their due titles: At which I ſmiled, and made no reply. He ſaid, I was ill to the biſhop. I told, that I aſſerted the truth. He ſaid, that he never took the covenant, and ſo could not be perjured I anſwered, Prelacy itſelf was abjured by the whole nation. He told me, That the whole council found, I was a man of great parts, and alſo of good birth. I replied, For my birth, I was related to the beſt in the kingdom, which I thought little of; and for my parts they were ſmall; yet I truſted ſo much to the goodneſs of that cauſe for which I was a priſoner, that if they would give God that juſtice as to let his cauſe be diſputed, I doubted not to plead it againſt all that could ſpeak againſt it. It was caſt up to me both at the council and here, that there were not two hundred in the nation to own our cauſe. I anſwered at both times, That the cauſe of Chriſt had been often owned by fewer. I was preſſed to take advice: I anſwered, I would adviſe with God and my own conſcience, and would not depend on men, and refuſed to debate any more, ſince it was to no purpoſe, being troubleſome to me, and not advantageous to the cauſe. At the council, ſome ſaid, I was poſſeſſed with a devil; ſome one thing, ſome another. The chancellor ſaid, I was a vitious man: I anſwered, While I was ſo, I had been acceptable to him; but now, when otherways, it was not ſo. He aſked me, If I would yet own that cauſe with my blood, if at liberty? I anſwered, Both our fathers had owned it with the hazard of their blood before me. Then was I called by all, a murderer. I anſwered, God ſhould decide it betwixt us; to whom I refer it, who were moſt murderers in his ſight, they or I.

Ye have an account, as near as I can give, of what paſſed among us. Be ye, and deſire all others to be, earneſt with God in my behalf; for I am weak, and cannot ſtand without conſtant ſupplies of the graces of his Spirit. O! I am afraid left I deny him: I have rich promiſes, but I want faith. Pray and wreſtle in my behalf, and in behalf of the reſt. And ſhew this to my friends in that cauſe with me, eſpecially D. K. Let all ly before the Lord, that he would ſhew us the cauſe of his anger againſt us: and let me know with the firſt occaſion who of us were ſlain. Commend me to all friends: and let none ſtumble at the cauſe, becauſe of this. It was often in my mouth to almoſt all, *That if we purged not ourſelves of the public and particular ſins among us, God would break us, and bring a delivery out of our aſhes.* Let none murmur at what we ſhould think our glory. And let miniſters and others be afraid to be more tender of men than God's glory. And however it be a ſtumbling to ſome, let it be a token of the love of God, to his church, to you, and all that love his truth. Pray for the out-lettings of all the graces of God's Spirit to me, and all the reſt. I have need of patience, ſubmiſſion, humility, love to, and zeal for God; hope and faith above all, without which I am but a frail worm, and will fall before theſe enemies of mine, inward and outward. And thus recommending you to his grace, who hath bought us with his precious blood, and remembering my love to all friends, I am,

Yours in our ſweet Lord, and Sympathizer in our afflictions,

Sic ſubſcribitur, DAVID HACKSTOUN.

P. S. You may let others ſee this, but have a care of keeping it; becauſe I have no double, and it may be all my teſtimony. Send nothing to me, for I am fully ſeen to, and have met with kindneſs from all ſorts, only friends have not liberty to ſee me. My love to you and all friends. I ſaid to Clerk Paterſon, That I ſhould have ſeen Mr. Cargil's Papers, before I had anſwered anent them.

The copy of another Letter written by DAVID HACKSTOUN *of Rathillet, to a gentlewoman of his acquaintance. Dated from the tolbooth of Edinburgh, July 28. 1680.*

Madam,

THE bearer shows me, your Ladyship desires to know what I mean by the Achan I mentioned in my other; which I shall explain: and alas! that I have such a wide field to walk in, when I name such a thing; for I know not how to find out the man that is free of the accursed thing among us, for which God is contending against the land; especially against such as would be most free of the public sins, and most downright for God. Only I desire both to reverence, and admire the holy wisdom and loving kindness of God, that is, by these dark-like dispensations, purging his people, that he may bring forth a chaste spouse to himself in Scotland. These are tokens of his fatherly love: and I fear a delivery, while we stand guilty of such things, as are so open whoredoms against our married Husband, might rather be looked upon as a bill of divorce, than joining again in a married relation. And first, I must explain the national sins, according to the light God hath bestowed upon me, out of his free grace, who is not tied to any, but chooseth and revealeth himself to whom he will; and often glorifies his free grace, in making use even of the greatest sinners, as I confess I have been one: which national sins are contained in our national decrees.

And *first*, the whole land is become guilty of idolatry, as it is established by the Acts of Supremacy, especially in the Act Explanatory; wherein all the declarative glory and prerogatives of Jesus Christ are given to the king, which is fearful idolatry, in ascribing that which he hath purchased with his precious blood, and received from his Father, as his gift, and hath reserved as his peculiar glory; giving this, I say, unto a creature, whom, by this blasphemous decree, we have set up in the room of Jesus Christ, as governor and absolute head and judge in all ecclesiastic affairs: And by the same decree, all acts and laws contrary to it are rescinded, and the whole word of God, contained in the scriptures of both the Old and New Testaments, are a law contrary to it, and

The laſt Speech and Teſtimony

ſo by this are reſcinded. Now, beſides this ſin of Idolatry; by the Act reciſſory, all other acts, oaths, covenants and engagements, that the lands are lying under, ſworn to God, and in his name, are reſcinded, and declared null: and in contempt of God, to whom, and in whoſe name they were ſo ſolemnly ſworn, and ſo often renewed, are burnt by the hands of the hangman, thro' ſeveral places of theſe covenanted kingdoms. This is a legal perjury and breach of covenant, unparallelable in ſacred or profane hiſtory. Beſides, in contempt of the preſence of God, ſeen at the meetings of his people conveened in his name, they have declared them rendezvouſes of rebellion: and by another act, have accounted it preſumption for a miniſter to preach without doors. Thus contemning the call of Chriſt; whereby they ſet themſelves above God. I could inſtance many horrid things acted and done by them, in their proſecuting their deſign of having that idol of theirs fixed in the uſurpation of the prerogatives of Jeſus Chriſt; yet not doubting but your Ladyſhip knows many of them, I ſhall for brevity's ſake omit: only the land is filled, from the one end to the other, with innocent blood, ſhed on that account; and with other terrible abominations deteſtable among Turks and Heathens: I think in God's righteous judgment, theſe men are given up thereto, for the up-filling of the meaſure of their iniquity, that he may be glorified in the ſtroke of his juſtice upon all ranks, which is faſt haſtening, and that inevitably.

But *next*, to mention who are guilty hereof; I know not how to do it; only I may ſay, I know none can be called free, and a freeing of any, or ourſelves thereof, is but a hardning ourſelves againſt God, and a defending ſin againſt him, who is a *ſwift witneſs*, and *will not be mocked*, but *will bring forth the hidden things of diſhoneſty to light*. And therefore, not to mention the idol of the Lord's jealouſy, or theſe that are proſecuting his wicked commands under him, nor Prelates and their adherents, I judge, and I fear, God will eſteem all guilty of theſe forementioned ſins, that have any way owned any of theſe, after their wickedneſs was diſcovered, and much more ſuch as have by their perſonal deeds homologate theſe wicked decrees, and that either by paying ceſſes for ſtrengthening them in their down-bearing of the meetings of God's people for his worſhip, met in oppoſition to theſe wicked *of David Hackstoun of Rathillet.*

decrees, which is their consent to, and contribution for, the strengthening them in all their wickedness against God: or yet by subscribing any manner of bonds to them, which is, an acknowledging them in that relation wherein they stand, and are designing to fix themselves; when they are pursuing, taking, imprisoning, and letting them out on these bonds again: for their end in all their prosecutions of this nature, is to confirm themselves in this usurpation of the crown of Christ, as head of the church: And a subscribing any manner of bond prescribed by them, is and will be, in the sight of God, an acknowledging them as head of the church, in the several stations wherein they have stated themselves; the king as head, and they as factors under him, prosecuting his will, and putting in execution his commands; and an acknowledging any other head, any manner of way, over the church, is directly a denying of Christ before men, in his kingly office, which is a plain denying of him, and hath sore threatenings annexed thereunto.

I could mention many other circumstances, wherein this generation has touched the accursed thing, and has bowed the knee to that Baal-like idol of the Lord's indignation and anger; but I shall only mention besides these two, a *third*, of some who have appeared in arms against God, for, and in company with his enemies. Now that way of giving and taking satisfaction for these sins, which some are for, I cannot consent to: For *first*, These sinful practices being practices immediately against God, and the first table of the law, no satisfaction to man can be sufficient. I close not that door that God hath opened in mercy to the really penitent, but, I say, real evidences that God has forgiven, should be, before a joining with such in society. I know the gospel should be preached to all, that they may repent, that being the means God hath appointed for conversion, when men have sinned: but O! when men after light fall into these things, and others counsel and advise them to such things, fearful shall their doom be, if God prevent them not in his mercy! Now, Madam, there were some such among us; and, as I have observed, God has still punished that party that has been appearing for him, when they have taken in, and joined with, the men of these abominations; and has, as it were, laid by such as have complied with the times apostacy, I doubt not, reserving

G 2

them to the general ftroke he is threatning the whole lands with. O that one and all were making their fouls intereft fure with God!

Madam, I fhall not mention the feveral fteps of apoftacy and defection from God in thefe lands, in complying one way or other with the ftated enemies of the living God, to the ftrengthening them in their ufurpations of Chrift's crown and privileges, and hardening them in their fin, in fhedding, fo many ways, fo much innocent blood, and their other wicked courfes: Neither fhall I mention that idolizing of men that is among us, to the provoking of God, to let, yea, caufe them fall: neither that felfifhnefs that is among us in our appearances for God, which cannot away with a holy, fpotlefs and jealous God, who *will not give his glory to another*. Oh! that one and all were mourning for, and acknowledging our own and the land's guiltinefs in thefe things, and were feeking brokennefs of fpirit, which is a facrifice well pleafing to God, that God might be reconciled to us, and fet up by his Spirit, his ftandard, and gather in his own people thereto; and might let out his Spirit to one and all that are called by his name. I doubt not but God will fave a remnant, but it will be of fuch in whom his free grace will be glorified, and not of the great ones, that have not rendered to the Lord, according to the talents he beftowed on them. Remember me to my fellow prifoners, efpecially fuch as are keeping their garments clean of thefe pollutions; and be earneft with God in my behalf, that he would keep me ftanding, by his free grace, in this trial, in patience, humility, and godly fear. And I am,

MADAM,
Your Ladyfhip's, in all humility, in Jefus Chrift,
DAVID HACKSTOUN.

A copy of a third Letter written by DAVID HACKSTOUN, *during his imprifonment: To his Chriftian friend N. Dated July* 28. 1680.

Dear and Chriftian Acquaintance,

MY love being remembred to you and all friends in Jefus Chrift; thefe are to fhew you and all others that I know and love the truth, as it is this day owned by the fmalleft handful that pretend thereto; that I was yesterday before the lords of justiciary; they charged me with several things. I declined the king's authority as an usurper of the prerogatives of the Son of God, whereby he hath involved the lands in idolatry, perjury, and other wickednesses: and I declined them as exercising under him the supreme power over the church, usurped from Jesus Christ; who, in carrying on their designs of confirming themselves in their usurpations of the crown of Christ, had shed so much innocent blood throughout the land: and that therefore I, as an owner of Christ's right, and his kingly office, which they by their wicked decrees had taken from him, durst not, with my own consent, sustain them as competent judges; but declined them as open and stated enemies to the living God, and competitors for his throne and power, belonging alone to him; whereupon I was dismissed, and at night my indictment to compear to-morrow before an assize was intimated. Therefore I entreat you will, for I know you have moying with God, and cause other faithful friends set time apart, and enquire the Lord's mind concerning me; and be earnest with him in my behalf, that he will glorify himself in me. You may send your letter to —— with a sure hand, who will give it to me. Where-ever Mr. D. C. is, acquaint him with my case, or send him this line; for I know the mind of God is with him; and desire him to write to me. I think, I dare not misbelieve, but when fears assault me, I think there is a voice saying to me, *Fear not*. Let none stumble at our cause, because of the late dispensation; it is God's cause, which was and is in our hands, tho' he has punished us with his fatherly chastisements, because of sin amongst us. *Every tree that bringeth forth fruit, he purgeth it, that it may bring forth more fruit*. But that which decayeth and goeth backward, is laid by as useless. John Pollock has been in the boots, but I am informed, he is not discouraged, but is likely to be well again. My wounds are very sore, but, blessed be God, he keeps me in a good temper, both of body and mind. I am kindly enough used, wanting nothing. I recommend you, and all the faithful, to the protection of him, who is the almighty God, and everlasting Father. No more, but rests,

Yours in our sweet Lord Jesus Christ,

DAVID HACKSTOUN,

A Letter to his Sister.

Loving Sister,

I Received yours, and the other with it, both to my contentment and satisfaction: It makes me afraid, that the eyes of many should be on me. Let all look to God; I am frail, but Christ is strong: I have his promise of through-bearing, and assurance that he should honour me in his cause, before this. Ly low before the Lord, and let others that are yet faithful be earnest on my behalf: and do it in faith: *The prayers of the faithful avail much*. Have you nothing, and tell all friends to have nothing to do with such, as have ado with these that are sitting in that seat, and exercising that power, which belongs alone to Christ. The stroke of the Lord's anger is ready to be poured forth; and these that have received greatest talents from God, and have made that use of them, to strengthen enemies hands by bonds, or otherwise owning them, shall be most remarkable in the stroke; and shall not be honoured to testify for Christ, despised Christ, robbed Christ, contemned Christ, by this generation. Remember me to all relations and friends; and give warning to all to cleave to Christ's truths and interest. If the free grace of God be glorified in me, ought not all to praise him? *Christ came not to call the righteous, but sinners*. Many of this generation think they have so much grace that they cannot sin; but I must tell them, grace doth not warrant from sin; and they may so think of it. *Sic subscribitur*,

DAVID HACKSTOUN.

The Dying Testimony of ARCHIBALD ALISON, *who lived in the parish of Evandale in Clydesdale, and suffered at the Grass-market of Edinburgh, August* 13. 1680.

THERE have been many such sights seen in this place of execution, since the year 1660, for this interest and cause, for which I have received the sentence of death; and here I am in your presence to lay down my life this day; for which, I charge thee, O my soul, and all that is within me, to bless and magnify the name of the Lord, who can perfect his praise, and bring a testimony out of the mouths of babes or sucklings; yea, before he want some to seal his testimony, even if it were from the beasts of the field, he will not want, as in Balaam's days, the dumb ass speaking with man's voice, gave a testimony against the madness of the prophet. Wherefore, unworthy as I am, I am come here, and begs your ear and attention; ye who are spectators and auditors, if the Lord shall permit me to speak a few words, and I shall be but brief.

There are many come here this day to hear and see me lay down this tabernacle of mine, that hath various ends, but our Lord knows you all and your ends both: it is true, God is my witness, that I judge myself the unworthiest person of any that have lost their blood for this honourable cause. He has been pleased to take a testimony from noblemen, gentlemen, ministers, and poor plowman lads, and tradesmen of several sorts, which is a token for good, that he has yet a kindness for these covenanted lands. And I bless the Lord with all my heart, that ever he called me with his heavenly calling: I bless the Lord, that I have a life to lay down for his sake; glory to the Lord, that I shall have blood and wounds in his cause.

But to come more particularly to the purpose in hand, the articles of my indictment were these. *First*, They charged me with rebellion, for joining with these they call rebels, and declared enemies to the king, and enemies to all good government: for my own part I never called them so. I declare here where I stand before him who will be my judge within a little, my design in coming forth with arms, was to hear the gospel preached truly and faithfully, and I know it was the design of that poor handful to defend the gospel, and to keep up a witness and testimony against the abounding corruptions that this land is filled with from end to end, and to plead with the Lord that he would not make a total removal therefrom. Yea, I heard Mr. Richard Cameron say, " My friends, we are not to compare ourselves
" with Gideon's three hundred men, no not at all; our
" design is to have you examined, how ye are, and
" what ye are; to choose two or three of the foot and
" two or three of the horse, that are found fittest quali-
" fied for elders, to try your principles, to try your life
" and conversation, and to have you being Christians,

"Our number was more the last day, and we gave them
free leave to go home, and only but a few handful to
stay; for we design not to fall upon any party of the forces, except they be few in number, and oppose us in
keeping up the gospel in the fields, for I am persuaded
that one meeting in the fields has been more owned
and countenanced by his presence with his people,
than twenty house-meetings as they are now bought;
and therefore make no strife among yourselves about
officers, because they are but men; yea, I think there
is not a man among you all meet for it; we are not
meet to be a minister to you, only we are to wait till
the Lord provide better; and ye that are not satisfied to stay in defence of the gospel, good-morrow to
you, whatsoever ye be." And so I thought it was
rational and warrantable both from the word of God,
and our solemn vows and covenants, which you and the
whole land are engaged unto. Now ye see what was
my motive to join with that handful, and in this I have
peace, and on this ground I lay down my life. There is
a second motive I had, for which I thought myself bound
to own that persecuted cause and interest of my blessed
Lord and Master, Jesus Christ: I being about two years
ago in Carrick, and hearing the precious gospel of Jesus
Christ; in these glorious days, the shining of the countenance of our Lord was discernibly seen there, both upon his ministers and people; I thought it my duty to
mark it. The Lord did so soften and animate my heart
at that time, that I made it my work how I might win
to clearness how to state myself, being among the deceitful indulged ministers, and finding several places of
Scripture calling me out from them, as that known Scripture, *If the Lord be God, follow him; but if Baal, then
follow him. Come out from among them, my people, and
touch not the unclean thing,* &c. *Touch not, taste not,
handle not, which are all to perish with the using.* I
thought it was dreadful to be halting between two opinions. On the other hand, I had some Scriptures concerning the cross that attends pure religion and undefiled. The Lord who has called me here to day, to seal
these truths, wrought with an irresistible power on my
heart, that good word of his in the xviii. Psal. 46, 47,
48 verses, *The Lord liveth, and blessed be my rock,* &c.
This makes me rejoice. *The Lord of hosts is on my side,*

b is my defence, &c. O so strongly as this ―― es me to suffer, and count all joy now to ―― er! And I had occasion to be at several ―― I bless the Lord for it: I bless the Lord ―― ide choice of me, who was a miserable ―― own my life for his cause: and so I die not ―― force, but willingly at his command. ―― her clause in my indictment, and sentence ―― say, That I walked up and down the ―― ring, destroying, and oppressing the sub- ―― say, I did never mind the like. And so ―― they have done to many an one) assized - ―― ne wrongously; for I did never mind to ―― iny man: Therefore I am clear to charge ―― my blood, and to give my testimony a- ―― murderers of the servants and people of ―― being about the service and worship of

――lace, I believe that all the Scriptures of ――w Testament are the word of the eternal God, given by divine inspiration; and commanded therein ought to be obeyed upon the greatest peril and hazard, and ――ked and false way should be avoided and ――t, whatever be the seeming advantages ――ompany the embracing of it, under the ――led forth with the workers of iniquity, ――ronounce peace on his Israel. *2dly*, I give ――join my adherence to the Confession of ――ger and Shorter Catechisms, National ――eague and Covenant, with our Solemn. ――nt of Sins and Engagement to Duties. ――to the church-government by general as- ――s, presbyteries, and kirk-sessions, accord- ――ablished in the year 1648. *4thly*, I give ――that faithful declaration at Rutherglen, ――ly 1679. *5thly*, I adhere, and give my ――declaration at Sanquhar, June 22. 1680. he paper gotten at the Ferry upon Henry 680. *6thly*, I give my testimony and set to ――he former testimonies sealed by the blood ――ave been murdered on scaffolds, in the ――ie sea, from the year 1660, to this day; imprisonments, and banishment of exiled.

and wandering ones, and by all the spoilings and robbings, oppression, stigmatizing, scourging, and booting, and other horrid cruelties, which have been committed by the enemies of our Lord Jesus Christ.

On the other hand, 1st, I enter my protestation before the Judge of all, both living and dead, before whom I am to appear within a little time, against all the encroachments made upon the prerogatives of our Lord Jesus Christ, particularly against Popery, Quakerism, and Prelacy, and all their underlings and the joiners with them; and against all supremacy that is contrary to the word of God; and against all Erastianism; and against both the indulgences first and last, and all the joiners with, connivers at, and supporters of it; and against the silence in watchmen at this day, in not giving faithful warning, according to that in Isa. lviii. 1. *Cry aloud, and spare not, lift up thy voice like a trumpet, shew Israel their sins, and the house of Jacob their transgressions.* And against her ambiguous and dark applications, so that the sin of the times is not touched, lest they irritate the magistrates, and bring themselves in hazard of our Lord's cross; which was an evil creeping in long ago, which the assembly condemned in the ministers; and ordered them to be suspended, if they did not amend; and seeing no humiliation for such a great sin, they were to be deposed. 2dly, I enter my protestation against all those who have declared themselves opposite to our Lord Jesus Christ, and have displayed a banner for Satan; not only tolerating, but acting and committing all manner of abominations, and horrid cruelties in things civil and ecclesiastical. 3dly, I enter my protestation against all declarations, proclamations, bonds, cess and militia-money, for keeping standing forces with a displayed banner against our Lord; and against all profanity, loosness and lukewarmness, and all the backslidings of the Church of Scotland, since our entering into covenant with God to this day.

Now Sirs, I have given you but a short hint of my faith and principles; and also of the motives which moved me to join with the serious seekers of God; and also the grounds of my indictment, and sentence of death: also some little glance at the corruptions of the times. I have here joined my testimony to the sufferings of the people of God, and I have entered my protestation against some open fins, which are obvious to all who have not willingly yielded themselves to work wickedness. O it is but little that I can say! it would take a long summer day to rank them up, and not win at them all: For my part, I am but ignorant, my capacity can but reach little thing. It may be, ye will take but little notice of what the like of me says, but I cannot help it. Now, as a dying man, I leave all these things to your consideration, if this prelatic and indulged party be the party to be meddled with and owned, pleaded for and defended; what think ye of them that have gone before us? What think ye of Argyle and Mr. Guthrie that were men of understanding? What think ye of Mr. Kid and Mr. King, and that gentleman that suffered last at the cross? Nay, what think ye of religion and the cost of it? What think ye of heaven and glory that is at the back of the cross? The hope of this makes me look upon pale death as a lovely messenger to me. I bless the Lord for my lot this day.

I shall come shortly to a close, only I beg leave to speak a word to two or three sorts of folks; and I think, all may be comprehended under these three. I intreat you take heed; I wish I may not be a stumbling-block to any, that is looking on me this day. *Blessed is he*, says Christ, *that shall not be offended in me*, and my followers. The first sort is the seekers of God; I have a word to you: Ye have kirk and state upon your top; ye get leave to weep a long night, and have none to comfort you: and if you cry, *Watchman, what of the night?* the watchmen are drunk and fallen asleep, they cannot tell. *Can these dry bones live? Lord, thou knowest.* Ye are seeing the godly cut off, one way and another; ye are hearing them that have the root of the matter in them crying up a sinful union; and ministers will not tell you what is your duty or danger. O my dear friends, cast not away your confidence; ye must come thro' many tribulations; but there is a begun heaven for you at night. *Seek ye the Lord, ye meek of the earth: ye shall be hid in the day of the Lord's anger.* There is no persecution in heaven, where our Lord's enemies shall never come: I shall not take upon me to say, who of them will not come to heaven; but this I may say, if they come, it will be more than ordinary humiliation they must have: As it is said of Manasseh; That *he humbled himself greatly before the Lord*

God of his fathers. Friends, give our Lor[d]
always good; but O he is good in a day [of]
will be sweet company thro' the ages of et[ernity]
is none like the God of Jeshurun, that rides
in thy help, and in his excellency on the sky.
are the everlasting arms, and he will save hi[m]
secondly, I have a word to say to you that a[s]
alas, you have wronged the cause; for wh[ich]
have lost the countenance of God, and wi[ll]
gain in haste; ye have *waxed fat and k[icked]*
flung at God, (so to speak) ye have said
with enemies for a false peace; ye have bee[n]
and union with the indulged, because t[he]
men. I say before the Lord, that ye, a[s]
men, have most basely betrayed the kirk c[ause]
shall go to heaven in a fiery chariot, ye sh[all]
leave to suffer but go away in a stink, for
ing and shunning the cross. *Thirdly,* A v[ery]
godly. O ye atheists and ungodly magi[strates]
perjury and bloodshed, ye have nourished
in a day of slaughter. The blood of the L[ord]
that has been shed these eighteen or ninete[en]
in this city, will be charged home upon
upon the assizers. Ye councillors, your v[ote]
warded. Ye criminal lords, remember,
judge the earth, and shall shortly be in eq[ual]
you; and they shall stand upon mount
Lamb, and give their consents against y[ou]
shortly cry *Hallelujah, hallelujah,* to your
And therefore I obtest you, in the bowe[ls]
Jesus Christ, that ye will desist from you[r]
ses, and ly in the dust, and mourn for all
tions; *Except ye repent, ye shall all likew[ise]*
ignorant and profane drunkards, swearer[s]
breakers, repent, or else ye shall likewis[e]
now I take my farewel of all the serious
for a short time: and you that are calm,
fessors, I leave you under process till you r[e]
ing off Christ and his cross, and for *brin[ging]*
report on the good land, and for your w[e]
cause. And ye rulers, farewel for ever
repentance and deep humiliation, for wro[ng]
and his people. Return my soul unto
Farewel all created comforts in time; an[d]

ther, Son, and Holy Ghoft, into thy hands I commit
my fpirit.
Sic fubfcribitur,
ARCHIBALD ALISON.

The dying Teftimony of JOHN MALCOLM, *weaver
in the parifh of Dalry, in the fheriffdom of Galloway,
who fuffered martyrdom at the Grafs-market of Edinburgh, Auguft* 13. 1680.

I Defire the audience of you, who are here fpectators
and auditors, to hear fome words of a dying man,
ready to offer up this tabernacle in your fight, who
would have it among my laft wifhes, that you would
confider your ways and your doings, that are not good;
and not harden your hearts as in the provocation; for ye
have to do with an holy God, who is quickly about to
come in flaming fire, to take vengeance on all the ungodly profane perfons, who are living at eafe in Zion, and
rejoicing in the afflictions of the people of God. I would
obteft you, in the bowels of our Lord Jefus Chrift, that
you would break off your pernicious ways, and make
peace with God while he would make peace with you,
left ye be deftroyed in the overflowing flood of his wrath.
There has been flockings and gatherings to fee others,
who are gone before me, that have been wonderfully
countenanced and owned with the evident prefence of
God, convincingly helping fome to go thro' the jaws of
death, rejoicing and looking profane on-lookers out of
countenance; and have given their teftimonies againft
the abominations committed in the land. And I am
come hither, who am the unworthieft of any that have
gone before me. Now, before I come further, I would
afk you, What you think of religion? What think you
can it be, that makes men go to death with fo great
peace and fweetnefs? Ye have heard what malefactors
have had to fay. Think ye not ftrange, that a rational
man can enter in upon eternity, leaving fuch a teftimony
as ye have heard? And I hope the Lord will help me in
lefs or more to be faithful and free in leaving my teftimony in the fight and prefence of him, who is the fovereign
Judge of all the earth, before whom I muft ftand in a
fhort time.

The caufe of my coming here this day is, becaufe I

was found with that poor persecuted handful, which is the people that was singly adhering to the honour and glory of God; now when he is threatning to bring in his sore plagues upon this apostate church, that has *played the harlot with many lovers*, for which he will bring on indignation, wrath and pain upon many. But this is ground of encouragement to the seekers of God, (1.) That he is keeping up a party in the land, that see it their duty to contend for his cause and interest, and shall *overcome thro' the blood of the Lamb, and by the word of their testimony, who are not loving their lives unto the death;* to contend for his cause and interest. For he hath said, Ezek. vii. 16. *But they that escape of them shall escape, and be like the doves upon the mountains, mourning every one of them for his iniquities.* Now, I seeing and considering upon the one hand, what treacherous dealings are hatched up among ministers and professors in this poor church, and on the other hand considering what the Lord had done formerly, I thought, I was convinced in conscience, and from respect to the honour of God, which I had before mine eyes, and the good of my own soul; I was constrained by an influence of the Spirit, bearing in that word upon my heart, which we have, 1 Kings xviii. 21. *And Elijah came unto all the people, and said, How long halt ye between two opinions? if the Lord be God, then follow him; but if Baal be God, then follow him.* The Lord determined me to join myself with that party, and I do not repent it this day. I count it my duty, and no sin nor rebellion. I think it my credit to serve such a noble master: And indeed I wonder at his condescendency, that ever he sought service from such a wretched sinner as I have been, who lived a stranger to him all my days; but O wonderful love! O wonder at the matchless acts of the Lord's condescendency, and incomprehensible ways with me! that he has made choice of such a poor, weak, frail, pickle of dust as I am; and has led me out and in, and has brought me to this place of execution, to give my testimony to his work, cause and interest; and has passed by the eminent, wise and prudent in the land, and has made choice of such a feckless nothing as I am; but blessed be his glorious name, that will have his word made out, that *out of the mouth of babes and sucklings, he can perfect his praise.* (2.) And this likewise is ground of hope to you that are weak, and cannot venture on suffering, being sensible of your own weakness; *To the weak he encreaseth strength.* And this is another ground of hope, that he takes the blood and wounds of poor weak things to seal his truths.

It cannot be expected that I shall be very formal in what I say, I being no scholar, nor yet old in experience. And besides, after I had received my sentence, I was taken out of a private room, and put in the irons among bad company, except two days before this. The ground of my indictment was, 1*st*, That I am against the king's forces, and fired upon them, under the command of Earlshall. I declare, I intended not to resist, but being put to it, in defence of the gospel, and my own defence, I did resist them to my power. 2*dly*, That I had been with that party in the months of April, May, and June. I was but two days with them, intending no other thing, but to hear the gospel, and for this I suffer; I bless the Lord, *not as an evil doer*, but for my duty: for ye know we are all bound in covenant both kirk and state, according to the coronation oath, the Covenants were owned and sworn, both by the supreme magistrate, the nobles, gentry, and commons of all sorts. The Lord did wonderfully shine upon this land, so that it became the glory of the whole world; the fame of it went abroad, and was renowned thro' the nations. I have heard, that if a stranger of another kingdom had come into a church of this land, there was such a frame of spirit among the people, that the stranger would have thought that they had been all saints. The church then was *fair as the moon, clear as the sun, and terrible as an army with banners.* But we have not been content with these days: Then the swearer was bound up from oaths, and the drunkard's throat ran dry, *iniquity stopped her mouth.* The Lord was with his people in those days: the gospel was successful: And yet I can say, there have been as great days of the gospel in the West of Scotland, in the foresaid months, in the fields, as were in Scotland, since it was Scotland. I am sure, the gospel preached by Mr. Richard Cameron especially, was backed with the power and presence of Christ; as much of Christ and heaven were found, as finite creatures on earth were able to hold, yea, and more than they could hold; the streams of the living waters ran through among his people at these meetings like a flood upon the souls of many, who can witness, if they were called to it, that they would not have been afraid of ten thousands: *The shout of a King was heard among them;* the fruits of it, I am hopeful, shall appear after this. All the troopers and dragoons in the three kingdoms will never get that fire of love that is kindled in the breasts of some in that country quenched; it will never be quenched: it will not rot. The fathers will be telling the children of it, when they are old men, who are not taken away from the wrath that is coming on, to avenge the quarrel of a broken covenant; they will be telling, ' That ' in the year 1680, there were as great days as there ' are now, (when there were Prelates through these ' lands) upon the mountains up and down this West: it ' was then that I got on the zeal of God upon my soul.' And they shall say, ' Who were they that preached in ' mosses and mountains, and not in the kirks nor houses? ' Did not all the godly ministers, when the apostate Pre' lates were in the land, go out and witness and testify a' gainst them, with their lives in their hands?' And the fathers will say, ' Know, my children, they had run well ' for a season, but they wearied, and yielded up the ' church's liberties to a tyrant king, of the name of ' Charles; and he set up the Prelates, and they made ' the land full of curates under them; and after that, ' some that stayed off a while, then turned council-cu' rates, and these council-curates beguiled the rest of ' them, and Erastianism was universal; but the mode' rate indulged in judgment, would have silenced Mr. ' Richard Cameron from preaching, but the Lord had ' said to him, *Go, and I will go with thee;* and so he ' was wonderfully helped. Indeed the Lord countenan' ced him after that, and deserted them, and he died a ' martyr, and had his head set up upon a port, beside ' other three of his brethren; and many that wrote a' gainst him, and had him in derision, went away with ' a stink.' They will have this to say, and tell to the young ones yet unborn; *The righteous man shall be had in everlasting remembrance.* Indeed, my friends, if any such be hearing me, I may say, truly a great man in our Israel fell at Airsmoss the 22d of July, 1680. And now, if I were set at liberty, with a provision that I were not found with Mr. Donald Cargil, whom I pray the Lord may keep from sinning, I would yet again join with that perfecuted party, altho' they fhould ufe me, as they did that eminently worthy gentleman that fuffered before us. So I am not in the dark how and for what I fuffer. I am clear that I was in my duty, and I have peace in it fince, and I grow ftill clearer in it, glory to his name: for it is true that after I got my indictment, and received my fentence, I wanted the countenance of God; for I never knew that the Lord loved me, but fince that time; but I was never in the dark about the righteoufnefs of the caufe: I knew it would bear a fuffering unto blood and death. And now, I am clear of my intereft, and clear as to the grounds that I am laying down my life for this day. I could wifh that every hair of my head were a life for his fake, and his perfecuted caufe. I die in the faith of the true Proteftant religion, in doctrine, difcipline and worfhip, as it was received in the year 1638, and in the year 1649. I join my adherence to the government of this church, as it was reformed from Popery, Prelacy, Eraftianifm and fupremacy. And I join my cordial teftimony to the church's laws and ftatutes at that time, as fhe was governed by general affemblies, fynods, prefbyteries, vifitations and feffions; and to days of humiliation for fin, folemn days of thankfgiving in receipt of mercies beftowed, and cenfures for trying out perfons of erroneous principles, either minifters or private perfons. I adhere to the Confeffion of Faith, the Larger and Shorter Catechifms, the Solemn Acknowledgment of Sins and Engagements to Duties, the National and Solemn League and Covenant, and the Proteftation at St. Johnftoun. I join my teftimony to and approbation of thefe papers at Queensferry, the 3d of June, 1680. I adhere to that faithful teftimony at Rutherglen the 29th of May, 1679. I join my teftimony to that laft teftimony or declaration affixed upon the market-crofs of Sanquhar the 22d of June, 1680. I witnefs my teftimony to the late appearance at Airfmofs the 22d of July, 1680, where the Lord's worthies fell. Likewife I witnefs my teftimony, and fet to my feal againft that horrid murder of that eminently worthy and famous, godly gentleman, David Hackftoun of Rathillet. Likewife againft all the blood fhed in the fields, fcaffolds, and the fea, thefe nineteen years. I enter my proteftation againft Popery, Quakerifm, Supremacy, Eraftianifm, Indulgences firft and laft; and againft arbitrary power over civil and ecclefiastic matters, further than the bounds appointed by the word of God. Likeways I witnefs my teftimony againft the pleaders for union, fiding, joining, halfing, with ufurpers of Chrift's crown, filence in watchmen, and all their contrivances, impofitions, inftructions, or limitations, they put upon the young men to be licentiate, prefcribing a rule to them, to order their miniftry fo and fo; their papers and pamphlets they have put on lately, to lead men over to that woeful Indulgence, under the fair pretext of union, which is dreadful under-hand dealing, to bring the people under the fhadow of the Lord's adverfaries. I enter my proteftation againft the national declaration put forth in the year 1661, and all their declarations fince, and all their bonds and oaths impofed upon the Lord's people. Likeways againft the paying of cefs and militia money; and againft their imprifonments, ftigmatizing, booting, and burning with fire-matches, fining and confining, robbing and fpoiling, banifhment, oppreffion, rigour of mafters of tolbooths. And becaufe of that miftake, that they fay in my indictment, that Prefbyterians, and I amongft the reft, had caft off all fear of God, and are againft all good order and civil law; I declare I adhere to kingly government, but not to perjury and tyranny, turning upfide down church and ftate, contrary to the word of God, our Covenants, and the laws of the nation; and contrary to the declaration at Dunfermline, the coronation-oath, and the acts of general affembly, and acts of parliament, ratifying prefbytery, and abjuring this prelatic hierarchy, which is now eftablifhed, and prefbytery refcinded. And I bear my teftimony againft thofe that have been, and yet are pleading for the favour (as they call it) of the Act of Indemnity, after the murdering of Mr. King and Mr. Kid, who were execute that day the proclamation was read over the Crofs, the 14th day of Auguft, 1679; and againft their jufticiary courts, to infnare and pannel the poor people of God in the Weft of Scotland.

 I fhall draw to a clofe fhortly; but I might (if I had time) enlarge further upon thefe. I will fay only this to you, who are looking upon me this day, That my lot is hard, but I blefs the Lord for it; *The captain of my falvation was made perfect thro' fuffering.* No man has wronged me by counfel or advice; fo I am perfuaded that the caufe is the Lord Jefus Chrift's caufe, and he will own it. *And whosoever touches any of his people, touches the apple of his eye.* For *he sends none a warfare upon their own charges,* and in his own time *he will make inquisition for the blood of* all *his saints,* because *it is right precious in his sight.* And when he makes inquisition after their blood, and searches them out that troubled his people, I would not be the king of Britian, nor a counsellor, prelate, or malignant, for a world; and whatever I be, yet I am persuaded, they have the blood of his dear saints in their skirts, which are this day under the altar, crying, *How long, O Lord, holy and just, wilt thou not avenge our blood on them that dwell on the earth!* You got Mr. King's advice on the scaffold, to be more sparing of shedding more blood; for within a short time, he told you, he would be on equal terms with you that judged him guilty of death: but that doth not warn the rulers of this kingdom. Do not think that I am quarrelling for the taking of my blood; No, it is love to your souls that obliges me to speak thus. O what can be expected, but that the Lord has his sword furbished for blood, and he will have a day of nobles blood! The Lord has been smiting and wounding his church and people, and blood has touched blood. Pentland-hills hath touched Mr. Guthrie's blood; and Bothwel touched Pentland; and the drowned in the sea touched Bothwel; and Airsmoss the drowned in the sea; and our blood toucheth that which was spilt the 22d of July last: O that at last ye would be persuaded to desist, and spill no more blood; O that the Lord himself would stop the effusion of more innocent blood, if it may stand with his honour. But if any more be for his honour and service; Lord, keep thy people when they are called to it, to say with David, *Here am I, let him do to me as seemeth him good.*

I am also apprehensive, that the Lord hath a great sacrifice of the bodies of multitudes, and that he will give the flesh and blood of many to the fowls of the air; and he minds to give the fowls and birds a feast of flesh and blood. O Scotland! wilt thou never be wise, until thou be betrayed into the hands of thine enemies? Truly, I think it is incredible, that this land will get leave to pass long, and not be sweeped with the besom of justice: The Lord is really angry with this land; for I know no person, no not one, but he has just ground of controversy with. It is astonishing to me, to think on the sparing

mercies of God towards these lands. For my part, I am glad that he calls me away after this manner, for which I desire with my soul to bless him, for his kindness to me, in taking this method and way with such a wretched sinner as I am, who deserves nothing but wrath, and only wrath; but glory to the riches of his grace, who *came into the world to save sinners, of whom I am the chief*: He is a noble high-priest indeed. I must draw to a close; I intreat your patience a little, and I shall say but these three or four things shortly. 1*st*, I would intreat you that are strangers to God, Make haste and flee in unto God for your life; from this consideration, that all who had union and communion with God are now landed in glory, have died in the faith of it, that there are glorious days coming, and that the Lord will reckon with his enemies, and pay them liberally, for all the wrongs done to his cause and people. *And it shall come to pass in that day, that the Lord shall punish the host of the high ones that are on the earth, and the kings of the earth, upon the earth: they shall be gathered together as prisoners are gathered into the pit, and shall be shut up in the prison, and after many days they shall be visited; then the moon shall be confounded, and the sun ashamed, when the Lord shall reign over mount Zion and Jerusalem, and before his ancients gloriously.* You may read it at your leisure, in the 24th chap. of Isaiah from the 21st verse to the end. There is another word in the xxxvi. of Job 18. verse; It is a word of advice, given by Elihu to Job; *Because there is wrath, beware lest he take you away with a stroke; then a great ransom cannot deliver you.* 2*dly*, It is my comfort this day, that my enemies are God's enemies. It is the allowance he bestows on poor things, in the following of their duty; tho' they have not much knowledge in religion, nor great experience, yet if they be faithful in the little, he helps them to be faithful in much. Ye know he says, *Because thou hast been faithful in what I committed to thee, have thou rule over five cities.* I know, that it is commonly reported, That they have not much grace that adhere to this persecuted way; as I take in myself among them, who never had great gifts, nor parts, nor heart experience; yet he has told me, since I received the sentence of death by men who are the Lord's sword, " That faithfulness in this juncture of time, in not de-
" nying his name, shall be an excuse for many infirmi-

of John Malcolm.

" ties." Among all the strong contenders, none get the prize but the sincere man, the resolute man, and they who are determined, as Esther was, to go, tho' it should cost them their life. And this is the time that the people of God should be at holding and drawing, rugging and riving, or ever the enemies of our Lord possess his crown, and bruik it with peace. And this I must add to these that are byassed, I shall be a dying witness against ministers and professors that made it their work to brand and cloath that faithful minister and martyr of Jesus Christ with odious names and notorious lies, in calling him a Jesuite, and saying that he received the pope's gold, and that he was a great favourite of the duke of York, a declared Papist; which I know, and many eminent Christians know, that he hated him as a limb of Satan; and also they said, that the troopers had commission to pass him by, rather than any man, even after the declaration came out, to give 5000 merks for him dead or alive. Go and ly in the dust for what you have said of him; and what you have said of Mr. Kid: I bless the Lord that ever I saw his face, and that ever I heard him preach. 3*dly*, Give me leave to say this much; I am afraid the apostacy of Scotland, the neutrality and formality that is among both ministers and professors, have shapen out this church and land of Britian in length and breadth, with the church of Laodicea, whom the Lord threatens *to spue out of his mouth*, as a loathsome thing, and then he will have pleasure in his Zion. Yet ye see, he is snedding down a Guthrie, a Welwood, a King, a Kid, a Brown, and a Cameron, and the like of a Henry Hall and a Robert Dick, that were contending for the truth, and for restoring the privileges of the church: and these were counted disturbers of your sinful union with the enemies of the Lord. Lay it to heart; now their blood is shed for the cause, and ye are not free of it; but ye can wipe your mouth, and say, ye are innocent? Remember that in the 1. Psalm, and 18. verse. *When thou sawest a thief, thou joinedst with him; and this the Lord hath seen, and kept silence:* Remember and mourn for it, *lest he tear you in pieces, when there is none to deliver.* The court favour is too short a covering, it will not hide you: therefore as a dying man, I warn you as from the Lord, *Consider your ways and your doings, that have not been good,* and cast yourselves out of the court

favour, otherways I declare ye shall not
of God. 4thly, If ye will set about some d
ation before the Lord, and take with you
the sin of crying up this clatty liberty, wh
of blood. *If ye will return to the Lord, th*
all your heart; for he is merciful and gracio
him of the evil that he threatens, neither wil
his anger. He did so to me; I no sooner
to him, but he made me welcome, and pu
tho' I be but young, and know nothing:
of me, he took me to Bothwel-bridge, to
and I had many temptations to stay; wha
ther, and from one hand and another; l
for my soul stay behind; I thought it m
myself with that party against the Lord's
the Lord was good to me there many way
my head in the day of battle, and suffere
of my head to fall to the ground, and he
better than me a thousand times, to fall
me; so I thought then I held my life of
Lord brought me to the Gray-friars chur
came almost naked, yet he mounted me b
I was before with cloaths, and wonder
for me, beyond many others. I bless
mother's sickness did not keep me from B
and when I was in the Gray-friars chur
threatened with death by the justice-gene
a great oath, That I should die if I wou
bond. I told him, as it was true, Tha
than I had been hanged; but I was brou
hand; and the Lord took me to the sea,
me from the ragings thereof, when he
better to lose their lives. And when h
upon me by sickness, he made me to be
my enemies; he healed me, and brought
then he called me out to hear the gospel
desire to bless him, and within a little
praise him for it.

The Lord was so seen amongst his pe
ful there, that he did engage me to join
were hazarding their lives upon the fiel
was at that late engagement, and the L
work off my hand there; and has brou
place, this day, to lay down my life for

this is the laſt combat I ſhall have; I ſhall work no more: I muſt take my leave of you all, and ſo reſt in his love. I go where *all tears ſhall be wiped away; where the ſervant is made free from his maſter.* To the land where *the inhabitants ſhall not ſay, they are ſick.* Now, be not diſcouraged at the ways of God's providence to me; for I can aſſure you, the cauſe is his own, and he will own it. *For lo, thine enemies ſhall periſh.* I would have every one of you ſeeking the favour of God: for ye will have ado with it at death and judgment: the greateſt perſecutor or malignant will have ſore miſſing of his favour in that day. O ſeek him in time! and the Lord help his poor young wreſtling people well thro' their trials; the Lord help them to be faithful, and to endure to the end; for they have the promiſe of being ſaved. Join with his people, and caſt in your lot with them, and do not ſtand on the other ſide; let his cauſe be your cauſe in well or wo. O noble cauſe! O noble work! O noble heaven! O noble Chriſt, that makes it to be heaven! and he is the owner of the work: O noble Mediator of the new covenant! O noble Redeemer, who is powerful to help in time of need, and will help ſuch as truſt in him. There was never one that truſted in him that came to loſs, he made them always up, ſometimes with an hundred-fold in this life, and heaven after.

I lay down my life, not as an evil doer, but as a ſufferer for Chriſt. I ſhall ſay no more, but a word or two. One is anent that which ſome would be informed in, Whether I took the bond that was tendered to the priſoners? I acknowledge, there was a ſupplication drawn up, containing two articles: One was, craving the benefit of the act of indemnity: The ſecond was, That I ſhould not lift arms againſt the king, or any in lawful authority: but becauſe it was not authority only, but lawful authority, it was not granted. And, at that time, there were pains taken by ſome perſons of note, that perſuaded me to take the bond as it was tendered by the bloody council. Indeed it hath been a thing heavier than the ſand to me, and hath made me groan. I think for that, and for many other private failings, the Lord did not give me his countenance; the Lord pardon that, as I hope he will, that I ſhould have put my hand to a pen, and blackened paper in that ſupplication: But for the bond, I bless the Lord, I did not subscribe it. The second thing I am reputed guilty of, is, That I supplicated for a delay some short time, and that I called it rebellion that I was Airsmoss. Indeed I subscribed no such things; but it was only this, That it might please them to grant us some more time, for we were in confusion, because of the shortness of the time; we desired some more time, that we might get our souls case laid to heart, and our peace made with God thro' Jesus Christ. I shall say no more, but wish that ye would all seek repentance in time, before it be hid from your eyes. I recommend my soul and spirit to him, *that is able to save to the uttermost all that come to him thro' Christ;* and desire to take my leave of all created comforts. Farewel all relations, farewel world, farewel sin. Welcome Christ, welcome heaven and glory for evermore. *Sic subscribitur,*

JOHN MALCOLM.

The last Testimony of Mr. JAMES SKEEN, *brother to the laird of Skeen, who suffered at Edinburgh, December 1st,* 1680.

His Interrogations and Answers before the Privy Council, related by himself, in a letter to his brother.

Dear Billy,

TO satisfy your desire, I send you this line, to let you know, that when I came before the council, (York and Rothes being there, two bishops, viz. Burnet and Paterson, the advocate, Clerk Paterson, Linlithgow, and many more, sitters and standers, Dalziel the general, being porter, walking proudly up and down, not as a servant) none was admitted to come in with me. I saluted them all civilly, and keeped off my hat, because they keeped off, that they might not say that I was a Quaker. Rothes asked me, Was I at Bothwel or Airsmoss? I answered, I was at home in the North both these times. They asked, If I did own Sanquhar Declaration, and the testimony at Rutherglen? I told them, I did own them both. He asked, Did I own the king's authority, I said, in so far as it was against the Covenant and interest of Christ, I disown it. He asked me, Thought I it not a sinful murder the killing of the

Arch-prelate? I said, I thought it was their duty to kill him, when God gave them opportunity; for he had been the author of much blood-shed. They asked me, Why I carried arms? I told them it was for self-defence, and the defence of the gospel. They asked me, Why I poisoned my ball? I told them, I wished none of them to recover whom I shot. He asked me, Why I carried a durk? I told them, they might ask Mr. George M'Kenzie, if it was not our country-fashion; and he presently told the chancellor that it was so. They asked, if I knew Cargil? I said, it was my comfort I knew him. Then they reproached him, and me for conversing with him. I said, I blessed God, he gave me sweet peace in it. They asked, Would I kill the soldiers, being the king's? I said, it was my duty if I could, when they persecuted God's people. They asked, if I would kill any of them? I said they were all stated enemies of our Lord Jesus Christ, and by the Declaration at Sanquhar I counted them my enemies. They asked, If I would think it my duty to kill the king? I said, He had stated himself an enemy to God's interest, and there was war declared against him. I said, the covenant made with God was the glory of Scotland, tho' they had unthankfully counted it their shame. And in direct terms, I said to the chancellor, I have a parchment at home, wherein your father's name is, and you are bound by that, as well as I. They asked, Why I called the chancellor, Sir! I said, Sir, was a title for a king, and it might serve him. The chancellor asked, if I knew his Royal Highness? I never saw such a person. York looks out by (for he sat in the shadow of Bishop Burnet) and said, Why did I wish the king so ill? I told, I wish no ill to any; but as they were in opposition to God I wished them brought down: and he spoke no more. The chancellor said, Would I not adhere to the acts of parliament of this kingdom? I said, I would not own any of them which were in opposition to God and his Covenant. Mr. M'Kenzie said, If the king were riding by in coach, would you think it no sin to kill him? I said, by the Sanquhar Declaration there was war declared against him, and so he needed not put that in question. So Mr. M'Kenzie came out by to the bar, and said, I know your relations and mine are sib; be ingenuous in all that is demanded of you, and I will save you from

I

torture. I said, Sir, I know you, and ye
my relations; I have been as free and ingen
imagine, because I reckon it my credit, an
give a full and free confession for my bless(
rest, that is reproached and born down.
where I saw Cargil last? I said, I met]
West-bow, to my comfort. They asked r
owners of the house? I said, I really coul(
I knew them not. They said, Would I kn
I said, Yes. They said, Would I show it
they would send with me? I told them,
what concerned myself, but to hurt any el
mar my peace with God; but if they wei
go out of the house, I should show it the
desired me to go my ways. The general o]
and rounded in my ear, Ye must go down
diers, and show them that house. I said,
to hurt any; these indwellers must be ad
the house first.

Then I was ordered to the guard, which
gow's soldiers, which took me, and walke
bald Stewart and John Sproul, who wer
the Tron, and back to the council house
being alone, and only six soldiers with me
prayer, and was comforted; and then
meat and drink; and then worshipped in
soldiers. At night, a person from J——
me, and brought me bread and ale, and f
confected carvel. After that I was carrie
tee, where were present the Chancello
terson, Justice-Clerk, Wigtoun and Lin
they shewed me two letters of mine to
wherein I owned the Declaration at San(
I would do much to persuade many th
from Mr. M'Ward's advice that was giv
ners. I owned the letters, and told their
could to dissuade professors from paying th
they ordered for bearing down the go
they laughed. The chancellor said, Wh
him Lord? I told him, were he for Cl
would honour him. Then he said, he c:
honour; but he would have me to know
cellor. I said, I knew that. He said, I v
man but a Scots-beast. At which Wigt

him, and he laughed. He then rounded to me, that he would be my friend, would I be ingenuous. I told him, I wished him no ill. They asked me, What Mr. William Alexander was it that I wrote of? I said Mr. Paterson the bishop, and Mr. Ross at Glasgow knew him, and persecuted him unjustly: I then related to them how it was. Paterson said, I told that which I knew not to be truth; he pitied me. He said to the chancellor, Certainly I forgot to write. I was before the justiciary court, where my confession was read, and after I read it again, and told them, I thought it my honour to subscribe to it. I assented to all that was recorded by the clerk; I owned it, and counted it my honour so to do. The justice-clerk, Hatton's son being there, said, He pitied me, I being a gentleman; he knew my friends. I said, were I an earl's son, I would esteem it my honour. I desired them to canvass well that they did, for they would be panneled before God for it. He said, I might prepare for another world. I said, I hoped the Lord would prepare me.

Now, dear Billy, I have have given you an account of the truth, as I confusedly remember; but I entreat you take all the praise you give me, and put it upon my Lord, for I am but a poor, simple, sinful worm: It is from him I had this courage. Wigtoun and the justice-clerk, desired me to shew them that house, saying, That I was free enough in all except that; and if I were obstinate, I might belike get the boots. I said, let them do with me what they pleased, in what concerned myself I was free, but to do hurt to others I would not, to bring them under their wrath; I would not mar my peace with God so far. The general said, he would parole to me, that the indwellers of the house should be advertised. I said, I would not have his parole. The chancellor boasted me for denying his parole. I said to the chancellor, I was a gentleman that had blood relations to his relations, the earl of Mar's mother and I being sister-bairns. He said, he was sorry I was so related. I said, the cause I was there owning honoured me; and I would it befel my friends. So this, I hope, you will not too critically reflect on my confused writing, since I am in haste; ye know, it may be, I may be cited before these bloody men this forenoon. I will not order for my funerals till I know my sentence: I may possibly not be allowed a burial. My Lord comforts me, and I leave all on him to

The laſt Speech and Teſtimony

bear me thro' this ſtorm, thro' the valley and ſhadow of death. Dear Billy, bid all ye fee of our ſerious friends help me with their prayers that I may be helped of the Lord to be faithful unto the death: and that he will give me the faith of aſſurance, that I ſhall enjoy my Lord's love thro' all eternity: the want of this clouds me much, I am ſo unworthy a wretch. I am,

Dear Billy, your unworthy friend, and loving brother,

JAMES SKEEN.

From my Lord Jeſus his houſe, which he has made a ſweet palace, wherein he ſhews me his wonderful free love, the cloſe priſon above the iron-houſe, in the high tolbooth of Edinburgh, Nov. 1680.

P. S. I told the chancellor, the cauſe was juſt, for which the king and others were excommunicate; tho' I was not there, yet I adhered to it.

Another Letter from Mr. JAMES SKEEN, *to all profeſſors in the ſhire of Aberdeen, eſpecially, Mr. William Alexander, Mr. William Mitchel, and Mr. John Watſon, my dear acquaintances. Being the laſt teſtimony for the intereſt of Chriſt from Mr. James Skeen, now in cloſe priſon for Chriſt's intereſt, in the tolbooth of Edinburgh.*

Dear Friends,

THE Lord having dealt ſo graciouſly with me, in wonderful free love, as to bring me to the love of himſelf, his truths, and deſpiſed intereſt, as that he engaged me in a particular covenant with himſelf, which, by his honouring me to make me a priſoner to evil men, for his deſpiſed intereſt, he has evidently confirmed to me, that he accepted of my bargain with himſelf, when moſt unworthy and wretched; tho' many times, by reaſon of a prevailing body of ſin and death, I provoked him to caſt the bargain; yet ſtill by new obligations he engaged me to renew it. My mercy has been great, that providence ordered ſome time my coming South, where moſt ſuffering has been for our Lord; and for that reaſon, moſt light has been given to profeſſors here, that they might fee what was clear duty in theſe trying, tempting and backſliding times. And whenever the Lord helped me to fee our covenant-obligations, which are the glory of Scotland, I was serious and zealous, ye know, to impart to all of you, whom I was acquaint with: The Lord always making my love to him to abound, I thought no travel ill-wared, or any hazard too great on any occasion, whereby I might propagate his despised interest among you. You know how much I have contended with you for paying of that cursed cess, ordered by the convention of estates, for bearing down the gospel; as I was honoured to witness against it at a committee on Saturday last at night: you are not aware how you bring the blood of saints on your heads, by this obedience to the stated enemies of our Lord Jesus Christ, your opposing of that which was, and is the judgment of the most tender professors, in withdrawing from indulged ministers; and from these ministers that favoured them, and so did not, nor would not declare against the indulgence as a sin, that most hainously and rebelliously dishonours our blessed Lord as head of the church, and set up a tyrannous usurper in his place, was a particular I much contended with many of you; in my hearing you pleading for a sinful union with these who have conspired to dethrone our blessed Lord; some of you opposed that which was an honourable testimony for our Lord at Rutherglen, and that declaration at Sanquhar; and the testimony or covenant that was taken at the Queensferry, calling these rash and inconsiderate, whom the Lord called out to be valiant contenders for his truth and interest, which is now contemned by a wicked apostate generation, and to seal all of them with blood: By all these the Lord has been calling his people to come from among Babel's brood; its cursed brood, who by many subtile satannical ways; what by Prelacy, Quakerism, Arminianism, Latitudinarians, and Indulged Ministers, and ministers and professors, that love so their quiet that they will not declare against, and decline that usurping traitor on the throne, Charles Stuart, and all the cursed crew of pretended magistrates in Scotland, having forfeited their right of government, as appears by their wicked and unparalleled apostacy from that Solemn League and Covenant, upon that foul pretext, that we are not in a probable capacity to extirpate them, or put them out of office. When in our place and station, we give our witness against these usurpations, we so far contend for God, and witness for his troden-down and despised interest, and testify our unwillingness, that our Lord should totally give up with this poor land. O! this hath been many times a sad heart to me, ye have looked more to the credit of men than the glory of our great Lord God. I fear this testimony be unacceptable and hazardous to you to mantain; becaufe of that they call treafon in it; but ah! there is fo much done to advance a mortal creature, a stated enemy to Christ, a furious hafty cruel murderer of God's faints, that there is fear of difowning of God, and a palpable denying of him before men, when you own tyrannous oppreffors. Your estates you cannot part with; your credit and pleasures, and your quiet in the world you will not part with: You will rather imagine arguments to cheat yourselves in defending your practices that are clear breaches of covenant: if your too great carnal love to the world did not blind you, and your unwillingnefs to quit your life for Christ, which foon will come to an end, however with lefs comfort, than you would certainly have when you adventure all for our blessed Lord.

As for you, Mr. Alexander, I may fay, I have found you willing on good information, to be for tender cleaving to your dear Master, and bad information, making it a question, if it was duty to dethrone the pretended king? which Mr. T. H. and Mr. R. M. oppofing, byaffed you from that principal duty; by which we are fingularly known to be true covenanters, and leave thefe that are blind, and follow your dear Master in the duties he calls his people to, and he will own them, and I am persuaded he has owned them who have owned him in this duty. You did quarrel at field-meetings, enemies ordering againft them, and confenting that houfe-meetings be enjoyed; but here is your testimony, when you keep the fields you declare that our Lord's church has liberty to keep her meetings and ordinances where fhe pleafes, and ought not to be at the arbitriment of men.

To Mr. Mitchel I fay, I have had a great esteem of you as a true lover of piety; and I doubt not, the Lord has fealed your ministry fometimes, and fome witneffes of it I have known: But O Sir, what a fearful fnare are you in, by complying with curates in hearing them, and taking both facraments off their hands! Oh! if ye quit not all carnal love to the world, to credit, and friends, that will oppofe your coming off, the hazard is great, the Lord may rank you with them that have oppofed the rifing of his kingdom: however, I am fure, he will make you mourn for it, and I doubt (if ye fhortly come not off from that accurfed crew) that the Lord will fend you a forer trial, than fufferers for him meet with.

To Mr. Watfon, I write this as my laft teftimony; O how unfaithful is his miniftry! he dare not, for fear of loofing his miniftry, declare againft the hainous breach of covenant by all the pretended magiftrates in the land. I grant your clearnefs as to other things was much one with my own. O Sir, quite men as they quite Chrift's way and intereft, elfe you will never be clear in truths, as the Lord lets out light, and increafeth it. And this is moft dreadfnl, to be fo enfnared to walk in darknefs, and fo be in oppofition to our bleffed Lord! O let love to the Lord Jefus Chrift affuredly overcome you, and then admiring of men, and cleaving to them who are out of Chrift's way, will be no fmall matter, but a hainous fin. Oh! will you adventure your falvation on it, to cleave to them who are reproaching our Lord, his people and intereft, by mixing in with the curfed curates? that perfon ye cleave to, draws on him the guilt of all the faints blood that is fhed in maintaining his intereft and covenant, whofe judgment ye cannot decline, he being Judge of all the world. Ye may fay much more, every one of you that know me: I was many times negligent of a tender walking, by feeking of fettlement, and if that had been my lot ye had not heard of this teftimony. You know every one of you, this teftimony I gave you formerly; even when with you, I many times wifhed from my heart the Lord would not order a fettlement to me among you. My heart was broken with your lukewarmnefs and indifferency. And this I teftified to feveral of you, and I rather choofed, I faid often, to be a fheep-keeper in the fouth, where I might be encouraged in godlinefs, than to live in pomp and eafe at home, with an ill-confcience; and when I came away laft, I was forry at my purpofe of leaving Scotland, when I heard all were agreeing to apoftacy, in my judgment then, from our beft covenanted God, and I was determined for Ireland then, being ill informed of every one of the kingdoms, there not being a people tenderly owning the covenant in Ireland, but all fome way owning the ufurper Charles Stuart; but in poor Scotland, here in the south, I found a poor handful, and about one faithful minister, whom the Lord called out, viz. Mr. Donald Cargil, to be his messenger to his people, and give witness against the apostacy of ministers and professors; even those who were great lights in the land are now in obscurity, and avowedly reproaching our Lord's interest and people, whom yet the Lord will cloath with shame and make their peace they boast of, and quiet sleep, to their great confounding. As for the call I have to suffer, I found it my only peace to quit thoughts of Ireland, that I might not be involved in their guilt of denying to have our Lord Jesus Christ to be king over them. O that poor party I find only for maintaining his prerogative royal, to which I am joined. Mr. Donald Cargil being the only faithful ambassador our Lord has in Scotland, I following the ordinances on Friday last, being as well armed for defending the gospel and myself as I could; beyond expectation, a party of Linlithgow's soldiers is sent out to my lodging, and not dreading danger in the day time, I thought our persecutors had never heard of my name; I was apprehended, and now at last brought hither to close prison, the Lord having honoured me to give an ample testimony before the council and lords of justiciary for my wronged Lord Jesus, and supposing I must seal it with my blood, I leave this testimony to you, my friends and acquaintances in Aberdeenshire, and subscribe it, November 17. 1680.

JAMES SKEEN.

From my delectable prison, in which my Lord has allowed me his peace and presence, and comforted me with that, I shall reign with him eternally, for I am his, and bought with his precious blood.

To his friend and fellow-prisoner. N.

Much honoured friend in Christ,

I Give it under my hand, I have no cause to rue my sweet bargain. His cross is easy and light yet; and that which is most terrifying, I hope he will make comfortable. O lovely Lord! what could make him to chuse me to suffer for him! what is all the world to me if his honour be at the stake? If his honour be advanced by my death, O happy me! I have oftentimes wished a suffering lot. I heard and saw so much of God's goodness, that I thought the cross and comforts of Christ could not be separated: And I have no reason to complain; the Lord is oft the joy of my heart, that I am forced to wonder at it; leaving further troubling you, hoping you will be as good as your word. Be much in prayer, for these two or three days. It is likely on Thursday next I will need no help of prayers, being come to the immediate vision of my Lord, to see him as he is: I will be stupified, as it were, and amazed at it. If his merits were not of infinite value, I might question, What would I do? But he has promised, *That I shall reign with him.*

JAMES SKEEN.

To his friend and fellow-prisoner N.

My dear friend in Christ,

I Received yours, encouraging me to hold on in my blessed Lord's way, which he hath pathed to me. I am not unmindful of you, as I can; and I desire you to pray, that none may offend at the Lord's interest for me, there being willingness on my part to suffer, tho' justly they cannot condemn me; for they offer me a delivery, if I would submit to the duke's and council's mercy; but it is often evidently seen, that *the tender mercies of the wicked are cruelty.* I find no liberty to deny my Lord for fear of death: I hope he will make up my loss in himself. All I can desire of you is, to pray much for me, that the Lord will own me, for his own cause, before the adversaries, and in my dissolution. I wish the Lord to comfort his people, and tenderly own his despised interest. Mr. Carstairs said, " He was a-
" shamed of that principle we maintained; and that we
" were not found Presbyterians; and wished the Lord
" might preserve him from the like." I am no whit troubled at this, I bless my Lord. They would have me conferring with him: I said, I would not notice him if he came near me. Tell my friend, I would have written, but had no time. I wrote yesternight to him. I need both your helps, by supplications, and strong cries to the Lord, to carry me thro' the valley and shadow of death. I must leave here; wishing the Lord to bear you up under all trials. I thought you should have been in

eternity before me; but now I think, I shall leave you in the vallies, when I shall arrive at the blessed harbour. I am,

Dear friend, your well-wisher, and Christ's prisoner,

JAMES SKEEN.

P. S. A double of my confessions you may have from a friend whom I shall desire to send it to you. I got my summonds for eternity with sound of trumpet yesternight, and my indictment with five shouts of the trumpet, and pursevants in their coats, at seven of the clock, was a grave sight; but my Lord helped me not to be afraid at it, since all was from him.

The last Speech and Testimony of Mr. JAMES SKEEN, *brother to the Laird of Skeen; which he intended to have delivered on the scaffold, December 1st, 1680.*

Dear people,

I Am come here this day, to lay down my life for owning Jesus Christ's despised interest, and for asserting that he is a King, and for averring that he is head of his own church, and has not delegated or deputed any, either pope, king, or council, to be his vicegerents on earth. Since my blessed Lord Jesus Christ has in his love engaged me by a particular covenant, in his own terms, to renounce and resign myself to him, in soul and body, assuring me by his word, and testifying his acceptance of my resignation by his holy and blessed Spirit; promising to redeem me from all sins, giving me assurance of a saving interest in himself; and now having called me in his providence, contriving this my suffering, by permitting his ungodly enemies to apprehend and take me prisoner, having wickedly plotted my taking; in my going on the way to attend what the Lord had to work on my soul by his preached gospel, to give a testimony for his covenant, interest and people that are reproached and born down by a perjured, God-contemning generation: and to seal my sufferings and testimony with my blood, I most willingly lay down my life for his interest. I leave my testimony to the National Covenant, and the Solemn League and Covenant, which are founded on the Scriptures, the word of God, which are written by the prophets and apostles in the Old and

New Testament, which has Jesus Christ, the blessed object of our faith, for the chief corner-stone of the building. I also leave my testimony to Mr. Donald Cargil's paper taken at the Queensferry, called a new covenant, according as they agree to the true original copy.

I adhere to Presbyterian government, and the whole work of reformation of the church of Scotland, the Confession of Faith, the Larger and Shorter Catechisms, consulted well, and written by the Assembly of Divines, except that article about magistracy, when ill expounded, in the 23d chapter.*, because our magistracy is but pure tyranny, exercised by the lustful rage of men, yea, rather devils in shape of men, whom God has permitted in his holy and spotless wisdom, for a trial to his people, and a snare to some others, to oppress, tyrannize, and blasphemously tread under foot his truth, interest and people; yea, that article is expounded in the National Covenant, where we have vowed to the almighty God, not to maintain the king's interest, when he disowns the Covenant, and well settled church-government by presbyteries, synods, and general assemblies of the church of Scotland. I adhere to the testimony for the interest of Christ at Rutherglen; at which time the wicked acts of parliament, and the blasphemous declarations, by which they have sworn to be enemies to the interest of Christ, were solemnly burnt. I adhere to the Sanquhar Declaration, whereby we that were true Presbyterians did depose that tyrant Charles Stuart; who is head of malignants and malignancy, from his exercise of government as to us: and we do no otherways than the people of Libnah, 2 Chron. xxi. 10. *The same time also did the people of Libnah revolt from under the king of Judah, because he had forsaken the Lord God of his fathers.* And this practice is not so gross that I own, in declaring against that monstrous tyrant on the throne of Britain, as many conjecture, if seriously folk would consider the unjustice practised in civil matters, by himself, and all his adherent inferior magistrates (yea inferior tyrants,

---

* Let none mistake this sentence, as if this worthy gentleman thereby disowned that unshaken principle of the Protestant religion, that " infidelity or difference in religion does not make void the magistrates just " and legal authority;" for it is plain, he rejects only the false sense that was then put upon it, to make it an argument for defence of tyranny and arbitrary power.

for he is the head and supreme tyrant) that no poor man that has a just cause, if he be not as profligate and wicked as themselves, can have justice; and his usurpation in ecclesiastic matters; which is too great a task for any on earth, since they must take upon them to dethrone our blessed Lord Jesus Christ, *who is given to be head over all things to the church.* Eph. i. 22. Psal. ii. 8. You would canvass the justice of disowning his authority, which to do, you are engaged by oath to God, he overturning the whole work of reformation, which was the great ground of his inthronement in Scotland, to maintain the covenant and work of reformation. His wicked burning of the Covenant, and Causes of God's Wrath, is cause enough to me to disown his authority, which is so maintained by perjury; Ezek. xvii. 15. 16. 17. 18. 19. *Shall he break the covenant, and prosper?* Consider likeways his oppression, in ordering military forces to oppress God's people, to obstruct, impede and hinder the worship of God, the ordinances in houses or fields, and compel them to join with a cursed crew of prelates, curates, and some indulged ministers. Yea, his tyranny is so great, that he ordered an host of armed men in the year 1678, to invade a peaceable country in the West; who robbed, stole from, and oppressed poor people, for no other reason, but because they would not pollute their consciences, and be subject to Prelacy; which Erastian government he has contended for these several years, and keeped up in this land. If there were no other cause of his rejection, they might suffice to justify any, who were engaged by God, having time and place to cut him off: for, by the law of God, murder, adultery, and oppression, are punishable by death, and kings are not exempted, far less tyrants, that are lawfully excommunicate. But to these horrid impieties is added, the shedding of the blood of poor innocents, which aggravateth his guilt; so that tho' the Lord should make him penitent, he deserves death by the law, according to which, *blood cannot be expiated, but by the blood of him who shed it.* For confirmation of what I have said, see Ezek. xxi. 25. 26. 27. read also Ezek. xliii. 9. *Put away the carcases of your kings far from me, and I will dwell in the midst of you for ever.* Consider how our fathers contended for truth, and must we lose what they have gained? Ah! this atheistical generation of perjured, adul-

of Mr. James Skeen.

terous, and bloody powers, are ripe for God's vengeance! I give my teſtimony againſt the curſed perſecuting ſoldiers; the blood of God's ſaints is on their heads, and mine is laid on them, eſpecially Serjeant Warrock who apprehended me; my blood is on the juſticiary†, who ſubſcribed to my ſentence, and on the fifteen aſſizers, James Glen ſtationer being clerk; and on the chancellor, and on Mr. George M'Kenzie who pleaded for my condemnation; and Thomas Dalziel who ordered my taking; and upon Andrew Cunningham who condemned me; and upon all the reſt who are acceſſory in the leaſt thereto: yea, the privy council are to be accountable for my blood; and my blood is on the head of Mr. J— C— who condemned my teſtimony againſt theſe bloody tyrants, aſſerting me to be a Jeſuite. I leave my teſtimony againſt receiving that accurſed traitor James Duke of York, and all Papiſts, Quakers, Prelates, Curates, Latitudinarians, indulged miniſters, and their favourers; the Hamilton Declaration, and other papers and actings, directly or indirectly againſt the truth. I leave my teſtimony againſt the luke-warm profeſſors, who write and ſpeak grievous things to reproach the truly godly, and who keep ſilence when God calls them to give a free and full teſtimony for his deſpiſed covenant, and whole work of reformation, againſt a treacherous, backſliding, and adulterous generation. And as in this place, or any other of my papers, I could not have deſigned God's enemies any otherways than by their pretended offices; thus far, dear people, I crave your liberty, and let none think, that thereby I own them in the leaſt point.

Likewiſe, whereas my ſufferings were delayed, the Lord, in whoſe preſence I muſt appear ere long, knows what a ſoul grief it is to me to remember it. When the day I was ſentenced to die for my dear Lord's intereſt came, I vainly expecting that my relations that were

K

† Theſe and the like ſentences, which may poſſibly be met with in ſome other teſtimonies, ought not to be miſtaken, as the effects of a revengeful ungoſpel ſpirit, but rather as a ſimple declaration of their being guilty of blood in condemning them, to ſerve as a warning to the perſecutors, not to proceed further in theſe wicked courſes, and to waken them to repentance, if poſſible, for what they had already done; and is much paralleled in its nature with that of Jeremiah, in his apology before the princes, chap. v. 15.

great in court, who had seen me, should have procured a reprival for me; but being disappointed, a fear of death surprised me, hearing that all were presently making ready for my execution, and then my carnal relations almost weeping on me, engaged me, by their insinuations, to supplicate that bloody crew for it myself. A carnal well-wisher drew it up in these terms: *James Skeen prisoner, earnestly desires your lordships to grant him a reprival for some days, till he canvass these things he was sentenced for with learned and godly men; and your lordships answer.* After I subscribed it, a great confusion and horror of spirit fell on me; I went to prayer, wishing in my heart it were not granted; but such was my trouble, I could not say any thing but nonsense. My heart was afflicted sore with this straitning, and the more when the reprival was granted. I thought, I having shifted the cross, my Lord might deny me that credit again, and put a worse on me in requital of my slighting him. I judge the Lord left me thus to slip, to humble me; and that he hid his face to make me examplarily punished for untender carrying under his cross, which he had chosen for me, to warn others under the cross that they would be circumspect and zealous for keeping from being polluted with any compliance with the defections of the times, that they may have a cleanly suffering. From this backsliding I recovered not for two days after, but found it sad for my soul, the Lord hid his face from me: but now my God has had compassion on me, and this time of the eight days reprival, he has preserved me from such a backsliding, when the devil by his emissaries has had much artifice to turn me aside from the way of the Lord. Yet I will say this far, all I have done was not in order to own that wicked council as lawful rulers; but my life being in their tyrannous hands, I thought then I might desire as much favour of them as of a robber, that had the dagger at my breast: and I truly look on all their actings in courts, either higher or lower judicatories, in matters civil or ecclesiastic, that they act as murderers, oppressors, and tyrants only.

And now these bloody oppressors say, because I will not sinfully renounce my Lord and his interest, and look on them as magistrates, and say, I spake rashly what I did, on which terms, craving them pardon, I would soon get remission, and be at liberty, that they look on me as guilty of my own blood: but I hope my God will not account me guilty, who knows I dare not fo finfully difown him, for all the hazard of my poor life; there being a dilemma in my cafe, either I muft fin or fuffer: I have found it my only peace with my Lord, to choofe fuffering, and hate the way of finning. And this I thought good to infert in my dying teftimony, that others may beware of an untender walk with God, *who is a confuming fire to all impenitent finners*. Now my Lord has fealed my remiffion for this extravagance, and has entered into a new covenant with me, and I have refigned myfelf wholly to him, to be at his difpofal; and it is my rejoicing that he is calling me out to honour me fo much as to fuffer for his fake. A poor country-man with us, would think it his credit to be called to fignify his loyalty to a nobleman who were his mafter, whofe courage obliges him to fight for his fafety to the lofs of his life: But O! what a difparity is in my cafe! I am but a bafe, wretched, finful worm, and I am called to fignify my love and loyalty to the King of glory, before treacherous and perfidious powers that fit at eafe, and difown, yea, declare againft my Lord, that he is not our covenanted King and Lord. And the two defpifed covenants are not defpicable, but our glory. I will firft declare they are traitors, and ought to be difowned as magiftrates or lawful rulers; and fo many of them as have imbrued their hands in the blood of the faints, either by commiffions, or votes in councils or other courts, or have lived oppreffing God's people, in adultery, uncleanntefs, wickednefs and witchcraft, they are guilty of death. And when there are no other magiftrates who will duly punifh thefe impieties, it is my duty, out of zeal to the Lord, I fay it again, if the Lord would imploy me, to cut them off: as that zeal of Phineas, tho' mocked at by them in their proclamation, is a good example.

Thus I end, wifhing what I have here penned for a teftimony to the Lord's defpifed intereft, may have weight with any, who confider, that what I have written, I muft ere long reckon for; and fo I have laboured to be fingle-hearted before the Lord in it.

Now, having touched every thing I can remember, concerning my judgment of things controverted, as alfo fome reafon of my principles, afferted in face of a great council, and twice before the justiciaries, which I gladly sign with my subscription, glorifying the Lord, who owned me, so that I was not ashamed but judged it my glory to give my full and free testimony for my blessed Lord's despised interest, against that wicked and treacherous pack of God's declared enemies. Now, farewel all dear friends; I hope the Lord will have a glorious church in Scotland, and he will raise his glory out of the ashes of a burnt covenant. Now, farewel sun, moon, and stars; farewel holy Scriptures. O I am going to a life, where I shall no more be troubled with a body of sin, and death; O! I am going to a mansion of glory, that my Lord has prepared me. I shall have a crown of life, because I have been, by my blessed Lord's assistance, (though I slipped aside) made faithful to the death. Now, welcome Father, Son, and Holy Spirit, thou hast redeemed me by thy price, and by thy power: O Lord God of hosts, into thy hands I commit my spirit,

Sic subscribitur, JAMES SKEEN.

In the close prison of Edinburgh, November 30, 1680, being the day before my execution, according to the unjust sentence of a perfidious court.

The Testimony of ARCHIBALD STEWART, *who lived at Borrowstounness, and suffered at the cross of Edinburgh, December 1, 1680.*

Men and Brethren,

IT is like, the most part of you are come here to gaze and wonder upon me, rather than to be edified; but I hope there are some here, that are witnessing and sympathizing with me: But while ye are strangers to God, and ignorant of his word, and what our Lord has suffered for us, and that he has told us, That *thro' many tribulations and afflictions we must enter into the kingdom of God,* it is no wonder ye count us fools; for while I was in black nature myself, I was as mad as any of you all; but blessings to his holy name, that *whereas once I was blind, now I see,* and therefore *I abhor myself in dust and ashes:* And I desire the more to magnify his free grace, for all that he hath done to me; it is nothing in myself. Therefore, why should I not be content to follow the footsteps of my blessed Master, that has gone before me *of Archibald Stewart.*

from time to eternity, tho' in this manner it is unpleasant to natural sense? and he is calling for my mite of a Testimony for his despised truth. For it was by the hearing of the gospel by his suffering servants, both here and in Holland, that I was brought to the love of God, and his only Son Jesus Christ: Since which time he has engaged my heart to seek him in the same way, I found him, where he was most eminently holden forth, and witnessed for, and my sins and the sins of the land holden forth to me: And it is for this that I am accused and condemned of men; for my following the gospel preached in the fields; because I was following that poor handful that fell at Airsmofs, where Mr. Richard Cameron had been preaching, and was to preach; and because, when the bloody soldiers came upon us, we offered to defend ourselves; whatever other causes they have to lay to my charge.

And that ye be not mistaken with me, and the Lord's people and his way; tho' they alledge that we are of bloody principles, (as the indulged ministers give it out that we are of jesuitical and bloody principles;) yet the Lord knows, and I declare, that I have desired to know his will, and walk in it; and I have been studying that which all the land are obliged to, which is, to hear and keep up the gospel, and defend my own life and the lives of my brethren, who have been so long hunted, and to defend the gospel, which has been so long born down. So then however I and that suffering remnant be mistaken, in that they give out in their declaration, that I said, I would kill the king or any of the council; it is an untruth and forged calumny, to reproach the way of God, more like themselves and their own principles, who have killed so many of the people of God, both in the fields and upon scaffolds, and us among the rest, to please that bloody tyrant Charles Stuart's brother, who has been thirsting for the blood of these three nations; and to make men believe that we have been contriving a plot to murder them: Tho' indeed, if they were brought to any trial of a just law, according to the word of God, or the laws of the land, most of them have done, or consented to more than might take their lives, both against the people of the Lord, and his born down truths, and against the commonwealth and laws of the land. But I never said, that I would do it; and when I was before them, especially in the justiciary court, upon trial of my life, they would hardly give me leave to speak for, or explain myself; more like men designed to catch advantage, and to cheat me out of my life, than just judges. I know, they must answer to their great Judge for what they do.

And this being the testimony of a dying man, they that fear the Lord will believe my declaration before their proclamation, which may be easily seen to be a plot in them, and not in us, to blind the eyes of a secure generation, and make strangers approve of their persecution, and believe they do it justly, and laugh at our calamity, until they can win to bring about that bloody Popish design against all that will not follow them in the three nations: altho' they now spare some men, and flatter them to take favours from them, whereby they engage them to ly by, till they destroy his remnant, that dare not but witness against them, and the common sins of the land, for which I desire to mourn, and pray the Lord's people to mourn over them, and witness against them, as they desire to be marked with the mourners mark, when a holy God shall come to take vengeance on all ranks that have so forsaken and betrayed his Christ, and set up a man in his place, which will be found to be the great idol of jealousy, besides the many other idols that have drawn away the true and kind love and fear that the generation owes to God. And because we desire to love and fear God, and to follow his sweet Christ, we are reproached and staged with tongues of many, as these that are out of the way, and are of jesuitical principles. I declare, I have in some measure been desiring and intending to know, love and follow the truth, both in obedience to his commands, and for the hope of glory, tho', I confess, thro' much weakness and infirmity.

I am a Presbyterian in my judgment, tho' I be looked upon as otherwise, because of my declaring my thoughts freely before men: and I own and adhere to that work of reformation, the Larger and Shorter Catechisms, the National and Solemn League and Covenant, the Acknowledgment of Sins and Engagement to duties, the Causes of God's wrath. Also I own all the testimonies of of our worthy sufferers, that have gone before us: As also I own the Sanquhar Declaration, and that Excommunication at the Torwood. At the writing hereof, I

of Archibald Stewart.

prayed that the Lord would open their eyes, and let them fee their fins, and grant them repentance, all of them that are of the election of free grace; and they that are not, I pray that the Lord would ratify in heaven what was done on earth by his faithful fervant, as it is according to his will; which has been all our defires.

Now I leave my teftimony againft the curfed Prelates, and all their hirelings, who have been the inftigators and drivers on of the council and bloody foldiers, to all the tyranny, oppreffion, and blood which they have fhed. And I leave my teftimony againft the woful indulgences, and all that have been either embracers of them, or any that have been ftrengtheners of their hands, or their favourers: They have broken and divided the people of the Lord, more than all the former perfecutions could ever do. I leave my teftimony againft all lukewarm and unfaithful minifters and profeffors, that have turned their back upon Chrift and his caufe, and have fallen away from their firft love, and the doing of their firft works; for they are pulling down what they firft builded. I leave my teftimony againft the oppreffion, tyranny and robbery done againft the people of God, either by one or other, and efpecially by thefe wretches, Glencairn and Halyards, whofe names fhall be recorded for generations to come, as robbers of the widow and fatherlefs, *who have lien in wait againft the dwellings of the righteous, and have fpoiled his refting place;* and have turned many a widow and orphan out of their dwellings.

I leave my teftimony againft thofe tyrants that have forefaulted all the rights that they now lay claim to, and ufurp over the people of the Lord and the whole land, and all their unjuft laws; but efpecially that accurfed fupremacy, by which they fet up a miferable, adulterous wretched man in Chrift's room, who thinks to wrong our Lord, and carry his crown; but it will be too heavy for him, tho' all the wicked Lords, Prelates, Malignants, and Indulged be joining hand in hand to hold it on, down it fhall come, and whofoever wears that crown. And it is becaufe of his wearing my lovely Lord and king's crown, and wronging him that I am contending; and as he and they have proclaimed me a rebel and traitor to man, fo I difown him and them, and declare him and them traitors and rebels to God and his Chrift, my defirable and holy Lord and King. But let me intreat you, that defire mercy, to forfake your wicked ways, and fall in love with Chrift, and feek peace with God thro' him, who is the only peace-maker; for there are fad judgments coming on the land; and all your peace with thefe wicked men will not keep you from the dreadful wrath of God coming on the land, becaufe of flighting of the gofpel, when it was to be had in God's own way; and the perjury, covenant-breaking, idolatry and profanenefs, treacherous backfliding, apoftacy, and other abominations, that all ranks of the land are guilty of; and becaufe of their receiving and entertaining of this bloody Popifh Duke, who muft be welcomed with a draught of our blood now, as he was the laft time with the blood of our brethren.

I blefs the Lord, I have great fatisfaction in my owning this defpifed way of God, for which I lay down my life; and alfo, that the Lord has drawn my heart after him, and made me heartily willing to be at his difpofal: and I have fweet peace in what I have done, and would entreat all to more tendernefs, and to watch over all their ways; for there are many looking on us, and waiting for our halting in the way of God: O that the Lord would help you to wait on him, *until the day break, and the fhadows,* and all thofe clouds, *fly away!* for this is a heavy day upon the church of God. O! to be labouring to ly in the duft, and to hide ourfelves, and fhut our mouths, and be filent; for the Lord hath rubbed fhame on all faces, becaufe of many backflidings and upfitting in duty, and that both public and private, which, I think the Lord is contending for this day. O! dear friends, all ye that defire to keep the way of God, and be carried faithfully through amidft all thefe tribulations and aftonifhing difpenfations, forfake not your Chriftian fellowfhips, wherein fo much of the power and prefence of God hath been found, among thofe that meet together out of love and zeal for God, to pour out their hearts before him, and converfe one with another. I think the forfaking and upfitting of Chriftian meetings, is as fad a token of God's leaving the land, as any that I fee; and therefore I not only exhort you to this duty, but, as a dying man, I charge you, as you will anfwer at the great day, to fet about that duty with fear, love, and zeal to God, having his glory before your eyes: and let love to Chrift be the principle and motive to draw you to this, and all other duties. Let none be ſtumbled at the way of Chriſt for what we are ſuffering, (if I durſt call it ſuffering) for all the ſteps of the way are eaſy to me, thro' faith in a ſlain Mediator: for it is thoſe that keep the word of his patience, that he will keep in the hour of temptation. O! labour to keep up theſe lovely field-meetings, wherewith my ſoul has been refreſhed. And let it be your work to keep patience, whatever ſufferings ye meet with from enemies, or reproaches from pretended friends, who, I fear, will be found ſecret and heart-enemies to God. This I leave to you as my laſt advice.

And now I bleſs God for all that he hath done for my ſoul, and for this way that he hath taken with me, in carrying me to the land of praiſe, where I ſhall ſing that ſweet ſong throughout the ages of eternity, which ſhall never have an end. O! long to be with him; for if ye knew what I have got of his love and preſence, ye would whiles be giving a look to time, and bidding it be gone. Now even let it be gone, that I may enjoy my beſt beloved. Now I take my farewel of all friends and relations, and all earthly comforts, and all created glory; and welcome ſweet Lord Jeſus, into thy hands I commit my ſpirit.

Sic ſubſcribitur, ARCHIBALD STEWART.

P. S. Upon the ſcaffold he ſung the ſecond Pſalm, and read the third of Malachy; but they would not ſuffer him to pray publickly, for when he began to ſpeak, ſaying, " O Lord, what wilt thou do with this gene-
" ration? what wilt thou do with bloody Charles
" Stuart?" incontinent the drums were beaten, and his mouth ſtopped, that he got no more ſaid.

The Teſtimony of JOHN POTTER, *a farmer, who lived in the pariſh of Uphall in Weſt-Lothian, and ſuffered at the croſs of Edinburgh, December 1ſt,* 1680.

ALL you ſpectators and auditors, I deſire your attention to a few words, and I ſhall be brief. And before I begin, I muſt tell you, you muſt not expect ſuch a teſtimony from me, as ye have had from ſome of them that went before me, I not being a learned man, as ſome of them have been; however, I deſire to look to God, who not only can give me what to ſpeak, but can

The laſt Speech and Teſti

alſo bleſs what I ſpeak; ſo as it may be
and the good of them that love him, ar
coming, which is the deſire of my ſoul.
ſtep out of time into eternity, I hope you
that I ſhall ſay any thing now, but what
binds me to ſay.

In the firſt place, I muſt tell you for w
here this day to lay down my life: it is {
adhering to my ſworn principles. I am ;
and herein I do rejoice, that I am to ſuff(
only; for adhering to the word of God,
feſſion of Faith, Larger and Shorter C;
Covenants, National and Solemn Lea
with our ſolemn Acknowledgment of Sin
ment to Duties, wherein all Scotland we
ed, and thought it their duty and honour
this is the reaſon for which I am ſentenc
men; but God, to whom vengeance dot
avenge himſelf for all the wrongs done
cauſe, intereſt, and people. I was born
light of the goſpel, and was taught to
King in Zion only, and head of his own
this I own to be my duty: but I am here
rebellion, which I deny, becauſe I was n
pinion, that it was rebellion to hear the
word of God binds us to it, as our du
why ſhould God have told us, that *we ſh(*
to ſea, to ſeek the word of the Lord and ſh(
And the practice of our Lord and his apo
ing of the goſpel to the people that heard
ficient ground to prove it to be duty to h
whether in fields or houſes, when it cann
where; and if it be duty to hear the goſpe
certainly it is duty to defend the goſpel,
in purity; according to the word of Goc
ing to the ſixth article of the Solemn Lea
nant, wherein we are bound to aſſiſt and (
enter into covenant with us, and to the
power, with our lives in our hands, mu(
fend the goſpel, which teaches us the fun
ciples of our holy religion.

And to take away that vile and malic
which they caſt upon us, charging us wit
to have murdered the duke of York, an

him; I declare, I had never such a principle as to murder any man; neither did I hear ever of it, till the council told me; which I knew to be a vile and hell-hatched aspersion, cast upon the way and people of God: but they judge others by themselves, for that is their principle to murder the gospel of God, as they also do. Next, I was charged, whether or not I adhered to Sanquhar Declaration? I answered, I not only adhered to it, but also will lay down my life cheerfully and willingly, as I do this day, for adhering thereto; yea, if every hair of my head were a life, and every drop of my blood were a man, I would willingly lay them all down for him and his cause. I come here to tell you, 1*st*, That I adhere to all the written will and word of God; and I adhere to the Confession of Faith, and our Catechisms, Larger and Shorter, and to our Covenants, National and Solemn League, and to the solemn Acknowledgment of Sins and Engagement to Duties, and to all the covenants made betwixt God and us, wherein I stand engaged. 2*dly*, I adhere to all the testimonies that have gone before me. 3*dly*, I adhere to all that has been done for maintaining and defending the gospel, against a tyrannizing and bloody enemy, when the actors thereof had the glory of God before their eyes, as the chief motive that drave them thereto, whether at Pentland, Drumclog, Glasgow, Bothwel, Airsmoss, or any other place in Scotland, where there has been any rencounter of that kind. 4*thly*, I adhere to that action of excommunication at the Torwood, it being according to the word of God, and done by a faithful minister of the gospel, and in as legal a way as the present dispensation and circumstance of time could permit: and also the persons excommunicate being guilty of such crimes, as justly do deserve that act to be passed against them. 5*thly*, I adhere to the testimonies of all that have born testimony against silent and unfaithful ministers, by their withdrawing from them, which is a declaring that they do not own them as faithful ambassadors of Jesus Christ, because of their unfaithfulness: and I hope, none will condemn me for saying, that I have not had clearness to join with them, while they remain so unconcerned with the cause of Christ, and the oppression of his people. 6*thly*, I adhere to the way of salvation agreed upon betwixt the Father and the Son before the creation of the world, that thro' the Son we should be made perfect, which I hope to obtain, before this body of mine be cold, and in his perfection I shall be made perfect, and thro' his suffering I shall be conformed to him, *who suffered without the gate, bearing his reproach.* And I am well pleased with my lot this day. *O my soul, and all that is within me, bless his holy name, for all that he hath done for my soul,* and for his way of bringing me here this day to lay down my life for him. I am not afraid of grim death; I know that God has taken away the sting of death, thro' the suffering of his Son.

In the next place, being here as a dying witness for Christ and his cause, I do therefore leave my testimony against all abominations done in the land against a holy God, and in contempt of his image; particularly, 1*st*, I testify against all that woful and hell-hatched Act of Supremacy, wherein they acknowledge the king to be head of the church, and thereby have invested a mortal creature with Christ's crown, sword and sceptre. 2*dly*, I bear witness and testify against the breaking of the National and Solemn League and Covenant, and making them to be burnt by the hand of the hang-man at the market cross of Edinburgh, and elsewhere thro' Scotland, so contrary to their solemn engagements. 3*dly*, I witness and bear my testimony against the reception of Prelacy, so contrary to the word of God, and our Covenants; for then it was that the Covenanters in Scotland should have withstood both king and council, and all that joined with them in that head, and should have testified against them with their swords in their hand, until they had resisted unto blood, according to the 6th article of the Solemn League and Covenant. O! that all that are alive this day, that were men when the Covenant was burnt, were taking with their sin, and were lying in the dust; every one for his share in that sin, and every one for the land's guiltiness. 4*thly*, I leave my testimony against all the horrid bloodshed that has been in the land, whether of noblemen, gentlemen, ministers, or any others, that have suffered in Edinburgh or any other place, whether on scaffolds, on gibbets, in open fields, or on the sea; particularly that horrid act of murdering so many men after they had taken them prisoners, and promised them their lives, which was done by Thomas Dalziel, called general, who took them prisoners, and after promising to set them at liberty, delivered them up to the bloody council, who most cruelly murdered them, against, and without all law and reason, never speaking of conscience, for they had lost all of that that they ever had, when they burnt the Covenant, and murdered the marquis of Argyle, and my Lord Warristoun, and that eminent minister Mr. James Guthry, who were murdered against the very act of their own laws. 5thly, I bear witness and testimony against the cutting off heads and hands, and setting them up upon the ports of Edinburgh, and elsewhere thro' the kingdom of Scotland, as if they had been thieves or malefactors. 6thly, I testify and bear witness against all the imprisonments, finings and confinings of the people of God, for adhering to his word and our covenants. 7thly, I testify and bear witness against the pressing of the Declaration against our Covenants upon the consciences of the Lord's people. 8thly, I testify and bear witness against the imposing and paying of cess and militia-money, both for oppressing the consciences, and grinding the faces of the poor. 9thly, I testify and bear witness against that cruel and hell-hatched act of sending the Highland Host, and the rest of that cabal, to oppress and plunder the people of God. 10thly, and lastly, I bear witness against all the oppression, spoiling, robbing, and hunting of the people of God, and that against all manner of law and reason. I shall be a standing witness against them, ay and while they repent. O! that the Lord would pour out of his Spirit upon all that have so grievously turned aside, and make them to ly in the dust, and to take with their sins; but I fear a holy God has given them up to themselves, and sealed their hearts with obduration, and so they are become proof against all dispensations; but sure such as will not bow to God, shall be broken by the mighty rod of iron that is in his hand to bruise the nations. I have here left my testimony against the perjury, bloodshed and oppression of the people of God, which has been done by him who is called the king of Britain and Ireland; and the perjury and bloodshed acted by noblemen and gentlemen, that have been assisting and strengthning his hand in bloody and cruel courses; and therefore I leave my testimony against them, and my blood upon their heads, and especially against such as were present in the

L

council when I was examined, and thefe perjured lords of the criminal court, where I was fentenced to die here in this place of execution; and alfo I leave my blood upon the head of affizers, and all others who faid amen to my fentence, whatever they have been, and yet are, except they repent, my blood fhall be charged upon them. Likewife I leave my teftimony againft all who carried arms to guard me to this fcaffold, they fhall be guilty of my blood, if mercy and grace prevent it not.

Likewife I bear witnefs, and leave my teftimony againft the reception of the Duke of York, firft and laft, that profeffed Papift, who has been laying out himfelf to carry us back to Rome, and that not only by the bloody council, and other perjured noblemen and gentlemen, but alfo by the city of Edinburgh, that went out of the port to receive him, as tho' he had been a king, with fhooting of guns, founding of trumpets, beating of drums and kindling of bonfires; which is contrary to the word of God and our covenant, after he had been caft off juftly by the other kingdom of England: I fhall be a witnefs againft that action in the great day. And particularly, I leave my blood upon that wretch and bloody tyrant the Duke of York; for it is to fatisfy him, and to quench his implacable thirft after blood, that I am brought hither this day. The laft time he came to Scotland, he got a facrifice of the blood of thefe five that fuffered at Magus-muir, who were indeed highly honoured, and nothing fhort of thefe that went before them; and now he muft have this our blood to quench his thirft upon; but that heart of his that is fo rejoicing at the hearing and feeing of our death, ere long fhall tremble, when my heart fhall fing Hallelujah to the Lamb of God, and join in my note, and pafs my fentence with the great Judge againft him, and all the enemies of God, if great repentance and free grace prevent it not.

And with refpect to that for which I am fentenced to death, becaufe of many miftakes, even among the godly, thro' wrong information; I here as a dying man declare, I had before me no defign but only the glory of God, and the coming of Chrift's kingdom, and his reigning as king in Zion. And for this I am fentenced, and for this I lay down my life this day, and I do it willingly and chearfully, and not by conftraint; for if I had been left of a holy God, so far as to quit one hoof of his truth, I might have redeemed my life as some have done, that were as deeply engaged to stand by the truth, even to the resisting unto blood, as I was; and seemed to be as deeply concerned as I was. How they have come out of prison I know not, but God knows, and to him they will, and must give account thereof, and to him I leave it; but I think there are few that come out of prison now, that can say, they have neither touched, tasted, nor handled the abominations of these times wherein they live: Therefore I leave my testimony and witness against all that have come out of prison, by taking of the bond, if it were but to compear before these bloody enemies of God, in as far as they were convinced that it was sin; as some of them were, otherwise their tongue and pen have lied; which I leave to God and their own conscience to determine, whether or not they have sinned in so doing. Next, I here as a dying man, do declare, that if the blotting of paper to them would save my life, I would not do it at that rate; for I see they are setting themselves to ensnare poor things; and I see neither ministers nor professors to give their advice in this matter, if it be not to make them take the bond, as they did to these poor things in the Church-yard. Also, I leave my testimony, and bear witness against all the unfaithfulness of ministers and professors. First, I bear witness against the unfaithfulness of these ministers that were with the public resolutions, to bring in, or keep in, any of these men that were open and avowed malignants and enemies to God, so contrary to our covenant. 2*dly*, I bear testimony against that act at Glasgow, wherein six hundred ministers and upwards did quit their charge and turn their back upon their flock; and since, many of them are turned ravening wolves and greedy dogs that cannot bark, according to that word, Ezek. xiii 4. 5. *O Israel, thy prophets are like the foxes in the desart, who have not gone up to the gap, neither made up the hedge for the house of Israel to stand in the battle, in the day of the Lord.* Had it not been their duty to have stood by their charge until they had been driven out of their pulpits? 3*dly*, I leave my testimony against both indulgences, first and last, and against all that comply and go on with them in that sinful course, ay and while they repent, I shall be a standing witness against them. Surely, if

they be found with clean fingers when Go
quire after blood, I am miftaken: But (
they anfwer, when Chrift will fay, 'Come
' me an account of your talent: What di
' your miniftry? laid ye it afide at the
' Charles Stuart and the bloody council
' more delight to be a doctor or chambe
' had to be a minifter?' Oh! let the unfa
remember that word in Ezek. xxxiii. 6. *Bu
men fee the fword come, and blow not the tr*
people be not warned, and if the fword com
perfon from among them, he is taken away
but his blood will I require at the watchman'
that the blood of many fouls will be require
of the moft part of the minifters of Scotlaɪ

I bear witnefs, and leave my teftimony
faithfulnefs of many minifters, who have l
ed love and burning zeal, which they h
ventured upon the high places of the earth
the gofpel. And now, in the laft place, l
ny againft all that have preached, writt
reproached that poor party that were oc
at Airfmofs, only for the hearing of the g

And now, when I am ftepping out of t
nity, I declare that I adhere to all the do
ver I heard Mr. Richard Cameron, or Mr
gil preach; and my foul bleffeth God tha
either of them; for my foul hath been ref
the voice and fhouting of a king among th
ings, wherein the fountain of living wa
made to run down among the people of C
manner that armies could not have terrifi
am fure the blood that has been fhed in t
on. fcaffolds in Scotland for the caufe and
fus Chrift, will have a glorious crop, in
and men; and I am fure, the feed fown at
have as glorious a vintage, as ever any fe
had.

And now, O ye that are the poor remi
to ftay behind, who are the butt of the
ly of the open and bloody enemies, but
minifters and profeffors, who have gone o
themfelves, and will not fuffer others to
have this to fay to you, be earneft and cot

ing of love to Chrift: Walk with more fear, left ye offend a holy and jealous God. O beware that ye quit not your integrity; there are many waiting for your halting, yea, and longing for it. Caft not off the way of Chrift becaufe of fuffering. If ye knew what of his love and comforting prefence I had, fince I was called to witnefs for him againft thefe bloody traitors, that are thirfting after the blood of the Lord's people, ye would long for fuch proofs of his love; feek him early, and ye fhall find him. Be not troubled becaufe of our death, it is not a death unto the foul, but an inlet of life to it; For *to be dead to the world is to be alive to Chrift. Bleffed are the dead that die in the Lord, from henceforth they reft from their labours, and their works do follow them.* And rejoice, O ye poor of the flock, that wait with fear and trembling, and with faith and love in exercife; it is to you that he will come: he meeteth him that rejoiceth in, and worketh righteoufnefs. *Bleffed are ye that weep now, for ye fhall be comforted. Bleffed are the meek; for they fhall inherit the earth. Bleffed are the merciful; for they fhall obtain mercy. Bleffed are they which do hunger and thirft after righteoufnefs; for they fhall be filled. Bleffed are the pure in heart; for they fhall fee God. Bleffed are the peace-makers; for they fhall be called the children of God. Bleffed are they that are* reproached *for righteoufnefs fake; for theirs is the kingdom of heaven. Bleffed are ye when men shall revile you, and perfecute you, and shall fay all manner of evil of you falfely for my fake.* O friends, it is only you that have ground to rejoice; if ye by him be helped to keep the word of his patience, he will keep you in the hour of temptation, which fhall come upon all the world, to try them that dwell upon the face of the earth.

O dear friends and followers of Chrift, hold on your way, weary not, faint not, and you fhall receive the crown of life. It is thofe that overcome by the blood of the Lamb, and the word of their teftimony, that fhall ftand, being clothed in white robes, before the throne, for thefe are they that came out of great tribulation. Remember, that there is a book of remembrance written, and the names of thefe are written in it, *that fpeak often one to another.* O my friends, let it be your ftudy to keep up private fellowfhip-meetings, wherein fo much of the power and life of religion is to be found. Remember, that here I, as a dying fufferer for Chrift, leave this charge to every one of you, that have any love to Chriſt: Set about this and other duties with more fervent love and zeal than heretofore hath been done; and be much in private prayer; wreſtle with God upon the account of Jacob's trouble. I will ſay this, that the more ye ſeek for Zion, the more ye will get for yourſelves. Let not the reproaches caſt upon the way of God ſtumble you. And ſee that when ye are reviled, ye revile not again; but rather with meekneſs and love, in the fear of the Lord, ſtudy ye to gain others; but if they will not hearken when this is done, then be free and faithful in teſtifying againſt them for ſo doing; but eſpecially let your converſation teſtify your diſlike of theſe ſinful courſes. And now, my dear friends in Chriſt, I leave you to him, who has promiſed to be with you in the fire and water, and bear the weight of all your reproaches, and *is afflicted in all your afflictions*.

As for you that are lying in black nature, I exhort you to repent of your ſins, and come out of that woful eſtate, wherein ye are now lying, and cloſe with a ſlain Mediator upon his own terms. O fall in love with the way of ſalvation. O can ye think of the way of redemption, and not ſtand and wonder at the condeſcendency of free grace? I tell you, *Except you repent, ye ſhall all periſh*.

I have a word to ſpeak to you that are cruel and open enemies to Chriſt and his cauſe. Remember, *The ſaints ſhall judge the world*; and then we ſhall not get leave to ſtand on equal terms with you; but we ſhall be ſet on thrones, with crowns on our head and harps in our hands, to ſing praiſe to the Lamb: And then we ſhall paſs our ſentence, with the great Judge, upon all the enemies of God, and you ſhall be turned into hell, with all the nations that forget God, if ye repent not. I pray that the Lord would open your eyes that you may ſee your ſins, and turn from them and live. I forgive all men the wrongs they have done, or can do to me; but for the wrongs done to Chriſt, in robbing him of his right over his church and people, I know vengeance belongs to God, and he will repay them; therefore I leave them under proceſs, ay and while they repent. And now I begin to enjoy him who is inviſible; for it is but little we can ſee of him now; but this I am ſure of, that I ſhall be made conform to him thro' his ſufferings. Therefore I take my leave of all the world, and the enjoyments thereof. I leave my wife and child to my covenanted God, who gave them to me, and willingly quit and give them up to him, hoping, that *he will be a huſband to the widow, and a father to the fatherleſs,* according to his promiſe. I hope that the friends of the Lord will remember the living for the dead's ſake. Farewel wife and child, parents and relations, and all friends and acquaintances. Welcome heaven, angels and ſaints; welcome God and Father ; welcome lovely Jeſus Chriſt; welcome Holy Spirit of grace, into thy hands I commend my ſoul and ſpirit.

Sic ſubſcribitur, JOHN POTTER.

The laſt Speech and Teſtimony of ISABEL ALISON, *who lived at Perth, and ſuffered at Edinburgh, January* 26. 1681.

The Interrogations of ISABEL ALISON *before the privy council.*

WHen I was brought before the council, they aſked me, Where did ye live, at St. Johnſtoun ? Anſwer, Yes. What was your occupation ! To which I did not anſwer. The biſhop aſked, If I converſed with Mr. Donald Cargil? I anſwered, Sir, you ſeem to be a man whom I have no clearneſs to ſpeak to. He deſired another to aſk the ſame queſtion : I anſwered, I have ſeen him, and I wiſh that I had ſeen him oftner. They aſked, if I owned what he had done againſt the civil magiſtrate ; I anſwered, I did own it. They aſked, If I could read the Bible ? I anſwered, Yes. They aſked, If I knew the duty we owe to the civil magiſtrate ? I anſwered, When the magiſtrate carrieth the ſword for God, according to what the Scripture calls for, we owe him all due reverence ; but when they overturn the work of God, and ſet themſelves in oppoſition to him, it is the duty of his ſervants to execute his laws and ordinances on them. They aſked, If I owned the Sanquhar Declaration ? I anſwered, I do own it. They aſked, If I owned the papers taken at the Queensferry on Henry Hall ? I anſwered, You need not queſtion that. They aſked, If I knew Mr. Skeen ? I anſwered, I never ſaw him. They aſked, If I converſed with rebels ? I anſwered, I never converſed with rebels. They asked, If I did converſe with David Hackſtoun ? I anſwered, I did converſe with him, and I

blefs the Lord that ever I faw him, fo1
ought in him but a godly pious youth. T
the killing of the bifhop of St. Andrews w;
I anfwered, I never heard him fay, that l
but if God moved any, and put it upon th
his righteous judgments upon him, I ha\
fay to that. They asked me, When faw ye
that pious youth? I anfwered, I have feer
asked, When? I anfwered, Thofe are f1
tions, I am not bound to anfwer them.
thought not that a teftimony. They asked
ye of that in the Confeffion of Faith, Th;
fhould be owned tho' they were heathens
It was another matter, than when thefe v
own the truth, have now overturned it, an
felves avowed enemies to it. They asked,
be judge of thefe things? I anfwered, the
truth, and the Spirit of God, and not n
overturned the work themfelves. They ask
the two Henderfons that murdered the
drews? I anfwered, I never knew any lord
They faid, Mr. James Sharp, if ye call hi
I never thought it murder; but if God m(
red them up to execute his righteous judgm
I have nothing to fay to that. They askec
not I would own all that I had faid? fo
you will be put to own it in the Grafs-1
they bemoaned me, in putting my life in h
a quarrel. I anfwered, I think my life lit1
the quarrel of owning my Lord and M
truths; for he hath freed me from everlaftir
redeemed me; and as for my body, it is a'
They faid, I did not follow the Lord's pra
anent Pilate. I anfwered, Chrift owned his
when he was queftioned on it, and he to
was a King, and for that end he was born.
that, that we are called in queftion this d
ing of his kingly government. The bifh
own it. I anfwered, We have found the fac
of the contrary. The bifhop faid, He piti(
lofs of my life. I told him, He had done n
hurt than the lofs of my life, or all the li
taken; for it had much more affected me
fouls were killed by their doctrine. The

of Isabel Alison.

Wherein is our doctrine erroneous? I said, That was better debated already than a poor lass could debate it. They said, Your ministers do not approve of these things; and ye have said more than some of your ministers; for your ministers have brought you on to these opinions, and left you there. I said, They had cast in baits among the ministers, and harled them aside; and altho' ministers say one thing to day, and another to morrow, we are not obliged to follow them in that. Then they said, They pitied me; for (said they) we find reason and a quick wit in you: And they desired me to take it to advisement. I told them, I had been advising on it these seven years, and I hoped not to change now. They enquired mockingly, If I lectured any? I answered, Quakers use to do so. They asked, If I did own presbyterian principles? I answered, That I did. They asked, If I was distempered? I told them, I was always solid in the wit that God had given me. Lastly, they asked my name. I told them, If they had staged me, they might remember my name, for I had told them already, and would not always be telling them. One of them said, May ye not tell us your name? Then another of themselves told it.

The Interrogations of ISABEL ALISON *before the criminal lords.*

BEing called before the criminal lords, they asked me, If I would abide by what I said the last day? I answered, I am not about to deny any thing of it. They said, Ye confessed that ye harboured the killers of the bishop, tho' ye would not call it murder. I said, I confessed no such thing. The advocate said, I did. I answered, I did not; and I told them, I would take with no untruths. He said, Did ye not converse with them? I said, I did converse with David Hackstoun, and I bless the Lord for it. They said, When saw you him last? I answered, Never since you murdered him. They desired me to say over what I said the last day. I said, Would they have me to be my own accuser? They said, The advocate was my accuser? I said, Let him say on then. Then they went over the things that past betwixt the council and me the other day; and put me to it, yea, or nay. I said, Ye have troubled me too much with answering questions, seeing ye are a judicature which I have no clearness to answer. They said, Do ye disown us, and the king's authority in us? I said, I disown you all, because you carry the sword against God, and not for him, and have these nineteen or twenty years made it your work to dethrone him, by swearing year after year against him and his work, and assuming that power to a human creature, which is due to him alone, and have rent the members from their head Christ, and one another. Then they asked, Who taught you these principles? I said, I was beholden to God that taught me these principles. They said, Are you a Quaker? I said, Did you hear me say, I was led by a spirit within me? I bless the Lord, I profited much by the persecuted gospel; and your acts of indemnity after Bothwel cleared me more than any thing I met with since. They said, How could that be? I said, By your meddling with Christ's interests, and parting them as ye pleased. They said, They did not usurp Christ's prerogatives. I said, What then mean your indulgences, and your setting up of Prelacy? for there has none preached publicly these twenty years without persecution, but these that have had their orders from you. Then they caused bring Sanquhar Declaration, and the † Paper found on Mr. Richard Cameron, and the Papers taken at the Queensferry, and asked, If I would adhere to them? I said, I would, as they were according to the Scriptures, and I saw not wherein they did contradict them. They asked, if ever Mr. Welch or Mr. Riddel taught me these principles? I answered, I would be far in the wrong to speak any thing that might wrong them. Then they bade me take heed what I was saying, for it was upon life and death, that I was questioned. I asked them, If they would have me to lie? I would not quit one truth, tho' it would purchase my life a thousand years, which ye cannot purchase, nor promise me an hour. They said, When saw ye the two Hendersons and John Balfour? Seeing ye love ingenuity, will ye be ingenuous, and tell us, if ye saw them since the death of the bishop? I said, they appeared publicly within the land since. They asked, if I conversed with them within these twelve

---

† This Paper being taken from him, at his death, by the enemies who slew him, no copy thereof, for ought I know, has ever been procured, and hence it cannot be certainly known what was the nature of it.

months? At which I kept silence. They urged me to say either yea, or nay. I answered, Yes. Then they said, Your blood be upon your own head, we shall be free of it. I answered, so said Pilate; but it was a question if it was so; and ye have nothing to say against me, but for owning of Christ's truths, and his persecuted members. To which they answered nothing. Then they desired me to subscribe what I owned: I refused, and they did it for me.

Account of what ISABEL ALISON *said before the Assizers.*

Dear Friends,

THESE are to shew you what past betwixt the black crew and me. They read my indictment, and asked, if I had ought to say against it? I said, Nothing. They read the papers as they did formerly, and asked, if I owned them? I said, I did own them. Then they called the assizers and swore them. Then I told them, All authority is of God, *Rom.* xiii. 1. and when they appeared against him, I was clear to disown them; and if they were not against him, I would not have been there: I take every one of you witness against another, at your appearance before God, that your proceeding against me is only for owning of Christ, his gospel, and members; which I could not disown, lest I should come under the hazard of denying Christ, and so be denied of him. And when the assize came, they asked, if I had ought to say against them? I said, They were all alike, for there would no honest man take the trade in hand. They said to the assize, It was against their will to take our lives: I said, If that had been true, they would not have brought me so far off, pursuing me for my life. This is the substance of what past, as I remember.

Account of Mr. Archibald Riddel's *examination of* Isabel Alison *and* Marion Harvie.

About seven of the clock at night the goodman of the tolbooth caused call us down, against our will, to be examined by Mr. Riddel, at the council's order. So we came down, and were brought to the west side of the house, to an empty room, where they brought him into us: The goodman of the tolbooth being present, and the keepers, and some gentlemen with them, and they caused us sit down. The goodman of the tolbooth said, Mr. Riddel, the council caused me bring you to confer with these women; to see if ye can bring them to repentance. Then we protested, and said, As for repentance, we know not what fault we have done: Then said they, You cannot be the worse to have one of your ministers to confer with. We told them, These ministers being their servants we looked no more upon them as ministers of Jesus Christ; and therefore he is no minister to us. Mr. Riddel asked, If the council would send Mr. Cargil to us, would we not confer with him? We said, He was not at their command; but if Mr. Cargil would do as ye and the rest of you have done, we would do the like with him. So he offered to pray; We said, We were not clear to join with him in prayer. He said, Wherefore? We said, We know the strain of your prayers will be like your discourse. He said, I shall not mention any of your principles in my prayer, but only desire the Lord to let you see the evil of your doings. We told him, We desired none of his prayers at all. They said, Would we not be content to hear him? We said, Forced prayers had no virtue. Then we said, What means he to pray with us more than he did with our brethren that have gone before us? Mr. Riddel said, Mr. Skeen conversed with Mr. Robert Ross. We said, He did not send for him, but he intruded himself upon him. The goodman of the tolbooth said, He conversed with Mr. Meldrum, and we smiled at that, and said, He might talk to him of his perjury, but for no other thing. So they urged prayer again. We said, It would be a mocking of God. They said, Why so? We said, Because we cannot join in it. So Mr. Riddel began to debate with us, and said, We would not find it in all the Scripture, nor any history, to disown the civil magistrate. We answered, There were never such magistrates seen as we have. He instanced Manasseh, who *made the streets of Jerusalem to run with the blood of the prophets*. We said, It was a question if he came the length in perjury. He instanced Joash: We answered, He was but a child when that covenant was sworn, and it was not so with these he now pleaded for. He then instanced Nero, how he set the city on fire, and robbed the churches; and yet notwithstanding the Apostle exhorteth submission to the magistrates then in being. We answered, It was in the Lord, and as they were a terror to evil doers. He said, Altho' they were wicked, yet they should not be altogether cast off. We said, Before their excommunication we would not have been so clear to cast them off. He said, There were but only seven in the excommunication, then why do ye cast at all the rest? We answered, These seven carried the great sway, and the rest came in under them. He said, How can one man take upon him to draw out the sword of excommunication, for the like was never heard tell of in no generation? We answered, Why not one man, since there were no moe faithful, and the church hath power to cast out scandalous persons, be they high, be they low. He said, Who is the church? We said, If there was a true church in the world, that little handful was one, tho' never so insignificant, of which handful we own ourselves a part: and tho' our blood go in the quarrel, yet we hope, it will be the foundation of a new building, and of a lively church.

He said, Thought we all the ministers wrong? We answered, We desire to forbear, and not to add; for we desire not to speak of ministers faults. And we desired him to forbear, and let us be gone; but he urged his discourse, and fell on upon the papers that were taken at the Queensferry, chiefly on that part of them; "When God gives them power, it is a just law to execute justice upon all persons that are guilty." And he came to us, and laid by his coat, and said, Would ye stab me with a knife in my breast, even now? And we smiled, and said, We never murdered any: But, said he, they swore to do so. We said, Why did he not debate these things with men, and not with lasses? For we told him, We never studied debates. He said again, Thought we all the ministers wrong? We answered, they were wrong, and forbade him to put us to it, to speak of ministers faults; for if he knew what we had to say of them, he would not urge us. So we desired to be gone. And he said, if ye come to calm blood, desire me or any other of the ministers to speak to you, and ye may tell the keepers and ye may have them: And there was a surgeon among them, and the goodman of the tolbooth said, He might draw blood of us, for we were mad. We said, Saw ye any mad action in us? This is all we can mind at present.

M

The last Speech and Testimony

The dying Testimony and last Words of ISABEL ALISON.

I Being sentenced to die in the Grafs-market of Edinburgh, January, 1681. thought fit to set down under my hand, the causes wherefore I suffer. I being apprehended at Perth, in my own chamber, by an order from the council, and brought to Edinburgh with a strong guard, and there put in prison, and then being examined first by a committee, and then by the criminal court; the manner of my examination was, *1st*, If I conversed with David Hackstoun and others of our friends? Which I owned upon good grounds. *2dly*, If I owned the excommunication at the Torwood, and the papers found at the Queensferry, and Sanquhar Declaration, and a paper found on Mr. Cameron at Airsmofs? All which I owned. Likewise I declined their authority, and told them, that they had declared war against Christ, and had usurped and taken his prerogatives, and so carried the sword against him, and not for him: So, I think, none can own them, unless they disown Christ Jesus. Therefore let enemies and pretended friends say what they will, I could have my life on no easier terms than the denying of Christ's kingly office. So I lay down my life for owning and adhering to Jesus Christ, his being a free king in his own house, for which I bless the Lord, that ever he called me to that.

Now in the first place, I adhere to the holy Scriptures of the Old and New Testament. And likewise I adhere to the Confession of Faith, because according to the Scriptures, the Larger and Shorter Catechisms; and our solemn Covenants, both National and Solemn League, as they were lawfully sworn in this land; and I adhere to the Acknowledgment of Sins, and Engagement to Duties; I adhere likewise to these fore-mentioned papers, and to the excommunication at Torwood, they all being according to the Scriptures of truth, and so both lawful and necessary. Likewise I adhere to the Rutherglen Testimony, and to all the testimonies of our worthies, who have suffered in Edinburgh, and elsewhere.

In the next place, I enter my protestation against all the violation done to the work of God these twenty years bygone. First, The burning of the Covenant made with God, and the Causes of God's Wrath, and the thursting *of Isabel Alison.*

in of prelates into the Lord's house, contrary to the word of God, and our sworn Covenants. I leave my testimony against Popery, which is so much countenanced at this day, against the receiving that limb of antichrist the duke of York. Likewise I leave my testimony against all the blood shed both on scaffolds and in the fields and seas; and against all the cruelty used against all the people of the Lord. And I leave my testimony against the paying of that wicked cess, for maintaining these profane wretches, to bear down the work of God. I leave my testimony against all unlawful bonds. And likewise against the shifting of a testimony, when clearly called by the Lord to give it. I leave my testimony against profanity of all sorts, and likewise against lukewarmness and indifferency in the Lord's matters. I leave my testimony against the unfaithfulness of ministers, first and last, their silence at the first, when their Master's work was broken down, for the most part they slipped from their Master's back, without so much as giving one word of a testimony against the wrongs done to him; and now are become a snare to the poor people in going to hear the curates, and poor things following their example are ensnared; my finding the sad experience of it, brings it the more into my memory. Yet notwithstanding of their being convinced of their error in this, many of them carry now, as if they rued that ever they came forth to the fields to proclaim their Master a free King in his own house: And now they are fallen in under the shadow of the sworn enemies, and alas they are become profound to lay snares; yea, *they are a trap upon Mispeh, and a net spread upon Tabor!* Oh, for the sad defection both of ministers and professors in Scotland! It is like our carriage may make many of our carcases to ly in the wilderness. I leave my testimony against the indulgences, first and last, and against all that comply therewith, or connive thereat. I leave my testimony against the censuring of worthy Mr. Cameron, or any other whom God raised up to declare the whole counsel of God, and to witness against the evils of this generation. I fear when God makes inquisition for blood, ministers hands will not be found free thereof.

As for charging my blood on any particular person, I cannot, for I have never gotten the certainty of what hath brought me to the stage; but if any have done it willingly, I leave it to God, and their own conscience. But I may warrantably charge it upon all the declared enemies of God within the land.

And 1*st*, I leave it upon the bloody council, that sent an order to take me, for they are guilty of it. 2*dly*, The sheriff clerk of Perth, and these that were with him when he took me, are guilty of it: the sheriff-clerk of Kinross, and the men that guarded me, are all likewise guilty of my blood: And I leave my blood on Sir George Mackenzie, and the rest of that bloody court; and I take the Lord to witness against them, whether or not it was on easy terms, that they offered me my life; they said only, they would not trouble me with their bishops; but I said, that Supremacy was as evil as Prelacy. And they said that I behoved to say, that the king was not an usurper, and pass from all my former confession, and that it was my duty to obey authority. I told them, that they were sworn enemies to God, so that it was impossible to obey God, and them both; so I told them, I would not retract an hair-breadth. They said, Thought I ever that he was our lawful king? I said, Yes; for he entered into covenant with God, and with the land: but he hath broken and cast off that tye, and hath exercised so much, both tyranny and cruelty, that I had just ground to decline him, and them both: Then they bade my blood be upon my own head; but I told them, they would find it on their heads, for it was for my owning of Christ's kingly office, that they put me to suffer, say the contrary who will. Now, I bless the Lord I am free from jesuitical principles. The Scripture is my rule, and when obedience to men is contrary to obedience to God, I am clear to disown them.

I leave my testimony against Mr. Riddel, for his obeying these wicked men to ensnare us, and to hold out to us, before these accursed enemies of Christ, that were seeking our lives for our adhering to the truth, that it was all delusion that we held. I many times rued that I bare so well with him; and now I hear, that he denies that which we wrote. But if ye will believe me, who am in a little to appear before God, there was nothing added, but rather wanting: I wish the Lord may forgive him. I bless the Lord, what strikes against myself only, I can very heartily forgive; but what strikes against God and his truths, I leave that to God, who is the Judge of all.

Now, I would only say this to you, who are seeking to keep your garments clean, *Be sober, be vigilant, for your adversary the devil goes about like a roaring lion, seeking whom he may devour.* And as I would have you be zealous for the truth, and not to quit one hoof; so I would have you labour against a spirit of bitterness; beware of self; and be more ready to mourn for the slips of others, than to make them the subject of your discourse; and labour to make earnest of religion, for I find there is need of more than a good cause, when it comes to the push. O the everlasting covenant is sweet to me now! And I would also say, they that would follow Christ, need not fear at the cross, for I can set to my seal to it, *His yoke is easy, and his burden is light.* Yea, many times he hath made me go very easy thro' things that I have thought I would never have win thro'. He is the only desirable master; but he must be followed fully. Rejoice in him, all ye that love him, *Wherefore lift up your heads, and be exceeding glad, for the day of your redemption draweth nigh.* Let not your hearts faint, nor your hands grow feeble. Go on in the strength of the Lord, my dear friends, for, I hope, he will yet have a remnant both of sons and daughters, that will cleave to him, tho' they will be very few; *even as the berries on the top of the outmost branches.* As for such as are grown weary of the cross of Christ, and have drawn to a lee-shore that God never allowed, it may be ere all be done it will turn like a tottering fence, and a bowing wall to them, and they shall have little profit of it, and as little credit. But what shall I say to the commendation of Christ and his cross! I bless the Lord, praise to his holy name, that hath made my prison a palace to me; and what am I that he should have dealt thus with me? I have looked greedy-like to such a lot as this, but still thought it was too high for me, when I saw how vile I was; but now the Lord hath made that scripture sweet to me, Isa. vi. 6. 7. *Then flew one of the seraphims unto me, having a live coal in his hand,—And he laid it upon my mouth, and said, Lo, this hath touched thy lips, and thine iniquity is taken away, and thy sin purged.* O how great is his love to me! that hath brought me forth to testify against the abominations of the times, and keeped me from fainting hitherto, and hath made me to rejoice in him. Now I blefs the Lord that ever he gave me a life to lay down for him. Now, farewel all creature comforts; farewel fweet Bible; farewel ye real friends in Chrift; farewel faith and hope; farewel prayers and all duties; farewel fun and moon: Within a little I fhall be free from fin, and all the forrows that follow thereon. Welcome everlafting enjoyment of the Father, Son, and Holy Ghoft, everlafting love, everlafting joy, everlafting light.

Edinburgh Tolbooth, } *Sic fubfcribitur,*
Jan. 26. 1681.

ISABEL ALISON.

BEing come to the fcaffold, after finging the lxxxiv. Pfalm, and reading the xvi. of Mark, fhe cried over the fcaffold, and faid, *Rejoice in the Lord, ye righteous; and again I fay, rejoice.* Then fhe defired to pray at that place, and the major came, and would not let her, but took her away to the ladder foot, and there fhe prayed. When fhe went up the ladder, fhe cried out, O be zealous, Sirs, be zealous, be zealous! *O love the Lord all ye his fervants*; O love him, Sirs! *for in his favour there is life.* And fhe faid, O ye his enemies, what will ye do, whither will ye fly in that day? For now there is a dreadful day coming on all the enemies of Jefus Chrift. Come out from among them, all ye that are the Lord's own people. Then fhe faid, Farewel all created comforts; farewel fweet Bible, in which I delighted moft, and which has been fweet to me fince I came to prifon; farewel chriftian acquaintances. Now, *Into thy hands I commit my fpirit, Father, Son and Holy Ghoft.* Whereupon the hangman threw her over.

The laft Speech and Teftimony of MARION HARVIE, *who lived at Borrowftounnefs, and fuffered at Edinburgh the* 26*th of January,* 1681.

An account of her anfwers before the privy council.

THEY asked firft, How long is it fince ye faw Mr. Donald Cargil? I faid, I cannot tell particularly when I faw him. They faid, Did you fee him within thefe three months? I faid, It may be I have. They faid, Do ye own his covenant? I faid, What covenant? Then they read it to me; and I faid, I did own it.

of Marion Harvie.

They said, Do ye own the Sanquhar Declaration? I answered, Yes. They said, Do ye own these to be lawful? I said, Yes; because they are according to the Scriptures, and our Covenants, which ye swore yourselves, and my father swore them. They said, Yea; but the Covenant does not bind you to deny the king's authority. I said, So long as the king held the truths of God, which he swore, we are obliged to own him; but when he brake his oath, and robbed Christ of his kingly rights, which do not belong to him, we are bound to disown him, and you also. They said, Do ye know what ye say? I said, Yes. They said, Were ye ever mad? I answered, I have all the wit that ever God gave me; do ye see any mad act in me? They said, Where was you born? I answered, In Borrowstounness. They asked, What was your occupation there? I told them, I served. They said, Did ye serve the woman that gave Mr. Donald Cargil quarters? I said, That is a question which I will not answer. They said, Who did ground you in these principles? I answered, Christ by his word. They said, Did not ministers ground you in these? I answered, When the ministers preached the word, the Spirit of God backed and confirmed it to me. They said, Did ye ever see Mr. John Welch? I said, Yes; my soul hath been refreshed by hearing him. They asked, if ever I heard Mr. Archibald Riddel? I answered, Yes; and I bless the Lord that ever I heard him. They said, Did ever they preach to take up arms against the king? I said, I have heard them preach to defend the gospel, which we are all sworn to do. They asked, If ever I swore to Mr. Donald Cargil's covenant? I said, No; but we are bound to own it. They said, Did ye ever hear Mr. George Johnstoun? I said, I am not concerned with him: I would not hear him, for he is joined in a confederacy with yourselves. They said, Did ye hear the excommunication at the Torwood? I said, No; I could not win to it. They asked, If I did approve of it? I answered, Yes. They asked, If I approved of the killing the lord St. Andrews? I said, In so far as the Lord raised up instruments, to execute his just judgments upon him, I have nothing to say against it; for he was a perjured wretch, and a betrayer of the kirk of Scotland. Then they asked, What age I was of? I answered, I cannot tell. They said among themselves, that I would be about twenty years of age, and began to regret my cafe, and faid, Would I caft away myfelf fo? I anfwered, I love my life as well as any of you do; but will not redeem it upon finful terms; for Chrift fays, *He that feeks to fave his life, fhall lofe it.* They faid, A roke, the code and bobboons, were as fit for me to meddle with, as thefe things. Then one of them asked, when the affize fhould fit? and fome other of them anfwered, On Monday. Then they asked, If I could write? I anfwered, Yes. Will you fubfcribe, faid they, what you have faid? I anfwered, No. They bade the clerk fet down, that I could write, but refufed to fubfcribe. Then they asked, If I defired to converfe with one of our minifters? I faid, What minifters? They faid, Mr. Riddel. I faid, What would ye have me to do with him? They faid, He might convince you of that fin. I faid, What fin? They faid, The fin of rebellion. I fmiled, and faid, If I were as free of all fin, as the fin of rebellion, I fhould be an innocent creature. They asked, If they fhould bring Mr. Riddel to me? I faid, It was an evidence he was not right fince they had him fo much at their will. And I told them, I would have none of their minifters. This is all I can remember, at this prefent.

Her difcourfe before the jufticiary court.

FIRST, I was brought and fet in the pannel, with the murderers, and they read over my indictment, and afked me, If I did confefs with thefe things? I anfwered, Yes. Then they read Sanquhar Declaration, and afked, if I owned it? I anfwered, Yes. They read that paper which they call the New Covenant, and afked, if I owned it? I anfwered, Yes. Then I protefted they had nothing to fay againft me, as to matter of fact; but only becaufe I owned Chrift and his truth, and perfecuted gofpel, and members, of which ye have hanged fome, others you have beheaded, and quartered quick. To that they replied nothing; but called the affizers who had no will to appear, till they were about to fine them, and then they came forward. One of them faid, He did not defire to be one of the affize, but they would have him. He bade them read our confeffion; for he knew not what they had to fay againft us. They bade him hold up his hand, and fwear that he would be true, and he could not, but fell a-trembling. The advocate *of Marion Harvie.*

bade the affizers look if I had any thing to fay againft them. I faid, I knew none of them, but what were all bloody butchers together. And when the affizers were fet in a place by themfelves, I faid to them, Now beware what ye are doing, for they have nothing to fay againft me; but only for owning Jefus Chrift and his perfecuted truths; for ye will get my blood upon your heads. So that man that fell a-trembling before, defired them to read my confeffion to him, and they read it. And after that the advocate had a difcourfe to them, and faid, Ye know thefe women are guilty of treafon. The affize faid, They are not guilty of matters of fact? He faid, but treafon is fact; and taking himfelf again, he faid, 'Tis true, it is but treafon in their judgment: but go on according to our law, and if ye will not do it, I will proceed. And when they had read my confeffion, they had fet down, that I had faid, The minifters had taught me thefe principles. I faid, That is a lie, and it is like the reft of your lies; for I faid, That it was Chrift by his word, that taught me. They anfwered nothing to that, but faid, Would I own the reft of my confeffion? I anfwered, Yes. The advocate faid, We do not defire to take their lives; for we have dealt with them many ways, and fent minifters to deal with them, and we cannot prevail with them. I faid, We are not concerned with you, and your minifters. The advocate faid, 'Tis not for religion that we are purfuing you; but for treafon. I anfwered, 'Tis for religion that ye are purfuing me; for I am of the fame religion that ye are all fwore to be of; but ye are all gone blind. I am a true Prefbyterian in my judgment. So they put the affize into a room by themfelves, and removed me without the guard into another room, then they read the delay till Friday at twelve of the clock: and I charged them before the tribunal of God, as they fhould anfwer there; for, faid I, ye have nothing to fay to me, but for my owning the perfecuted gofpel.

The dying Teftimony and laft Words of MARION
HARVIE.

Chriftian Friends and Acquaintances,

I Being to lay down my life on Wednefday next, January 26. 1681. I thought fit to let it be known to the world wherefore I lay down my life; and to let it be

feen, that I die not as a fool, or an evil
bufy body in other mens matters: No, i
ing to the truths of Jefus Chrift, and avov
king in Zion, and head of his church; anc
againft the ungodly laws of men, and their
of his rights, and ufurping his prerogative
I durſt not but teſtify againſt; and I bleſs
that ever he called me to bear witneſs aga
the times, and the defections of upſitten
profeſſors. 1ſt, I adhere to the holy and fv
of God, which have been my rule in all I
which my ſoul has been refreſhed. 2dly, 1
Confeſſion of Faith, becauſe agreeable to t
3dly, I adhere to the Larger and Shorte
4thly, I adhere to the Covenants, Nation:
League, and the work of reformation. 5
to all the faithful teſtimonies, which have b
faithful miniſters of Jefus Chriſt, either o:
fields. 6thly, I adhere to the papers found a
ferry on Henry Hall. 7thly, I adhere to t
at Sanquhar, and the teſtimony at Ruther
papers found on worthy Mr. Richard Cam
adhere to the excommunication at the To1
I adhere to the excommunication of the biſh
underlings; and I die in the faith of it,
hath ratified that in heaven, which his fai
have done on earth, as to caſtiüg out th
God out of the church. And now, I defi1
Lord for my lot: *My lot is fallen to me in ∤
and I have a goodly heritage.*

* I leave my blood upon the traitor that
throne: then on James Duke of York, w
in the council when I was examined the fi
I leave my blood on the bloody crew that c
rulers. And I leave it on James Henderſon
ferry, who was the Judas that fold Archi
and Mr. Skeen, and me, to the bloody f
much money. I leave my blood on Serje
who took me, and brought me to priſon
blood on the criminal lords, as they call th
eſpecially that execommunicate tyrant Ge(
zie, the advocate, and the fifteen aſſizers;
drew Cunningham that gave me my doom;

* Underſtand this paragraph with the caution given,

traitor Thomas Dalziel, who was porter
was firſt before them, and threatned me

ſtimony againſt the burning of the cove-
rere ſolemnly ſworn by the three nations,
1ands to the great God of heaven and
: my teſt mony againſt all the blood-ſhed
if the Lord's people, either on ſcaffolds
I proteſt againſt baniſhments and fin-
murderings, eſpecially the inhuman mur-
David Hackſtoun; I leave my teſtimony
ing of the ceſs, imployed for the bear-
preaching of the goſpel, and the taking
poor followers of Jeſus Chriſt. I leave
gainſt the profeſſors that ſay, this is not
od for which I ſuffer, and call the way of
I leave my teſtimony againſt Mr. Archi-
vho became ſervant to the bloody lords,
is work to make me deny Chriſt, and
to the ungodly laws of men, and
s of God, deluſions, which I am to
lood: and I rejoice that ever he counted
to do. O! I may ſay, *What am I, or*
er's houſe, that he ſhould have called me out
hs with my blood? Which truths, both
rofeſſors have counted prudence to diſown
which the land will be to mourn and fore-
e all be done. I leave my teſtimony a-
n Blair, that ſaid, I had no more grace
ad, and was witneſs to my ſentence, that
and his wife, that ſaid, I had no more
old ſhoes; as if grace were not free, and
ad not enough to give me. I leave my
nſt both miniſters and profeſſors, that
mſelves in any of theſe courſes of defec-
nemies, and are faſt in their camps.
teſtimony againſt Popery, Prelacy, Qua-
dulgency, and deſires to mourn for it,
ed with them in hearing them, or any of
nive at them. I leave my teſtimony a-
tical principles, altho' our profeſſors ſay,
o them; I deny it, and I take God to be
it I hate all opinions that are contrary to
hs of God. And ſince ever God called

me to follow his persecuted gospel, it was still my desire to stick close by him, and the rule he has set down for poor sinners to walk by. And it was always my rejoicing to serve him, and to act and do for his truth, and to vindicate it. And many a sore heart I have had with them, in vindicating his truths, when they have been denying them, and casting dirt in the faces of faithful witnesses of Jesus Christ; and I desire all these that are endeavouring to contend for Christ and his truths, that they would be faithful in their witnessing for him, and eschew the least appearance of sin. For I a dying witness of Christ, obtest you, as you will answer, when ye stand before him in the day of your appearance, that ye be faithful in owning him, in all his truths, and not yield a hoof to these ungodly, perjured, bloody and excommunicate traitors, and tyrants; for there is much advantage to be had in faithfulness for Christ; and that I may set to my seal to the truth of. And I think Christ is taking a narrow view of his followers at this time; for there are few that yield a hair-breadth of the truths of God, that readily win to their feet again; but go from one degree of defection to another.

And again, I desire to bless and magnify the Lord, for my lot, and may say, *He hath brought me to the wilderness to allure me there, and speak comfortably to my soul.* It was but little of him I knew when I came to prison; but now he has said to me, *Because he lives, I shall live also:* And he has told me, *I am he, that hath blotted out thine iniquity, for my own name's sake.* Kind has he been to me, since he brought me out to witness for him. I have never sought any thing from him, that was for his glory, since I came to prison, but he granted me my desire. For the most part, I have found him in every thing, that hath come in my way, ordering it himself, for his own glory. And now I bless him, that thoughts of death are not terrible to me. He hath made me as willing to lay down my life for him, as ever I was willing to live in the world. And now, ye that are his witnesses, be not afraid to venture on the cross of Christ. *For his yoke is easy, and his burden light.* For many times, I have been made to think strange, what makes folk cast at the cross of Christ, that hath been so light to me, that I found no burden of it at all, he bore me and it both. Now, let not the frowns of men, and their flatteries put you from your duty. Keep up your societies, and the assembling of yourselves together; for there is much profit to be found in it. Many times hath it been found comfortable to me, to hear of the few in Scotland, in which Christ was delighting; and that there was much love to God's glory, and zeal for his honour amongst them. Now, be humbled, and ly in the dust, and never give over crying in behalf of the church, which is so small, that it can scarcely be discerned, and never give over till he appear; for I think he is near at hand. O watch, and double your diligence, and *hold fast till he come, and let none take your crown, for he is good to the soul that seeks him.* If I were to live again, I would let that perjured crew see, that I should be more guilty of that which they call rebellion, in serving my lovely King, and in acting and doing for him and his glory, if he called me to it: And it is my grief, that I have not been more faithful for my master Christ. All his dealings with me have been in love and in mercy. His corrections have been all in love and free grace. O free love! O! I am oft made to wonder, what it was that made him take a blasphemer to witness for him and his truths. I may say, *I am a brand plucked out of the fire:* I am a limb of the devil plucked out from his fire-side. O! I am made to wonder and admire at his condescending love? Now, I leave my testimony against Jean Forrest, for saying, that I am going to the grave with a lie in my right hand, and charging my blood on my own head. O my friends, *come out from among them, and touch not the unclean thing.* It will never be well, till there be a separation from sin. I bless the Lord that ever I heard Mr. Cargil, that faithful servant of Jesus Christ; I bless the Lord that ever I heard Mr. Richard Cameron, my soul has been refreshed with the hearing of him, particularly at a communion in Carrick, on these words in Psal. lxxxv. 8.—*The Lord will speak peace unto his people, and to his saints; but let them not turn again to folly.* Now I leave my testimony against all the backsliding ministers, who, when I began to hear the gospel, preached the same truths, which I am to lay down my life for at this time; but now they are joined in a combination against God. And for the most part, are all at the enemies will; for when I got my sentence, the bloody traitors promised to bring any of our ministers to us, when before them; and so this gives me ground to say, they are become their servants.

Now the Lord knows, I have a sore heart to mention these things; but when I saw some of them there, and they offering us any of the rest, it gives me ground to set it down with a sore heart. Now what shall I say? I have sinned against him, and I am guilty of the defections, for which my carcase must ly in the wilderness, and not see the King come home to his habitation. But O! I am content, and heartily content, that he gives me my soul for a prey; and well is me for it, I think myself not behind. O my love! O my love! O my love! My altogether lovely Christ. The common report thro' the country is; That I might have had my life on very easy terms; but I could have it on no easier terms, than the denying of my Lord and Master Christ. First, They asked, If I would retract my former confession, and particularised all the papers I had owned before, and if I would not call Charles Stuart an usurper and the devil's vicegerent: I told them, I would not go back in any thing, for ye have nothing, said I, to lay to me but for the avowing Christ to be King in Zion, and head of his own church. And they said, they did not usurp Christ's crown: But I said, They were blinded and did not see. They said, There was but a few of us for these principles. I said, They had all the wyte of it, and it was most bitter to us, that our ministers had spoken against these truths. And indeed I think they had not been so cruel to me, were it not for these ministers. And so I think, our ministers are not free of our blood; for when they spake against us and the way, it hardened these bloody traitors, and emboldened them to take our lives.

I leave my testimony against them, for they have caused many poor things to err from the way of God, and many have made ministers their rule, and so the blind have led the blind, and both have fallen into the ditch together. And some think and say, " O can we quit so many godly ministers?" We dow not quit them; but I assure you, ye shall get a share of the wrath and stroke, which God hath prepared for these backsliders and betrayers of their trust. O I wonder what is the reason that men count it their wisdom to deny God, who has been so kind to them, and who have many a day delighted to commend his love to me, with the hazard of their lives;

for which I will be a witnefs againft them. Now I have no more to fay; be faithful unto the death; or elfe, Wo, wo, wo to you that are owning him at this day, if ye do not own him in all his offices, as King, Prieft, and Prophet: O my dear love! well is me that ever he let me know that his love was better than life. Wo to that creature, that will not love my lovely Lord Jefus Chrift.

Now, farewel lovely and fweet Scriptures, which were ay my comfort in the midft of all my difficulties: Farewel faith, farewel hope, farewel wanderers, who have been comfortable to my foul, in the hearing of them commend Chrift's love. Farewel brethren, farewel fifters, farewel Chriftian acquaintances, farewel fun, moon, and ftars. And now welcome my lovely and heartfome Chrift Jefus, into whofe hands I commit my fpirit throughout all eternity. I may fay, *Few and evil have the days of the years of my pilgrimage been*, I being about twenty years of age.

From the tolbooth of Edinburgh, the Woman-houfe on the Eaft fide of the prifon, Jan. 11th 1681.

MARION HARVIE.

THIS Martyr, tho' both young in years, and of the weaker fex, (which heightens the difcovery, how brutally furious and mad thefe perfecutors were) was fo fingularly affifted of the Lord in his caufe, and had fuch difcoveries of his fpecial love to her foul, that fhe was nothing terrified by her adverfaries: When fhe was brought from the tolbooth to the council-houfe, to be carried to her execution; as fhe came out of the tolbooth-door feveral friends attending her, fhe was obferved to fay with a furprifing chearfulnefs and air of heavenly ravifhment, Behold I hear my beloved faying unto me, *Arife my love, my fair one, and come away*. And being brought to the council, Bifhop Paterfon being refolved, feeing he could not deftroy her foul, yet to grieve and vex it, faid, Marion, you faid, you would never hear a curate, now ye fhall be forced to hear one, upon which he ordered one of his fuffragans, whom he had prepared for the purpofe, to pray; fo foon as he began, fhe faid to her fellow-prifoner Ifabel Alifon, Come Ifabel let us fing the xxiii. Pfalm, which accordingly they did; Marion repeated the Pfalm line by line without book, which drowned the voice of the curate, and extremely confounded the perfecutors. Being come to the fcaffold, after finging the lxxxiv. Pfalm, and reading the iii. of Malachy, fhe faid, I am come here to day for avowing Chrift to be head of his church, and King in Zion. O feek him, Sirs, feek him, and ye fhall find him; I fought him and found him, I held him, and would not let him go. Then fhe briefly narrated the manner how fhe was taken, and recapitulated in fhort the heads of her written teftimony, faying to this effect; "I going out of Edinburgh to hear the pefecuted gofpel in the fields, was taken by the way with foldiers, and brought in to the guard, afterwards I was brought to the council, and they queftioned me if I knew Mr. Donald Cargil? or if I heard him preach? I anfwered, I blefs the Lord I heard him, and my foul was refrefhed with hearing him, for he is a faithful minifter of Jefus Chrift. They afked if I adhered to the papers gotten at the Ferry? I faid, I did own them, and all the reft of Chrift's truths. If I would have denied any of them, my life was in my offer; but I durft not do it; No, not for my foul. Ere I wanted an hour of his prefence, I had rather die ten deaths. I durft not fpeak againft him, left I fhould have finned againft God. I adhere to the Bible, and Confeffion of Faith, Catechifms and Covenants, which are according to this Bible, (whereupon fhe clapped her hand upon the Bible) I alfo adhere to the teftimonies given by the faithful witneffes of Chrift, that have gone before us, on fcaffolds, and in the fields. I leave my teftimony againft all Quakers, Jefuites, Indulgences, and all profane and ungodly perfons, and mainly all covenant-breakers, and perfecutors, of his way and truths, which I am come here to feal with my blood; againft all payers of cefs, and bonders, and againft all oppreffion or murdering. They fay, I would murder, but I declare, I am free of all matters of fact; I could never take the life of a chicken, but my heart fhrinked. But it is only for my judgment of things that I am brought here. I leave my blood on the council, and the Duke of York." At this the foldiers interrupted her, and would not allow her to fpeak any: But fhe cried out, "I leave my blood on all ungodly and profane wretches." The moft of her difcourfe was of God's love to her, and the commendation of free grace; and fhe declared fhe had much of the Lord's prefence with her in prison, and said, " I bless the Lord, the snare is broken, and we are escaped;" and when she came to the ladder-foot, she prayed. And going up the ladder, she said, " O my fair one, my lovely one, come away;" and sitting down upon the ladder, she said, " I am not come here for murder, for they have no matter of fact to charge me with, but only my judgment. I am about twenty years of age; at fourteen or fifteen I was a hearer of the curates and indulged, and while I was a hearer of these, I was a blasphemer and sabbath-breaker, and a chapter of the Bible was a burden to me; but since I heard this persecuted gospel, I durst not blaspheme, nor break the sabbath, and the Bible became my delight." With this the major called to the hangman to cast her over, and the murderer presently choaked her.

The joint Testimony of WILLIAM GOUGER, CHRISTOPHER MILLER, *and* ROBERT SANGSTER, *who lived in the shire of Stirling, and suffered at the Grass-market of Edinburgh, March 11th 1681. Directed to the shire of Stirling.*

THE Lord in his holy providence having singled us out of that shire to seal his controverted truths with our blood; we could not but leave a line behind us, (we being Stirling-shire men) to let you know wherefore we are come here this day; to this place of execution; that it is for adhering to that which ministers and professors are disowning; and the Lord seeing it fit to honour us beyond others, now in this day of defection and backdrawing from the truth. We tell you, that it is truth we are to suffer for; altho' ye condemn us in it, and say that we have a hand in our own death; yet we durst not, for our souls, do otherwise, or else we would have been sure of the broad curse of God on us, and our life both. You may think that it is a novelty of our head that we are brought hither for; but if any of you had that love to the Lord, that you seemed to have once a day, you would count it your duty, as well as ours, to contend for the sweet truths of God, when you see ings so stately among the meetings of his people; that will not contend for lovely Christ. O! do ye not think that a sad day will come on you, for joining with God's enemies, who have broken covenant with him, and shed the blood of the saints, and trampled on the honour of God, and ye will not fear to join with them for all the blood they have shed, you will still go on with them; and tho' you profess that you have love to the Son of God, and that your zeal for the Lord God of hosts is not abated; yet you will go on with them; and bond and comply in paying of cess and militia-money to maintain a party against God and his work, which once in a day you were foreward to maintain, and would have ventured your life in the maintaining of it against all the Lord's enemies. You may justly take shame to yourselves, for your preferring the things of time to the sweet cross of lovely Christ. O Sirs! what think you will your doom be, that have done so much against the honour of a holy God? indeed you may look out for wrath, and that of the saddest sort.

Now, as dying men, we tell you, that there are sad days abiding you, for what you have done against the honour and glory of God, if ye get not speedy repentance. Therefore as you would answer in the great day, make conscience of what ye do. Remember that you will count and reckon for all that you have done, and will be reckoned as guilty of the blood of the saints, as the worst enemies amongst them all. Therefore as dying men we charge you to take with guilt, or else it will be worse for you. O Sirs! fear the Lord's wrath, and fall to and mourn for what you have done. O cry mightily for repentance, or else you will get Judas's reward. For you are the persons that have betrayed the Son of God, and expelled him out of your coasts. You were thinking that he was like to prove a costly Christ, and therefore you of that shire would consent to banish him away from among you. You would not hear tell of a field-preaching for fear of hazard. O Sirs! take it to consideration, and lay it to heart what a hand you have in banishing Christ and the gospel out of Scotland, and we are sure, it was not your parts to have done so. No, no, it was not your part to have given lovely Christ such an affront; the sweet days that you have had long since might have made you give royal Jesus better quarters, tho' you should go to the gibbet for it, and lose your gear. For your doing as you have done is a denying of him before men. Take it as ye will, we must tell you, as in the sight of a living God, before whom we are now to appear, and get our sentence for all that we have done; You are the only shire that has denied lovely Christ quarters, for he sent an offer to you to the Torwood, and ye would not hear it. Well, it is likely there are many of you that will never get another; there are some of you that would not go to hear, but forbade others to go, and thought it was duty not to go; and some of you were at that preaching and made a bad use of it. O remember, Sirs, you have rejected Christ. We tell you it, as dying men, you will count for it ere it be long, for our Lord did not send the gospel to the Torwood for nought, but it will accomplish that for which it was sent. O Sirs, be afraid and tremble, for judgment is at the door, and indeed your sentence will be sore to abide, it will be more tolerable for open enemies in the day of judgment than for you. We are afraid, when we think, what judgments will be on you shortly, for considering what pains has been taken on you of that shire, and how tender the Lord has been of you, in training you up for suffering, and has given you trials, and you have endured them, and he has taken them off again, and given you sorer trials, and he has delivered you out of these. It had been better for you that you had been at that preaching tho' you should have gotten the gallows the very next day, than to have done what ye did, and that you will find ere it be long.

O what of his kindness have you met with at such places! You dare not say, *That he hath been a barren wilderness, or a land of drought* to you. Testify against him if he was not kind to you, so long as ye abode by him he abode by you, and he was tender of you so long as ye kept faithful to him; but after ye turned into the enemies camp then he turned to be your enemy, and fought against you, and in all you do God will be seen to be against you. You may thrive in the world, but it will be a dear thriving to you, you will get the wrath of God with it. But ye have done with thriving in the worship of God. Indeed there are many of you that hold your life no more of God. Remember we tell you of it, who are within a few hours of eternity. Now it is like you will not notice what the like of us say, but will alledge that we are dying as fools, and have no Presbyterian principles, but notions; but we say the contrary: We say, we are not fools as to that, however the world may think and look on us as such: We say, we have Presbyterian principles, and are Presbyterians in our judgments, and will make it appear that we die as Christians, and as those that own the truths of God, and are standing to what ministers once taught us, altho' this day, they are turned to the contrary, and condemning us, and saying, that we have nothing but notions of our own heads, that make us do such things, but they will not find it so in the day of accounts.

And first, you may say, That it is not a Presbyterian principle to cast off magistrates. We grant with you; but where are the magistrates? Indeed they were once placed such; but they cast out themselves when they brake the covenant, and set up a cursed supremacy, insulting over the Lord's inheritance; and when they have done that, we think they are no more to be owned as magistrates by Presbyterians; but to be cast off and witnessed against; and when it comes to that part of the play, do ye not think that it was our part to contend for truth? O Sirs! do ye not believe Jesus Christ to be the eternal Son of God, and *that all things were made for him and by him, whether they be thrones or dominions, or principalities or powers?* What is not his? And that by free gift and donation, by an eternal decree intimate to us in the ii. Psalm, where, in a more particular manner, he is declared to be King in Zion, and all the Heathen promised to the enlargement of his kingdom. O Sirs, do ye not believe that Scotland became his with its own consent, as the product of that decree, and the fruit of his intercession and purchase; and that he allows no authority to be owned and submitted unto in Scotland, but only in so far as they keep the line of subordination to the Son of God? Or do you believe, that Scotland should have no other magistrates, but such as should be of God's choosing, *Men of truth, able men, fearing God, hating covetousness.* And that the land was bound by covenant to have such, *under the pains contained in the law, and danger both of soul and body in the day of the Lord's fearful appearance to judgment?* We believe, many a man's wit in that day shall be counted foolishness. Then if this be a ground, we are sure ye must say, That day that Charles Stuart was crowned, perjury became national; only professors as to this point were free.

Do ye think, we would without perjury and treachery to God, own Charles Stuart's authority any longer, when he held not his authority of God? but it being manifest, that in Middleton's parliament, he disclaimed that title to authority, we think, we were bound to witness our loyalty to another, and that we were freely absolved from obedience and fidelity to him then, and could not own his authority without gross perjury, he declaring, he would have no homage upon account of the covenant: Would ye not count him a distracted man that would cleave to him upon that account whether he would or not? Yea, and whoever does it, we know they will find themselves fools. Do you believe, that in the day that that Covenant was taken, any within the nation was not bound to perform and prosecute it, and that God would punish the destroyers of that covenant? Do ye think that Act Explanatory of the supremacy is not a plain renunciation of the word of God, the law of nature, the covenant, and human society, and setting up devilism and confusion, without a full, free and direct testimony to the contrary? We are sure that every public breach of covenant requires public repentance. We think, there can none be absolved without this: For in express terms our Lord says, *Whosoever denies me before men, him will I deny before my Father which is in heaven.* Now there should not only be a testimony given, but a walking according to it afterwards. O Sirs, Would ye have none to witness against the abominations of this day? Indeed you are all mistaken, for our Lord will not want witnesses to witness for him, however few and feckless they be; yet *He will make the things that are not, confound the things that are.* O Sirs! think ye it not a sin to join with them that have rejected the living God, and will not have him to reign over them? Do ye not think it duty to protest against them that are trampling our Lord's glory under foot? O Sirs, do not you think yourselves guilty of breach of covenant, that have connived at these men, that have their hands reeking in the blood of the saints, when you are strengthning their hands in the doing of it? We think you guiltier nor these wretches; because ye join with them in sin, whereas you should have

protested against them in the committing
We wot well, if ye read the Bible, ye will
selves as guilty as they are, and the guiltie
for it was your part to have contended f
and stood in defence thereof, unto the losin
liberties, and all that you had. The Lord
off, and yet you will do what in you lies
up, who shed the blood of those, who w
day your dear brethren. It may be, you v
Samuel knew that Saul was rejected of Go
did not cast him off? We answer, He di
his power to get him cast off; for he went
David in his stead, and durst not do it pul
cretly for fear of Saul, neither did Sar
much with Saul after that. Next you say,
heart smote him, for taking, and cutting
Saul's garment, and said, *That he would no
anointed.* Now we say, he had two reason
not. *1st,* He had that reason, that he w
anointed. *2dly,* It was his own particular
cause he was to reign in his stead. So
Charles Stuart is not the Lord's anointed
our particular quarrel, but in defence c
and in so far as he is an enemy to God an
salvation, which is sufficient ground to ca
son out of the church, and witness against
of the gospel, unto the losing of life, libe
ther things. And believe us as ye will, w
them Christians, that will not contend fo
and his sweet truths, in witnessing agair
excommunicate traitor, and not owning t
seeing they have disowned *the Just and*
are trampling on his sweet truths, and wo
them to rise again; but would have the sto
there might be no more mention made of
God. And you have a deep hand in this,
not faithful and free in witnessing for his
and if ye will not do it, *Delivery to the ch
from another airth*; and you shall be destroy
be up again in spite of all your hearts, an
your fears and theirs both come on you; f
inquisition for all his truths; and when he
we would not abide the reproof that you
of Stirling-shire will get, for all the go

there will be no excufe heard then; your wife and children, or lands, will be no excufe; for he hath told in exprefs terms, That *whofoever will not forfake all, and follow him, cannot be his difciple*. Wife and children, houfes and lands, muft all go for him; and you muft take up his crofs daily, and wander thro' at his back, it may be, hard beftead, with a borrowed bed, and a borrowed fire fide, and live upon providence: We wot well, there are fome of you that can fay to your fweet experience, that you never lived better than on God's providence, altho' now ye have rejected and betaken yourfelves to the world. Have you done fo: Well you may be doing; but ere long ye will rue it. Remember we told you it, when we were going into eternity, That you would meet with much wo and forrow, for what you have done againft the honour of God, if you repent not.

2*dly*, You fay, It is not a Prefbyterian principle to own that party that is jeoparding their lives for the honour of God, and witneffing for his defpifed truths, that this day is fo abufed and nick-named by you and others: But we fay, it is, and maintain it to be a Prefbyterian principle, to own that defpifed party, for they are the party that are only defigning the glory and honour of God, and have no other view before them but his fweet truths, which are dear to them; and they will quite with life and liberty, before they quite with an hoof of truth; which has been made out by their valiant fufferings. O but truth has been fweet and dear to them! They have not counted their lives dear unto them on the account of it. They have chearfully gone to the fcaffold for truth, and have been honourably carried thro', and the Lord's prefence feen in their through-bearing; as we hope, fhall be made out on us, ere it be long: Alfo they ftudy to fpend their time and ftrength for God. When all other means have failed them, they ftudy to keep up that mean of reading, finging and praying, as the Lord will affift and help them; altho' the indulged and their conforts have a great envy at them, and do what they can to get them off the earth; for they are the main actors in taking of that poor party; and all is, becaufe their practices condemn theirs; altho' they take the Scriptures for their rule, and ftudy to walk fo, as they may get God's approbation in the day of accounts.

3*dly*, You fay, It is not a Prefbyterian principle, to

own these papers, that our worthies have set out, or the work that they have done, which many of them have sealed with their blood: But we say, that it is a Presbyterian principle; because all that they did was agreeable to the word of God, and our covenants. For consider these papers when you please, you will find them consonant to the Scriptures, and just and lawful for Presbyterians to own; and say the contrary who will, we do not think them Presbyterians, nor yet covenanters, that will not own them; for there is nothing in them, but what we will with all our hearts seal with our blood as Presbyterians, and as having these principles.

4*thly*, You say, It is not a Presbyterian principle, to confess all these things: But we say, it is a Presbyterian principle, to confess and avouch him and his truths, before this adulterous generation: Now when the quarrel is thus stated, we should not put them to prove what is truth. Stephen made a free confession of his faith, and so have all our worthies. And now seeing we own these things, and they being the controverted truths of the day, and the Lord calling us to own and maintain them; we never thought it our part to smother and hide them, but with courage to avouch them, to the losing of our lives in the quarrel. We seeing our dearest Lord's truths trampled on, and a pack of you that seemed to be fair before the wind, for owning of truth, and witnessing for him, never so much as putting to your hand to help; but turning your back on truth, and the way of God. Indeed we fear, that ye shall never be honoured to witness for God any more; it is like, you care not for that honour; but we tell you, that you will rue it, when you will not get it mended: And remember we tell you it here, as dying witnesses for truth, you will meet with as sad a judgment, as ever a shire met with, if you repent not, your judgment will be unparallelable for your denying him before men.

We are come here this day to witness freely and faithfully against you, and all others, for their complying with the enemies against the work of God. And we say, as in the sight of a living God, you will count for it ere it be long. O! but we think it a sweet thing to be honoured this day to contend for truth, and to be *overcomers by the blood of the Lamb, and by the word of our testimony.* Indeed we are called to it, *to contend for the faith once delivered to the saints.* And we think, if we had not been free and faithful, before these bloody wretches, we would have held our life no more of God; if we did not speak for his truths before them, when he bade us speak; for he sought a proof of our love to him, and his nick-named despised way, and to poor Zion, whom no man is seeking after. And think you that we durst hold our tongue and not speak, when he bade us? Indeed our life was not dear to us, when his truth came in question. We might have gone away with our life, and the broad curse of God upon it, to go with us; if we had denied him at this time, we would have held our lives no more of him, of whom we held it all our days; and now we might chearfully lay it down at his command and bidding: For this we knew that devils or men could not stir a hair of our head, without our Lord's determination; and therefore we are the less afraid of what they could do.

And now as dying men, we charge you not to speak of that poor party, that this day is so reproached and spoken against by a party of them that are called ministers and professors. O take shame to you altogether; and as you will be answerable, in the day of accounts, we tell you, not to have a wrong thought of them, for all the reproaches that can be said against them; for they are a godly people, and have much of his mind. And if you go on with enemies, and others that have turned their backs on the way of God, go your ways; but *it were better that a milstone were hanged about your neck, and ye cast into the midst of the sea*, than that ye should speak at such a rate as ye do. For let you and others, reproach as you will, they design nothing but the honour of God, and have the Scriptures to be their rule, and walk as becomes the gospel, and they study a holy carriage: altho' there be many among them that have an unsuitable carriage, by reason of whom *the way of God is evil spoken of;* yet the way of God is not a hair the worse to be liked. It may be there is a Judas among the twelve; and what of that? We say, the rest are not be cast at for all that, seeing they keep the truth. We know there are many of you that say, that we do not keep by the Scriptures; but we declare the contrary; for with all our heart, we set to our seal and testimony to the holy Scriptures, which have been sweet to us; and our testimony to the National and Solemn League and Covenant, and to the Confession of Faith, as agreeable to the word of God, and to the Catechifms Larger and Shorter, and to all that our worthies have done in the defence of the gofpel : we join our hearty teftimony to all their appearances in the fields, both firft and laft.

And we proteft againft all the actings of the enemies againft the Lord's people in all their proceedings, both firft and laft, and every thing that they have done againft our worthies, when they were in defence of the gofpel; and we abhor and teftify againft Popery, Prelacy, Quakerifm, Eraftianifm, Indulgency, and all the connivers with them, be who they will; and againft jefuitifh principles, which you fay we hold, which fect we moft bafely abhor, and give our teftimony againft all fuch erroneous fects and principles: we give our teftimony againft all you that fay we have fuch principles, and that we have got new principles, and new light; but we do fay the contrary, and declare, that we hold by thefe principles, which minifters did teach both you and us to ftand to in the defence of, until we had loft our lives and all in that quarrel. Now, you that fay fuch things of us, we exhort you to repent, or elfe you will meet with a fore day of wrath, for it is not a light thing to fpeak of fufferers, as you do: Therefore we obteft you, in the bowels of Jefus Chrift, to be fober in your fpeeches againft that party, and make a right choice, and fairly fide yourfelves, and come out from among the tents of the wicked, and be feparated from among them, and join yourfelves to the poor fuffering remnant, and be not at eafe now in the day of Zion's trouble. Do not think that you will enjoy your ceiled houfes, and your warm fire-fides in fuch a day as this. If you be fingle for God, he will have you out from all thefe things, and denied to them all, for *woe to him that is at eafe* when Zion is in trouble, and is not concerned in all the afflictions of Jofeph; you muft either now get a wakening, or elfe you will get a wakening, when the wrath of an angry God comes on the land for fins.

Indeed, Sirs, we think, that religion has not coft you much heart-work. We think, you have not been at much pains in feeking of God, for as fair a fhew as you feem to have. Indeed when the gofpel was in its purity, and many feeking to preachings, the Lord feemed to be kind to you, and you feemed to have much love to him, and his defpifed way, and you feemed as if you would

have ventured your life in the defence of the gofpel; but
when we would have looked thro' you at preachings,
and going to them, and in coming from them, it would
have made fome of us a fore heart to fee your unconcernednefs and unfuitable carriage, even among you
that feemed to be the heads of them. And when we
would have been in fome of your companies, either coming or going, your talk did always fmell of the world,
and fo is come of it. O! repent, and come out from a-
mong your lufts and idols, that you are fo wedded to,
and take hold of a Mediator, and feek the Lord with all
your heart. O! you town of Stirling, and the fhire, repent, for fentence is paft againft you for what you have
done, altho' it be not put in execution yet; but it will
be put in execution ere long, if you repent not. Tho'
the Lord is feeing it fit to take us away from the evils
which are coming on this land, for breach of covenant,
and a flighted gofpel; we tell you, it may be, you will
find it when we are gone, it is better to endure all torments that devils and men can inflict on you here, than
to endure one drop of the wrath of an angry God, that
will be poured out without mixture on all ranks, that
have not the work of the day upon their fpirits, be who
they will, minifters or profeffors, indulged, or not indulged; for if they be not taken up and concerned with the
cafe of the church of God, this day, as it is ftated, he
will come and reckon with them all, and count them all
turners afide, and *will lead them forth with the workers of
iniquity, when peace fhall be on Ifrael*. Therefore we
would defire you to have a care, and look well about
you what you are doing, and beware of fpeaking againft
that party.

There are fome of you that fay, they are of bloody
principles. You fhould beware of fpeaking thefe things,
for the contrary is known, that they are not murderers,
nor have any fuch intentions, as fome of yourfelves
know, altho' ye be fpeaking the contrary, for you never
heard of their killing any, except it was in defence of
the gofpel, and their own defence.

Likewife you fay, that we are curfers and criers for
vengeance on the land. Now, we muft not ftay to argue
this out, we being this day to lay down our lives, but we
think any that has tender love to the Son of God, and
his caufe, cannot but be grieved to fee minifters and

professors so avowedly betray the truth, that is sweet and dear to us, yea, dearer than our lives; and when we think on what ye have done to the sweet truths of God, we cannot but pray against your courses: And as for any thing ye can do to us, we heartily forgive you; but the wrongs ye have done to a holy God, we cannot get them born, for they are weighty to us. If it were our enemies, we would bear with it, but when it comes from the like of you, we cannot get it born. Truly, Sirs, we think ye will embrace Popery ere it be long: your entertaining of that excommunicate Duke of York, a profest Papist, says, that you would do more yet. There was not one of you all in town, or shire, that moved your tongue against him, but as if you had been all profest Papists, you let him come in among you, and kindly entertained him; we leave our testimony against your so doing.

But we break off, having no more time, and request you to take these things to your consideration, and lay sin to heart, and mourn bitterly before the Lord, for what you have done. We here obtest you to come off these ways of yours, and make conscience of duty, as in the sight of a holy God, before whom ye must shortly appear. Slight not time, for it is precious, wrath is at the door: O! make haste, and lay these things to heart, and study to have a more tender respect to the honour of God. We desire to leave it on you now, when we are going into eternity, that you would mind your engagements and vows to God. And so we bid you farewel, and bid you mind the poor groaning kirk that we are to leave behind us, which was dear to us. Now, we bid farewel to poor desolate Zion, and pray the Lord may mind her case. Farewel all things in time, and welcome Father, Son, and Holy Ghost.

*Subscribed at the Iron-house, a little before we went out to the scaffold, March.*11. 1681.

WILLIAM GOUGER.
CHRISTr. MILLER.
ROBERT SANGSTER.

It is remarkable, that this martyr, William Gouger, had a little paper in his Bible, which he minded to throw over the scaffold; but when he was taken into the council-house with the other two, it was someway got by the murderers, who having read it, commanded the executioner to tye him ſtraiter than ordinary, ſo that he could ſcarce go up the ladder, and afterwards they ſtopped him from praying. When he was upon the ladder, he began to ſpeak, and ſaid, I am come here for owning Chriſt to be Head and King in Zion, whereupon they cauſed to beat the drums, ſeeking to damp and aſtoniſh him, that they might trample upon his conſcience; and when they offered him his life, upon condition he would own the king, he replied, I will own none but Chriſt to be King in Zion. Then they ſaid, Will ye not retract any thing, Sir? He anſwered, No, no; I own all, I adhere to all. Upon which they immediately called the executioner to throw him over, which he did incontinent, not allowing him to recommend his ſpirit to the Lord.

There are extant particular teſtimonies of theſe three martyrs, but becauſe it is doubted, that they may not be genuine, but vitiated by John Gib, or ſome of theſe that were tainted with his errors; therefore they are here omitted. And moreover, whereas ſome are ſuſpicious, that theſe three martyrs themſelves, or at leaſt the two laſt, were in ſome danger from the errors of John Gib; yet in regard that it was not upon any ſuch account they ſuffered, but for teſtifying againſt the eccleſiaſtical ſupremacy, they ought to be recorded among the reſt, as dying witneſſes for Jeſus Chriſt.

The dying Teſtimony of LAURENCE HAY, *weaver, who lived in Fife, and ſuffered at Edinburgh, July* 13. 1681.

Men and Brethren,

HAVING by ſerious conſideration, joined in giving a teſtimony againſt the enemies of God, and all that have joined with them in any thing which tended to the overthrow of the work of reformation; for which I am come, in your ſight, to lay down this life of mine, which I engaged to do in that teſtimony, thro' his ſtrength, if he called me to it; becauſe it was according to the word of God, and the covenanted reformation; and ſeeing I engaged in the ſtrength of the Lord to ſeal it with my blood, and now he in his holy and wiſe providence has put me to ſeal it; altho' I be the feckleſſeſt and unworthieſt of all that ſociety, I here in your preſence, with all my heart, ſet to my ſeal to it with my blood, as was promiſed at the end of the paper. And if all the hairs of my head were men, having lives, I would think them all little enough, to feal the caufe of my deareft and fweeteft Lord Jefus, who has been fweet and kind to me, in carrying me thro' every ftep of the work, which he put in my hand. O love him, Sirs! O but he is worth the loving! O but he has been kind to me fince I was apprehended! For he told me then that Satan would caft fome in prifon, that they might be tried; and he bade me *be faithful to the death*, and he promifed me *a crown of life;* and he hath helped me fince to fulfil the conditions, and hath alfo given me a right to the promife. And this was all my defire, *That the trial of my faith might be found precious, to the praife of his fweet name:* that his caufe might not be wronged, nor his ark get a wrong touch by me. And herein he hath heard my defire, according to that fcripture, *He will hear the defires of the humble, and the expectation of the poor fhall not be loft.* For *he keeps covenant with thoufands of them that love him, and keep his commandments:* And his commandments are not grievous, but *his yoke is eafy, and his burden light.* And he has faid, *He that forfaketh wife, or children, houfes or lands, for my name's fake and the gofpel's, fhall receive in this life an hundred fold, and in the world to come, life everlafting. And he that loveth father or mother more than me, is not worthy of me.*

Therefore, dear friends, give not over to contend for his born down truths, that this day are in debate betwixt him and his enemies in covenanted Scotland, according to that fcripture, *Contend earneftly for the faith once delivered to the faints.* O contend, contend, and give not over; for *he will arife for the oppreffion of the poor, and for the fighings of the needy;* for he will have an opportunity to be about with all his enemies, and he is weary with forbearing. Therefore truft in the Lord, *truft in him at all times; for they that truft in him fhall not be afhamed;* for they fhall ftand in the gate unafhamed to fpeak unto their foes. O Sirs! give him much credit; for he hath difappointed me of my fears, in that wherein I feared appearing before men, and helped me to ftand before them; fo that I had no terror, or amazement, more than they had been the meaneft of creatures; altho' I cannot fay, that *I have fought the good fight*, as that eminent apoftle faid; yet I can fay (praifed be God) *He hath given me the victory thro' Jefus Chrift my Lord,*

of Laurence Hay.

over principalities; and hath confirmed me, that *neither death nor life, nor any creature, shall separate me from the love of my sweet Lord Jesus Christ*; who is love-worthy, praise-worthy, worthy to be feared and honoured; who in his absolute sovereignty, set apart poor me, to give a testimony for his glorious and honourable work of reformation, *who am less than the least of all saints*, but he is an absolute Lord, and *shews mercy to whom he will shew mercy, and whom he will he hardeneth; And he keeps the souls of the faithful, and plentifully rewards the proud doer.*

Therefore, being called to suffer this day, in this place, for the following of my duty, and for that in particular, in giving a testimony against the dreadful defections of these times, by the means of these backsliding ministers, who have left our sweet Lord Jesus, with his back at the wall, and his poor flock *scattered upon the mountains, as sheep having no shepherd.* But dear friends, comfort yourselves in this, that in his own time, *he will search his sheep, and find them out;* altho', alas! I fear left they shall be sorer scattered than yet they are: But wait on him; 'for he that shall come, will come, and will not tarry. 'And his reward is with him, and his work is before 'him. And the Lord whom ye seek, shall suddenly come 'to his temple, even the messenger of the covenant.' But, O dear friends, labour to be 'stedfast and unmove-'able, always abounding in the work of the Lord. And 'give all diligence to make your calling and election sure; 'and if you do these things, you shall never fall. And 'commit the keeping of your souls to him in well doing, 'as unto a faithful Creator: for he is able to keep that 'which is committed to him, against that day, and pre-'sent it spotless before the Father.' Altho', alas! I was loth to adventure, or to credit in his hand; but now he hath discovered to me, that he is the best hand that I can venture on; and has gained my consent, and has become the surety for me of a better covenant, *well ordered in all things and sure.*

Therefore, considering my engagements to him, I leave my testimony to the holy Scriptures of the Old and New Testament, and the version of the Psalms in metre, and to the work of reformation, Covenants National and Solemn League, the Solemn Acknowledgment of Sins and Engagement to Duties, the Causes of God's Wrath, the

Confeſſion of Faith, as being conform to the
and the Catechiſms Larger and Shorter; I g
herence to all the faithful teſtimonies given t
thies, to the maintenance of the work of r(
from the year 1660, until this day, either b
pearances in the fields, or on ſcaffolds, or i
I adhere to the Sanquhar Declaration, th
Excommunication, and the Papers found at th(
to that joint Teſtimony given in the ſhire
that ſociety, whereof I was a member, tho'
one, and I adhere to all things contained t
cauſe they are according to the Scriptures.
my teſtimony to the faithful preaching in the
to the keeping up of ſocieties, and chriſtian
commanded in the word of God, *Not forſakiı*
bling of yourſelves together, as the manner of ſoı
much the more as you ſee the day approaching
now when his glory is at the ſtake, which
worth than our ſouls; and when men are ſee
his work razed, and the name of Iſrael blott(
it may be no more in remembrance.

    Likewiſe I leave my teſtimony againſt all
have joined with the declared enemies of the
Chriſt, both miniſters and profeſſors; and
theſe, who maintain any principle contrary
of God, eſpecially theſe who deny the auth
Scriptures, and all the work of reform
have razed the fundamentals of true Chriſtiı
of them the Lord has given up to ſtrong d
believe lies, and to deny Jeſus Chriſt to be
God, and maintain new lights, in meddlir
decrees of God, which his word never app
againſt every one of their principles. Likew
my teſtimony againſt all who brand us with ı
faith; which one declared to myſelf in my he
room below where I was a priſoner; which I
if he durſt in conſcience ſay, That I lived l
cite faith, or the example of others? So he
there were ſome in the room with me tha
murderers of others who had ſuffered. And
that the xv. Pſalm reached him a very ſad ı
ſpeaking evil againſt his neighbour: and alſo
ſpeak what we do know, and teſtify what we
And I declared that I had ſeen no ſuch thing

was in the room with me; but you have wronged (said
I) God and his caufe, by fhifting his crofs, and therefore
you will not ftand to wrong your neighbour.

And as for our being branded, that we hold our principles of men, and are dying to pleafe men, I altogether abhor fuch afperfions, for I hold my principles of none but of God and his word; and that which carries the fway with me is, the controverted truths of Jefus Chrift, that are at this day in debate betwixt him and his enemies; efpecially his kingly office, on which I dare venture life and liberty, and my falvation alfo, becaufe the Father hath declared him to be *King on his holy hill of Zion by an unalterable decree; and there to reign till all his enemies be brought under his feet.* Therefore, as I have left my teftimony againft all who caft fuch afperfions on me, or any other who have fuffered in this manner; I leave my blood alfo to witnefs againft them, who will adventure to do it, whether enemies or pretended friends. Likewife I leave my teftimony againft the encroachments made upon the rights of our Lord Jefus Chrift and the privileges of his church, by that ufurper Charles Stuart, and all the bloody crew under him. Likewife I leave my teftimony againft that excommunicate traitor the duke of Monmouth, for his appearance againft the work of God and his people, joined for the defence of the gofpel and intereft of Jefus Chrift, and all that joined with him. Likewife I leave my teftimony againft that avowed Papift York. Alfo I leave my teftimony againft that defigned parliament to put power in his hand. Alfo I leave my teftimony againft thefe abominable wretches that fat in thefe affociations and falfly accufed and fentenced me to death, and againft thefe fifteen affizers who gave me my fentence, and againft that wretch called the clerk, and Andrew Cunningham who gave me my doom. Likewife I leave my teftimony againft all who have joined with the declared enemies, whether minifters or profeffors, efpecially in the fhire of Fife, who have delivered up the teftimony to thefe abominable wretches, particularly Balgrumma and Vederftar. Likewife I leave my teftimony againft Popery, Prelacy, and that woful Eraftian fupremacy and indulgences firft and laft, which hath been the *dagger, the haft whereof hath gone in after the blade*, and hath wounded the church in the innermoft part of the belly, and the dart that has ftricken her thro' the liver. O! how sharp are the wounds of a friend? *They* go down *to the innermost part of the belly. If it had been an enemy, I would have born it.* And it is evidently seen that our mother-church hath been, and is this day wounded in the house of her friends; for which the Lord will sadly reckon with all such as have done so, if they do not repent and mourn for it. Likewise I leave my testimony against all them, that are any way instrumental of bearing down our poor mother-church, either by appearance in arms, or furnishing of others for that effect, by paying of cess or militia-money, or any other way, homologating the acts, or strengthening the hands of her declared and avowed enemies.

Now dear friends, being straitned for want of time, I am forced to draw to a close; only desiring you to be earnest in contending for the broken down work of reformation, that this day is brought very low: but be not discouraged, altho' his ark be tossed this day upon the waters, like the poor ship in the midst of the sea, and the poor disciples afraid lest they should sink, and the Master asleep (as it were) upon a pillow; yet go to him and cry, *Master, Master, save us, else we perish;* for he is easy to be intreated, and he likes well to have his poor people coming to him in the time of their distress; for *he is a present help in the time of need, a God rich in mercy, and near to all that call upon him in truth.* But, O dear friends, beware of backdrawing, for he hath said, *If any man draw back, my soul shall have no pleasure in him; and he that putteth his hand to the plough and looketh back, is not fit for the kingdom of heaven; but he that endureth to the end, the same shall be saved.* Be not ashamed of him, *For if any man be ashamed of him, or his words, of him also will he be ashamed before the Father and the holy angels.* O dear friends, the more that ye see a perverse generation crying him down, be ye the more at the work of crying him up; for he is well worth the commendation of all that can commend him. O dear friends, *in all things let him have the pre-eminence, and count all things loss and dung that ye may win Christ; and press towards the mark for the prize of the high calling of God in Christ Jesus;* Looking unto Jesus who is *the author and finisher of our faith; who for the joy that was set before him, endured the cross, despising the shame, and is set down at the right hand of the throne of God.* Strive to enter in at the strait gate; *for many shall seek to enter in, and shall not be able.* Now friends, beware of sinning, and beware of snares; for they are at this day very thick and many; but our God has promised that he will not suffer his poor people *to be tempted above what they are able, but will with the temptation make a way that they may escape.* So I bid you all farewel; desiring you to be kind to my wife and children when I am gone; Farewel sweet Bible by his blessing; farewel sun, moon and stars; farewel meat and drink; farewel all created comforts and enjoyments, wherewith I have been abundantly supplied; farewel my dear wife and children, the Lord be better to you than ten husbands, when I am gone; farewel mother, brethren and sisters; farewel sweet societies, and preached gospel, whereby I have been begotten by the seed of the word; farewel sweet prison and reproaches for sweet Christ and his cause. And welcome Father, Son and holy Ghost; welcome, everlasting life, and the spirits of just men made perfect. Lord, into thy hands I commit my spirit.

At the Iron house, July 13. 1681.

LAURENCE HAY.

The Testimony of ANDREW PITTILLOCH *Landlabourer in the parish of Largo in Fife. who suffered at the Grass-market of Edinburgh, July* 13. 1681.

Men and brethren,

WHerefore are you come here this day? will you tell me, if that be your intention, to be edified by the words of a poor thing, witnessing for my lovely Lord Jesus Christ? And if that be your intention in your coming hither, it is well: Now when I am going off time, to bid farewel to you all, O that I could commend my lovely Lord Jesus and his sweet cross to you. O Sirs, will you come *taste and see that God is good.* You will never do better, nor come and see; for since the Lord honoured me to be his prisoner, he has letten me know nothing but love; he has made my prison no prison. O Sirs, *All his ways are ways of pleasantness, and his paths peace.* And his cross is sweet and easy; altho' worthless I cannot commend it to you. But O sirs, fear not at the sweet cross of royal and sweet Jesus; but contend for him and his noble cause, for I can assure you, I had never such a sweet life as I have had since he brought me to the like of thir trials. O fweet indictment! O fweet fentence for my lovely Lord! O fweet fcaffold, for contending for the caufe, covenant and work of reformation! O Sirs, quit all for holy Jefus, for I can promife you that you will never die better, than for contending for King Chrift. Indeed Sirs, minifters and profeffors, as they call them, fay, That we are dying as fools, and giddy headed profeffors; but glory to his holy and fweet name, that has made it out to my foul that it is otherwife: And now, that my confcience doth not condemn me, how dare any mortal creature condemn me?

O friends! what is the reafon that you will not take him, who is the *chief among ten thoufands, that is altogether lovely*, and without compare? *There is no fpot in him.* O prefer him to your chief joy! There are many of you who have preferred other things to him. O fear and tremble for wrath will be upon you very fuddenly! O be afraid, for our Lord has faid, ' If ye will not quit ' all for him, you cannot be his difciple.' And fo you have neither part nor lot in our fweet Lord; you may read the x. of Matt. from the 16th ver. to the end. O Sirs, go not with the Indulged, nor yet fide with them, cleave to the Lord with all your heart, and be not put off with any but himfelf. O he is fweet to be with; O his way is fweet to keep, but I cannot commend him to you, his fweetnefs is without compare. O take him, and be reftlefs till ye get him to *your mother's houfe, and to the chamber of her that bare you*. Pray much for your motherchurch, that minifters and others have wronged: I witnefs and teftify againft them, for their unrighteoufnefs, both firft and laft.

Firft, For leaving of their kirks, without a public teftimony againft enemies, at the incoming of Prelacy. *2dly,* For their conniving at one anothers fins. *3dly,* For their leaving the fields when there was fo much need of preaching to poor things, when wrath and judgment were coming on the land, they did not fet the trumpet to their mouth, and give the people a faithful warning. They fay, we have caft them off, but they are miftaken, for they have caft themfelves off, by changing their head; and the Scriptures have caft them off, and I cannot join with them. I would with all my heart have a miniftry; but I would have it according to the word of God. Men that will *preach in feafon, and out of feafon,* whether people will hear, or whether they will forbear; that will be faithful in preaching againſt ſin of all ſorts, and will hide nothing of the mind of the Lord; but they that do play faſt and looſe in the matters of a holy God, and will not witneſs againſt enemies; I own none of theſe, but I leave my teſtimony againſt them for their unfaithfulneſs. They will preach to poor things to ſtand for God and his truths, and not yield a hair, for the ſaving of their lives; and yet they yield and comply themſelves; and when they come before enemies, never a word of a teſtimony before them, but paſs the ſworn covenant and work of reformation in ſilence, and for fear of their lives will not hit them on the ſore. Indeed they will wale their words ſo, as they may not give their enemies offence. You condemn us, becauſe we do that, that once a day you would have accounted it your honour to do; and ſay, That we are all diſtracted, and have diſtracted notions in our heads. And ſay you ſo? Wilt thou tell me man, if thou thinkeſt that a diſtracted notion, to confeſs the covenant and work of reformation? But you will ſay, It is not for that that I lay down my life, but for the ſubſcribing of that paper; And I do think it well worth the ſealing with my blood; and will you tell me what could we do leſs? You ran away and left the work, and the enemies were carrying all before them; and we durſt not but leave a teſtimony againſt them. My heart was like to bleed, when I ſaw enemies carry the day, and robbing the Lord of his rights, his crown and kingdom, and not ſo much as one to move their tongue againſt them, and ſay, that is ill done that they have done. I leave it to God and your own conſcience, whether or not it be duty to contend for truth this day when it was ſo much neglected. I leave my teſtimony againſt you and your hearers, and the joiners with you, ay and while they repent. I bid you repent and come off, and witneſs for the Lord, and if you will not do it, as ſure as God is in heaven, he will be about with you; eſcape who will, ye will not eſcape; for it is like he will begin at the ſanctuary.

Take warning in time, I leave it on you now, when I am going into eternity; for I am perſuaded, this is the way to the kingdom of heaven; for the Lord hath confirmed it to my ſoul, and hath made my life a ſweet life to me. O read Iſaiah xli. for it was ſweet to me when I was taken, and O that I had as many lives to lay

The laſt Speech and Teſtimony

down for him as there are hairs on my head, I would think them all too little! O what is my life? Nothing in compariſon of his glory. O wo to you, idle ſhepherds, for ye deceive poor things! *If it were poſſible*, I think, *ye would deceive the very elect;* you take God to be your witneſs, that ye are in his way yet, and have not quit one hoof; but your practice condemns you. You may read Malachy ii. 1. 2. 3. ' And now, O ye prieſts, this ' commandment is for you. If ye will not hear, and ' if ye will not lay it to heart, to give glory to my name, ' I will even ſend a curſe upon you, and I will curſe your ' bleſſings: yea, I have curſed them already, becauſe ye ' do not lay it to heart.' Therefore ' behold, I will cor- ' rupt your ſeed, and ſpread dung upon your faces, even ' the dung of your ſolemn feaſts, and one ſhall take you ' away with it.' Matt. vii. 15, 16. ' Beware of falſe ' prophets, which come to you in ſheeps cloathing, but ' inwardly they are ravening wolves: Ye ſhall know them ' by their fruits. Do men gather grapes of thorns, or ' figs of thiſtles?' And that xxxiv. of Ezek. 2 ver. ' Son ' of man, propheſy againſt the ſhepherds of Iſrael, and ' ſay unto them, Thus ſaith the Lord God unto the ſhep- ' herds of Iſrael, that do feed themſelves; ſhould not ' the ſhepherds feed the flocks.' I leave my teſtimony a- gainſt them that ſay, We hold our principles of men, and that we die for pleaſing men; but it is not ſo, for I never thought that little of my life as to lay it down for the pleaſing of any; for it is a moſt baſe aſperſion of ſome, caſt on us, becauſe our practice condemns theirs, and they can get no other thing to brand us with but that. And glory to the Lord, the contrary is ſeen both by our practices, and our throughbearing: and it is made out, that we hold our principles of none, but of God and his word.

I leave my teſtimony againſt the four men in the Can- nongate tolbooth, or any other that join with them, for wronging of the holy and ſweet Scriptures. Some brand me with that, that I am of their judgment, which thing I exceedingly abhor and deteſt, as the mire in the ſtreets; and I count them guilty of death, for wronging of the Scriptures. If we had judges in the land, that were for G d, they ſhould not live. I leave my teſtimony againſt th t tyrant on the throne, and all his underlings; and, I ſay, it will never be right with our land, ' till Haman

' and his ten sons be hung up before the sun.' I leave my testimony against them that rule as judges; and I leave my blood on the assizers, doomster, soldiers, and all of them, and all that acknowledge or aid them as magistrates, ay and while they repent. I leave my testimony against all enemies of all sorts; and against all sorts of compliance in less or more, and against all that has been done against the work of God these twenty years bygone; against the test, and compliance with, or compearing before God's enemies in less or more. I leave my testimony against the ministers and professors in Fife, for the wrongs they have done to my lovely Lord and his sweet cause; and my head shall be a standing witness against them, and preach to them from Cupar tolbooth, ay and while they repent. As for any thing that they have done to me, I freely forgive them, and pray that the Lord may forgive them. I leave my testimony against all them that will not hear Mr. Donald Cargil, and own him as a faithful minister of the gospel, and none but he is faithful this day. I leave my testimony to the holy and sweet scriptures, which many a day I have been refreshed with, I bless the Lord, that ever I could read a line of them. Now, I adhere to the faithful preached gospel, and to all that our worthies have done, which I need not particularly mention here.

And you that are the people of the Lord, O be ye busy and improve your time, and make use of your Bibles, while you have them, for it is like there may be a bonfire made of them yet, as well as of the Covenant. And covenant with him and contend for him to the utmost of your power; for I have found more of his sweet love, in contending for him, than ever I got in prayer, or hearing the word. O his sweet work, let it not slip thro' your fingers. It is like ye will have sad days of it, when I am gone. Popery is begun, and it is like to overspread the whole land, and there is none to move their tongue against it, although the land be sworn in solemn oath against it. O Sirs! ' lift up your voice for ' the remnant that is left.' Fast and pray, cry and weep, let not the apple of your eye cease, the wrath is like to be great, that will overtake us. O cry, that the days may be shortened, for the elect's sake, left no flesh should be saved. O look out for sad days, dear friends; it may be you will get the saddest stroke that ever a poor land was tryſted with: ye may read thro' the Scriptures, and ye will find what judgments followed ſuch ſins, peſtilence, ſword, and famine, which ye may look for. I leave it on you, that ye be not ſlack-handed, for it may come to that, that 'the tender and delicate women may 'eat their own children for ſtraitneſs in the ſiege.' It is to be feared, that the plagues that are coming on Scotland, for a broken and burnt covenant, will make their ears to tingle that hear of them; but I will not be to ſee it. The Lord is taking me away from the evil to come, which was often my deſire; for the ſad hearts that miniſters and profeſſors have made me, with their complying and wronging his glory, made me oft wiſh to be away; and now it does not trouble me to lay down my life in your preſence this day. O it is ſweet to be a ſufferer for truth! I wonder what doth ail the generation to fear at him or his ſweet croſs; for there is no cauſe of ruing or wearying, for all that is come. There is a beauty in holineſs. O! commend him, Sirs! O bleſs and praiſe him that ever he honoured ſuch a wretch as I am, to be a martyr for his ſweet truth! O ſweet honour he puts on poor things! O Sirs, caſt in your lot with the ſuffering remnant that this day is in the furnace. Sink and ſwim with his church. O prefer Jeruſalem to your chief joy! But O be perſuaded to come and taſte of his goodneſs: This is the way, altho' the whole world ſhould condemn it. It will not be the learned clergy, or great heads of wit, that he will honour with carrying on of his work, for they have all denied him. There are none of the miniſters that will witneſs for him, nor yet any that the Lord has beſtowed great parts on; their wit leads them by the croſs, and beyond ſuffering. They will not ſuffer if petitioning will do it, or hiring of advocates, or learned ſpeakers; they can put in petitions, and ſay, They never intended the death of any man, but in the defence of their life; but never a word of the defence of the goſpel, the work of reformation, or the ſworn covenant. Nay, if they had done that their life would go. But they were bound by covenant to own and maintain religion againſt Popery and Prelacy, Quakeriſm, Indulgence, and whatſoever elſe is contrary to ſound doctrine, with their lives in their hands; and to quit with all 'for the faith once delivered to the ſaints:' And tho' they never mention a word of all this, yet they will ſay,

of Andrew Pittilloch.

they came clearly off. But I say, now when I am going into eternity, that God's wrath will be on such a liberty, and God will count with them for what they have done against his honour; for there can none come clearly out from among their hands, that is once before them, without wronging his glory. O fear and tremble, Sirs! you that get the favour of God's enemies, and yield your conscience to the lusts of men. I leave it on all persons, now when I am to appear before my Judge, that they do nothing but what is according to the holy and sweet Scriptures; take them to be your rule, and go no farther than they allow you. They do not bid you petition enemies for your liberty, nor yet hire advocates.

Now, my advice to you that are taken prisoners is, that you seek no favour of God's enemies; black not paper with them, in good, cheap nor dear; stand for your sweet Lord with your life in your hand; own and avouch him to be *King and Head of his own church:* Count not your life dear unto you, when it comes in competition with truth. And now, as for you that are the poor seekers of the Lord, O act faith on him, give him much credit. Live as brethren, dwell in unity; let peace and truth be among you: but good Lord, let never peace be without truth. Keep up fellowship and society meetings; for my soul hath been often refreshed in the fellowship of the saints. O stand for your despised Lord, and his wronged glory.

Now I being straitned for want of time, it being short, I forbear, and bid you *be strong in the Lord, and the power of his might.* Now, farewel my dear friends; farewel holy and sweet Scriptures; farewel sun, moon, and stars; farewel sweet reproaches and crosses for my sweet Lord Jesus; farewel all things in time, reading, praying, and all duties; farewel relations; farewel my dear wife, the Lord be to you better than ten husbands. Glory be to his great name, that made me so sweetly to submit to his will, whatever he trysted me with. Farewel mother and sisters, and all relations; farewel all my christian acquaintances for a while; farewel sweet society in Fife, the Lord's blessing be on you all. And now welcome Father, Son, and Holy Ghost; welcome sweet company of angels, and the spirits of just men

made perfect; welcome everlasting songs of praise. Now, into thy hands, holy Father, I commit my spirit.
Sic subscribitur,
ANDREW PITTILLOCH.

The Testimony of WILLIAM THOMSON, *who lived in the shire of Fife, and suffered at Edinburgh, July* 27. 1681.

Men and Brethren,

I Being a prisoner for Christ's sake, and for my adhering to truth, being taken at Alloa, coming out of Fife from hearing of the gospel preached by Mr. Donald Cargil, the last sabbath of June, this present year; and not knowing when I may be taken and murdered by the stated enemies of our Lord (for they neither walk after the equity of their own law, nor God's law) I have for fear of inconveniencies, laid hold of this opportunity to set down, under my hand, or from my mouth, an account of my life and conversation, and my testimony to the truth of Christ, and against all the abominations of the times.

I was, before the year 1679, running away with the rest of this generation, to God-provoking courses; and about that time, when I saw the people of God going to draw together, to adventure their lives in the Lord's quarrel, the Lord took a dealing with me at that time so that I could neither get night's rest, nor day's rest, til I resolved to go with them. And on the other hand, was afraid lest I should have been the Achan in the Lord's camp; but again I remembered the Lord's promise, that is held out in the word,—*Return unto me, and I will return unto you, saith the Lord of hosts*, Mal. iii. 7. Now I do with all my heart bless the Lord, for his wonderful workings with me, since he began with me. I think when I look on his dealings since that time till now, I must say That I am a brand plucked out of the fire. O that my heart and soul could praise him, for all that he hath done for me! And now I am content to die a dyvour to free grace, and in Christ's debt. I was charged with being guilty of rebellion against their prince: I answered, was not so, for I was there a prisoner of Jesus Christ and for his sake: And told them, I adhered to his covenant, and all things in it. I am not convicted from th word of God of any crime, as to him whom they call king; nor any thing worthy of death committed againſt any man, either in thought, word, or deed : So my blood ſhall cry, with the reſt of the innocent blood ſhed in the land, for vengeance from heaven, on the inhabitants of the earth, great or ſmall, who are in the leaſt acceſſory thereto, ay and while they repent. It is not my doing, but their own that hath procured it; and God is juſt to ſeek after them for the ſame : neither is it in any man's power to forgive that, as being a breach of God's holy law, without repentance, nor then neither ; for the furtheſt they can come is, but to declare unto them from God's word, That that and their other ſins ſhall never be charged upon them, if they have truly received Chriſt upon his own terms, and *walked worthy of the Lord, unto all well-pleaſing*. But now the thing is clear, the ground whereon they intend to take away my life is, the diſowning Charles Stuart for my king, becauſe, he will have no homage upon the account of the covenant from me, or any other, and God only requires the performing of vows, and keeping and fulfilling the covenants, Pſal. 1. So in this caſe, I cannot ſerve two maſters, and I reſolve to obey God rather than man.

Now, I here as a dying man, ready to ſtep into eternity, having health and ſtrength, and being in my right mind, declare, I adhere to the Proteſtant religion, as that which is God's true religion, and the Chriſtian religion. I adhere to the holy rule of the word of God, the Scriptures of the Old and New Teſtament, containing the will of God to man, and anent man ; and that the Scriptures are a full rule of faith and manners to us. I adhere to the work of reformation in Scotland, to the Covenants National and Solemn League, the ſolemn Acknowledgment of Sins and engagement to Duties, the Confeſſion of Faith, in regard it agrees with the foreſaid writings ; the Larger and Shorter Catechiſms, as moſt ſeaſonable, found, and according to the Scriptures, and well worth the reading, conſidering and practiſing what is therein ſet forth. I ſay, I adhere to the Rutherglen Teſtimony, to the paper commonly called Mr. Donald Cargil's Covenant, of the date of June, 1680 : I adhere to the original copies of theſe papers, as they were correCted and reviſed by the authors. And likewiſe I adhere to every ſound paper, tending to the good of religion ; as, the

Directory for Worship and catechising; an
to the doctrine, discipline, worship, and
the church of Scotland. I bear my testi
the lawful wrestlings of the people of God
in the defence and preservation of their civ
divine rights and privileges, contained anc
the foresaid papers against all encroachers
betrayers thereof; especially by the sword,
lawful and commanded of God, to be mad
quarrel; which is to be carried to preachii
assemblies of the Lord's people, and so m
as the enemy discharges it, as the case nc

In the last place, I give my testimony ;
on against all wrongs and injuries done to
people throughout the whole world this d;
particularly, against all that hath been
land, since the beginning of the work of rei
to this day, in prejudice of God's glory,
people: and especially these crying sins:
ruption of the worship of God, profanati
things, mocking, misbelieving, and bel)
and carrying as if there were no God;
worse, saying he approves of all that the
heaven-contemning generation! 2*dly*, A
frauding, mocking, murdering and oppre
ple'of God, in their bodies, consciences ar
punishing them as evil doers; yea, as the
of cruelty, and that only for following th
making them to stink, as it were, above
and making their names to rot by calumnies
es, and doing all they can to drive them to
blaming them as the main instruments of a
vous villanies and abuses in the land; so t
to that with it, *The man that departs from
himself a prey.* And scarcely can these wh
sty get a night's quarters in any house ir
that the people of God are become *a scor
and a fear to their friends, and especially rep
who are their nearest neighbours,* as the Psalr
3*dly*. I leave my testimony against all tha
with the stated enemies of God, these C1
these heaven-contemners, and non-such f
God; whether by bonds, oaths or promise
persons worthy of no credit nor truit,. whc

faith nor truſt upon any account, but where it may contribute for fulfilling their luſts, and profecuting their wicked defigns and hell-hatched enterpriſes. If they were brought to ſtraits, poſſibly they might feign themſelves; but he is unwife that will give them fo much truſt as a dog: as Solomon ſays, *When he ſpeaks fair, believe him not, for there are ſeven abominations in his heart*; which I have a proof of in my taking, by a poor wretch who hath fold foul and confcience to the luſt and arbitriment of a faithleſs apoſtate wretch like himſelf. And if ye will not be perſuaded to leave off ſeeking their peace, and covenanting with them by bonds, oaths, and promiſes; well, fee what David the king of Iſrael ſays, by the ſpirit of God, when he is making his teſtament, 2 Sam. xxiii. 6. 7. ' But the ſons of Belial ſhall be all of
' them as thorns thurſt away, becauſe they cannot be ta-
' ken with hands: but the man that ſhall touch them
' muſt be fenced with iron, and the ſtaff of a ſpear; and
' they ſhall be utterly burnt with fire.' But ye that are much more ſeeking peace with enemies than with God, think with yourſelves to which of them are ye moſt beholden, and which of them have done you moſt good; which of them have moſt power over you; which of the two hath the beſt quarrel by the end; which of the two is the moſt precious and lovely; and which of the two will be your judge at the laſt day. Well, if you have done well in ſeeking the peace of enemies, with the loſs of the peace of God; then rejoice ye in them and with them, and let them do ſo with you: And if otherways, the Lord, no doubt, will reward you, as the cauſe requires, for what ye have done to God's work, cauſe, covenant and people. 4*thly*, I leave my teſtimony againſt all that contribute of their means, for the downbearing of God's works and people, and upholding his and their enemies, ſeeing it is ſo expreſly againſt the Covenant, and in that caſe they being called to ſuffer, and not to fin, to which practice is annexed a gracious promiſe; ' He that loſeth life, lands, goods, or relations,
' for Chriſt's ſake, and the goſpel's, ſhall receive an hun-
' dred fold in this life, and in the world to come life ever-
' laſting.' And againſt all that otherways waſte and abuſe them to God's diſhonour, but only uſing this world, as not abuſing it: for all within the nation being dedicate and given away by covenant to God, and this being

often renewed, calls all men to be tender
God, and fee how they adminifter their ſt[e]
to him they muſt be accountable. But, ala[s]
count which many of them have to mak[e]
teſtimony againſt the rendering up the po[w]
and ſtate into the hands of malignants. I
they have been all dreaming, or wilfully o[r]
ning againſt the light of their own confci
God hath difcovered them fince, in an
and now they fin more and more : they h
they refuſe to let it go, and will not return
profeſſors and miniſters, I mean, in a ſp
but more particularly the miniſters : for [w]
was to ſpeak they held their peace, and ſlip
Maſter's back, without ſo much as teſtify
horrid fins then committed ; and did ne[v]
make up the hedge, and build that whi
down : And, as I am informed, a great [p]
dreadful complyers with, and conformer
courſes of this apoſtatizing generation ; y
cutors of their more godly and faithful b
ſters and profeſſors ; and now they are the
ers of the work, and perfecutors of the g[o]
der hand, and to their faces ; and inſtead [of]
binding up the weak, ſtrive to break all t
cially when they are among the enemies]
laſt place, I bear my teſtimony to the cro
the only defirable upmaking and rich lot
of God this day in Scotland. O it is the [p]
things, who defire to feek God, and d[e]
the land ! I think they want a good ba[r]
want it ; and I think they want nothing
and get leave to carry it heartſomely, and [b]
der it. I would adviſe you all to take it
thus much for your encouragement, tha[t]
ſweet. There is no better way to carry
than to caſt all our care upon Chriſt, an[d]
all things, and uſe our fingle endeavours
and ſpeak what he bids us, and obey his vo[ice]
Now, I declare I hate all ungodlineſs. [I]
things, wherein I have been troubled
world, and evil heart of mifbelief, a fubtil,
malicious devil, and tempted with a co[r]

who have shaken off the fear of God. Now, welcome Lord Jesus, into thy hand I commit my spirit.
Sic subscribitur, WILLIAM THOMSON.

[This following Testimony having a large preamble, wherein he gives his private opinion concerning some things then in debate, which do not relate to the causes of his suffering, and which are of no use now, these vain janglings and unprofitable strifes of words being ceased, and his opinion about them not being a testimony for the truth, nor espoused by any of the godly as a head of suffering or contending for; the encouragers of this work have thought fit that the preamble be past by, and the testimony itself only published.]

The last Testimony of WILLIAM CUTHIL, *seaman in Borrowstounness, who suffered at Edinburgh, July* 27. 1681.

I Here, as one ready to step into eternity, and one of the subjects of a kingdom covenanted to God, and one of Christ's sufferers, enter my protestation, and give in my testimony against all that hath been done against Christ's reigning, and the thriving of his kingdom in Scotland, since the beginning of the work of reformation. And more particularly, against all the several steps of backsliding: As,

1st, The admitting Charles Stuart to the exercise of kingly power *, and crowning him, while they knew he carried heart enmity against the work and people of God, and while in the mean time there was so much of his treachery made known to the parliament, by his commissionating James Graham earl of Montrose to burn and slay the subjects of this kingdom, that would not side with, or would withstand him in the prosecuting of his wickedness; which is recorded in the Causes of Wrath, and the Remonstrances of the gentlemen, ministers, and commanders attending the forces in the West, in the year 1650.

* This ought not to be understood of the manner of his coronation, which is owned by all Presbyterians to have been most consonant to God's word, and the national constitution of Scotland, but of his disposition and practice which was too evidently contradictory to the sacred engagements he came under.

2*dly*, Against the unfaithfulness, connivance and compliance of ministers, and others, at the wickedness perpetrated in the land during the time of Cromwel's usurpation; for, as I am informed, few testified against him, for trampling all the interests of Jesus Christ under his feet, in giving a toleration to all sectaries (whereof the abominable and blasphemous Quakers are a witness, whose religion is nothing but refined Paganism at the best, yea, I think it is much worse) which was to set up their thresholds beside Christ's, and their altars beside the Lord's, in a land covenanted to God, never to suffer the like, and lying under the same bonds.

3*dly*, Against the Public Resolutions, for the bringing in malignants to the places of power and trust; which have been the rod in God's hand above the heads and upon the backs of God's people, ever since they lusted after them; and now, I suppose, they are convinced (at least some of them) that God hath given them on the finger-ends for it: but we have not seen them confessing before God and his people, in public (for it should be as public as the sin was) that *they have added this sin to all their other sins, in asking them a king, whereas the Lord was their king.*

4*thly*, I bear my testimony against that unparalleled practice of ministers, in quitting their charges; and that, which doth more aggravate their guilt, at his command, who had no power to act, nor right to be obeyed, neither in that, nor yet in civil things; for then he had unkinged himself; and their going away without almost ever a testimony who should have been the main men that should have told the people what to do. Oh and alas, for that practice! Yet they were put away without being convicted of any crime done against him; but is it not against Presbyterian principles, that a king should depose ministers of the gospel, tho' he had a just right, all that time, to rule the civil state? For it was without controversy that he had imprisoned some of Christ's ministers, without being ever summoned, or treated by any legal procedure, as Naphtali records, and usurped the ecclesiastic officers seat to depose the rest of them.

5*thly*, I hold it as one of the causes of God's wrath against the land, and one of the causes of God's breaking and scattering that poor handful of men at Pentland, that renewed the covenant at Lanerk, and did not keep out his interest out of it; for it only binds us to its maintainers, not to its destroyers.

6*thly*, I bear testimony against the procedure of the ministers, when they came to the fields again after Pentland, because they did not first begin with public and private fasts, and make up the hedge and gap for the church of God in Scotland: And then only preaching to cases of conscience, and not catechising the people, nor informing them in the duty of the day; but did let them pay curates stipends, and other revenues of that nature. But I think they were engaged to God under the pain of losing soul and body, in the day of God's fearful judgment, to tell the people to chase them out of the land. Seeing Prelacy was abjured and cast out like an abominable branch, as it was, were they not worthy to die the death, that would, against so much light, defile God's land with that abjured abomination? but forsooth, to this day, they must be fed like birds in a cage upon the fattest in the land, and the spoils of Christ's crown.

7*thly*, I bear my testimony against that course carried on by the ministers; their conniving at, countenancing of, and complying with these indulged, that have quit Christ, and taken on with another master. O the treacherous dealers have dealt very treacherously! Yea, they were open persecutors of the really godly, thereafter for their faithfulness, and were about to stop their mouth, and to make that indulgence the door by which all the ministers were to enter to their ministry.

8*thly*, I bear my testimony against their treachery at Bothwel-bridge, in stopping the drawing up of the causes of God's wrath, and keeping a fast day, and changing their declaration; and in hindering the purging of the army: And to mend all, they raised the ugliest clamour and report among them that minded and spoke honestly and truly, that could be.

9*thly*, I bear my testimony against their treachery at Edinburgh, when a proclamation came out to the view of the world, blaspheming God's true religion, and declaring that all that belonged to God was due to Charles Stuart, which is the plain sense of the act; and they sat in an assembly, and voted for a liberty coming from him to preach by; tho' the very same day that that was proclaimed, two of their more worthy and faithful brethren were murdered: I think this people are grown like brute beasts. O how much pomp and jovialty was that day in rejoicing over the ruins of the work of God and his people, yea, over himself! There was first a scaffold made on the east side of the cross, and a green table set down on it, and two green forms; and then the cross was covered; and about twelve hours of the day, the pursevants, and lyon-heralds, and lyon king at arms, and eight trumpeters went up to the cross, and fourteen men on the foresaid scaffold, and seven of them with red gowns of velvet, and seven with black, and then that act was read, and at night the bells were ringing, and bonfires burning. O I think it was a wonder, that God made not all the town where such wickedness was acted against and in despite of him, to sink to the lowest hell.

10thly, I leave my testimony against them, for running away and leaving God's flock after Bothwel-bridge, when they had drawn them to the fields: the Lord be judge this day between them and his flock, and let their sentence come out from before his presence, and let his eyes behold those things that are equal. O their skirts are full of the blood of souls! they say, the people hath left them, but it is more evident than that it can be gainsaid, that they have left the people. Does not the Scripture say, That they who are in the watchmens place, should warn the people when they see the sword come; and have not the ministers of Scotland had the first hand in all these courses of backslidings? should they be pure with unclean-hands, and the unjust ballance (so to say) and the bag of deceitful weights. Well, their sins are known to be no more sins of weakness, but sins of wickedness.

11thly, I bear my testimony against them, because they did not join with their brethren in the work of the day, in preaching to the people in the fields, with Mr. Richard Cameron and Mr. Donald Cargil. And will ye tell me, altho' there were never one to open their mouth in that thing, does not the work of the one confound them to silence, and the work of the other justify and plead for them? But there is one thing, I have learned from the practice of all this people, and God's dealing with them. They have fought their own, and one anothers credit, more than God's, and he hath discovered their wickedness in their uglness.

12thly, I bear my testimony against their obstinacy, in refusing to return and amend their manners. They hold fast wickedness, and refuse to let it go, and that against the light of God's word, their own consciences, their vows and engagements to God, the cries of bloodshed, the cries of wrong done to God and his work, and against these their former preachings and practices; that they will not come out and rid the ground, so to speak, and seek out the causes of God's wrath, and set days of humiliation apart, and see that they be kept, and renew their engagements, and carry themselves like ministers of Jesus Christ afterward. Is this erroneous? Is not this according to Presbyterian principles? Does not the confession of our faith, say, these who offend the church, and their brethren shall make their repentance as public as their offences have been? Is not this the plain meaning of that article, yea the very words almost, of the Confession of Faith, chap xv. art. last? without which thing be done, (if any would take my counsel, who am looking to receive the sentence of death every hour) I would say, meddle not with them, for they have not only sinned against the church of God and their brethren, and their own souls, but against God: And have they not been light and treacherous? whereof many instances may be given. Have they not polluted the sanctuary? Have they not done violence to the law? Have they not been unfaithful? Are they not walking very openly amongst God's stated enemies, while the people of God dare not be seen? I fear, If they make not haste to come off these courses, that God's wrath shall overtake them, ere it be long. And *lastly*, I bear my testimony against them, for their untenderness to weak consciences, and making use of their gifts and parts to wrest the word of God, to put out that light which God has given poor things; of which I, among others, have a proof; for one of them came into the prison, and told me, That he had been dealing with him, who had been pursuing us to death, (the king's advocate) that he would not take innocent blood upon him; and out of love and tenderness to our souls, he came to pay us a visit; and said, he was neither a curate nor an indulged man, but a minister of the gospel: So he said, That we would be well advised what we were doing, for the advocate had said, we were shortly to be before the criminal court. And I asked, What he advised us to do? and began to tell him the ground whereupon we were accused, which was this,

The last Speech and Testimony

That Charles Stuart, having broken and burnt God's covenant, and compelled all that he could by his forces to do the like, and slain many upon that account; upon this head, I declined his authority; and being hard questioned, confessed, that I thought it lawful to kill him, but I did not say by whose hands: and he said, All that would not free me from being his subject, and instanced Zedekiah's case to prove it: But I was not in case to speak to him, (being confused with a distracted man who was in with us) only I told him, there was as great a difference betwixt that of Zedekiah, and this in hand, as east was from the west. And he called us Jannes and Jambres who withstood the truth, when we would not hear him? and said, There was no such thing as any condition holden out in the form and order of the coronation, that did free us from allegiance to Charles Stuart upon that account. But what? do they think, that every one can reason and debate with them, or else that they are not Christians, but gainstanders of the truth? Hath not God given to every man his measure of light and grace both? If they know not this, and walk not accordingly, they were never worthy to be ministers of the gospel. He said, that he would send me any of the ministers whom I pleased to call for: I said, That I heard tell Mr. Donald Cargil was taken, would he send him to me, and I would take it as a great kindness off his hand; but he said, that he had taken a way by himself. But what shall I say, my heart is like to sink, when I think on them, and the case of the land. O I think, it is a desperate like case! only I know God can, and I hope he will cure it.

Next, I bear my testimony against all that pay cess and locality to uphold Christ's enemies, the bloody soldiers, or any of that cursed crew; yea, against all that give them meat or drink, when they come to their houses, it being so expresly against Christ and the covenant; and against all that pay customs or duties, belonging to the crown of Scotland, unto Charles Stuart, his officers, collectors, or tacksmen; seeing all that is employed against Christ, and against all that shall do it, till they wit well that it be otherwise employed; and against all bonders with them, or to him, or any in his name, or delegated by him, or cloathed with his authority; seeing they are persons worthy of no credit; whereof I have a proof in my taking. Ye would do well to believe the wife man Solomon, who fays, *When he speaks fair, believe him not, for there are seven abominations in his heart.*

Next, I leave my teſtimony againſt all that fide with, or ſtrengthen the hands of the adverſaries of the Lord, in leſs or more, againſt clear conviction from the word of God,' or ſound reaſon; and particularly againſt this duke, that bold and truculent Papiſt, who hath defiled the Lord's land with his altars and images. And I proteſt againſt this enſuing parliament, for putting power in his hand to do what he pleaſeth; for by the word of God, and the laws of the land, he ſhould die the death. And alſo, I bear teſtimony againſt theſe who have ſided with, or ſtrengthened the foreſaid enemy, and will not come off again. O, if they will not help the people of God, that they would let them alone, and not help their adverſaries.

Next, I leave my teſtimony againſt the gentry and commonalty, for letting ſo much innocent blood be ſhed, ſome of which ranks, I think God hath a turn to put in their hands yet, if they would eſpouſe his quarrel, and turn to him with all their hearts, and not ſuffer the work to go as it does; but indeed they muſt keep company with God's ſtated enemies, and learn the court faſhion. I will tell you one thing, Ye have loſt the manners of the court of heaven, by learning the manners of the courts of men. O what think ye to do? Or how think ye to be countable to God?'Will ye but ſpeak your minds; who, think ye, hath the beſt end of the controverſy? Will ye let the fear of men and the devil prevail with you more than the fear of God? Or what think ye this duke would do to you, when he ſees his opportunity? Will ye truſt bloody Papiſts? It may be, ye may be put to ſuffer on worſe accounts yet, if ye will not own God and his people; but there are but very few of you now, who are ought but mockres. Will ye turn to the Lord with all your hearts. Is it any ſhame to you to take ſhame to yourſelves, in glorifying God by confeſſing your ſins, and turning from them? But will you tell me now, who think ye can be at one with you, while ye are ſtanding out againſt God? Will ye read but the firſt chapter of Iſaiah, and conſider it, and the firſt two chapters of Jeremiah, the ſecond of Joel, the prophecy of Haggai, Isa. xxii. Ezek. vii. O consider, and if not, the Lord and you take it between you. Read and consider Psal. l. 5.

Now, what shall I say to you, who own and adhere to God's cause, against all the enemies? O that I could let you see the inside of my heart! Will ye learn Christianity; seek the Lord and get him on your side. I think, it is a good token of a sanctified heart, that longs more to be in God's company, nor other folks, that sees the worst of evil lies in committing sin. Beware of heart-risings and grudgings one against another; know, that there is a great difference between sins of weakness, and sins of wickedness; ye may not mark every failing, for if ye do, ye shall not have two to stay together in Scotland. O but there be much need of the gospel, and these ministers will not come out and contend for Christ! without which, tho' I were at liberty, God knows, I durst not meddle with them, and I would rather keep a-back from them nor other folk; for I think, there are many of them either unconcerned, or then dreadfully misted, for how can it be otherwise, not bearing with tender consciences, for they will rather strive to break folk than build them up; but how can any that has love to Christ look on them with good-will: I do verily think, if ever they turn again, the world shall hear tell of it. It is beyond all controversy, that they have quit their first works, and their first love. O will ye learn to be sober and grave. Cleave to your covenants and engagements: I say, mind your engagements; look what becomes of covenant-breakers. I would say unto you, Take no courses by the end, till God give you clearness; but indeed, I know, that God will reprove many in this generation, because they put away light from them. Now ye are deprived of all cleanly preaching; but will ye observe Christ's answer to the spouse in the Song, when she says, ' Where makest thou thy flocks to rest at noon?' He says, ' If thou know not, O thou fairest among wo-
' men, go thy way forth by the footsteps of the flock,
' and feed thy kids beside the shepherds tents:' Beware of ' turning aside after the flocks of his companions.' Beware of these ministers of Charles Stuart, these indulged and these Prelatic, these mockers of God, and contemners of the godly, these Christ-deserters, these under-valuers of heaven, these scandalous and insignificant time-

fervers, whom God hath blafted, to the conviction of all the generation that fee any thing; thefe monfters of men, the difgrace of the miniftry, the juft contempt of the generation. God hath fometimes had a church without a miniftry, but he never had a miniftry without a church. Doth not the Scripture fay, *That for many days Ifrael fhall be without a prieft, without a teraphim,* &c. Do we not fee in the Revelation, *The two witneffes flain, and ly three days and an half:* But O cry to God, *That he would fend forth labourers to his vineyard; for verily the harveft is great, but the labourers are few.* If there be a cafting at the gofpel on the people's fide, then I think they fhall be in extreme hazard of lofing their foul, if God's mercy prevent it not; for then they refufe to be guided by God: But if *when the hireling fees the wolf come, he run away, and leave the fheep, becaufe he is an hireling,* then I think the mercy of God is engaged for the fheep, becaufe *they have no fhepherd.* It is not the firft time that Ifrael has been *fcattered as fheep having no shepherd;* But it is as fure as the fun fhines, none can keep himfelf, nor guide himfelf: *It is not in him that walketh, to direct his fteps.* And God hath 'fown a joyful light to the upright;' And he has faid, ' Him that fitteth in darknefs, and hath no ' light, let him truft in the Lord, and ftay himfelf upon his God.' But could the fpoufe reft in Jerufalem, and her hufband not to be found? It is beyond debate, that fhe made all the fields ado before fhe wanted him. Can the fpoufe fee another wear her hufband's cloaths, and be well fatisfied? yea, one that has robbed, fpoiled, and fhut him to the doors, with difgrace, contempt and fhame, and as one unworthy to manage the affairs of his own houfe; and has defyed him to take any thing back again, and has fet up legs and arms, heads and hands, and quarters of the children, as trophies of victory over the Goodman of the houfe, and has triumphed with fpite and contempt, and is only feeking it of the poor widow, the wife and the bairns to be quiet, and accept of him for a hufband and father : So I fay, Shall the wife and children of fuch a Hufband and Father be peaceable to fee this ? I trow, there are few earthly folk would do fo: But O ! who can fhew the difference here, as to fearching out it cannot be. The Lord keep you from dwelling at eafe, under one roof, with fuch an one. Beware of making any treaty of peace with fuch a robber and murderer as this; beware of feeding thefe his foldiers, or giving them quarters, when they come to your houfes. O but the kings of Aſſyria knew well enough, that *the kings of Iſrael were merciful kings!* If ye will not ufe the fword at God's bidding, God will put it (as he hath) into the hands of his and your enemies, to ufe it againſt you. Indeed I think, ' till Saul's fons be hanged up before the ' Lord, the plague of famine fhall not be ſtayed from If- ' rael.'

Now, in the next place, I witnefs by this my teſtimony, my adherence to the Scriptures of truth, the holy Bible, the Old and New Teſtament, which has been made fweet to me. The fault is not in them that we underſtand them not, but in us, and this we have as our old father Adam's heirfhip. I witnefs my adherence to the Covenants National and Solemn League; Confeſſion of Faith; only there is in it fomething concerning the magiſtrate's calling a fynod of miniſters, by virtue of his magiſtratical power, which ought to be cautioufly underſtood, according to the general aſſembly's explication. I adhere to the Catechifms Larger and Shorter, Pfalms in metre, Directory for worfhip, Form of Church-government; the doctrine of the church of Scotland, as it is held out in the word of God, and laid down in the forefaid papers. I adhere to all the faithful teſtimonies for truth in Scotland, of one fort and another, and particularly thefe three, the papers found at the Queensferry of the date of the 3d of June, the Sanquhar Declaration, the Rutherglen Teſtimony, and every other paper tending to the good of religion, particularly the Caufes of Wrath; and I requeſt all to read and confider them. I leave my teſtimony againſt them that fay, That I am a felf-murderer, becaufe I fpake that which God gave me to fpeak, before his adverfaries: and I think that it is my great mercy, that he hath helped me to be free before them in matters of truth, relating to the difowning of them, and ſtanding to our God's, and our own rights. This paper I leave as my teſtimony, and formed and deliberate thoughts; and requeſt all to bear with faults of weaknefs, efpecially when the fword of the adverfary is above a man's head. Now, farewel world, and all things in it. Welcome Lord Jefus Chriſt, into thy hands I recommend my fpirit.

Sic fubſcribitur, WILLIAM CUTHIL.

The dying Testimony of ROBERT GARNOCK *hammerman in Stirling, who suffered at the Gallowlee betwixt Leith and Edinburgh, October* 10. 1681.

Men and Brethren,

I Having received a sentence of death from men for adhering to the truth, against Popery, Prelacy, Erastianism and Indulgences first and last, and all that was contrary to sound doctrine; am now to leave a line behind me, as the Lord will help me to write, and to tell you, That however this generation may condemn me, as having a hand in my own death, I declare that it is not so; for I die a Presbyterian in my judgment. For I considering, how solemnly Scotland was bound to defend truth against all encroachments made thereon, with their lives and liberties, and how they of this nation had so easily broken their vows and engagements; and then seeing thro' the Scriptures, how deep covenant-breaking draws, and what a great and heinous sin this is in the sight of God; could do no less than give in my protestation against all their proceedings, in their hell-hatched acts that were so contrary to the word of God, and our sworn covenants; and it is for that, that I am come in your presence this day, to lay down this life of mine; for which I bless the Lord that ever he honoured the like of me with a gibbet and a bloody winding-sheet, for his noble, honourable and sweet cause. O will ye love him, Sirs! O he is well worth the loving, and quitting all for! O for many lives to seal the sweet cause with! If I had as many lives as there are hairs in my head, I would think them all too little to be martyrs for truth. I bless the Lord, I do not suffer unwillingly, nor by constraint, but heartily and chearfully. O but the Lord hath taken great pains on me to train me up for this great work. I bless his holy name, that ever he counted me worthy of such honour; his love hath been to me beyond many. I have been a long time a prisoner, and have been altered of my prison; I was among, and in the company of the most part who suffered since Bothwel; and was in company with many ensnaring persons, tho' I do not question but they were godly folk; and yet the Lord keeped me from hearkning to their counsel. Glory, glory be to his holy and sweet name. O but it is many a time a wonder, how I have done such and such things! but it is he that hath done it: He hath done all things well, both in me and for me; holy is his name. O if I could get my royal King Jesus cried up, and all the world down! O will you fall in love with Chrift! friends, what ails you at him, and his sweet cause? I can affure you, he is no hard master to serve. O he is lovely! *He is white and ruddy, the chief among ten thousands*. I defire none of you to think, I suffer *as an evil doer, or as a busy body in other mens matters*; or that it is out of blind zeal, that I am come here this day: No, for it was after ferious confideration that I did it, and after great weights and preffures. It was great grief of foul to me, to fee my Master's truth fo wronged, trampled on and abused by a God-daring generation, and none to speak for him. And now my Lord is highly honouring me for that; glory to his great name for it. For he hath honoured me, and my neighbours with irons, and the thieves hole, which were fweet and refrefhful to us, and then honoured us wonderfully to go in before these bloody men, and get our fentences.

Our interrogations are known, I have not time to write them. But I difowned them, for difowning of the Covenant, and adhered to my proteftation given in againft them: and now am come to the Gallowlee, to lay down my life, and to have my head cut off, and put upon a port. It is known, how barbaroufly I have been ufed by them, and how honourably fuch a filly wretch as I am, hath been carried thro': Glory be to his fweet name for it. Indeed it was the bargain betwixt Chrift and my foul long fince, that thro' his ftrength I fhould be for him, and at his bidding, whatever piece of work he put in my hand; and he promifed, *that his grace fhould be sufficient for me;* and *that his ftrength fhould be feen in my weaknefs;* and that go whither I would, he would go with me, *thro' fire and water*, the flames would not fcorch me, nor the *waters overflow me*. O take him, Sirs! for *he is faithful who hath promifed*, and he will perform. Now, as a dying martyr for Chrift, I would leave it on all of you to make hafte, and prepare for ftrokes, for they are at hand; and do not think, that they will not come, becaufe they are delayed. No, he will come, and that *as a thief in the night*, and will furprife many of you, if not all; *Watch and pray, that ye enter not into tempta-*

tion. I would not have you secure, but take warning in time, before his wrath break forth. He hath waited long on Scotland's repentance; it is like, he will not bear much longer. Do not sleep, as do others, but rise, make haste, *get on the whole armour of God, that ye may be able to stand.* It is dangerous now to be out of God's gate; it is not good siding with God's enemies: It will be dangerous to be found in their camp. I would not be in their stead for all the gold of Ophir, who have saved their lives with prejudice to the work and people of God. I would have them take warning. They say, They have done nothing, but what was lawful and right; but they commit transgression, and (with the whore) *wipe their mouth, and say, They have done no evil.* Indeed they may put off men so, but they will not get God and their own consciences put off. They need never go about the bush, for I see not how any that is faithful, being once brought before them, can win honestly off; for if ye will but say, ye disown their authority, then your life must go. For they had as little to lay to my charge as to any, yet I could not win off with a good conscience, but to the gallows I must go: And glory to his great name, who hath honoured me; or that ever he gave me a head to be set on a port for his sweet name and cause. Now, as for what I own or disown, I being straitened by reason of the want of time, cannot get it set down here; and another thing I see, that martyrs testimonies are of no value, and very lightly esteemed.

I give my testimony to the holy and sweet Scriptures, Covenants, Confession of Faith, which are according to the Scripture, Catechisms Larger and Shorter, the Acknowledgment of Sins and Engagement to Duties, and to all that our worthies have done, in defence of the gospel, at Pentland, Loudon hill, Bothwel-bridge, and Airs-moss; to Rutherglen Testimony, and Sanquhar Declaration, Ferry Papers, and Torwood Excommunication, the Fife Testimony, D —— ie, K —— le, and P ---- s Protestations, and all that have been done in defence of the gospel, where-ever it hath been done. And I, as a dying martyr for the truth, give my testimony against all the encroachments on our Lord's rights, in less or more, as Popery, Prelacy, Erastianism, and Indulgences first and last, and all that side with them. And I, as a dying witness for Christ, desire friends to the cause of Christ,

to beware of them ; ' For, if it were poffi
' deceive the very elect. They will n
' kingdom of heaven themselves, nor wi
' thers to go in thereat.' Beware of the
for they and the devil thought to have
with my lovely Lord Jesus Christ, tha:
betwixt him and my soul. O ! but the]
generation are evil and bitter against th
the Lord, and his poor people.

 Next, I give my testimony against al
God, and all that join with them, in p;
lity, militia-money, or whatever is for
ing of their hands. And now I leave i
that ye would not brand me with havin
own death ; for I could not get my life
had taken upon me all the blood of the
and owned that as lawful authority whi
way my dear brethren's lives; and said,
and right what they had done. And inde
more of any, if they will but own them :
They think, they are right enough in :
lives, when they who are called Presbyte
and their tyranny to be authority. A:
am to go away, I would have you to la
deeply owning of them draws, and he
wrath of God ye draw on you in so de
would have you beware, and look what
ness it is ; and *obey God rather than man*. :
I am this day to step out of time into ete
no more troubled than I were to take a
earth, and not so much. I bless the Lo
peace of conscience in what I have d
think it a very weighty business for 1
twelve hours of eternity, and not troubl
Lord is kind, and hath trained me up f
now I can want him no longer. I will g
this night ; for ' I will be with him in p
' a new song put in my mouth, the song
' the Lamb ;' I will be in amongst ' the
' of the first-born,' and enjoy the sweet
and his Son Jesus Christ, and ' the spi
' made perfect :' I am sure of it.

 O dear friends, I would, as one going
test you, that you make good earnest in

restless until you get a clearness of an interest in Christ; for it is a dangerous time to live in the dark. I would have you consider what a weighty business it is to deny the Lord of glory before men. There has strange things of this nature fallen out in this our day. O! look to yourselves, I would entreat you, to be for God, and he will be for you; confess him, and he will confess you. As good soldiers endure hardness, wax valiant in suffering. Resist unto blood, for it is the cause of God that is at stake. O! there are none of you lamenting after God; ah! is there none of you that hath love to the Lord, and will take part with him, against all his enemies? O! but it be sad to see you with such whole hearts, and so little grief among you, for the robbery that the Lord of glory is getting. I declare my suffering is nothing, but when I see you who are professors, what an unconcerned people ye are, it makes my soul bleed to see you in such a frame, when the church is in such a condition. I wish the Lord may help poor young ones, that are brought up under you with the want of the gospel. O for the gospel back again to Scotland! Oh for one faithful minister in all the land! O but the harvest be great, and the labourers few! As for my part, now when I am going into eternity, I declare, I see not, nor hear not of a minister in all Scotland, who is at the duty the Lord calls for at ministers hands, in preaching against all sorts of sin; *in season, and out of season, rebuking, reproving, and exhorting.* As for my part, I cannot join with them who are not so.

Now, my Lord is bringing me to conformity with himself, and honouring me after my worthy pastor, Mr. James Guthrie; altho' I knew nothing when he was alive; yet the Lord hath honoured me to protest against Popery, and to seal it with my blood; and he honoured him to protest against Prelacy, and to seal it with his blood. The Lord hath keeped me in prison to this day for that end. His head is on one port of Edinburgh, and mine must go on another. Glory, glory to the Lord's holy and sweet name, for what he hath done for me. O set days apart, and bless his holy and never enough exalted name, for what he hath done for me. O Sirs! his cross hath been all paved over with love to me all alongst, and it is sweeter now than ever. O will ye be persuaded to fall in love with the cross of royal Jesus? O take him. Will ye be entreated to come and taste of his love! O sweet lot this day, for me to go to a gibbet for Christ and his cause! I think the thoughts of this do ravish my heart and soul, and make me to fall out in wondering, that I am within so few hours of that endless joy, that paradise, among these flowers and trees, that are on each side of that *pure river, clear as crystal,* where the tree is, that *bears twelve manner of fruits, and the leaves of the tree are for the healing of the nations.* O that I could leave this weight upon you; yea, with as great weight as it lies on my spirits, to see how few of you are travelling to that land. O be much above, and be here as strangers; I mean, in respect of conformity to this world, tho' hated of it, and studying to live the life that our Lord hath commanded in his word. And ' suffer affliction with the people of ' God, rather than enjoy the pleasures of sin for a sea- ' son.' Now, I bless the Lord, I am not as many suspect me, thinking to win heaven by my suffering; No, no: I know there is no winning of it, but thro' the precious blood of the Son of God. Now, ye who are the true seekers of God, and so the butt of the world's malice, O be diligent, and run fast; time is precious: O make use of it, and act for God, contend for the truth, stand for God against all his enemies. Fear not the wrath of men. Love one another. Wrestle with God mutually in societies. *Confess your faults one to another;* pray with one another; *Reprove, rebuke, exhort one another in love.* Slight no commanded duty: be faithful in your stations, as ye will be answerable in the great day.

Now, having no more time, I bid farewel to you all. Farewel holy and sweet Scriptures, wherewith I have been refreshed many a day. I would have you read much of them, and pray over them to the Lord, that ye may get his blessing with, and the right use of them. O! make use of your Bibles, my dear friends, so long as you have them. Seek not counsel from men. Follow none further than they hold by truth. Now, I request you have a care; this land is like to come under great errors. Now, farewel sweet reproaches for my lovely Lord Jesus, tho' once they were not joyous, but grievous, yet now they are sweet; I bless the Lord for it. I heartily forgive all men, for any thing they have said of me: I pray, that it may not be laid to their charge in the day of accounts. As for what they have done to God and *of Patrick Forman.*

his caufe, I leave that to God and their own confciences. Farewel all chriftian acquaintances and relations, father and mother, brethren and fifters; farewel fweet prifon for my royal Lord Jefus Chrift; it is now at an end: farewel all croffes of one fort and another; and fo farewel every thing in time, reading, praying, and believing. Welcome eternal life, and the fpirits of juft men made perfect; welcome Father, Son, and Holy Ghoft, into thy hands I commit my fpirit.

Sic fubfcribitur, ROBERT GARNOCK.

The laft Teftimony of PATRICK FORMAN, *who lived in Alloa, and fuffered at the Gallowlee, October* 10*th,* 1681.

I Thought it fit, being fentenced to die within three days, to write this teftimony, to fhew you, that I die not as a fool; and I declare I am in my right mind, and not prodigal of my life, as fome alledge, but I love life as well as any, and would do as much to fave it; but when my life comes in competition with the truths of Jefus Chrift, I dare not buy it with the denial of the fmalleft truths (if any may be called fmall) but know, that the leaft of the truths are of greater moment than the whole world, and the inhabitants thereof. Now, therefore, do not afperfe me when I am gone, with not being a Prefbyterian, for tho' in great weaknefs, I am a Prefbyterian, both in profeffion and practice, tho' my failings be many.

1*ft*, I believe there is but one God, Father, Son, and holy Ghoft; one Redeemer, one way of falvation, and that it is thro' Jefus Chrift, according to that word, John xxiv. 6. *Jefus faith unto them, I am the way, the truth and the life; no man cometh unto the Father, but by me.* And likewife I leave my teftimony to the holy Scriptures of the Old and New Teftaments; and my foul defires to blefs the Lord, that ever they were in our mother-tongue. My foul hath been refrefhed in converfing with them, when the Spirit of the Lord has backed them; but I knew likewife, they are but a killing letter without the Spirit: Yet this I would advife you, as a dying martyr for Chrift, to fearch the Scriptures, and feek the Lord's mind in them; for there are none noble, but thefe who fearch the Scriptures; and O that I could recommend them to you, as they have been fweet and refrefhful to me; yea, they are as a garden of fweet-fmelling flowers; in them are cures for all difeafes, and remedies for all diftempers; yea, they commend themfelves, they need none of my commendation. Make good ufe of them, while ye have them; for if idolaters get their will, they will not be long amongft you; I pray the Lord may prevent it.

2dly, I leave my teftimony to the Confeffion of Faith, Larger and Shorter Catechifms, the Solemn Acknowledgment of Sins, and Engagement to Duties. I bear my teftimony to the National Covenant, and Solemn League and Covenant. Likewife I adhere to all the faithful teftimonies that have been given for the truth, fince the year 1638; efpecially that Sanquhar Declaration, and Rutherglen Teftimony, and the papers found on Henry Hall at the Queensferry, called the New Covenant; and to the lawfulnefs of Torwood excommunication, and all the teftimonies of the martyrs, who are gone before me, according to truth, both in fields, on fcaffolds, and in the feas; and likewife I leave my teftimony to that poor perfecuted remnant that are yet left as berries on the tops of the utmoft branches, wandering about, being defolate, afflicted and tormented, groaning under the fad yoke of tyranny. O Lord deliver them in thy own way and time; and encourage them now when there is no encouragement from men, and their eyes cannot behold their teachers. And now, my friends, I tell you, being within few hours to ftep out of time into eternity, that ye beware of cafting afperfions on any of the Lords people, for owning their duty, which is avowing and declaring Jefus Chrift to be King in Zion, head of his people, and only Lord of your confciences; and declining all powers which are contrary to and inconfiftent with our Lord's kingly power. And now I declare, I own magiftracy, as it is an ordinance of God, and offered my willing fubjection unto them; but when the magiftrate becomes a tyrant by overturning the whole law of God, and the juft laws of the nation, he or they being once covenanted to the contrary, then I think it my duty, as I am bound by the Scripture, and our Covenants, and my own confcience, to fhow, in my ftation, my diflike of the wrongs my lovely Lord and Mafter is getting; for as the Scripture declares, *There are no powers but of God, and the powers that be are ordained of God.* Then confequently that power cannot be of God, that murders the people of God; otherways ye muſt ſay, that the Lord is the author of evil, which were horrid blaſphemy. Now therefore, my dear friends, ſuppoſe that they will take away our lives, under the name of treaſon and rebellion, (as they have done to our brethren theſe twenty years) yet it is not ſo, but for religion and loyalty to our Lord and Maſter, and to every ordinance of man, as it is confiſtent with the law of our Lord Jeſus Chriſt. Therefore, as ye would be anſwerable at the day of our appearance; when we ſhall ſtand naked and bare before the Judge of all the earth, ſpeak not againſt us, left ye be reckoned amongſt the fighters againſt Jeſus Chriſt; for I declare, I have owned nothing, but that which is the duty of the whole nation, as well as mine. And I doubt not but the Lord will reckon with this generation, ere it be long, for maintaining that throne of iniquity theſe twenty years.

And now, I declare, as a dying man, that it is but juſtice that is come upon this poor nation; for when the Lord ſet them free from that yoke of bondage they were lying under, by that old tyrant Charles I. who deſigned to cut off the Lord's people, which he put in practice, in murdering the Lord's people in Ireland, by the hands of the bloody Papiſts, and thought to have done ſo to England and Scotland, but the Lord prevented him, and put a ſtop to his tyranny, by ſuffering men to take away his life, and cauſing his family to be baniſhed; and brake the yoke off our neck, and became our Lord, King and head; we ſoon wearied of the Lord, and caſt him off, and ſaid, *We will have a king to rule over us, like the nations;* and ye may judge, whether he has reigned Saul-like or not? And I doubt not but he ſhall be taken away in wrath, becauſe he was given in the Lord's anger; and tho' his time has been a groaning time, yet his end ſhall be terrible, and the people ſhall find the ſmart of it, as the children of Iſrael did, when they fell at Gilboa. Friends, look for ſad days, when we are gone. O therefore, I intreat you, as ye would tender the glory of God, and deſire the ſalvation of your own ſouls, mourn for the wrongs ye have done to the glory of God, in your owning of that tyrant, who is the malignant's head and god. And now I am ſure, ye are left without excuſe, if ye will not caſt him off; and they who will ſay, he hath power over civil matters, must say, God is unjust, and he is the author of evil, which were horrid blasphemy.

The matter of my condemnation is, becaufe I will not yield to their iniquitous laws, and call tyranny authority, and a constitution of wickednefs, a constitution of God; which I dare not, for my foul, have the leaft thought of. And now, my friends, I am to die for protesting against Popery, and the inbringing of that Papist the Duke, to defile the Lord's land; and declining their power, becaufe they had murdered my brethren thefe twenty years, and testifying against all the wrongs my lovely Lord and Master hath got. Therefore I charge you, to beware of speaking against me, or any of my brethren; for my head and my right hand shall be a witnefs against you, who shall condemn us; whatever I have been, I am now highly honoured to witnefs for Christ's caufe. And now, my dear friends, I must tell you, That grace is free, and I am a debtor to free grace, and I am as a brand plucked out of the fire; yet my Lord hath loved me with an everlasting love. And I blefs the Lord, I am in my right mind, and has hatred against no man's perfon, but in fo far as they are fighting against my God, and plotting against his holy child Jefus; but as it is written, Pfal. ii. 9. *Thou shalt break them with a rod of iron, thou shalt dash them in pieces like a potsherd.* I leave my testimony against Charles Stuart, for his breach of covenant, and for his setting forth that hellish act of supremacy; whereby he refcinded the law of God, and the just laws of the land, that he might murder the Lord's people. I likewife leave my blood upon him, and thefe bloody counfellors, justiciary and affizers; becaufe they take away my life, and the lives of my brethren, without a shadow of law or justice; for there were none of us guilty of action or crimes, and the protestation we gave them, shall be a standing witnefs against them. 2*dly*, I leave my testimony against Prelacy, becaufe they have taken upon them the place of Lords, which is proper to none but Jefus Christ; for we have but one God, one Lord, one Saviour and Master, &c. and they have our blood upon their heads. I leave my testimony against all the proceedings against the Lord's people, for their murders in the fields, and in the sea, and on scaffolds. I leave my testimony against the bringing home of that tyrant Charles Stuart, after they knew that he had broken *of Patrick Forman.* 199

all bonds that could bind men, and was no more to be believed. I likewise leave my testimony against the duke of York, and against the reception of him, first and last, because they knew he was a professed Papist, and was seeking nothing but the lives of the Lord's people, as his actions declare; First, he behoved to have a draught of these five mens blood at Magus muir, and next, of Mr. James Skeen, John Potter, Archibald Stewart, and the rest of our brethren since; O bloody wretch! he is filling himself drunk with the blood of the saints; and when he was declared vice-roy and high commissioner, as they call him, he behoved to have a draught of blood to sit down with, viz. of that faithful minister of Jesus Christ, Mr. Donald Cargil, and the other four; and then they sat down to their parliament, for enacting these hell-hatched acts, placing Charles Stuart and his succession for their god; and that they call law and authority for their bible. And now when they have taken their breath, they must have our blood to flocken them. I leave my testimony against the parliamenters, and my blood upon them, I am sure they will find it, and my brethren's lying heavy upon them. I likewise leave my testimony against bonders, cess and locality payers, for strengthening the hands of these wicked ruffians, the troopers and soldiers, who destroy the Lord's people. Now therefore, dear friends, I warn you, as you would fly from the wrath to come, shake yourselves of these things, if so be there may be hope; it may be if ye be serious, ye will be hid in the day of the Lord's anger: Take warning, and fly from the wrath that is to come.

Likewise I leave my testimony against the unfaithfulness of the watchmen of Scotland, for they have not fed the flock, but fed themselves. Therefore I, as a dying man, must tell you, that it will be a wonder, if ever ye be honoured to be faithful, for your turning your backs on your Master, when all men are set against him, and your seeking to save your lives, when the Lord is calling you to suffer, rather than to yield, or quit one hair of the truth, Ye think nothing to call tyranny lawful magistracy, and by that ye say, That all the martyrs, who have suffered under tyranny these twenty years, have suffered justly. If that word be true, *There is no power but of God;* then certainly Charles Stuart's power must not be of God; for his unheard of murders, perjuries and adulteries. Now I say, those who call him a magistrate, they say, That God is the author of sin, which is horrid blasphemy; and I think, there are few ministers in Scotland, who are free of that horrid sin, and are not in some sort guilty of their brethren's blood; for ye are an upcast to poor sufferers. Now therefore, I advise you to repent, for I shall wish you no wrong. I might say much to that purpose, but I shall forbear, only I desire the Lord may forgive you, for your lukewarmness, neutrality, indifferency and sinful silence, where there is none to speak for Jesus Christ. And now I advise you that are his people, to take warning from me as a dying man, not to join with them, till their repentance be as visible as their sin hath been. O seek teachers from the Lord, for he will not want ministers, when he hath an errand to send them. Wait on the Lord, for he doth all things well. Now, my dear friends, who desire to live godly, look out for tribulation and affliction, and the scourge of tongues, and the envy and malice of devils. The ministers will reproach you and condemn you, and the worldly-wise professors will advise you to run at leisure, and not condemn the godly for their failings: It is true, I grant the godly my fall and rise again; but alas! their apostacy in denying their Master, and defending it, will be found very hard and terrible, in the sight of the Lord.

Now, I must not tarry, being surprised with shortness of time, having the king of terrors to grapple with. Only this I say, (my dear friends) make haste, get your peace made with God, and in your stations contend for him: Labour to have nothing before your eyes, but the glory of God, and ye shall undoubtedly get employment of him; make it your main work to seek the Lord. And now, that I am to step out of time into eternity, I bless the Lord for the way he hath taken with me; for all that I have met with, hath been in loving kindness; and I can say, that from my experience, he hath been kind to me in my wanderings and imprisonments; irons and stocks, have been made sweet to me; yea, evil company hath been made useful to me. Yea, these antiscripturists were made instructive to me; for I saw these four men (I mean John Gib and his followers) were once as fairly on the way, by appearance, as any I knew; but I see gifts are not graces, and now I think, they are *of David Farrie.*

hopeleſs; and I adviſe none that tenders the glory of God to meddle with them; for they are turned horrid blaſphemers, and deniers of the Scriptures. Beware of them; for I have no time to give you a particular account of them.

Now, my dear friends, farewel, with whom I have been refreſhed many times: the love of God be with you, and carry you thro'. Farewel holy Scriptures, wherewith I have been comforted; farewel praying; farewel ſweet impriſonment; farewel ſweet ſtocks and irons for Chriſt's ſake; farewel wanderings and ſweet reproaches for my Lord's ſake; farewel ſun, moon and ſtars; farewel day and night; farewel all created comforts. Welcome death; welcome gallows, for Chriſt's ſake; welcome eternity; welcome angels; welcome ſpirits of juſt men made perfect; welcome praiſes that ſhall never have an end. There I ſhall reſt thro' all the ages of eternity, in Immanuel's land. Welcome Father, Son, and Holy Ghoſt, into thy hands I recommend my ſpirit.

Sic ſubſcribitur,
PATRICK FORMAN.

The laſt Teſtimony of DAVID FARRIE, *who ſuffered at the Gallowlee. Edinburgh, October 10th, 1681.*

Dear Friends,

I Deſire to bleſs the Lord, that I am ſentenced to be a martyr for Chriſt and his cauſe, by wicked men, whoſe actions prove what they are; yet glory be to the name of God, that this day, I do not ſuffer as an evil-doer, but for the teſtimony of the truth, in owning Jeſus Chriſt as head in his church; yea, in the church of Scotland, and not only ſo, but covenanted to be ſo, as he was with the children of Iſrael, in the ſight of the nations; which covenant, made betwixt Jeſus Chriſt and this land, I bleſs the Lord, that, by his ſtrength, I have been enabled to own, before all theſe accuſers of mine, eſpecially the bloody committee, the bloody council, and the dreadful bloody aſſizers of the people of God, and givers of them their ſentences of death, all inſtituted by Charles Stuart, who was once by his profeſſion, and by his oath, an owner of that covenant. Now the grounds of my ſentence are to be ſeen in my interrogations before the committee, council, and juſticiary ſo called: At which

I was asked, If I owned my former spe
What I had said, I had said: But in case
think, that I had heart-malice at him w
king; I told them, I wished neither h
nor their souls, any more evil nor I w
but since he had broken the covenant v
turned out all our ministers, obtruded]
Church, and overturned the whole work
I could not own him as king, and them a:
he and his emissaries were proceeding to
ry into the land; and I disowned them
and told them, There was a day coming
and I would be arraigned before a judge,
and receive righteous judgment, and tha
would be a witness against them for the
sentences against the people of God, and
ous proceedings against us, to take awa
owning and adhering to the word of
sworn covenants. And when I was asked
questions, I answered, what I had said,
I had said as much as would be for the
row of all present, except those that were p
let men judge whether or not it becom
Charles Stuart as king and them as judg
have broken the covenant, and overturn
reformation, and shed so much of the p
their blood; and not only so, but also
duke, Popish by profession, heir to the cr
door whereat they may receive Popery
For I think there are none, but in some n
low Popery, that will not witness against,
him and them in their proceedings, espec
test, which that wicked parliament hath
mongst all their other proceedings, thes
against God, his work and people; whe
turning our ministry and thursting in of P
lawful acts of indulgence first and last,
murdering of the people of God, in fields
and seas, in one place and another are a
great witness, that is, and will be standi
said Charles Stuart, and his unlawful co
liaments, and all their proceedings! Th
second commandment threatens his wra
children for the fathers iniquity, unto

of David Farrie. 203

fourth generations of them that hate him; and if the Lord visit not the succeffors of this generation aforenamed, with dreadful judgments, I am miftaken; yea, and all thefe that join and comply with them, either minifters or profeffors, I mean the indulged, and all thefe that bond with the enemies, or give them clats of gear for their liberations, when they are brought to prifon upon the account of owning the truth; or in any manner of way acknowledge them as magiftrates; I fay, (without repentance) I fee no way that they can mifs God's wrath.

But I think, I need not infift much on thefe fubjects; for all the warnings they have gotten (which are many) by minifters and profeffors, one way or other, efpecially on fcaffolds, fince Mr. James Guthrie to this day, have not been effectual; their actings prove them to be more hardened in their fin than when they began. Therefore I think it feems, that the Lord will either give them no more warnings, or elfe take them fhortly away, or both: indeed he may give them more warnings, but if ever they do the moft part of this generation any good I greatly queftion, I mean thefe whom I have named; for I think, with feveral others who are gone before me, and are going off the ftage by death, That there will be dreadful judgments to follow on this generation, for breach of covenant with God, and open rebellion againft him, by thefe iniquitous laws of theirs, in taking away the lives, liberties and privileges of the people of God, and not only fo, but in making Charles Stuart head of the church, which becomes not him nor any mortal; for Jefus Chrift is head of his own church, and Lord over the confciences of men. And as for me, I would not have my confcience tied by Charles Stuart's belt, nor any who are called his fubjects, tho' I were to live an hundred years; no, tho' I could have the whole world for my pains; for I might as well ty my confcience to the devil and my own corruptions, as do it, by yielding fubmiffion to his iniquitous laws, by either bond or cefs, or any thing relating thereto. Now I blefs the Lord, I hope, that he who hath led me hitherto, will lead me away from him, and his, and my own corruptions, and the devil, ere the tenth day of this month pafs over.

And as for my own particular intereft, I blefs the

The last Speech and Testimony

Lord, I am in some measure, as clear of my interest in Christ, as I am that my pen is writing on this paper; for I hope, that the Lord will carry me honourably thro', and give me that which he hath promised: ay when I asked him faith, he gave me faith, life, light, and a heart to believe, and love to him, and his glory, interest, cause, covenant and work of reformation, and strength to stand, and withstand my enemies inward and outward, who many a time have assaulted and tempted me, striving to drive me away to sin. Indeed it is true, I lived most lewdly, ay till within a little more nor these four years. O if I could go to the stage, blessing and magnifying the Lord, that it hath pleased him to bring me from the devil's fire-side, as it were, and draw me out to hear the gospel of Christ! I bless the Lord, the first field-preaching that ever I heard, I entered in covenant with him to follow him, tho' it should cost me my life; and at a communion in Irongray in Galloway, I had the clear manifestation of my interest. O free grace! O free love! O free mercy! what am I, that he hath been so kind to me! O me! O poor me! and not only so, but also when he discovered the evils of the woful indulgence, from the supremacy, that he made it known to me, and also made me to stand and withstand that woful evil, and to join with that party, by the bond found upon Mr. Richard Cameron, whom he honoured to witness against it; and for this I desire to bless him. O! I think, it is Scotland's mercy this day, that he hath opened the eyes of the blind, to see these abominations, especially among the ministers, I mean, the indulged, and those who plead for them! O! Scotland's mercy hath been great, that notwithstanding of their rebellion, and joining with rebels by that supremacy, the Lord opened the eyes of the blind to see these abominations, and to testify against them: O! I say, this is Scotland's mercy; tho' some may think otherwise; for if the Lord had not opened up that evil to poor things, it had been a token that he would have gone his way, and not owned his covenanted land any more; but it is a token for good yet to the land, that notwithstanding of all our rebellions against him by breach of covenant, he continues yet to discover to his people, what is sin and duty. And this also is a token that the Lord will not leave Scotland, tho' he may chastise it very sore; his taking the blood and lives of his saints, on fields, seas and scaffolds, to witness for his covenants; for the blood of the martyrs is the seed of the church. And this is another token for good to the church, that there is a remnant (though small) that is weeping and lamenting over the broken case of the church, and over the unconcernedness of the people of God, or of these who say they are the people of God, and that there are so few to keep clean garments, and to wrestle, and witness against the sins of this generation of covenant-breakers and usurpers. O Sirs! is not this a sweet cordial yet, for all that is come upon us? O Sirs! take courage, and plead with the Lord, and also, thro' his strength, plead with your whorish-mother, viz. the indulged, and their deeds, which they have done, and those that plead for them. O plead, and plead in patience; let not self rise, let not passion rise and vex you; *Be sober, be not soon angry;* fear not reproaches; but beware of giving the enemies, or professed friends, just ground of reproach; walk in the sight of God and man both, without offence and reproach; and then if men will be offended, let it be for your duty, and not for your sin. But O be tender of the glory of God: let there be no vain janglings, or foolish and unlearned questions among you, knowing that they gender strife. Be tender one of another. Do not reprove every small circumstance, till ye have God with you in your reproof, and the thing be a known sin. Avoid evil company, and rather draw yourselves to prayer alone, and with company when ye can have the occasion, and miss no occasion; for it will be the ready way to cause the Lord leave you and the land; and then, *Wo to you, if he depart from you.* O invite one another to prayer, especially young folks; for I think, if the Lord do good to this generation, it will be to young folk. O babes and sucklings set to the work; for the Lord hath promised, that *out of the mouth of babes and sucklings, he will perfect praise:* Who knows, if ye be at your duty, but the Lord will yet send teachers, who will stand in the gap, to hold away wrath; but till the Lord send them, stand in the gap yourselves; and when ye have got them, lay not all the stress upon them, lest the last plague be worse than the first.

O keep warfare against corruptions, and the devil, in every thing. O do not make an idol of the godly, tho' they be really godly, zealous, judicious and pru-

dent; I do not mean the prudence that
Chriſt and his kingly office mean. Let G
God, and not another. Uſe all things to
fying, and ſtrengthning one anothers har
maintain your brother's juſt cauſe, when
hearing, eſpecially in the matters of Go
one another, *but not to doubtful diſputatic*
and own the godly who are penitent, tho
and failings, providing they be ſenſible
*for the Lord maketh more of one prodigal
ſheep that is come home, or is found, than h
nine, who went not aſtray.* So ought ye
yourſelves; but beware of any ſinful u
grip after miniſters till they at leaſt come
work where Mr. Donald Cargil left it.
them honeſt till ye find them ſo: for I
none who will venture all for Chriſt ar
mean their lives, liberties and fortunes, til
and there are none but ſuch who can be
ful, for he hath ſaid, *He that loveth father
or children, houſes or lands, better than m
of me;* and that they who do ſo, *cannot*
Therefore ye muſt of neceſſity look to theſ
yourſelves, till the Lord ſend ſhepherds
for the flock; and not leave, nor tear tl
livering them into the hand of their enem
the ſad experience of it this day. O! I v
the caſe of the miniſters of Scotland th
world. Conſider Luke xvii. 10. *So lik
have done all theſe things, ſay, we are unpre*
Let the law of God be your rule; and v
done all to keep the law; yet conſider,
merit any good thing, but ye muſt lean on
and ſuffering of Jeſus Chriſt: But yet th
obſerved and obeyed. It is true, *no mere
feƈtly to keep the commandments of God;* b
be your ſnare, for it is the ſnare of many
tion.

O Sirs! ſtudy the Scripture; walk by
the law of God, and the liberty of the g
but do not abuſe your liberty, to cauſe t
be evil ſpoken of. I ſpeak as a dying ma
I have learned from the word of God, ar
of diſpenſations. O! he hath taught m

and gofpel, and the teaching of his Spirit, many things that I cannot exprefs, not one of a thoufand. O! he hath filled my mouth many a time with arguments, till I could go no further. I defire to fpeak it to the commendation of free grace. O if the enemies knew what true grace were, they would not do as they do: But truly I think, the judgment fhall be terrible that they fhall be tryfted with. O! it hath been weighty to me, to think on their deftruction and mifery, which I have thought upon many a time to be eternal; and yet I have thought upon the other hand, that it was my duty, when God's juftice paffed the fentence, to fay, Amen, (as it were) and fo have defired that the Lord would let his determination be execute upon them. Now, there needs none of the fuffering remnant be difcouraged, for God is God, and his word is his word; and there is no change of times, nor alteration of difpenfations, but the word will clear all, in fome place of it, and there is no fin that can be committed, but there is a reproof in the word of God to fuit it; nor one objection in the heart, but there is an anfwer for it from the word: So ftudy the word of God, and implore his prefence in reading of it.

Make much ufe of the Confeffion of Faith, the Larger and Shorter Catechifm; mind our Covenants National and Solemn League. Be not drawn away with the tyranny and perjury of the time. Know that God is God, and that he will not fit with the wrongs he hath gotten by the tyranny and perjury of thefe men; I mean him whom they call fupreme magiftrate Charles Stuart, and thefe under him. God be thanked, his church is well quit of him, tho' a gallows be fet up for the church, and all the Jews; yet, it is like, Haman muft have a fwing of his own weight on the gallows he hath prepared, or elfe fome difgracefuller death. Mind Rutherglen Teftimony, and Sanquhar Declaration, and the papers found at the Ferry: do not think that thefe will fall to the ground. Mind our martyrs teftimonies, and every thing confiftent with the word of God. Do not think but God will be about with this generation, for letting fo light of fuch things, and cafting them behind their backs. For I declare, I adhere to every found writing, that is according to the word of God, be the author who will; I fay, I declare it as a dying man. Indeed this generation think no better fport, than to take any person and cast him into prison, and if they but find, when they have searched them most barbarously, a paper that there is any religion in, be they man or woman, lad or lass, presently they impeach them with treason; yea, but I am sure of this, that God will not sit with such things, but he will be about with them, be who they will. O! but it is sad to see such things; this land doubtless is ripening for a stroke, and a judgment will pursue it. O! who would have thought that Scotland would have quit with their covenanted God, and have trode upon all who have the image of God, in any manner to be seen in them. It is true, *all things work to the good of them that love him:* It is this that makes a prison, a banishment, a gallows (where none uses to be hanged but murderers) sweet indeed. They think it will be for our disgrace, ignominy and shame, to take us to the Gallowlee to be execute; but they are all beguiled, it will be for our honour; our God is wise enough for all that. They think it is the disgrace of the Presbyterians in Scotland, to have our heads hanging, and to be hanged up before the sun. Nay, but they are all beguiled; for it will be recorded from one generation to another, That there was a party of ministers and people, who sealed the covenant with their blood, and their heads were set up for a token of the Lord's kindness to the land. But for my part, I think myself unworthy to be reckoned among such, yet I hope that it shall be said amongst them in these days, that if there had not been a party, to suffer in our cities, they would have had nothing but vile Popery in the land; and will be rejoicing that ever there was any to suffer for Christ in Scotland. O Scotland! is there any land so highly honoured as thou art? None that is to be seen or heard of; but yet thou hast been of all nations the most treacherous and bloody. Was there ever a land so blood-thirsty!

I can say no more, but O be earnest with God, and do not leave off your duty, or otherwise I can see nothing, but that the dreadful judgment of God shall both pursue you and the land; indeed if ye remain at your duty, it may be that ye shall prevail with the Lord, both for yourselves and for the land. But I must leave you to him, who is your God, to lead and guide you in all truth and honesty, both towards God and man. So I leave you to him. Now, farewel thou vile Scotland;

farewel thou highly honoured Scotland; farewel ye friends in Chrift, and all friends and acquaintances; farewel life, and liberty in this life. Welcome Chrift, heaven, and eternal falvation, for ever and ever.
Sic fubfcribitur,
DAVID FARRIE.

The laſt Speech and Teſtimony of JAMES STEW-ART, *who fuffered at the Gallowlee, Edinburgh, October* 10. 1681.

Dear Friends,

I Being in prifon for Chrift, and his perfecuted caufe, tho' fome may fay otherways, and that upon the account of my taking; but I do not care what they fay, for I have had, and yet have great peace in my fufferings. But fome will be ready to fay, That it was an imprudent and an unfure action, and fo might have been forborn: And fuppofe it be fo, it is not the head of my fuffering, for it was not that upon which I was ftaged, for I was prefently ftaged for the truth, the next day after I was taken, being brought before a committee; tho' indeed I was not fo free as I fhould have been. There is a paffage, Acts xxi. of Paul's going up to Jerufalem, which, fome fay, he might have forborn, but more efpecially his going up to the temple, and doing thefe things which are according to the law; he might, I fay, have forborn this, and walked confonant to his former practice, doctrine and writings: But tho' his going to the temple was the occafion of his taking, yet not the head of his fuffering; fo, I fay, tho' that which I did in relieving my brother, was the occafion, yet my fuffering was ftated on another head. But I cannot fee, how it is as ye fay; for I feeing it my duty, and finding opportunity, had a clear call for all that I did. And befides all that, we being bound in covenant to defend and maintain one another, we are bound as well to relieve one another out of prifon, when there is a probability feen. But I need not ftand much in making this out, it being the way that the Lord took to bring me to my fuffering; and I am heartily content with my lot, and defire with my foul to blefs him for it. Tho' I was dreadfully afperfed when that bond of liberation was offered to us, for tho' fome had clearnefs to take it, yet I could never

The last Speech and Testimony

have thoughts of taking it in peace; and I bless the Lord who kept my hand from it: it was neither strength nor sharp-sightedness in me, that withheld me from yielding to the temptation; but the Lord hath shewed himself graciously favourable and kind unto me, now when I am set up like a beacon upon the top of an hill, and the eyes of many being upon me, and all are wondering at me, and calling me distracted, and saying, I am a fool, but (the Lord be thanked) I have all the senses that ever I had, tho' distressed, yet I despair not. Neither am I suffering as a fool; for I know assuredly, this is the way to obtain the promise. There is nothing in it meritorious, I confess; for all my suffering he may put me into hell; but I say, the suffering of reproaches and the scourge of tongues, is a symptom or mark of his way, when it is for his sake, Matth. v. 11. *Blessed are ye when men shall revile you, and speak all manner of evil against you, and persecute you for my name's sake.* It is for his name's sake that I am suffering, and this confirms me of it, Matth. x. 22. *Ye shall be hated of all men for my name's sake; but he that endureth unto the end, shall be saved.*

Now, it is for Christ's kingly office that I am suffering; and this being the main head on which my suffering is stated, even that great truth, viz. Jesus Christ is King and Head of Zion, I desire and charge you to beware of misconstructing my sufferings, and saying, that I was suffering for disowning of authority, and declining of judges; for it is not so, I being a Presbyterian in my judgment, and owning both magistracy and ministry, according to the word of God, and as he hath ordained them: but if Charles Stuart's authority be according to the word of God, I am mistaken. If he be exercising his power, to the terrifying of evil doers, and the encouraging them that do well, I die in an error. I say, beware of your judging, for I am a Presbyterian in my judgment, and a member of the church of Scotland, and am to seal it with my blood.

I adhere to that blessed transaction between the Father and the Son, that holy device devised from all eternity, the Father to send his Son, and the Son to come and satisfy divine justice, and so redeem lost man. I adhere to all the Scriptures of the Old and New Testaments, which are all standing in force until this day, and obligatory upon us, except the ceremonial law, with

of James Stewart. 211

a part of the judicial, which is now abrogate and abolished by our Lord's coming, he being the end of the law. I adhere to our glorious work of reformation, Confession of Faith, Larger and Shorter Catechisms, Acknowledgment of Sins, and Engagement to Duties, tho' they be abused and misconstructed by many. And I adhere to the Sum of Saving Knowledge, wherein is held forth the life and marrow of religion. I adhere to all the testimonies that have been given. Mr. Guthrie, Argyle, and Wariftoun, they gave in their testimony according to the light that the Lord gave them; and I do not condemn their testimony, as some say, for at some times the Lord gives more light than at other times; so it cannot be said, that we contradict or disown their testimony, tho' it hath pleased the Lord, thro' continuance of time, to give more light of the abounding abominations that are still growing and abounding in this generation; and so whatever they omitted through want of that light, which it hath pleased the Lord to let us see, makes no contradiction. I adhere to the Rutherglen and Sanquhar Declarations. I adhere to the paper found upon Mr. Richard Cameron at Airsmofs, July 22. 1680. I adhere to the papers that were found at the Queensferry upon Henry Hall. I adhere to any writings that are according to the word of God, for truth is truth, come by whom it will. Now, as a dying man, I adhere to all these things. I have received an unjust sentence from men, for owning and adhering to the same, and for protesting against the inbringing of Popery, to defile the land. And likewise upon these accounts, I disown Charles Stuart to be my king and sovereign. First, because of that hellish Act of Supremacy, and that Act Rescissory, whereby they have overturned and wrested all the laws, acts and constitutions of the land: for in the foresaid act, he assumeth that unto himself which belongs properly to our Lord and Master, and says, That he rules over all things both spiritual and temporal; and then, when he hath made himself supreme over all things, he rescinds the laws that are of God, and sets up other laws, to satisfy his own lusts, in murdering, killing and destroying the Lord's people; and this is the reason why I disown him: and likewise his dreadful perjury and blasphemy in his covenant breaking. I decline them as judges, for the opening a door there to

Popery, which they have done, by receiving that popish duke in among them, which I proteft and leave my teftimony againft; it being contrary to our engagements to fuffer Papifts to dwell amongft us, and to have a profeft Papift to ufurp over us, it being repugnant to our principles. I leave my teftimony againft Prelacy, it being a limb of that antichriftian whore of Rome. I leave my teftimony againft all the abominations of this generation as blafpheming of the holy name of the Lord, drunkennefs, ftealing, whoring, Sodomy, and all manner of uncleannefs. I leave my teftimony againft all indifferency and lukewarm neutrality in our Lord's matters. I leave my teftimony againft the indulgences firft and laft, as having a greater hand in breaking of the church of Scotland, nor all the enemies living in it could have done; for they fold their Mafter's truths, and give away their pleafant things with their own hands, and fo came in under Charles Stuart, and took him for their head, and have caft off their rightful head Jefus Chrift; Eph. i. 22. *And hath put all things under his feet, and gave him to be head over all things to the church.* Wo will be unto them for what they have done to the poor kirk of Scotland. I leave my teftimony againft filent and unwatchful minifters. Remember, there are many taken away, and it is to be feared, in their iniquity; and do ye think that ye are free of their blood? Ye may look what warning ye have given, and if it be faithful; then ye may fay, that ye are not guilty. But there is not a minifter this day, who dares fay, he is at his duty. They refufe to give counfel when afked at, as I myfelf can witnefs; for when that liberation was granted, I fent to one of them, and charged him, as I judged him faithful, to tell me his mind, which he refufed; and faid, filence might ferve for an anfwer, I was not fuffering for truth. But I heartily forgive him, and all men, what they have done to me, as for my own particular; but how they have reproached Chrift and his way, it is not mine to forgive them.

O the minifters of Scotland are become light and treacherous perfons, as well as revolters; they are become ravening wolves; fo I cannot fee, how they have not unminiftered themfelves. If Abiathar was turned out of the prieft's office for leaving David, and following Adonijah; how much more ought the minifters of Scotland, for leaving of him, who is the true Head of the church, and chufing Charles Stuart for their head? It is not long fince they were preaching that to be fin, which they are now practifing. I have no doubt, but ere long there fhall come out fire from Abimelech, and deftroy the men of Shechem, and fire from them, and devour him. And ere long Mr. Donald Cargil, and Mr. Richard Cameron their names that now ftink among minifters and profeffors fhall have a fweet fmell; and thefe that calumniate and afperfe them, their names fhall go away with a ftink, and fly away with a fmoke; but I am fure, that that now glorified martyr Mr. Donald Cargil, his name fhall laft from generation to generation; and he fhall have caufe to rejoice in his King, Head and Mafter, who is Jefus Chrift; when thofe who condemned him, fhall not know where to flee for fhelter, and fhall be weary of their head, king and mafter, who is Charles Stuart; and what brethren (difaffected as they were) did caft upon him as a fhame, was his glory and decorement. He was of a high heroic fpirit, and was free of a bafe and Simonain carriage. He was a man hated of his brethren; but the great Elijah in his time was fo. Time and tongue would fail me to fpeak to his commendation. He was the man who carried the ftandard, without the help of any vifible: but he had the help and affiftance of his Mafter, at whofe command he was ay wandering here without refidence, yet knew of one above, and had full affurance of his dwelling-place.

I leave my teftimony againft uplifting, or caufing uplift cefs or excife, or any thing, for the maintaining that tyrant, or any of his emiffaries; it being for nothing, but maintaining thefe ruffian troopers and foldiers, who are kept for nothing, but to fupprefs and bear down the gofpel, and banifh it out of the land. I leave my teftimony againft all declaration-takers and bonders, efpecially the taking that bond of liberation as they call it, of the date of Auguft 5. 1680. as far as they were convinced it was fin, as fome of themfelves faid it was. I leave my teftimony againft that teft, and all the reft of their proceedings, and acts of parliament. I leave my teftimony againft jailor fee paying; it being an acknowledgment of their tyranny to be lawful, which how unjuft it is, I have a proof among others; for that night I was before York, and the reft, being October 1ft, 1681. I being examined

by Sir George M'Kenzie, York and Mr. \
son coming unto me, when I was silent, ;
answer to some things they asked at me,
to take out my tongue with a pair of pinc(
not: And he held him as a witness against
I told him, that he was a judge the oth(
would ye hold him as a witness against t
justiciary? yet they did it; which was nei
to law nor reason. If there were no mor
passage, it proves them to be unjust judge
many worse than that is. I leave my te[
the mounting of militia, and uplifting of
service. I leave my testimony against ev
may strengthen his hands, or weaken the ha
ple of the Lord.

Now, I desire you, as a dying man, v
forty-eight hours, or little more, of etern
Charles Stuart to be your king and sovere
you so to do, as you would have peace wi
never knew what true peace was till I di
Jesus Christ for my king and lawgiver. 1
I disown kings or kingly government, for
but when their actions are such as his ar(
nanted king as he was, we cannot in con{
him; for he hath murdered the Lord's pe(
ren: and when we acknowledge even his (
I cannot see what way we are clean of the
ing by a shadow of law and authority that
their lives, and so we cannot own him in
own him in ecclesiastic matters, I think the
so absurd, as to say, we should do that, :
thing to do in church matters: he only
sceptre in his hand, to be a hedge about,
her against all opposition; and now ye m
hath destroyed her, instead of defending h(
it in short, and desire you to ponder and c
ye will not find me so mad, as many of :
for I am not prodigal of my life, neither
in my own death; for I love my life as we
bours, and it is as dear to me as any of y(
but when it comes in competition with my
I dare not seek to save my life with preju(
Neither am I wearied of my life, tho' it.
there is nothing here to be coveted, that

to weary one, neither am I wearied of it; therefore I charge you, that ye do not brand me with afperfions when I am gone. I leave my blood on all the affizers, who after we had given in our proteftation againft all their proceedings, both in their council and jufticiary, and told them, That it was for no action that we were fuffering, but only on the matters of confcience and judgment that we were panneled; yet notwithftanding of our charging them with our blood, they moft unjuftly took away our lives. Do not think this flows from a fpirit of malice, fpite, bitternefs or revenge; for I defire to blefs the Lord, I am free of the fpirit of bitternefs or revenge: but they take away my life without and againft any juft law; I cannot get it paffed. Do not think that I am an enthufiaftic, and take on me a bare impulfe of the Spirit for a call to fuffer on, or the word as it lies literally, for a call; for it is not fo; I having defired and ufed fome endeavours, tho' it has been in great weaknefs I confefs; yet I dare fay, in fome refpect, my defire to the Lord about it hath been fincere, that he would help me to get his word and my own confcience confulted, and try the word by the fpirit, and the fpirit by the word; for it is but a dead letter without the fpirit. And likewife my blood is lying, and will be heavy on that popifh duke. And I will not fay but the Lord will permit him to ufurp the crown of Scotland, but the blood that he hath got to welcome him home to it, and to fatisfy his own luft, will weigh him down from the throne; but indeed, I fear, that he get his defign drawn to a great length, and get the ark carried away, even to your apprehenfion, out of Scotland; but remember the Philiftines carrying away the ark, and the men of Bethfhemefh looking into it, how the Lord fmote them: and fo I think, when they have got the kirk banifhed and deftroyed, and the witneffes all killed, when they will look on the church as carried clean away, and thereupon fhall turn fecure, will not the Lord be avenged on them, and charge them with all the blood they have fo heinoufly fhed? But indeed we have deferved no lefs than the Lord's leaving of this land, and to give them into the hands of our enemies: but as long as there is no appearance of a better church in the whole world, ye need not fear that the Lord will enhance Scotland's right of a church to any other. He fuffered the children of Israel many a time to fall into, and ly under the hand of their enemies; but he never forsook them altogether until there came a better in their place. Likewise my blood is on all these parliamenters and councellors, these of the justiciary, as they call it.

Now, dear friends, I am going to eternity, ere it be long, from whence I cannot return ; and as a dying man I give you warning, and bid you take heed what you are doing. Be tender of the glory of God, and take no unlawful gate to shun suffering, nor sinful shifts to come by the cross. But when there is a cross lying in the way, see that ye seek not to go about it; and venture upon suffering before sinning; for he never sent any a warfare upon their own charges. If any knew the sweetness of a prison, they would not be so afraid to enter upon suffering; ye would not join with the Lord's enemies as ye are doing. O dear friends, take warning now for it is a question if ever ye get any more warnings of this kind : for it is a sad juncture that your lot and mine is fallen into; but now I am going away home. O the Lord is kind to me, who hath honoured me so highly, and is also taking me away from the evil that is to come: For, indeed I think, there are sad days abiding poor Scotland. O Sirs! be busy, and venture all upon him, and put all in his hand; and whatever you have been, let not that fear you ; if you have been a great sinner, I say, let not that hinder you from coming to him, and closing with him ; for the greater sinner you be, the more free grace is magnified in reclaiming you I may speak this from my own experience ; for I was as a brand plucked out of the fire : and he hath brought me thro' many difficulties, temptations and snares, and made my soul escape as a bird out of the cunning fowler's net and brought me to a prison at length, to suffer bond for him. He made all things sweet to me, the company sweet to me, even bad company; he made reproache sweet. I have been made to wonder at his kindness and love to me-ward; and now he hath brought me this length, without being feared what enemies can do to me and that is a great confirmation to me of true love, that perfect love casts out fear. Now, he is faithful into whose hands I commit my spirit and soul, and he will keep it against that day.

Now when I am going, farewel all friends and christi

an acquaintances; farewel fweet and holy Scriptures, wherewith my foul hath been refrefhed; farewel reading, finging and praying; farewel fweet meditation; farewel fun, moon and ftars; farewel all created comforts. Welcome death; welcome fweet gallows, for my fweet and lovely Lord; welcome angels; welcome fpirits of juft men made perfect; welcome eternity; welcome praifes; welcome immediate vifion of the Sun of righteoufnefs. *Sic fubfcribitur,*

JAMES STEWART.

THere fuffered alfo at the fame time and place, one Alexander Ruffel, whofe teftimony differing nothing in fubftance from the reft, and being in fome things not very conveniently expreffed, it is not thought neceffary to be publifhed at large; only thefe heads in it are remarkable. *Firft*, He declares, That for the fpace of fourteen years, while he heard the curates, he was a perfon given to all manner of licentioufnefs keeping company with the profane; drinking, fwearing, fabbathbreaking, and reproaching the people of God. *2dly*, That the firft field-preaching ever he heard, to which he went merely out of curiofity, it pleafed the Lord to convert him. *3dly*, That the means of his being called out to the help of the Lord's people at Bothwel, was the death of three of his children within ten days fpace, which extraordinary providence impreffed his heart fo, that he durft not fit God's call to that work. *4thly*, He confeffed his having taken the bond for living orderly (as it was called) and with great remorfe acknowledges his failings, in that he took not opportunity to confefs that fin publicly. All the other heads do coincide with the teftimonies of the other four who fuffered with him.

The laft teftimony of ROBERT GRAY *in Northumberland, who fuffered for the truth, in the Grafs-market of Edinburgh, May* 19. 1682.

His Interrogations by a committee of the Council, May 13.

ROBERT GRAY being called before the chancellor, and a committee of council, appointed for public affairs, and interrogate, If he knew John Anderfon prifoner at Dumfries? He declared, he did not know him, but had writ a letter to him; and that letter being produced to him, he owned the same, as he testified under his hand write and subscription, at the end thereof. And being asked, If he thought of the king and government, as is expressed in that letter? He said, he did, and he owned that in his judgment. And being asked, If he thought the king a tyrant? He said, He had written so, and owned it, and that he wrote this letter to John Anderson, as his duty to his brother.

Follows the foresaid letter, which was all the ground of his indictment.

Dear Friends,

I Received yours, and am much refreshed to hear of any in this day, that is holding by the truth, and is helped to witness against the wrongs done to our Lord and Master, which is the main thing that we are called to at this time, by which God is glorified, and which shall bring peace to us at the end of the day. As in answer to that, about owning this tyrant in ecclesiastic matters, I hope, it is without all doubt and debate, with all the zealous exercised Christians in Scotland, that he should not be owned at all in it whatever the time-servers, that will sail with any wind that blows, do, we are not concerned; who are like Esau, who sold his birth-right for a mess of pottage. And as for owning him in civil things, to me it is very clear, now as matters are stated, that he should not be owned: In a word, for his breach of the civil law, his pardoning and setting free murderers and bougerers, and murdering of poor innocents, and making his will a law, and placing none in public trust but these that have taken that black test, utterly to disown the whole work of reformation; with which way I cannot meddle directly or indirectly, without saying a confederacy with them.

There might be more said upon this head, if time would permit; but I think this, with what our late worthies did in casting this tyrant off, and out of the church, might give full satisfaction not to own them in any thing, seeing they have acted for the devil more than ever; and it has prospered more in their hands than formerly. Indeed, if we consult men at this time in the matters of godliness, no wonder we be in the dark; but O beware of that, and fly to the holy word of God. Beware of looking out at any back-door, or halting betwixt two opinions; for of a truth there is a halting this day, that will not be approven of God, in meddling with this malignant party directly or indirectly. It is a thousand to one if they see it. As anent Barscob, and Major Lermont, they got their sentence on Fridy last, to die on the 28. of this instant, and other two, Hugh Micklewraith and Robert Fleming, got their sentence on that day too, and should have died on this Wednesday last; but they have got a remission to the 28. day, and it is reported, that Barscob and the rest have offered to take the test, and they have sent up to the tyrant on that account, to save their lives; and as for John M'Clurg and R. N. there is no word yet what they will do with them; I shall give you an account afterwards. My soul is grieved to see the treachery that is used in the matters of God among the prisoners, and their seeking sinful shifts to shun the cross of Christ. O dear friends, seek to be kept stedfast in the day of trial. Now, I can say no more; but leaves you in his hand, who has brought you to the trial, and can carry you cleanly through it. I rest, your fellow-prisoner and friend,

ROBERT GRAY.

The last Testimony of ROBERT GRAY.

Men and brethren,

I Having got my sentence of death from men, who are unjustly taking away my life, merely for adhering to my principles, and have no matter of fact to prove against me; but only adhering to the truths of Jesus Christ, and testifying against their sinful laws and actions, which my indictment will testify. They take away my life for declining their authority, and calling Charles Stuart a tyrant, and speaking against their test, that they have made to overturn the whole work of reformation, in calling it the Black Test. Now many may condemn me, and no doubt do, in my writing that letter to John Anderson, whom I own as my brother in Christ, suffering upon the same heads in Dumfries prison. I do not much care what the time-servers say; but I hope none of the zealous exercised Christians in the land that are concerned with the wrongs done to their Lord and Master Jesus Christ, will do it; I having a right call to do what I did, he writing to me, and I giving him an answer, in which

I have great peace, notwithstanding it has brought me upon the trial, and my God has owned me in it. And let such as will condemn me, mind that Scripture, *It is God that justifieth, who is he that condemneth?* I bless the Lord, that ever I was honoured to testify against the wrongs done to my Lord and Master Jesus Christ, either by word or write. O wonder! what am I, that ever he should have chosen the like of me, who have been one of the vilest of sinners! If the world had seen me as he saw me, they would not have chosen me, no, not to have kept company with: But O wonder, that his condescending love has not only taken me to be a servant, but to be one of the children of the family! and has said to me, as John xiv. 19. *Because I live, ye shall live also.* He has chosen me, and not I him, John i. 15. Isa. xlviii. 10. *Behold, I have refined thee, but not with silver; I have chosen thee in the furnace of affliction, for mine own sake, even for mine own sake will I do it.* Now, I had his promise before ever I came to a prison, that he should honour me. As Psal. xci. 14. 15. *Because he hath set his love upon me, therefore will I deliver him; I will set him on high, because he hath known my name. He shall call upon me, and I will answer him; I will be with him in trouble, I will deliver him, and honour him.* Now, this is the ground upon which I have walked, and the grip I have got, which I have holden till now; I mean, when I covenanted with my God, to take him upon the terms of his offer. It is a year bygone, being the first week of May, 1681. since I personally subscribed my name to be the Lords; for before that I played many times fast and loose with God, for which I take shame and confusion of face to myself, (which is my due) but since I have been kept free of what formerly I was guilty of, tho' the assaults of Satan have not been wanting. I durst not look back, nor yet take my word again; but desired to act and contend for my Lord and Master Jesus Christ's rights, and not to quit them to any, which he helped and owned me in.

O dear friends, all of you that are contending for Christ's truths, get once a right in himself, and ye cannot then, nor dare not but contend for him: But while ye are in the dark about your interest, ye can never walk upon sure grounds; but like a man walking in the dark, that has hopes of getting to his lodging, but knows not the way: and the thing that steals many of this generation off their feet, is, They go to seek the way from others that are also in the dark of it themselves, and they seek the way from men, and follow the example of men, becaufe they think they are godly men, and by their practice they think they have the image of God; and becaufe of that they follow them, and take their advice, and do what they do, thinking they cannot do wrong; but I am clear of it, that is not the way of God in this dark day, to feek it from blind guides, and not from the true guide Jefus Chrift, *who is given for a leader and a commander to his people*, and ought to be led by none, nor have counfel from none but himfelf; for the Spirit of God fays, Ifa. xxx. 1. *We to the rebellious children, faith the Lord, that take counfel, but not of me; and that cover with a covering, but not of my Spirit, that they may add fin to fin; and walk, and go down into Egypt, and have not afked at my mouth.* O but this is the very thing, that I have feen at this day, efpecially fince I came to prifon. O the treachery againft God, which has been there, which was my only burden and grief, and made me weary of the prifon, and defire to be gone; they taking counfel from men, and placing vile and unworthy men, to agent and plead for them in Chrift's matters, and dare not truft him- with it themfelves; and fo it is no wonder, that he leave them, and they go a black gate. I take the walls of the Cannongate tolbooth (which I was prifoner in near ten months) to be witnefs againft the wrongs done to my Lord and Mafter Jefus Chrift there, both before and fince; and I take the good maintenance they have had, to witnefs to their confcience at the great day of accounts. They had never reafon to complain of wants, or to fay, That our Lord was a hard mafter; and yet they wrong him, moft treacheroufly and cunningly hiding from the eyes of the world their compliance with their agents; and like the whore, wiping their mouth, and faying they have done no evil, and faying, they have peace. O but my foul trembles to think of that peace, to feek peace with the enemies of God, and fay, they have peace in it. I'll not fay, but ye may have peace at prefent, when ye go out of prifon, becaufe you are going home to your idols and Delilahs whatever they be, either your wives or children, or lands or enjoyments; but I will fay this, that if you have wronged the work of God for them, they shall be accursed to you, and prove a snare to you; and then you shall see what peace you will have. Let such as have meddled, or are meddling with these perjured men, see that Scripture as anent their peace, Isa. lix. 8. *They have made them crooked paths; whosoever goeth therein shall not know peace.* And I am convinced of it, that these that meddle with them directly or indirectly, when called to witness for truth, or staged thereupon, and yield to them in their desires that are sinful, shall break their peace with God, and shall hinder themselves to get the bargain made with him; and if they have made it, it will be very much if the bargain stand, without drawing a new engagement, and deep mourning for the wrongs done to him: For our Lord is now taking a narrow look of Scotland, and seeing who did put the hand to the plough to carry on the work of reformation, to banish Popery out of Scotland; and now he is seeing who is countenancing Popery, and this Popish duke, that has gotten in his foot in Scotland, which will be the blackest sight ever poor Scotland saw: But whoever of the nobles or gentry of the land is guilty; yet I will assure you, as sure as the Lord is in heaven, ministers, yea, Presbyterian ministers, are not free of Popery's coming into the land; because they have not testified against it, who should have set the trumpet to their mouth, and have given faithful warning, and so they would have delivered their own souls and the souls of others, whereas now poor things are ensnared; but their blood will be required at ministers hands: and ye that are old wily professors, that have taken the lee side of the brae, and are advising others to do so, ye are not free of the innocent bloodshed in Scotland, and the loss of poor souls, because of your practice of seeming piety and holiness, so ye blind their eyes, and what ye do, that is a godly man, in the town and country parishes, in going to hear the curates, that have taken that black test, or any other thing, because ye do it to save your gear, they follow your practice; but assure yourselves, the loss of their souls will be required at your hands, who are ring-leaders in an evil course, be who ye will, in prison, or out of prison; our Lord is now near his coming, and is begun to tread upon Scotland's sea, and will within a little tread upon the necks of his enemies, and come and deliver his church, which I die in the faith of: But it will be a coftly delivery.

Now, I adhere and give my teftimony to that glorious work of reformation, in reforming this land from Popery. And I adhere to the National Covenant, and Solemn League and Covenant, Confeffion of Faith, Larger and Shorter Catéchifms, Acknowledgment of Sins and Engagement to Duties. I adhere to the teftimonies of our worthies that have gone before, and thefe of late, that are fo much condemned by the Profeffors of this generation; but this I will adventure to fay, that thefe who are condemning them, whom God hath juftified, fhall never be honoured to give a teftimony to the truths of Chrift, and againft his enemies. I adhere to all the meetings and affemblies of the people of God, that have been in Scotland in defence of the gofpel. I adhere to Pentland, Drumclog, Bothwel, and Airfmofs, where our worthies fell; which blood (I die in the faith of it) fhall have a glorious fpring: which quarrel the God of heaven, the covenanted God of Scotland, will refent. I alfo adhere to and heartily join with the Rutherglen Declaration; and I difown the Hamilton Declaration, becaufe it took in the malignant intereft. I adhere to the Sanquhar Declaration, and Queensferry Papers, and the excommunication at the Torwood, as lawful and right, in cafting off Charles Stuart, and the reft of the malignant party: And it fhall be feen within few years, that that party that the Lord ftirred up for that ufe, was in their duty, and thefe that lay by were not. I alfo adhere to and heartily join with that noble teftimony given at Lanerk, againft that black parliament that fat laft, to overturn the whole work of reformation, and made that black Teft, that has defiled the whole land, and made an open door for Popery to come into the land. I leave my teftimony againft all thefe that have taken it, or againft thofe that have or may take favours from men, that have taken that Teft efpecially. I leave my teftimony againft prifoners, who being in upon the account of religion, do tamper any way with thefe black tefters to wrong the intereft of God. Wo, wo, wo, will be to them that give the enemy fuch ground to fay, we are but fanatics, and will do any thing before we lofe our lives, which I myfelf heard fome of them fay, which was a grief to my soul, and did sting me to the heart. I leave my testimony against such professors and preachers, as can sit in such company, and hear such talk, and not resent it; it being an acquiescing to the discourse to keep silence. I leave my testimony against all giving bond and caution, or petitioning the stated enemies of our Lord Jesus Christ. I leave my testimony against all these cess payers, and doing any other thing that strengthens the enemies hands, and against jailor fee paying, for by so doing it says, we have done wrong to them; which I deny that we have done any, but they have done to us.

I leave my testimony against these ministers that sat in a presbytery against worthy Mr. Richard Cameron, that highly honoured martyr of Jesus Christ, and thought to have deposed him from his ministry. I also leave my testimony against that meeting that sat at Sundowal in Nithsdale, which I was a witness to: ye will see it more fully spoken to in that paper of mine which was found at Kelso, which I own, and desire that it may be put in with this *; and they may go together, and my indictment with the letter. I am called to set to my seal to the faithfulness of that worthy man's doctrine, viz. worthy Mr. Richard Cameron, who was the man the Lord made use of to establish me in the faith. I bless the Lord that ever I saw him, or was honoured to be in his company. I bless the Lord that ever I was in the company of worthy Mr. Donald Cargil. I am likewise here to bear witness to the faithful warning these two worthies gave in Northumberland. I likewise leave my testimony against the professors in Northumberland, that *came not out to help the Lord against the mighty;* when I myself gave them warning, some of them mocked at me; for which I will be a witness against them, at the great day of accounts. I leave my testimony against the giving bond to assizers or sessions, or answering their courts. My work, while I am here, is only to witness against the sins of the times wherein I live, and the wrongs done to my Lord and Master. I leave my testimony against these four men that were prisoners in the Cannongate tolbooth, John Gib, and the other three that held his principles; I disown, detest and abominate their principles, though some were pleased to brand me with them since I came to prison. I heartily forgive them what-

---

* This cannot be done, no copy of that paper being found.

faid of me, as I defire to be forgiven of
ch is in heaven.
ne here is but fhort; and I think it need-
y more, the teftimonies of the worthies be-
ued by this generation, that nothing will
and judgments, that tho' an angel fhould
m heaven, it will avail nothing; for no-
e but wrath, wrath, wrath; judgments,
judgments coming on this land very fud-
' eyes fhall be clofed, and I fhall not fee
me for this; therefore I am content,
ɔntent, feeing I get my foul for a prey.
a fhort word to fay to the remnant of the
hat is to be left behind, who was only my
world: my foul trembles to think what
ɔu this day, efpecially thofe of you that
ind in contending for the truths of our
rift: whatever has fallen out among you
ve fallen back, feek to reclaim them, that
·ought in again. Let felf be done away,
and let the way of God be taken in time,
ut fhort that ye will have it: And think
I wait for better times and opportunities;
it, for ye have time and opportunity now,
ɔt have afterwards; and if ye get not to-
y, you fhall meet with fome thing fhortly
you blyth to be together; and *let thefe*
re ftanding, take heed left they fall. Now,
: gone out from us, by complying with
party, and pleading for Baal's intereft, I
ituart's intereft, and taking fhelter under
have lefs hope of them than any. If ye
face to God, and fay, That ye never durft
lefe tyrants and ufurpers, to wrong the
I for the lofs of your life, or gear; then
u of your foul for a prey. Tho' ye have
have in the world, your children fhall fee
d ye fhall have all your wants made up,
et Chrift himfelf.
ftay no longer, nor take up my time no
work is finifhed, and I have fought the
I finifhed my courfe. Strong have been
I trials that I have had from the devil,
ɔth minifters and profeffors, but my God

hath helped me to withstand them, for wl
holy name, and desire to praise him while
let all the zealous godly in Scotland pra
behalf, that he chose the like of me, who
sinner. Now, I am this day free of the bl
in the world. I desire to forgive all m
done to me, as I desire to be forgiven
which is in heaven. But for these who ha
taken away my life, simply for adhering
for no matters of fact, for my part I for
my God shall resent it, with the rest of my
blood, that has been shed on fields and sca

Now, farewel all creature comforts in
sweet societies of the Lord's people, that
delight in the world; farewel holy and sw
which only were my comfort in all my f
all friends and christian acquaintances; fa
brother, and all relations in the world; ai
moon and stars. Welcome scaffold, for
Jesus Christ; welcome gibbet; and we
welcome immediate presence of God, an(
Christ, who only has redeemed me by h
come angels, and the spirits of just men
where we shall never part again. Now,
hands I commit my spirit, that is thine
Lord Jesus Christ; come quickly and re
to my resting place, where my portion is.

ROBE

Account of some of his last words in the co
on the scaffold.

THIS worthy martyr coming out o
to the place of execution, was tak
tom is, first into the town council-house, v
council desired, that he would purge the c
And he told them, that judgment woul'
city, for the innocent blood shed therein,
assure themselves of it, for it was withou
said to him, that he had access to pray
He told them, That he had committed
already. Then they said, if he had not
were there who would pray for him;
round, said, He saw none whom he \
but he had an Advocate with the Father

brought from thence to his execution-place, after a little
difcourfe to the pretended magiftrates of the city, fome
of them being prefent, he fung the lxxxiv. Pfalm, and
read the xv. chapter of the gofpel according to John,
and after the reading thereof, he faid to the multitude,
Sirs, ye would remember that that is the word of God,
and not of man, and that we are to follow no man further than he follows the word of God : And faid, if light
had not come into Scotland, they had been more excuf-
able, but now they have no cloke nor excufe for their fin,
and their wrongs done to God ; and becaufe of defpifed
light, and the defpifed gofpel, there is affuredly great
wrath coming upon them. And then he prayed, and
after prayer went up the ladder, and looking about to
the multitude faid, Sirs, you are feeding your eyes upon me, but what fee you upon me ? Surely you fee not
the wrath of God upon me : but if ye would look up to
the heavens, ye may fee the wrath of an angry God a-
gainft yourfelves. And he faid, I am brought out of a-
nother nation to own that covenant which ye have bro
ken, and to feal it, and the glorious work of reformation
with my blood. Which covenant ye have not only broken, but ye have given it under your hands, that ye fhall
never own God any more, nor have any more of him.
And he bleffed the Lord, faying, Glory, glory, glory be
to his name, that ever he gave me a life to lay down for
him, in witneffing againft his enemies, and the wrongs
done my Lord and Mafter Jefus Chrift. And faid, The
Lord be judge between me and you, who have taken a-
way my life, which of us have been in the wrong to o-
ther ; and affure yourfelves there is wrath, fad wrath,
hanging over this city, for the innocent blood fhed therein. But as for you, who are the remnant of the Lord's
people, I would fay this to you, keep your ground, and
beware of turning afide to one hand or another, and I
will affure you, the Lord will prepare a Zoar for you.
Cleave to truth, and cleave to one another, and as fure
as God lives, ye fhall yet fee glorious days in Scotland ;
for I die in the faith of it, that he is on his way, returning to the land : but wo, wo, wo will be to thofe
who are enemies and ftrangers to him. Then praying a
little within himfelf, when fome bade put him over, and
others cried out, Spare him a little ; he cried, I am ready. Whereupon the executioner threw him over.

The laſt Teſtimony of JAMES ROBERTSON, *who lived in the pariſh of Stonehouſe, and ſuffered at the Graſs-market of Edinburgh. December* 15, 1682.

His Interrogations before the council.

Queſt, 1. IS the king your lawful prince, yea, or not? *Anſ.* Since you have made your queſtions matters of life and death, ye ought to give time to deliberate upon them: but ſeeing I am put to it, I anſwer, As he is *a terror to evil doers, and a praiſe to them that do well*, he is, or is not. *Q.* 2. Were Pentland and Bothwel acts of traitory? *A.* They being in their own defence, and the defence of the goſpel, they are not acts of traitory or rebellion; ſelf-defence being always lawful, which I prove by the Confeſſion of Faith, in that article whereon ye ground yourſelves; which is, That ſubjects may reſiſt unjuſt violence and tyranny. *Q.* 3. But wherein lies his tyranny? *A.* If robbing the privileges of the church be not an act of tyranny, I refer it to be judged. *Q.* 4. Is the king a tyrant? *A.* I refer it to his obligation in the coronation oath, and his preſent actings and practices, in robbing the privileges of the goſpel, with the uſurpation of the churches liberties, and the prerogatives royal of Jeſus Chriſt, the anointed of the Father, in making himſelf ſupreme: and I refer it to perſons at home, and nations abroad. *Q.* 5. Was you at Bothwel-bridge? *A.* Ye count it an act of traitory, and alſo rebellion, which is criminal: bear witneſs of it, and ſo make it evident. *Q.* 6. They ſaid, Purge yourſelf by oath, and ſo we offer to ſet you at liberty. I anſwered, I will ſay no more of it, for when I told the truth to ſome of you, I was not believed. One of them ſaid, Now I will try if ye be a man of parts. *Q.* 7. There was an act of parliament, when the Confeſſion of Faith was made, declaring, that the king was ſupreme, and it was owned by the preſbyterians of that time. *A.* How could that be owned, ſeeing the Confeſſion was owned. And I called for the act, but it was not brought. *Q.* 8. Was the biſhop's death murder? *A.* When I am judge ſet on the bench, I ſhall paſs ſentence thereupon. Being queſtioned further anent it, I ſaid, I have anſwered that already, I will ſay no more to it. *Q.* 9.

Own you Lanerk and Sanquhar Declarations? *A.* I cannot own any thing, till I see and consider it. *Q.* 10. Keep you your parish kirk? *A.* If the minister have ought to challenge me with, he may do it. *Q.* 11. Now as a test of your loyalty, will you say, *God save the King*? *A.* Prayer ought to be gone about with composure and deliberation, and I am not in a composure for it. *Q.* 12. Would ye not seek a blessing if at meat? *A.* If ye were present ye would see. One of them said, These principles will condemn you. I answered, If I be absolved of God, it is the less matter though men condemn me.

The last Testimony of JAMES ROBERTSON.

Dear friends, true lovers of Zion's righteous cause,

IF I could speak or write any thing to the commendation of the covenanted God of the church and kingdom of Scotland; I have surely many things to do it for. 1*st*, That he trysted my lot to be in a nation where he hath set up his pure worship, whereas he might have letten my lot be among the Pagans and heathen nations that know nothing of the true God. Or, 2*dly*, He might have ordered it to be among these that are worshiping Antichrist, that whore of Rome, that monstrous beast, that 'sitteth upon many waters;' whose sentence may be read, Rev. xiv. 9. ' And the third angel followed them, saying with a loud voice, If any man worship the beast and his image, and receive his mark in his forehead, or in his hand,' ver. 10. ' The same shall drink of the wine of the wrath of God, which is poured out without mixture, into the cup of his indignation; and he shall be tormented with fire and brimstone, in the presence of his holy angels, and in the presence of the Lamb; ver. 11. ' And the smoke of their torment ascendeth up for ever and ever: and they have no rest day nor night, who worship the beast and his image, and whosoever receiveth the mark of his name.' &c. So that it is as sure as God is God, and the holy scriptures are his word, according to which all men that have heard or seen it, shall be judged, having the sentence of absolution or condemnation past according thereto. Rom. ii. 12. ' For as many as have sinned without law, shall also perish without law; and as many as have sinned in the law, shall be judged by 'the law.' So that it is clear, that the firſt will ſurely periſh, viz. All infidels, Atheiſts, and Pagans, that know not the true God, nor his law. *And as many as have ſinned in the law, ſhall be judged by the law*, &c. So that whatever vain hopes Papiſts may have of being ſaved, living and dying Papiſts, or whatever charity looſe Proteſtants have upon that account to give them, they are as far from being ſaved in that unconverted condition, as devils which are eternally caſt out of his preſence. 3*dly*, I have him to bleſs for this, that, my lot is not in and among the corrupt Proteſtant churches abroad, Lutheraniſm, and other corruptions and abounding errors, both in doctrine, worſhip, diſcipline, and government, ſectarian, epiſcopal, or eraſtian; but in the reformed church of Scotland, where all theſe things have been caſt over the hedge, as not plants of his planting; and where Chriſt hath been owned in all his three offices, King, Prieſt, and Prophet; tho' alas! he may ſay of us, in a great meaſure, as to the church of Iſrael of old, 'I have planted her a noble vine, but how is ſhe 'become a degenerate plant of a ſtrange vine unto me!' In that day of planting, we could have ſung that ſong, Iſa. xxvi. 1.—' We have a ſtrong city, ſalvation will 'God appoint her for walls and bulwarks,' &c. Lam. iv. 11. 'The Lord hath accompliſhed his fury, he hath 'poured out his fierce anger, and hath kindled a fire in 'Zion, and it hath devoured the foundations thereof.' ver. 12. 'The kings of the earth, and all the inhabi-'tants of the world, would not have believed that the 'adverſary and the enemy ſhould have entered into the 'gates of Jeruſalem.' ver. 13. 'For the ſins of her 'prophets, and the iniquities of her prieſts, that have 'ſhed the blood of the juſt in the midſt of her:' ver. 14. 'They have wandered like blind men in the ſtreets, they 'have polluted themſelves with blood, ſo that men 'could not touch their garments,' &c. This may be our regrete before God, as it is in the ſeventh verſe here in this chapter, 'Her Nazarites were purer than ſnow, 'they were whiter than milk, they were more ruddy in 'body than rubies, their poliſhing was of ſapphire.' ver. 8. 'Their viſage is blacker than a coal, they 'are not known in the ſtreets; their ſkin cleaveth to 'their bones; it is withered, it is become like a ſtick;' &c. And O! how unnatural like were it for the mother to let her child, the son of her womb, perish for lack of the breasts; were she free of the child's blood, it perishing for want of its natural food? And O! how many are this day perishing for want of the lively preached gospel; ver. 3. ' Even the sea monsters draw out the ' breasts, they give suck to the young ones; the daugh- ' ters of my people are become cruel like the ostriches in ' the wilderness.' 4*thly*, I have him to bless for this, that I am not this day fighting against him in an open war; and so bearing arms against him, his work and people, for there is no more in me as of myself, than these that are deepliest imbruing their hands in the blood of the saints. 5*thly*, I have him to bless for this, that ever he hath opened my eyes to see the mystery of iniquity that abounds and hath its seat in the heart, and also in some measure hath given me a sight of the remedy in the blood of Jesus Christ, with his Spirit engaging me to himself, letting me see himself to be altogether precious, making me see that it is better to be *a door-keeper in the house of God, than to dwell in the tabernacles of sin:* Psal. lxxiii. 24. *Thou shalt guide me with thy counsel, and afterward receive me to glory.* Ver. 25. *Whom have I in heaven but thee? and there is none upon earth that I desire besides thee.* 6*thly*, I have his holy name to bless, that ever he made me to know any thing, how small soever, of his controverted truth, viz. The privileges of his crown and kingdom, now when by their acts and laws they have taken his crown and sceptre, and royal robe, and settled the whole government of his house upon a man that is but a worm: But this I believe, his decree will stand, oppose it who will; Psal. ii. 6. *Yet have I set my king upon my holy hill of Zion,* &c. Isa. xlii. 8. *I am the Lord, that is my name, my glory will I not give to another, nor my praise to graven images,* &c. Now, is not that his declarative glory, which that usurper hath taken to himself? yea, he that *leadeth captivity captive,* according to his royal word, will reclaim his own glory; he it is alone that hath given Christ to be the sure foundation whereon all the building is fitly framed: ' That stone which the ' builders rejected is made the head of the corner.' Isa. xxviii. 16. ' Thus saith the Lord God, Behold, I lay in ' Zion for a foundation, a stone, a tried stone, a precious ' corner stone, a sure foundation : he that believeth, shall ' not make haste.' Ver. 17. ' Judgment also will I lay to

'the line, and righteousness to the plummet, and the hail
'shall sweep away the refuge of lies, and the waters shall
'overflow the hiding place.' 7thly, I bless and magnify
the holy name of my God, that hath called me to be a
sufferer for his work and interest, counting it not my
shame, but a high privilege and dignifying of me, when
many famous in this generation have been denied of it,
though indeed most of this generation have brought up
an ill report upon the cross, endeavouring by their practice to render it of none effect; but I have this scripture
for my encouragement, 1 Pet. iii. 13. 14. 15. 16. 17.
*And who is he that will harm you, if ye be followers of that
which is good?* &c. 8thly, I have this great and glorious
Prince to praise for this; and O! let all the true children of Zion laud and praise this only praise-worthy God,
that hath not only called me to bear witness to the truth,
but hath helped me not to deny his name, titles and attributes; for that is the thing that the enemies and u-
surpers of my lovely Lord's crown are seeking, to deny
allegiance to him, *who is given of the Father to be a leader
and commander to the people,* even he, *on whose shoulders
the government is laid,* committing the ordering of his
house to faithful stewards, to order his affairs according
to his own appointment in his holy word, and hath not
left it to the prudence of men, how learned soever. Ga-
maliel that learned Pharisee and doctor of the law, erred in the exposition of the law, not knowing Christ to be
the end of the law for righteousness to every one that believeth.
And seeing these great learned rabbies erred every one in
that which was the great and main end of the law, viz.
Christ, *to whom Moses and all the prophets bear witness;*
now much more shall they err where it is left to their
own wisdom, having no plat-form to walk by, as the
maintainers of the prelatic hierarchy would be at. Solomon was as wise as any, yea the wisest man that ever
was, or ever shall be, and he erred, having the rule of
the law to walk by: Were not all the laws and forms of
the house given by God to Moses, as well for manner of
worship, as the matter thereof?

And further, as to that which is so much pleaded for
by this generation, his authority in civil matters, which
as matters now stand, cannot be given, neither will they
have it without the other: for by their acts of parliament
they have made them equally essential to the crown:

cannot be an authority without a founda-
all say, He hath it from that which he
admiſſion to the government, as he enter-
rms of the coronation oath. To this I
th reſcinded that, in and by that act re-
rſt parliament; for when he annulled and
from which he had his power and autho-
y reſcinded his own authority alſo: So
ie hath no juſt power, having oftener than
 covenants, which were his coronation
which he could not enter the government.
id, That the foundation of his power is
teſt, wherein he is made abſolute ſupreme
l matters and perſons, as well eccleſiaſti-
ʼhat is ſo far from giving him a right,
him a complete monſter, having one head
; and if that authority ſhould be owned.
free-born member of the church of Scot-
Chriſt's myſtical body, and in my bap-
ʼen away to him, and having given my
nce to him as King and head of his own
own that authority, without being guilty
 againſt the King of Zion; and ſo of the
of ſacrilege? 2*dly*, I ſhall thereby deny
o God Creator, under whom the magi-
le in a direct line; he ruling by his own
hich is contrary to our obligations in co-
ng bound in covenant to defend the civil
rties of the crown and kingdom, as we
ts thereof. 3*dly*, That which they have
nning the true ſons of the church, and
kingdom, to death, which is open mur-
:olour of law: Now that it is ſuch, theſe
ve proceeded againſt, being adherers to
od, which is the only rule of faith and
ng God as God, Chriſt as Redeemer, the
 Sanctifier; and they having nothing to
ith, but their adherence to the true Chri-
 and they ſentenced upon the ſame heads;
deepeſt of murder. 4*thly*, Theſe being own-
reformed religion, and all the fundamen-
church and kingdom; and they refuſing
ntence according to the word of God, ac-
:h all ſentences of life and death ought to

pass, as also refusing to judge according to the laws, as they received them at their admission to the government; which was, not to rule the law, but it to rule them, and they to rule the people according to that law, and the people remaining in subjection to the law of God, and the ancient and fundamental laws of the land, and the persons of lawful governors, being made treason; this must certainly not only be a murdering of men, yea, true Christian men, but also a murdering of justice. And thus the land is defiled with blood. Read the sentence of such, Num. xxxv. 33. *So ye shall not pollute the land wherein ye are; for blood it defileth the land; and the land cannot be cleansed of the blood that is shed therein, but by the blood of him that shed it.* Such as are owning and pleading for this present power, let the end of magistracy be considered, Rom. xiii. 3. 'For rulers are not a terror to
' good works, but to the evil; wilt thou not then be afraid
' of the power? do that which is good, and thou shalt
' have praise of the same.' ver. 6. ' For this cause pay you
' tribute also; for they are God's ministers, attending
' continually upon this very thing.' 1 Pet. ii. 14. 'Or un-
' to governors, as unto them that are sent by him, for the
' punishment of evil doers, and for the praise of them
' that do well.'

Now, it is undeniably evident from what is aforesaid, that piety is suppressed, and iniquity nourished, and the sword in their hand used against these that do most entirely cleave to the Scripture rule, and the sworn principles of the church of Scotland, and the ancient fundamental laws thereof. Prov. xx. 8. *A king that sitteth on the throne of judgment, scattereth away all iniquity with his eyes,* &c. Now I dare herein appeal to the sentence of all single, unbyassed, and judicious persons, whether or not the present exercise of their power be not both injustice and tyranny, for there is no public power in the land, but what is founded on perjury, sacrilege and tyranny, and exercised according thereto. And seeing it is so, ye that are owners of such a power, ye must needs be upon the matter, owners of all these; compearing before their courts, and paying them tribute, placing advocates, and pleading your cause before such unjust judges: and more especially such as are prisoners for the truths of the gospel, and so ought to witness a good confession for his trampled-upon truths, who was not ashameed to witnefs a good confeffion before Pontius Pilate, to wit, that he was a King; John xviii. 37. *Pilate therefore faid unto him, Art thou a king then? Jefus anfwered, Thou fayeſt that I am a king. To this end was I born,* &c.

Now, ye who are charging me this day, and others of my brethren, fufferers for truth, to be guilty of felf-murder, and fo a breach of the fixth commandment, which is very falfe, for felf-prefervation muft ftoop to truth's prefervation. Did our bleffed Lord eftablifh an advocate to plead for him? Did that valiant champion Stephen do it? But was free and pofitive in afferting his teftimony. Or did Paul do it? Or fhew me any fuch precept or practice from Scripture? Yea, confider the nature of witneffing, it proveth the contrary. But I prove fuch as do this to be actually guilty of the breach of the fecond commandment, which is, that *Thou ſhalt not make unto thyſelf any graven image,* Exod. xx. 4. For as I have proved before, he is fet up in Chrift's room, and exerciſeth authority in and by that abominable arrogate fupremacy, and having intermixed things civil and eccleſiaſtic, by their acts of parliament, making them both alike inherent to the crown; and fo cannot be owned in neither without facrilegious idolatry, and fo a breach of this commandment; as alſo of the fifth commandment, which concerneth natural and civil parents, which are to be owned and obeyed only in the Lord, which cannot in the leaft allow of any man's being abfolutely fupreme, even in civil matters, it being the ordinance of God, and a lawful magiſtrate the minifter of God, bound to difpenfe his ordinance, according to the rule in the word, and according to the ancienr laws of the kingdom: For in the obeying of lawful power, it is obedience to this commandment: fo upon the contrary, the owning and obeying an unlawful power, (fuch as theirs) certainly muft be a breach of it. And can any deny that to be an owning of them, to eſtabliſh one of the members of their court, to plead for no other effect, but to hale men out of the true principles and practices of the true reformed church of Scotland, when the pannel is called by his lot, to witnefs for them and give a confeffion thereof, before fuch an evil and adulterous generation, thefe being Chrift's truths queftioned; and truth is himfelf, *I am the way, the truth, and the life,* &c. If any fhould object, and fay, they are fmall things. To this I anfwer, No truth is small. Luke. xvi. 10. *He that is faithful in that which is least, is faithful also in much; and he that is unjust in the least, is unjust also in much,* &c. And such as are supplicating the enemies, are guilty here; for a supplication ought not, nor can be given in, but to a lawful power, and for a lawful thing. 3*dly.* Such are guilty, who are coming out of prison upon bond and caution, binding themselves to compear before their judicatories, at such a particular time, or at demand; for we ought not to bind to compear or answer before a judicatory, but a lawful one, such as theirs is not; so that such are actually guilty, but especially such who formerly joined in declining them.

This generation seems to be a generation in a great measure, given up to work all manner of wickedness with greediness, considering what profanity and robbing of God, mocking him and religion, instability, and the giving away his and the church's due: Mal. iii. 7. 'Even from the days of your fathers, ye are gone away 'from mine ordinances, and have not kept them: return 'unto me, and I will return unto you, saith the Lord 'of hosts: But ye said, Wherein shall we return?' ver. '8. Will a man rob God? Yet ye have robbed me: But 'ye say, Wherein have we robbed thee? In tithes and 'offerings.' ver. 9. 'Ye are cursed with a curse; for ye 'have robbed me, even this whole nation,' &c. I am not to take upon me to speak any thing for future times, but this generation seems to have the marks and evidences of a generation of his wrath; fitted for judgment and destruction. Take these Scriptures as an evidence, Micah vi. 16. *For the statutes of Omri are kept.* Isa. xxiv. 1. 2. 3. 4. 5. 6. *Behold the Lord maketh the earth empty,* &c. Now read Israel's sins here, and compare them with Scotland's sins, and see if they be not parallel: And seeing it is so, what can be expected, but the punishments and plagues shall be parallel also. I cannot shake the thoughts of this off my spirit, but that there is a fourfold vengeance to be poured out upon this land. *First,* The vengeance of God, for the intrusions on, and usurpations of his sword, crown, sceptre and robe royal. 2*dly,* A temple-vengeance, which is not a small one, for the laying his sanctuary desolate. 3*dly,* A gospel-vengeance, viz. for the slighting of the great and rich offer of Christ and salvation offered in such purity and plenty. 4*thly,* A

covenant-vengeance, for the great perjury and apoſtacy in the breach of, and falling from the proſecuting the ends of theſe covenants; which the Lord highly honoured this land with, to bring it into covenant with himſelf, and make it Hephzibah and Beulah unto him, Iſa. xxxiv. 5. 6. 7. 'For my ſword ſhall be bathed in hea-
' ven, it ſhall come down upon Idumea, and upon the
' people of my curſe to judgment,' &c. Jer. xxii. 6. 7. 8. 9. ' For thus ſaith the Lord unto the king's houſe of
' Judah, Thou art Gilead unto me, and the head of Le-
' banon; yet ſurely I will make thee a wilderneſs, and
' cities which are not inhabited,' &c. This land hath not only departed from God, in and by their own ſins, in refuſing the rich offer of the goſpel; and breach of covenant; but have homologate that broken and deſpiſed idol's ſin, that hath overturned the work of reformation, by their owning of him now, when he hath taken the whole privileges of Chriſt's crown and kingdom to himſelf. And this I am perſwaded of, that if there be a family in the Chriſtian world, that comes under Amalek's curſe, *viz. With whom he will have war for ever*; it is that family, called the Royal Family; whom, I think, God is about to ſweep off the throne, ſo that no root thereof ſhall be left to exerciſe in the government, Iſa. xl. 23. 24. *That bringeth the princes to nothing; he maketh the judges of the earth as vanity*, &c.

Now, as to the articles of my indictment, whereon my ſentence of death is founded, is, *Firſt*, The owning and maintaining, that it was lawful to riſe in arms at Pentland and Bothwel-bridge: Which I did with great chearfulneſs and boldneſs, they being in their own defence, and in the defence of the goſpel; and took that article for proof in the Confeſſion of Faith, that they have given out to be the confeſſion of their own faith, profeſſing to build that abominable and ridiculous teſt upon; which ſhews, that they are ill builders, the building being ſo far off the foundation. But I refer you to the draught of a paper, which I drew as my teſtimony againſt that teſt; which with the conſent and advice of others, was affixed on the pariſh kirk door of Stonehouſe: And I am of the mind, that this proof, as it did enrage them, *being like a wild bull caught in their own net;* ſo it did give them no ſmall damp.

A ſecond was, ſpeaking treaſon (as they call it) and

declining their authority, which confifteth in this Firſt, when aſked, If their king, or rather their idol were a tyrant? I referred it to his obligations in his coronation oath, to be confidered with his prefent actings and practices, with his ufurpations upon the privileges of the church, and prerogatives royal of Jefus Chrift, *who is the anointed of the Father :* and the refufing to fay, (God fave the king) which we find was the order that was ufed in and among the children of Ifrael, at the king's anointing to that office; and ufed in our own nation at the coronation. Now, this being only due to a lawful king, ought not to be given but to a lawful king, and fo not to him, being a degenerate tyrant: For if I fhould, I thereby had faid Amen to all that he hath done againſt the church and liberties thereof, and to all his oppreffion by unlawful exactions, and raifing of armies, for no other effect, but to deprive us of the hearing of the gofpel, and troubling or molefting the *fubjects*, both in their confciences and external liberties, and alfo their blood-fhed and murders made upon the people of God, and free fubjects of the kingdom; and fo *bid him God fpeed*, contrary to that in the Second Epiftle of John, 10 verfe. And feeing it cannot be given to any that have thus ufed their power to a wrong end, in fuch a meafure and manner; fo much lefs, when they have fet him up as an idol, in the room of God Incarnate. And fhall I pray, To blefs that man in his perfon and government, which God hath curfed? For it cannot be expected, but that he fhall be curfed, that thus ventureth upon the thick boffes of the buckler of God Almighty.

Now, I fhall here give in fhort, an account of my principles, which I fhall do, as in the fight of an all-feeing God. viz I am a true Chriftian, truly anti-popifh, anti-prelatic, anti-fectarian, anti-fchifmatic, anti-eraftian, a true Prefbyterian, owning the true proteftant religion, now owned and profeffed by the poor wreftling and fuffering remnant in Scotland: And whatever men have faid, or may fay of me, I have lived, and now I die thus.

Wherefore in the firft place, I give teftimony to the truth, fulnefs and authority of the Scriptures; and to all the truths contained therein, and warrantable therefrom. 2*dly*, I bear my teftimony to the way of falvation thro' Jefus Chrift; and that by his fatisfaction the moral law was not abrogated, but fulfilled: And that the moral law is as binding on the Chriftian truly interefted in him, this day, as it was that day that it was given to the children of Ifrael; only the condemnatory fentence thereof loofed to all fuch as are believers indeed. 3*dly*, I bear my teftimony to the work of reformation, as it was reformed from Popery, Prelacy, Eraftianifm, and other errors; as it is contained in the Confeffion of Faith, Larger and Shorter Catechifms, Covenants National and Solemn League, Solemn Acknowledgment of Sins and Engagement to Duties, the Sum of Saving Knowledge, Directory for Worfhip, the Caufes of God's Wrath, drawn up by the general affembly of this church, after the evil in meddling with that rotten-hearted malignant Charles Stuart was feen. 4*thly*, I bear my teftimony to the faithful actings of the remonftrators againft malignants and the malignant interefts, which are the very things this day contended for, by the true Prefbyterians of the Church of Scotland. 5*thly*, I bear my teftimony (not to go further back, feeing it homologates the reft) to that noble teftimony given at Lanerk, againft that tyrant, and the teft enacted by the late parliament; which I could not but look upon, in the time of the carrying on of it, and yet doth, that the remnant was therein owned of the Lord. 6*thly*, I bear my teftimony to all the faithful teftimonies of the martyrs that have gone before us, on fcaffolds, in the fields, or in the feas. 7*thly*, I bear my teftimony to all the appearances in arms, for the defence of the gofpel. 8*thly*, I bear my teftimony to the faithful manner of the delivery of the gofpel, that hath been in the open fields, by the faithful and fent fervants of Jefus Chrift, exercifing according to his own commiffion: preaching days, communion days, and fafts, particularly one holden at Auchingilloch by three minifters, two of them now glorified, viz. Mr. Donald Cargil and Mr. Richard Cameron; where the land's guilt was freely and faithfully difcovered. 9*thly*, and *aftly*, I bear my teftimony to the fellowfhip-meetings of the Lord's people particular and general, and my foul hath many a time been refrefhed in them.

Likewife on the other hand, I leave my teftimony againft the public refolutions for taking in that malignant intereft; for which this poor church is this day fmarting, and feeling the weight of that tyrant's hand, for fuch

eager lusting after a king. 2*dly*, I leav[e]
against Hamilton declaration, which is o[ne]
thing with the resolutions. (1.) For tak[ing]
said interest, contrary to the land's engag[e]
nant. (2.) For corrupting the army.
more fully of this, with several other
the excommunication, tyrant's interest, c[c]
is more fully expressed in a paper, intit[uled]
grievances, set down by way of query; whic[h]
ed by a minister being preaching near t[he]
residence, and some falsely accusing m[e]
ministers, and so at ministry: and to she[w]
hearing was not from any schismatical de[sire]
science of duty, judging him deficient an[d]
being faithful. I therefore drew my g[rievances]
presented; and referreth to this and the
paper, as a part of my testimony against t[he]
to a holy God in this backsliding age. 3[dly]
testimony against all unfaithfulness in
For their dark and ambiguous manner o[f]
not giving free, full and faithful warni[ng]
and dangers of our day. (2.) They ei[ther]
leaving off preaching, as if seeming
hazard loosed them from that comman[d]
preach in season and out of season, &c.
edge of their doctrine against the most
land, and taking the faults and failings
Scripture, to defend them in their sinful,
niving and complying courses; which
the Scripture, for these are set down fo[r]
on, not to split upon such rocks. And
professors are guilty also in this matter,
ny it to be a fault, viz. such and such t[hings]
cannot state their sufferings on them. N[ow]
this is a presumptuous sinning, venturing
God is merciful; this is a daring of h[im]
Surely David was not of this mind of it,
' Who can understand his errors, clean[se]
' secret faults.' ver. 13. ' Keep back
' from presumptuous sins, let them not h[ave]
' ver me,' &c. Numb. xv. 30. ' But th[at]
' ought presumptuously, whether he be b[orn]
' or a stranger, the same reproacheth
' that soul shall be cut off from his pe[ople]

ny against that erastian indulgence, and
th them, because they entered not by the
t by the order of the usurper, whereas
ily door. John x. 1. But this I will say,
will not, nor dare not take that usurper's
ey be defiled thereby, *their countenance
he other, and be fatter and fairer in the day
o be proved before the king*, Dan. i. 15.
my testimony against all the hearers of
le tested curates throughout the land; so
gainst the corner of that land, viz. Kilmar-
country thereabout, where I was appre-
I was then perswaded of, and yet am,
ordered, that I might in particular wit-
em for their compearing at courts, sub-
, paying fines, which includeth in it an
nt of a fault, building that which former-
troy, and destroying that which formerly
and that according to God's word; and
merly were leaders in the way of truth,
professors, are now as active by example
he present course, and so are a stumbling
. *Offences must come, but wo to them by whom
'er it were, that a milstone were hanged a-
, and they were cast into the midst of the sea.*
have formerly known the way of truth,
ore stability, and let not your liberty be-
ng block to others. 6thly, I bear my tes-
all profanity and profane persons, against
nd Athiests practical and professed; not
eny the true God by profession, but even
y practice, belying their profession: A-
usiasm and enthusiasts, altho' these black-
ian writers, are pleased to call the way
lowed by the poor remnant, such; yet my
ve always been to be both cleared in mat-
nd practice, according to the word and
his I think, that the Lord is about to let
stumble, fall, and break their necks up-
arnal wisdom, and each of them upon a-
nind this, *That the world by wisdom knew*
seems, it is the nothings of this age, that
se of: *Out of the mouths of babes and suck-
rfect his praise.*

The laſt Speech and Teſtimony

Now, I would ſpeak in ſhort to three ſorts: 1ſt, You that are ſtrangers and enemies to this lovely Lord, let your eſtrangement be done away; break off your ſins by repentance; conſider the hazard you are in, even of eternal wrath and ſcorching hell fire for ever. O this condeſcending love of God, that is laid out in this manner! O ye that are enemies to his intereſt and people, mind that juſtice, even wrathful juſtice, is ready to be poured out upon you! O therefore come off! repent and turn in unto this ſo favourable and merciful a God: leave off your perſecution, come unto him, *there is mercy with him that he may be feared;* and if ye will not return, then his wrath will be upon you to all eternity. 2*dly*, Ye that have ſometimes known what it was to be in God's favour, and had much love and tenderneſs for him, his work and intereſt, cauſe and covenant, as it was reformed in this land, and now are fallen from your firſt love, O endeavour to have in mind the love of your eſpouſals, when ye and Chriſt were hand-faſted: O conſider aright what a great difference there is between your love, faith, zeal, tenderneſs now, in regard of what it was. Therefore take a right look of matters, and weigh them aright in the balance of the ſanctuary, both as to your own particular caſe, and the caſe of his church; and turn to him with ſpeedy and unfeigned repentance; for he that turns aſide to crooked ways, *ſhall be led forth with the workers of iniquity*. O therefore turn in time, leſt *repentance be hid from your eyes*. O! as ye love the glory of God, the good of your own ſouls, and the advantage of the church, if ſuch an one as I may be ſo bold as to invite you, now going out of time into eternity; as ye would not be partakers of the plagues that are to come upon ſuch a generation, come off with ſpeed. 3*dly*, You that are in good terms with God, and helped to keep by his way, break not your peace by turning aſide to crooked ways, entertain love, keep and hold faſt your integrity, in this day, when many have broken the bargain with him, now when the language of many is this, *Theſe are hard ſayings, who can bear them?* And now, that this is his language to you, *Will ye alſo leave me?* O! let this be the language of every ingenuous ſoul, *To whom ſhall we go? for thou haſt the words of eternal life.* Make ſure ſalvation to yourſelves, thereby ye ſhall be the more fit to follow him in this day, when he is calling forth his *of James Robertson.*

narching. Many follow him when the
:ace is flourishing; but they are ill wor-
t, who will not take part with him in the
arpest sufferings; for what is the greatest
at can come from man, coming upon his
;ard of what he suffered for us, even the
" God, which would have prest us down
ugh all eternity: and may not the confi-
s oblige you? I can speak it to his com-
it he can make the cross light and easy,
· it and you both. And seeing everlasting
neath, have you not ground to expect that
his own arm be crushed. He can straw
'ith roses. I dare not say that ever I met
r when the strait hath been greatest, then he
lnefs most. O the rich manifestations that
: soul under the cross! Yea, it is all paved
ho would not go thro' a sea of bloody suf-
m and for him? He is *the rose of Sharon,*
vallies; he is fair and ruddy, the chief among
thousands: O! who can describe him?
' precious object, *altogether lovely.* If he
known, who would not love him? he is
d loving. The soul may solace itself in
: greatest of straits. Now, ye that have
valk worthy of him. O! who knows what
ohn iv. 17. *Herein is our love made perfect,*
ve boldness in the day of judgment; because
we in this world. How is that? *Though*
:et not of the world. Ver. 18. *There is no*
it perfect love casteth out fear; because fear
he that feareth is not made perfect in love.
on of our love is, ver. 19. *We love him be-*
rved us. Now, dear friends, ye that are
) by him, think it not strange tho' the
u, it hated himself: *He was a man of sor-*
inted with grief. If ye were of the world,
' love its own. Should we not be as pilgrims
travelling, seeking an heavenly country.
t for the people of God, and to whom is
ated, but to the weary passenger.
given out by the enemies and professors,
igal of my life, and leading of my two
: death; but they are both false charges:

for I have found more straightness and sted
them, than I can find in myself. As for th
have so much of humanity, that I love my life
not redeem it with the loss of my integrity, an
any of his precious truths. I durst not make
have any favour of the enemies, nor to touch
handle with them, for their dainties or decei
And there is one scripture which at my first
prison confirmed me, Philip. iv. 6. *Be care,*
thing: but in every thing by prayer and supplic
thanksgiving, let your requests be made known un

Now, dear friends, encourage yourselves in
and stand fast in one spirit, striving together fc
of Jesus: Let nothing damp your courage, ze
ness, and faithfulness, for this so lovely a l
let brotherly love always continue. Beware
both on the right and left hand; we have bea
for both, to our sad experience, in this poc
beware of peremptoriness, passion, and pride
may be, and I fear is, a spiritual pride, as w
tural. Carry suitably to these who are wi
to them that are within. Endeavour to hav
in the Lord obtained, and entertained. Mix
of true zeal with the wild sparks of carnal pa
let meekness of spirit, with a christian, godly
ful conversation, adorn the doctrine of God ot
The breakings of the remnant, I may warra
have lyen heavier upon my spirit, than all t
met with from the enemy. And if ye will r
gether, wrath will be upon you. O! for that
they shall be made ' one stick in his hand,' wl
be as in Isa. xi. 13. ' The envy of Ephraim als
' part, and the adversaries of Judah shall b
' Ephraim shall not envy Judah, and Judah sh
' Ephraim.' Ver. 14. ' But they shall flee upor
' ders of the Philistines towards the west, and
' spoil them of the east together,' &c. And
ture, ' Suffer not sin upon thy brother's soul,
' wife reprove him.' Seek to reclaim them tl
len: ' Ye that are spiritual, restore such an
' spirit of meekness.' Follow a gospel metho
of self-seeking, ' And let him that thinketh h
' take heed lest he fall,' &c. I am not hei
to these that are going on in homologating thes

yoking, Chrift-difhonouring, church-ruining, and land defolating courfes; but to the wreftling remnant.

Now death is not a whit terrible to me, 1 Cor. xv. 55. 'O death, where is thy fting? O grave, where is thy 'victory? Ver. 56. The fting of death is fin, and the 'ftrength of fin is the law. Ver 57. But thanks be to 'God, which giveth us the victory, through our Lord 'Jefus Chrift.' I think this is his language to me, Micah. ii. 10. 'Arife ye and depart, for this is not your 'reft: becaufe it is polluted,' &c. 2 Cor. v. 1. 'For we 'know, that if our earthly houfe of this tabernacle were 'diffolved, we have a building of God, an houfe not 'made with hands, eternal in the heavens.'

Now, as to his way with his church, it is myfterious; *his way is in the deep, his paths in the mighty waters;* but the thoughts of this I cannot put off my fpirit, but that he hath thoughts of good and not of evil; to give this poor church an expected end. But I am perfuaded of this, that he hath fome other work ado, before that be accomplifhed, for falling from her firft love, and the great ingratitude for the great and high privileges formerly enjoyed: But be not difcouraged, nor finfully anxious, neither about the church nor the remnant, but wait on God in his own way, and commit all to him, and he fhall bring it to pafs: It may come in a way leaft expected (I have no doubt about it) that his power, infinitenefs, and fovereignty may yet appear.

Now, I declare I am free of the blood of all men, and tho' man had never public fcandal to charge me with, yet I am one of the chief of faved finners. And in refpect of original, actual, and omiffional fin, there hath been as much guiltinefs in me, as might and would have weighed down to the pit the whole world; but my lovely Lord hath fhewed me warm blinks of his love. O for love to give to this lovely Lord Jefus, according to that fcripture, *Come and I will tell you what the Lord hath done for my foul.* Upon the day before I received my fentence, I met with a great meafure, and a full gale of the Spirit, wherein my heart was both melted and enlarged, winning near to him, both alone and with the reft: but a little thereafter going to him alone, I found him hiding, and being fenfible of it, my heart, in fome meafure panted after him, yet abfent; fo going to the word, was directed to 1 John v. 14. 'This is the confi-

'dence that we have in him, that if we aſk any thing
'according to his will, he heareth us. Ver. 15. And if
'we know that he hear us, whatſoever we aſk, we know
'that we have the petitions that we deſired of him:'
Which did in no ſmall meaſure ſettle and comfort my ſpirit; ſo meditating a little, and conſidering how theſe two
could conſiſt together, was anſwered thus; *Becauſe they
have no changes, therefore they fear not God*. And ſince,
I bleſs his holy name, I have had great compoſure of
ſpirit.

Now, according to my bleſſed Lord's command, I am
not prepoſſeſt with malice, or a ſpirit of revenge, but
can bleſs when curſed: As for theſe men that are unjuſtly taking away my life, not only contrary to the law of
God, and the ancient and fundamental laws of the land,
but even contrary to their own law; for what they are
doing againſt me as I am in myſelf, I can freely forgive
them and all others; but as they do it againſt the image
of God in me, and upon his truth's account, and ſo a-
gainſt himſelf, that is not mine to forgive, but I leave it
to him to whom vengeance belongeth, to deal with them
as he may beſt glorify himſelf. Now, I rejoice in my lot,
for it hath fallen to me in pleaſant places; and I have a
goodly inheritance; I would not exchange it with the
greateſt monarch upon earth. O! let heaven and earth
praiſe him, ſun and moon praiſe him: O! all the creation praiſe him, angels and glorified ſaints praiſe him,
and my ſoul ſhall praiſe him thro' all the ages of eternity. Now, farewel all things in time, farewel holy Scriptures; farewel prayer, meditation, faith, hope; farewel
all true friends. Welcome heaven; welcome Father,
Son, and Holy Spirit; welcome angels, and the ſpirits of juſt men made perfect; welcome praiſes for evermore. *Sic ſubſcribitur*,

JAMES ROBERTSON.

The laſt Speech and Teſtimony of JOHN FINLAY,
*who lived in the Muirſide, in the pariſh of Kilmarnock,
and ſuffered in the Graſs-market of Edinburgh, December* 15. 1682.

Men and brethren,

SHewing you that I am condemned unjuſtly by a generation of bloody men, who is thirſting after the

blood of the saints of God, and upon no other account, but for my being found in the way of my duty in the fight of God; glory to his holy name for it, tho' gone about with many failings, much imperfections, for adhering to Chrift and all his offices, as Prophet, Prieft, and King; and for my following him in all his perfecuted gofpel truths. The articles of my indictment, were for, 1ft, My keeping company with the perfecuted people of God, minifters and others, for which, with my whole foul, I blefs him that ever he honoured me with fuch company; and in token of his countenance he hath kept me in that company. 2dly, For my being in company and converfe with Mr. Donald Cargil; (for which, with my whole foul, I defire to blefs and magnify the riches of his grace, that ever he conferred fuch company upon fuch a finful wretch) and Mr. King, Mr. Richard Cameron, Mr. Kid, in particular. 3dly, My refufing to call the bifhop's death murder, which I durft not do, it being God's righteous judgment upon him. 4thly, My not calling Bothwel-bridge, rebellion; it being in defence of themfelves and of the gofpel, which is lawful in God's fight; and therefore I durft not call it rebellion. 5thly, My giving meat, drink, and comfort to the perfecuted people of God; which I did willingly and with my whole heart; and herein I have fweet peace this day; as in Matt. x. 43. ' And whofoever fhall give
' to drink unto one of thefe little ones, a cup of cold wa-
' ter only, in the name of a difciple, verily I fay unto
' you, he fhall in no wife lofe his reward :' Which he hath made out to me abundantly to the full. 6thly, For my being commanded to fay, *God fave the king*, which I durft not do for my very foul; their bidding us to do it in the teft of our loyalty, to fave him in his perfon and government, and authority, which is a perfect owning of him in all that he hath done, in his ufurpation upon Chrift's prerogatives and privileges, they having made him fupreme head in all matters and caufes, civil and ecclefiaftic; which if I had done, it had been a flat denying of Chrift, and a joining with him and them, I mean Charles Stuart, in all that they have done in overturning of the glorious work of reformation in thefe lands, and all the wrongs done to the gofpel and people of God in this day, which would have made me odious in the fight of God, and before the world; for which I blefs

him, he hath kept me from: as the scripture saith, *He that is not faithful in little, will not be faithful in that which is much.* 7thly, Being asked, if I would not pray for the king? I said, Yes. Do it then. I said according to the scripture. They said, he will pray for him as he is a man, but not as he is king, which is high treason and rebellion. Now, my friends, I being conscientious to myself, that my owning him as my king, was a casting off Christ Jesus who is head and King of Zion, and taking on with him, and so would have incurred the wrath of God, and homologate all the blood-shed, and all the horrid bloody abominations they have committed in the land, with avowed defying of the great God. O who dare join with such avowed enemies of our God, and so cast off the society of the saints, and give the hand of fellowship to such bloody and mansworn wretches, that is making it their whole work to root out godliness out of this covenanted land, that the name of Israel shall no more be made mention of: but they will be all beguiled, for Christ will reign till all his enemies be made his footstool.

1*st*, I give my testimony to the sure word of God, which is the Scriptures of truth. 2*dly*, I give my testimony to the way of salvation thro' Jesus Christ, and that by his satisfaction. 3*dly*, I bear my testimony to the work of reformation, as it was reformed from Popery, Prelacy, Erastianism, and other errors, as it is contained in the Confession of Faith, Larger and Shorter Catechisms. 4*thly*, I give my testimony to the Covenants National and Solemn League, and solemn Acknowledgment of Sins, and Engagement to Duties, Sum of Saving Knowledge, Directory for Worship; and to the Causes of God's Wrath, drawn up by the general assembly of the church, after their meeting with the rotten-hearted malignant Charles Stuart. 5*thly*, I bear my testimony to the faithful actings of the remonstrators against the malignant interest, that is the very thing contended for by the true Presbyterians of the church of Scotland. 6*thly*, I give my testimony, not to go farther back, seeing it homologates the rest, to that notable testimony given at Lanerk against that tyrant, and the test, intimated by that late parliament, which I could not but look upon it in the time of carrying on of it, and yet doth, that the remnant was owned of the Lord. 7*thly*, *of John Finlay.* 249

I bear my teſtimony to all the faithful teſtimonies of the martyrs, that have gone before us, whether on ſcaffolds, or on the fields, or in the ſeas. 8*thly*, I bear my teſtimony to all appearances in arms, for defence of the goſpel. 9*thly*, I bear my teſtimony to the faithful preaching of the goſpel that hath been in the fields by the faithful and ſent meſſengers of Jeſus Chriſt, according to his own miſſion, preaching days, communion days, and faſt days, by Meſſrs. Cargil, King, Kid, Cameron and Douglas. 10*thly* and *laſtly*, I bear my teſtimony to the fellowſhip-meetings of the Lord's people, particular and general: my ſoul hath been many a time refreſhed with his preſence in company with them.

Likewiſe I bear my teſtimony, 1*ſt*, Againſt the public reſolutioners for taking in the malignant intereſt, for which this poor church is ſmarting for this day, and feeling the weight of the tyrant's hand, for ſuch eager luſting after the king. 2*dly*, I bear my teſtimony againſt Hamilton Declaration, which is one and the ſame with the reſolutioners, for taking in the foreſaid intereſt, contrary to the land's engagements in covenant. 3*dly*, For corrupting the army, and other things, ſuch as the excommunicate tyrant's intereſt, ceſs, and all other impoſitions of that nature, for the down-bearing of Chriſt's intereſt, doing it againſt a holy God. 4*thly*, I bear my teſtimony againſt indulged miniſters, for their not coming in by the door, but by the miſſion of men, John x. 1. *He that entereth not by the door into the ſheep fold, but climbeth up ſome other way, the ſame is a thief and a robber.* They being entered by the tyrant and not by the door, they are become men-ſervants, and not ſervants to Jeſus Chriſt, and ſo is become an eraſtian party, which hath wronged our Lord and King more than the bloody prelatic party hath done theſe twenty years by-gone, by their renting the churches bowels, and for dividing many a boſom-friend, to the great hurt of the goſpel. 5*thly*, I leave my teſtimony againſt all corrupt miniſters, ſheltering themſelves under their wings, ſtrengthening the ſtakes of that plantation, and for their dark and ambiguous preaching in not declaring the whole counſel of God: 6*thly*, I leave my teſtimony againſt all the enemies and wrongers of my Lord's glorious privileges and prerogatives, all in general. I leave my teſtimony againſt that bloody murderer John Reid, who murdered a wo-

man in the town of New-milns, and no
arms againſt Chriſt and his followers;
and confeſt to me that he had not an orde
againſt that party that carried me to Ed
eſpecially Alexander Gemmil, my neigh
vexed me more than all that party, for he
folk and baptized children, and mocked m
fully.

A line of advice to two or three ſorts of
that are old profeſſors and covenanters i
Scotland, and eſpecially in Kilmarnock pa
ye doing? Where are ye now be when ye
venant, and ſwore againſt Popery, Prelac
faction, ſide and party? How are ye pr
ends of that Covenant, now in the ſight
the oath of God, that ye ſwore with han
the moſt High, and before heaven and e
moon? O my ſoul trembles to think wha
ye are to the young generation, ye who ſh
as the he-goats before the flock, to train t
way of God, and the way of holineſs and
and now ye are leading them juſt the cont
ye not have been more tender of the blood
the young generation, as to turn your b
profeſſion, and turn in with the men of t
tions in all things? O fear the wrath of t
has ſaid, *Shall any break the covenant an*
Now therefore, I deſire, as ye tender y
that ye would turn again to your firſt h
was better with you than it is now. Next
the young generation, men and women, y
ing? Are ye following the footſteps of y
their courſes of defection, joining in hearin
ed curates, anſwering at their courts, jo
worſhip with them, in their abominabl
ſtroying courſes, contrary to the word of
lemn Covenants, and Confeſſion of Faitl
Shorter Catechiſms, the order of the chur
in diſcipline, worſhip, and government;
and I, are ſworn, with hands lifted up to
God, which no power on earth is able
undo, nor free from, no man, nor woma
the name of the Father, Son, and Holy G
fore take heed how ye think to anſwer b

in-revenging God, before whom I am to appear within a little fpace, and before whom I and all the world will ſtand and be judged with righteous judgment.

And likewife feeing that I dare not but fhew you my mind anent fome perfons and their carriage in this day of Jacob's trouble, when Zion is laying wafte and plowing like a field. *Firſt*, I give my teftimony againft thefe men called elders in my own parifh, becaufe of their complying with every courfe of defection and abomination that comes alongſt through the country. *1ſt*, They being thought to be faithful elders in the time of the Prefbyterian government, and then turned elders to the curate Carnagie, and then turned elders to Mr. Wadderburn, that indulged minifter, and now are feffioners to this curate. And feeing this is true, that they have fhewed themfelves to be men of no principles, and the Spirit of God faying exprefly, *Meddle not with them that are given to change;* who can blame me to difown them.

I give my teftimony againft John Boyd, called bailie of Kilmarnock, for his bloody courfes in many things, and efpecially in his uplifting of the cefs and bloody fines, and in oppreffing the poor in their confciences, and laying on of dragoons upon them moſt cruelly, which he laid upon me four times; I wifh God may forgive him for what he has done in that matter.

Now, according to my bleffed Lord's command, I am not poffeffed with malice, or a fpirit of revenge, but bleffes when curfed. As for thefe men that are unjuſtly taking away my life, not only contrary to the law of God, and the ancient laws of the land, but even contrary to their own law; now for what they are doing to me, as I am in myfelf, I can freely forgive them, and all others; but as they do it againſt the image of God in me, and upon his truth's account, and fo againſt himfelf, that is not mine to forgive, but leaves it to him, to whom vengeance belongs, that he may deal with them as he may moſt glorify himfelf. O if I could fpeak or write any thing to the commendation of the covenanted God of the church of Scotland, I have furely many things to fay, for that he tryfted my lot to be in a nation where he hath fet up his pure worfhip; whereas he might juftly have letten my lot be amongſt Pagans, and heathen nations, that knew nothing of the true God. Or, *2dly*, he might have ordered it to be among thefe that are worfhipping Anti-

chrift, that whore, that monftrous beaft,
many waters; whofe fentence may be rea
9. 'And the third angel followed them,
' loud voice, If any man worfhip the beaft
' and receive his mark in his forehead, or
ver. 10. ' The fame fhall drink of the win
' of God, which is poured out without mi:
' cup of his indignation; and he fhall be t
' fire and brimftone, in the prefence of th
' and in the prefence of the Lamb:' ver.
' fmoke of their torment afcendeth up for
' and they have no reft day nor night, wl
' beaft and his image, and whofoever recei
' of his name.' And fo, as fure as God is
holy Scriptures are his word, according to
that have heard or feen it, fhall be judge
fentence of abfolution or condemnation]
thereto, Rom. ii. 12. ' For as many as have
' law, fhall alfo perifh without law.' So i
the firft will furely perifh, viz, all Infidels
and Heathens, and Pagans, that know no
nor his law: ' And as many as have finn
' fhall be judged by the law.' And fo
hopes the Papifts may have of being fav
dying Papifts, or whatever charity loofe
on that head to give them, they are as f
faved as devils, which are eternally caft
fence.

3*dly*, I have him to blefs for this, tha
among corrupt proteftant churches abroa
and other corruptions and abounding error
trine, difcipline, worfhip and governme
Epifcopal, or Eraftian; but in the reforr
Scotland, where all thefe things have bee
hedge, as not plants of his planting, wher
owned in all his offices, Prophet, Prieft, and
may fay of us, in a great meafure, as to
Ifrael of old, ' I have planted thee a n
' thou art become a degenerate plant of
' unto me,' &c. In that day of planting
fung that fong, Ifa. xxvi. 1.—' We nave
' falvation will God appoint for walls a
Lam. iv. 11. ' The Lord hath accompl
' he hath poured out his fierce anger, an

1, and it hath devoured the foundations
. 12. 'The kings of the earth, and all the
f the world would not have believed, that
and the enemy should have entered the
alem. Ver. 13. For the sins of her pro-
1e iniquities of her priests, they have shed
:he just in the midst of her. Ver. 14. They
d as blind men in the streets, they have
nselves with blood, so that men could not
arments.' This may be our regret before
7. 'Her Nazarites were purer than snow,
iter than milk, they were more ruddy in
ubbies, their polishing was of sapphire:
: visage is blacker than a coal: they are
the streets: their skin cleaveth to their
vithered, it is become like a stick, &c.' O
l-like were it for the mother to let the
of her womb, perish for lack of the breasts;
f the child's blood, it perishing for want
ood? And O! how many are this day pent of the lively preached gospel: 'Even
ers draw out the breasts, they give suck
g ones; the daughters of my people are
like the ostriches in the wilderness,' ver.

e him to bless for this, that I am not this
gainst him in an open stated war, and so
gainst him and his people, for there is no
to myself, than these that are imbrewing
eply in the blood of the saints.
: him to bless for this, that ever he opened
ee the mystery of iniquity that abounds,
at in the heart: as also, in some measure,
emedy in the blood of Jesus, with his Spi-
1e to himself, letting me see himself alto-
s, making me to see that *it is better to be a
he house of God, than to dwell in the* pleasures
son: Psal. lxxiii. 24. *Thou shalt guide me
!, and afterward receive me to glory.* Ver.
e *I in heaven but thee? and there is none
I desire besides thee.*
c his holy name to bless that ever he ho-
know any thing, how small soever, of his
:hs, viz. his crown, kingdom and privile-
Y

ges, now when many by their acts and laws have taken his crown and sceptre and royal robe from him, and settled the whole government of his house upon a man that is but a worm; but I believe his decree will stand, oppose it who will; Psal. ii. 6. *Yet have I set my King upon my holy hill of Zion.* Isa. xlii. 8. *I am the Lord, that is my name, and my glory will I not give to another, neither my praise to graven images.* Now it is his declarative glory which that usurper hath taken to himself. Ay, but he that leadeth captivity captive according to his royal will and word, will reclaim his own glory: he it is alone that hath given him to be the sure foundation, whereon all the building is fitly framed, that stone that the builders hath rejected is made the head of the corner, Isa. xxviii. 16. ' Therefore thus saith the Lord God, Behold I lay in ' Zion for a foundation, a stone, a tried stone, a preci- ' ous corner stone, a sure foundation; he that believeth ' shall not make haste.' Ver. 17. ' Judgment also will ' I lay to the line, and righteousness to the plummet, ' and the hail shall sweep away the refuge of lies, and ' the waters shall overflow the hiding-place.'

7thly, I bless and magnify the holy name of my God, that hath called me to be a sufferer for his work and interest, counting it not my shame, but a high privilege and dignifying of me, when many famous in their generation have been denied of it, when so many are denying, and by their practice are rendering the cross of Christ of no effect. O my friends, bless and magnify your God for this, that ye are privileged with these things, and strive to walk worthy of him in your places, callings and stations, and relations, as a husband, as a wife, as a master, as a servant, as a Christian; study to have a blameless conversation, as becomes the gospel, as far as ye can, walk void of offence towards God and man. My dear friends, I have sweet peace in my lovely Lord; he has made my prison become a palace unto me, and he has made me many a time to bless him for my lot, for which my soul shall praise him thro' all eternity. Therefore, my dear friends, let none of you think it strange, concerning the fiery trial, as tho' some strange thing had happened unto me, for it is in his holy wisdom he hath made my lot sweet; for he has made out his sweet promises unto me, one of which is of more worth than all the world, giving me the witness of his Spirit, bearing

of William Cochran. 255
witnefs with my fpirit that I have a right to them all.

Now farewel all things in time; farewel holy Scriptures; farewel all Chriftian friends; farewel prayer and meditation; farewel faith; farewel hope. Welcome heaven; welcome Father, Son, and Holy Spirit; welcome angels, and the fouls of juft men made perfect; welcome praifes for evermore.

Sic fubfcribitur, JOHN FINLAY.

The laft Teftimony of WILLIAM COCHRAN, *who lived in the parifh of Evandale, and fuffered in the Grafs-market of Edinburgh, December* 15. 1682.

Loving Friends,

SEEING I am going off time to eternity, I think it fit now to leave my teftimony to the truths of God. And 1ft, I own the Scriptures, and acknowledge them to be the only rule to the church and people of God at all times, and under all difpenfations. 2dly, Jefus Chrift to be the only Saviour of his people, and head of his church, and fole governour of his houfe. 3dly, I adhere to the covenanted work of reformation, Confeffion of Faith, and the Covenants and Catechifms: And I think it my great honour and glory, that I was born a member of that church, and defire to bear my teftimony to all the privileges of that church: and alfo I defire to bear witnefs againft all her enemies, efpecially againft Supremacy and Prelacy, and all prelatic and Eraftian courfes, and againft all joiners and compliers whatfoever with fuch like.

Now I defire every believer in the church of Scotland, to take a look how matters ftand between God and their fouls, in fuch a day as this; for it feems to me, that that religion which would have done your turn at other times, will not do it now; for his way is now in the deeps, and ye would need look where ye ftand, when fo many are falling; and fee whether ye have made religion your only choice or no: For except Chrift be the only pearl of price to you, and his law your delight, ye cannot hold out; for it feems to be a great work to be felf-denied, and part with all things, when they come in competition with the truths of Chrift. Your going to kirks, and anfwering courts now, when they are founded upon perjury, and feated upon the ruins of the church; I cannot see, but it is a direct contradicting of the work of reformation, which we are sworn to maintain in its purity, in doctrine, worship, discipline and government, for we should not be divided directly nor indirectly; and a joining with the enemies of the truth, when we should neither touch nor taste with the men of these abominations. O look where ye are, and what will be the end, if mercy prevent it not; when once ye are fanged in their snares, ye stand stoutly to the defence of it, and of these that join with them in these ensnaring courses. I desire you would look through the causes, why the Lord contends with this poor land, and leaves them thus to consume away unto dross, for the whole land is involved in perjury, for they are all joining together to destroy that which we were bound and sworn to maintain both in kirk and state.

Ye know that the land was given away to the Lord by covenant, and we, with all our substance, lives and fortunes, sworn to defend it to the utmost of our power. O therefore consider where ye are now, you may date your perjury from the changing of the government, and the couping up of the work of reformation, and your being witness to it, and to the taking and beheading of Argyle and Mr. Guthrie, without either resisting or resenting of it, which is astonishing to me to think upon, for ye were bound to defend the lives of these two men, tho' all your lives should have gone for it: I am put to wonder at Scotland's blindness. Ye may see your crowning and entering into covenant with Charles Stuart hath been a thing contrary to the will of the Lord, for he and all his predecessors have still been known to be in opposition to the ways of the Lord. It seems that the Lord is still contending with the land, and will contend, until he consume him and the land, because the king's sins become the people's sins, when not witnessed against and withstood. Now we know how he hath ensnared the whole land by his acts, but especially his supremacy over the church, and intrusion on Christ's prerogatives; and so many ministers being in the land, and yet have not witnessed against it, but have either kept silence, and thereby declared their unfaithfulness to the Lord, and the souls of them they were set over; for the ministers ought to preach *in season and out of season, and set the trumpet to their mouths,* and give the people warning of every fin, or elfe the Lord will require their blood at the minifters hands; I fear the minifters of Scotland will be found very guilty of this; they have not given the people faithful warning againſt the hearing of the curates and indulged, for the peoples teſtimonies lay partly in forbearing to hear; for they were thurſt in by the king's fupremacy, and entered not in at the door: And the indulged have done more hurt to the church, than all the curates have done; for they were looked upon to be godly men, and poor things not confidering, but following them blindly, not looking to the Scripture, and the government of the church, and fo have broken and divided the people.

And our noblemen and gentlemen, from whom other things were looked for, have deferted the caufe to the ſtain of their memory to after generations. The minifters ought to have given the people warning, and not have been fo tender of men when truth was fo wronged: for the people many of them were like to have taken warning; but we fee that juggling with the Lord firſt and laſt hath been our ruin and wrack, and now we are brought to nothing, and our worldly wifdom is feen to be foolifhnefs with the Lord. But I perceive, within thefe two or three years, the Lord is beginning to let us fee our former ground again; and I defire you his poor people to labour to win at it, and to hold in it, and to be as tender of one another as ye can, without finning againſt the Lord; for we will be all found guilty of the defection in lefs or more: Therefore I defire you to humble yourfelves before the Lord, and to make confcience of mourning and heart-brokennefs and weeping; for if ye had the fenfe of it deeply impreſſed upon your hearts, as I have had fince I was a prifoner, and the heart-breaks that I have had both from one and another, but efpecially from miſtaken friends, ye could not but have weeped with all your heart. But dear friends, be not difcouraged, but hold on; for this way that I am now to fuffer and lay down my life in, is, and will be found at length to be the way of God. There is much need of tendernefs of, and zeal to God's glory, and of watchfulnefs; for I find there are fnares on all hands, and fear fome of the Lord's choice people will be permitted to fall. And likewife, I defire, dear friends, that ye would keep a fpirit of fympathy with one another; I fear your straits be but coming: And I defire, when ye fall upon debates upon the matters of the Lord, that ye would follow the methods of the Scriptures, and his Spirit there, and ceafe from your bitternefs, one of you againft another: *For the wrath of man worketh not the righteoufnefs of the Lord;* but be humbled under the fenfe of the public fins that have caufed us to be fmitten with fuch fharp difpenfations from the Lord. But I think Scotland's cafe is like the cafe of Jonah, who fled from the prefence of the Lord, till he could win no further, and the Lord purfued him unto the whale's belly, till he was forced to cry out unto the Lord. O! that ye would cry, and cry aright with broken hearts, and confefs to the Lord, and forfake. Lay it home to each one of yourfelves in particular, as David did, when he tranfgreffed againft the Lord, and numbered the people. O that ye would plead with the Lord, and come in his mercy, and plead for the young generation, that have not finned away the gofpel, as we have done, and fay to the Lord, What have thefe filly fheep done? O plead hard with the Lord, for I am perfuaded he hath a kindnefs for Scotland; he is dealing with the hearts of fome of the young generation, and as yet he has keeped up a party contending for his work, and will keep up fome witneffing ftill; yea, I think he will ftill keep a contending party for his work and truths until he return again: and I think the hopes of this fhould encourage your hearts.

Now, the main article of my indictment upon which I have received my fentence of death from men, was that I would not fay *God fave the king*, which (as they have now ftated him an idol in the Mediator's room) I could not do, without being guilty of faying Amen to all that he hath done againft the church and people of God, and true fubjects of the kingdom, and the antient and fundamental laws thereof; and have done contrary to that in the fecond epiftle of John, ver. 10. ' If there come any ' unto you, and bring not this doctrine, receive him not ' into your houfe, neither bid him, God-fpeed: for he ' that biddeth him God-fpeed, is partaker of his evil ' deeds.' And alfo ye know, that taking of the name of God in our mouths, is a part of worfhip, and fo a worfhipping of their idol; for before our faces they faid, That he was king over all perfons, and over all caufes; which is putting him in God's room. But they fentenced me, becaufe, faid they, that I difowned authority, which was a diving into the thoughts of my heart. Now, in obedience to what my Lord hath commanded, I can freely forgive, as I defire to be forgiven, any thing that is done to me, as I am in myfelf; but what hath been done againft me upon the account of truth, and fo ftriking againft God, I am not to fet myfelf above him, but I leave that to himfelf. Now, I have great fatisfaction in my lot, and I rejoice that he hath called me to it, and I blefs him that I have been all along helped to join with his defpifed work and people. And now many are pleafed to fay, That I had not been apprehended as a prifoner, if there had not been fome of the fuffering people of God frequently about my mother's houfe; which is a commanded duty, much commended by Chrift; *If any man give a cup of cold water to a difciple, in the name of a difciple, he fhall not want a difciple's reward.* Therefore feeing it is fuch, let none offend at fuch a work, who look upon themfelves as members of that body; what may follow, leave that in the Lord's hand, who doth all things well, and nothing can harm his people, being found rightly in the way of their duty. Now, as to thofe who count the pure way of truth a wild principle, I count it a greater mercy to be wild from the way of finning, than to be tamed thereunto; as, alas! moft of the generation are.

Now, farewel all true friends in Chrift; farewel holy and fweet Scriptures; farewel finning and fuffering. Welcome heaven and the full enjoyment of God thro' all eternity.

Sic fubfcribitur,
WILLIAM COCHRAN.

The laft Speech and Teftimony of ANDREW GUILLINE, *Weaver, who lived in the fhire of Fife, and fuffered at the Gallowlee, Edinburgh, July,* 1683.

My dear friends,

BEING here to die for my deareft Lord's precious truths, I thought fit to leave this with you, as my laft advice. Seek to do good to all in your day. Let your moderation be known unto all men. Study to be employing your God, for there is fudden wrath pronounced from heaven againft all that have been doing, or continue to do evil: for he hath said, Jer. x. 25. *Pour out thy fury upon the heathen,—and upon the families that call not upon thy name*. We had need to know what we shall answer, when we shall come before him, with whom we have to do; for he is a holy God, and *a consuming fire to the workers of iniquity*. Wherefore dear friends, study holiness in all manner of conversation; make it your earnest care to have your conversation as becomes the gospel, and then he will be forth-coming unto you. My friends, I leave you with the Lord, who hath promised to be the God of his people. He is given of the Father to be a leader and commander to his people, and he will lead them. And I entreat every particular person, never to be at rest, till they give away themselves personally in covenant to God, and promise thro' his grace, to be for him, and not for another. I leave you to him, who *leads Joseph like a flock*. If you would have him speaking peace to you in your life, and in your end, cleave to the Son of God and his truths. And remember, if speedy repentance do not prevent, you will utterly ruin your immortal souls. Now, my dear friends, ye that are desiring singly to stand for God, hold on your way, and wait for the Lord, and quit not a hoof of the truth: He will be an upmaking God to you, and he has promised to be a present help to you in the time of your need.

There is a great confluence come here at this time; I would wish with all my heart, they would get good by their coming. I am come here to lay down my life: I declare I die not as a murderer, nor as an evil doer; altho' this covenant-breaking, perjured, murdering generation lay it to my charge, as tho' I was a murderer, on account of the justice that was execute on that Judas that sold the kirk of Scotland for 50000 merks a year. And we being bound to extirpate Popery and prelacy, and that to the utmost of our power, and we having no other that were appearing for God at that day, but such as took away his life, therefore I was bound to join with them, in defending the true religion, and all the land. Every man was bound in covenant, when he had sold the church, they were bound, I say, to meet him by the way, when he came down from London, and have him presently put to the edge of the sword, for that heinous indignity done to the holy Son of God. But it is, alas! too apparent that men have never known God rightly, nor confidered that he is a holy God. O terrible backfliding! they will not believe that God will call them to an account for what they owed to God: But affure yourfelves, as he is in heaven, he will call every one to an account, how they have ftood to that covenant and work of reformation. I need fay no more; but I would have you confider, that in breaking the covenant, we have trampled under foot the precious truths of Jefus Chrift.

Now, being ftraitned of time, I muft leave off writing. Wherefore, farewel holy Scriptures, wherewith my foul hath been many a day refrefhed; farewel fweet focieties with whom I have been, whofe company was only refrefhful to me; farewel my mother, brethren, fifters, and all other relations; farewel all earthly pleafures; farewel fun, moon and ftars. Welcome fpirits of juft men made perfect; welcome angels; welcome Father, Son, and Holy Ghoft; into whofe hands I commit my fpirit. *Sic fubfcribitur,*

ANDREW GUILLINE.

The inhuman treatment this martyr met with ought not to be forgot, as a pregnant inftance of the hellifh rage and fury of thefe perfecutors, and of the Lord's rich grace, who wonderfully countenanced and ftrengthened him to endure the tortures inflicted upon him, with an undaunted bravenefs of fpirit: For befides the tortures he fuffered in prifon, they ordered both his hands to be cut off, while he was alive: And it was obferved by onlookers, tho' (by reafon the executioner was drunk) he received nine ftrokes in cutting them off, yet he bore it with invincible patience. And after the right hand was cut off, he held out the ftump in view of the multitude, faying, *As my blessed Lord fealed my falvation with his blood, fo am I honoured this day to feal his truths with my blood.* Afterwards being ftrangled a little, his head was cut off, and it, with the hands, placed upon the Nether-bow-port of Edinburgh; and his intrails being taken out, his body was conveyed to Magus-moor, and there hung up in chains, on a high pole.

The laſt Teſtimony of JOHN COCHRAN, *who lived in the pariſh of Leſmahego, and ſuffered at the croſs of Edinburgh, upon the 30th of November,* 1683.

BEING brought before the lords of juſticiary, they aſked, Where I went in to the rebels? I anſwered, I went in to the people of God, whom ye call ſo, at Drumclog. They aſked, if I had arms? I told them, I had a fork. They aſked, if I thought it rebellion? I ſaid, No. And they ſaid, What was it then? I told them, it was in defence of the goſpel. They aſked, if I did own the authority? I told them, as far as it did agree with the word of God. Then they aſked, if I would pray for the king? I told them, that prayer ſhould be gone about in decency and order. Then they aſked, if I would ſay, *God ſave the king?* And I refuſed. Then they ſaid, was I not bound to pray for him? I told them, that I was bound to pray for all that were within the bounds of election. Then they ſaid, Was the biſhop's death murder? I told, I was no judge. Then they aſked, if I was at Bothwel? I told, I was. They ſaid, Was it rebellion? I ſaid, No. Then I was taken back to priſon again, and the irons laid on me: but bleſſed be the Lord, that was no diſcouragement to me; for when the ſtorm blew hardeſt the ſmiles of my Lord were at the ſweeteſt. It is matter of rejoicing unto me, to think how my Lord hath paſſed by many a tall cedar, and hath laid his love upon a poor bramble-buſh, the like of me. And O! that I could bleſs the Lord for it, and ſay, ' Come all ye that fear the Lord, and I will ' tell you what he hath done for my ſoul.' And now I am made to ſay, ' That the Lord doth all things well, ' and holy is his name.' And as for my part, I have good cauſe to bleſs the Lord, that ever I was a hearer of the perſecuted goſpel; and however the world think of us, that our lot is hard in a world, yet remember, that he ſaith in his holy word, that ' whoſoever will ' live godly, muſt ſuffer perſecution; and whoſoever ' will not take up his croſs, and follow me, is not wor- ' thy of me.' And ' fear not him that can kill the body,' but he hath ſaid, ' I will forewarn you whom ye ſhall ' fear, fear him that can kill both ſoul and body, and ' caſt both into hell.' And ' if judgment begin at the

' houfe of God, where fhall the wicked 'and ungodly ap-
' pear in that day, when he fhall take vengeance on them
' that fear him not, and obey not the gofpel?' And
now, alas! I am afraid, that even much of the gofpel
amongft us, will be a witnefs againft us; for it was the
judgment of Capernaum, that fo many mighty works
were done in it, and yet they believed not: and yet for
all that came upon it, it was faid to be exalted up to heaven; and then we hear of its being thruft down to hell:
even fo I fear the having fo much light be the plague of
our land; for it was once a praife to all the earth; but
now a mocking, even among the heathens.

And now as a dying man, I do heartily declare my adherence unto all the holy Scriptures of the Old and New
Teftaments; and preaching of that bleffed gofpel, by a
faithful, fent, Prefbyterian, gofpel miniftry. As alfo, I
do, with all my foul and heart, agree with, and affent
unto the Confeffion of Faith, Larger and Shorter Catechifms the Sum of Saving Knowledge; the National
and Solemn League and Covenants, Directory for Worfhip, the Solemn Acknowledgment of public Sins and
Breaches of the Covenant, and Engagement to all Duties, together with all and whatfoever is contained within the forefaid book. And likewife I do hereby heartily
witnefs and teftify againft Popery, Prelacy, Eraftianifm,
herefy, and other errors, efpecially Quakerifm, and whatfoever is difconform and difagreeable to the holy Scriptures, and thefe other found writings above mentioned.
And fick-like I witnefs and teftify my abhorrence and de-
teftation of that abominable and blafphemous teft, which
is now fo violently preffed upon the people, tending to
the deftruction of their fouls. Moreover, I leave my wife
and fix fmall children to the care and protection of almighty God, who hath promifed *to be a father to the fatherlefs, and an hufband to the widow;* and my foul to God
who gave it, for whofe caufe I now willingly lay down
my life: And now I bid farewel to all earthly and carnal
comforts. Farewel all Chriftian aquaintance: And welcome Father Son and Holy Ghoft, into whofe hands I do
commit my fpirit. *Sic Subfcribitur,*

JOHN COCHRAN.

At the fame time alfo fuffered upon the fame heads of
truth, and adhering to the fame teftimony, thefe two pi-

The last Speech and Testim

ous martyrs, John Whitelaw and Arthu
were interrogate upon the fame things bef
or lords of justiciary, and do agree with
martyr in every respect, and express in th
the like satisfaction with their lot, and cl
der the cross, and their adherence to the f
and abhorrence of the same errors.

A Letter from JOHN WHARRY, *wh*
market-cross of Glasgow, June 11*th.*
during his imprisonment, to his mother
tions.

Dear mother, brother and sisters,

I Beseech you, in the name of my sweet
lovely, incomprehensible, matchless, p
tiful and glorious Redeemer, captain and
all his enemies, be not discouraged; for
love cast on me in black nature, who wa
of sin and wrath, I am now, by his ble
made free, by the laying down of his swe
sinners, of which I was one of the chiefest
that I might get life eternal, which is hi
stowed on me: And now, thro' his blesse
vidence, has made choice of poor unwortl
prisoner; who ordereth all things well t
he sets his love on; and *these whom he love*
the end. I do not question his all-sufficien
ther, do not ye question it, but that he
make me conqueror over my inward and
mies. O mother, bless the Lord that eve
a son, and flesh and bones, to be honour
ferer for his precious name, truths and
covenant, and concerns, according to h
his blessed word, which is contained in th
Testaments, agreeable to all truths con
O mother, will ye be intreated for his
give me back again to him in a free-will
am persuaded, that it would please my n
and then it would fare better with me,
O if ye knew what of the kisses of love
got, since I was brought to carts, stocks
unworthy I, that should be honoured wit
ther, I beseech you for his love's sake, t

repine, and thereby provoke the Lord to anger. O bless him, for making all things pleasant and delightsome, refreshful and comfortable to my soul, and my brother's. I cannot express what of love I have met with, since they apprehended me, and my brother. O bless him for dealing so with me. I beseech you, mother, be serious with the Lord, that what he hath begun, he may also perfect in us to his own glory, and for his own work in the souls of all that are within the compass of the decree of election of free grace. I cannot describe him, he is incomprehensible, and he is without compare. O he is beautiful and glorious, strong and almighty, powerful to break through difficulties, and to bring through his own elect: All which is necessary, and nothing less, that his own being cast in the furnace for the trial of their faith and patience, may be helped to endure; for he knows well enough to purge away the dross and the scum of his own elect. O! but some souls he plunges over and over; to others he limits and permits their winnowing by Satan. O! but true faith, believing and casting all the weight upon the promises, will bring you to the accomplishment, if ye endure with patience, he is the same always to poor sinners, to make them to conquer over all their inward and outward enemies, to these that have received him in the precious offers of the gospel, holden out to poor sinners freely, and to poor me: and he hath engaged my heart to fall in love with him, and to follow the blessed persecuted gospel, thro' good report and ill report, upon all hazards whatsoever through his strength. O! bless him, all that is within me, that ever he made me to act faith on his great and precious promises, and also to trust to the faithful outmaking of them to his own in particular straits, and also to the church in general, in his due season, against all oppositions that can come from a tempting devil, and a wicked, conspiring and desperate heart, and the wicked, flattering, deceiving and bewitching world. O! but these be three strong, arch, cunning and subtile enemies! I fear, if this question were asked at professors in the land, If they knew these? They would answer, They knew them very well; tho' I fear the contrary; and it appears much in our day and generation. Wo is us! where is this married land gone to, judge ye? I bless him that he has made me his prisoner, tho' I be unworthy; he has stooped low, and with his delicates has come to me in my irons and cords, in that chamber in Glasgow, with his own wine, apples and flagons. O! if ye knew what a life we have here; if ye knew the want of him, ye would have longed for him, and would not have thought a prison, cords, stocks, irons, hard to bear for his comely presence, and refreshing of our souls. O! glory to his blessed and everlasting name, whose loving kindness lasts for ay. O friends! give all the praise to precious and lovely Christ. O friends! wrestle and hold on; use importunity with him for your bleeding mother-church; for it is not time to be slack. O pray for us, that we may get more and more of his support, that we may be strong in our almighty God, who has done great things for his church, and is beginning to do great things for us in our prison. O! praise him all ye people; it may be nearer to the breaking of the day of our king royal, than ye are aware. God has long been silent, and conscience dumb amongst people. O be ye aware, that ye have not these two, when he arises to make war for all the wrongs he has sustained. We beseech you, in his own name, try whose ye are, what ye are, and in whose list ye are: Know ye not, that true *faith is the substance of things not seen, but hoped for* in him, and will be made forthcoming to the sensible feeling of his own elect.

JOHN WHARRY.

A Letter written by JAMES SMITH, *who suffered for the truth at the market-cross of Glasgow, June* 11*th.* 1683. *to his father and mother.*

Dear father and mother,

I Beseech you to forgive me all the offences I have done to you, for ye know it is natural to children to offend and grieve their parents. Now this I seek in his name, and for his sake, and I heartily forgive any provocations that my father has given me, as I am of myself, and desire the Lord may take a dealing with your heart, O my father. Now, my dear father, seek the Lord that your soul may live; and make religion your main work, and let it not be a by-business to you, but strive and wrestle to get time spent rightly in the fear of the Lord, minding always and at all times, that the eye of a holy and juſt God is upon you ; and be ſerious with God, and deal in earneſt with him, that he would help you to ſelf-denial, to be denied to all things beneath the clouds; and ſtudy to win at mortification, and let your affections follow nothing further than ye can be mortified to it ; and be ſubmiſſive to his holy will. Now the Lord himſelf perſuade you to fall in love with lovely Chriſt : And I deſire the Lord may give you unfeigned repentance, and faith in Jeſus Chriſt, and ſtrength to ſtand out and reſiſt theſe inſnaring courſes, viz. locality paying, and the compearing at courts, and hearing of curates, and the like. Dear father, mother, brethren and ſiſters, quit with me, and give me up to the Lord, who gave me to you. Give me up freely without any hankering and repining ; for he loveth a cheerful giver. I dare not ſay but he has been kind to me ; O matchleſs love ! O praiſe, praiſe him that ever he honoured the like of me with cords on my arms, and ſtocks on my legs; irons have been ſweet and eaſy to me, and no trouble. Now hold up my caſe to the Lord, and doubt not of his faithfulneſs and all-ſufficiency, for he is both able and willing, and he has ſaid, *In all your afflictions I am afflicted;* and he carries his and their croſs both, and he *ſends none a warfare on their own charges.* John. xii. 24. *Verily verily I ſay unto you, except a corn of wheat fall into the ground and die, it abideth alone ; but if it die, it bringeth forth much fruit.* And ver. 25. *He that loveth his life, ſhall loſe it ; and he that hateth his life in this world, ſhall keep it unto life eternal.* And I can ſay upon good grounds, I am well helped of my lovely Maſter in all that I have been tryſted with. I deſire with all my heart and ſoul to bleſs and praiſe the holy name of my God for his love, and that ever he looked on the like of me, a poor ſinful thing. O praiſe him, and rejoice with me, that it is ſo well with me. Now the manner of my taking, was not ſurpriſing to me : I was not afraid, for I dare not queſtion but it was the place, and alſo the time was come : glory to his name in ſo ordering of it. No more at preſent, but have my love remembered to you, and deſires you all to take up yourſelves with your duty. Now I quit you all to him *who is able to ſave to the utmoſt.* Be much taken up in the church's condition, and be not at eaſe in the time of Zion's trouble. My brethren, my advice to you is, to join yourſelves in a ſociety or fellow-

ship meeting, in the strength of the Lord. Now my lovely Lord, give thy blessing to all thine, and pardon the sins of all the elect. *Sic Subscribitur,*
JAMES SMITH.

These two zealous martyrs were precluded from having any formal testimony, by the rage and cruelty of the persecutors, who having suborned witnesses against them, to depone that they saw them kill a soldier at Inchbelly-bridge, in relieving a prisoner there, did presently take them forth to the cross of Glasgow, and with the greatest of inhuman rage, hanging them on a gibbet till they were half dead, caused cut them down, and laying them in that condition upon a cart, carried them to the said Inchbelly-bridge, to be there hung up in chains. And it is worth the recording to the praise of his grace, for whose royal dignities they witnessed, that they endured all these hardships inflicted upon them, with a great deal of Christian magnanimity and alacrity, even to the conviction of enemies.

The Interrogations proposed to JOHN NISBET *younger, who lived in the parish of Loudon, and suffered at Kilmarnock, April 4th, 1683. Sent by him in a Letter to some friends.*

Dear friends,

THE manner of my examination (as I remember) was this: *First Q.* When saw ye John Nisbet? *A.* I did not see him this good while. *Q.* But when did you see him, and where did you see him? *A.* Altho' I could, I would not answer, to discover my neighbours. The major said, He would make me tell, or he would make me sit three hours in hell. I answered, That was not in his power. *Q.* Are ye under an oath that ye will not tell of the rest of you? *A.* I am under no oath but what the Covenant binds us to. *Q.* Took ye ever the communion? *A.* No. *Q.* Did ye ever preach, or expound the Scriptures? *A.* I could never read the Rudiments. Yet (said they) there were men who did preach, that were not learned. I told them I knew none but the Quakers, whose principles I disown. Then said they, say, *God save the king.* I answered, It was not in my power to save, or condemn him. *Q.* Would you not say, *God save your beast,* if it were fallen into a hole? *A.* No; becaufe it is a taking of his name in vain. *Q.* Was you at Bothwel at the rebellion? *A.* Seeing you count it rebellion, it is criminal, witnefs of it. *Q.* Is the bifhop's death murder? *A.* I am not a judge to cognofce upon it. And being afked again my opinion of it, I anfwered, I had faid all that I could fay of it already. *Q.* Was Bothwel rebellion? I anfwered, It was felf-defence, which was lawful. *Q.* How prove ye that? *A.* By that Confeffion which ye build your Teft upon. Then they faid jeeringly, I was a grammarian. *Q.* Own ye a law? *A.* Yes. *Q.* Own ye the law as it is now eftablifhed? *A.* Since ye make your queftions matters of life and death, ye ought to give time to confider upon them. *Q.* Own ye the king in all matters civil and ecclefiaftic, and to be head of the church? *A.* I will acknowledge none to be head of the church but Chrift. *Q.* Who is lawgiver? *A.* Chrift. *Q.* Is the king the king, or not? *A.* He was once a covenanted king. *Q.* Is he the king now? *A.* I refer it to his obligations in his coronation oath, to be confidered. *Q.* Is he your king, or not? I told them, I would not anfwer any more fuch queftions at this time. This is all that paft, for the moft part, except a number of fenfelefs queftions. No more at prefent, but has my love remembred to all friends in Chrift. I am very well borne thro', bleffed be the Lord for it. *Sic Subfcribitur,*

JOHN NISBET.

The laft Teftimony of JOHN NISBET.

Dear friends, and true lovers of Zion's righteous caufe,

IF I could fpeak or write any thing to the commendation of the covenanted God of the church and kingdom of Scotland, furely I have many things to do it for. 1*ft*, That he hath tryfted my lot to be in a nation where he hath fet up his pure worfhip, difcipline and government; whereas he might juftly have ordered it to have been among thofe that are worfhipping Antichrift, that whore of Rome, that monftrous beaft that fitteth upon many waters, whofe fentence may be read, Rev. xiv. 9. 'And the third angel founded, faying with a loud 'voice, If any man worfhip the beaft and his image, 'and receive his mark in his forehead, or in his hand,' ver. 10. 'The fame fhall drink of the wine of the wrath

'of God, that is poured out without mi*x*
'cup of his indignation; and he shall be t*o*
'fire and brimstone, in the presence of h*i*
'and in the presence of the Lamb:' ver.
'smoke of their torment ascendeth up for
'and they have no rest day nor night, wh
'beast and his image, and whosoever rece*i*
'of his name.' 2*dly*, He might have ord
been among the corrupt protestant church
therans, and other corruptions, and abo*u*
but in the reformed church of Scotland,
as the moon, clear as the sun, and terrible a
banners. The day was, when we could h
song, Isa. xxvi. 1. *We have a strong city, sa*
Lord appoint for walls and bulwarks. 3*dly*,
name of my God, that I am not this day
against him, his work and interest; for th
in me, as of myself, than in these that
bruing their hands in the blood of the sa
bless and magnify his holy name, that e*v*
me out of the state of nature, and brough
state of grace and salvation, through the
blood of Christ; and exalted be his holy
hath given me a sight of my own weakn*e*
sight of the deceitfulness of my own evil
mystery, of iniquity abounding there; and
the remedy of the blood of Christ, with h
ging me to himself, and letting me see him
lovely and precious; so that I may safely
is none in heaven or in earth that I desire be
lxxiii. 25. And 5*thly*, I bless and magnify
of my God, who hath given me a sight of h
truths, now when it is come in question,
be head of his own house or not, where
truth clearer in all the Scripture; yet it m
ken of, if ye resolve not to suffer for it.
his name, that ever he counted me worth
him, counting it not my shame, but an
and dignifying of me, when many famou*s*
ration have been denied of it, and are e*n*
their practice to render the cross of Chri
7*thly*, I bless and magnify his holy name
keeped me from denying of his name, i*n*
attributes; for that is the thing which the

furpers of my lovely Lord's crown are feeking to have
me to deny allegiance to him, who is given of the Father
to be a leader and commander of his people; Ifa. xxviii.
16. 'Thus faith the Lord, Behold I lay in Zion for a
' foundation, a ftone, a tried ftone, a precious corner-
' ftone, a fure foundation, he that believeth fhall not
' make hafte.' Ver. 17. ' Judgment will I lay to the
' line, and righteoufnefs to the plummet, and the hail
' fhall fweep away the refuge of lies, and the waters fhall
' overflow the hiding-place' But this may be our com-
plaint, Lam. iv. 4. ' The tongue of the fucking child
' cleaveth to the roof of his mouth for thirft, the young
' children afk bread, and no man breaketh it unto them.'
Ver. 3.—' The daughter of my people is become cruel
' as the oftriches in the wildernefs.' Mal. ii. 8. ' But
' ye are departed out of the way, ye have caufed many
' to ftumble at the law: ye have corrupted the covenant
' of Levi, faith the Lord of hofts.' Ver. 9. ' Therefore
' have I alfo made you contemptible and bafe before all
' the people, according as ye have not keeped my ways,
' and have been partial in the law.' For now it is with
the land as it is in Ezek. xxiv. 7. ' For her blood is in
' the midft of her, fhe fet it upon the top of a rock, fhe
' poured it not upon the ground, to cover it with duft.'
Ver. 8. ' That it might caufe fury to come up, to take
' vengeance: I have fet her blood upon the top of a rock,
' that it fhould not be covered. Ver. 9, ' Therefore
' thus faith the Lord, Wo to the bloody city, I will even
' make the pile for fire great.' For the iniquities of a
land, many are the judgments thereof; therefore we had
need to mourn, for we will all be found guilty of the fins
of the land, in lefs or more. It makes me to tremble, to
think of Scotland's unfaithfulnefs in all ranks, for as it
is with the people, fo with the priefts, for all have wandered out of the way, and followed their idols, efpecially
the fins of the corrupt rulers; Micah vi. 16. ' For the fta-
' tutes of Omri are kept, and all the works of the houfe
' of Ahab, and ye walk in their counfels, that I fhould
' go far from my fanctuary; therefore ye fhall bear the
' reproach of my people.' Lam. iv. 11. ' The Lord
' hath accomplifhed his fury, he hath poured out his
' fierce anger, he hath kindled a fire in Zion, it hath de-
' voured the foundations thereof.' Ver. 14. ' They have
' polluted themfelves with blood, fo that men could not

'touch their garments.' Now his glory
der-foot; but he hath faid, Ifa. xlii. 8. '
'that is my name, and my glory will I r
'ther, neither my praife to graven imag(
Now, is it not his declarative glory, w
per hath taken to himfelf? Yea, but he th
tivity captive, and giveth gifts unto mer
his own glory, for *the government is laid up*
Ifa. ix. 6. Eph. i. 22. And hath put all ɪ
feet, and gave him to be the head of all thin
Now, I being a free-born member of t
kingdom of Scotland, and joining with
mental laws thereof, and they refufe to
tence me according to that law, that
doubt be murder: and further, they refu
cording to the Scriptures, which is an l
nefs. O what will come upon Scotland,
bominations committed therein? Surely
meet with odious judgments. Ifa. xxxiv. ɛ
fhall be buthed in heaven: behold it fhall coɪ
dumea, and upon the people of my curfe to j
I fee nothing appearing in this land, but
the way of truth; for there is no public
the land, but what is founded upon perjᴜ
and tyranny; Ezek. xxii. 6. *Behold, the pɪ*
every one were in thee, to their power to fhɛ
compare Scotland's fins with Ifrael's fins,
zekiel, and fee if they be not parallel. A
are fo, what can be expected, but that the
and plagues fhall be parallel alfo? For
mourning for all the abominations done ir

Now, thefe that are charging me witl
which is a breach of the fixth command,
falfe; for felf prefervation muft ftoop to t
vation. And further, I have that much
that I love my life, but cannot redeem iɪ
of my integrity; but I prove fuch as do
which they would have me to do, are actᴜ
the breach of the fecond commandment, ᴠ
fhalt not make unto thyfelf any graven image
not fay, but it is a worfhipping of image
them in thefe things, now when they hav
felves in Chrift's room: therefore I exho
beware of joining with them in their finɛ

in their plagues, now when they have
, that they will have no king but Charles
ore I think it is our duty to cleave to
ft either quit Chrift or Charles. Indeed
lk pretend to keep both ; but I defy any,
d to a public teftimony, but they muft
ift or Charles; for they will not have the
ut the ecclefiaftic; fo I cannot fee how
ned in either : for by their acts of parli-
e made them alike inherent to the crown :
authority be fo owned by me, being a
ber of the church of Scotland, which is
l body, without being guilty of high re-
God ? And further, he having broken all
ich was the tenor by which he entered into
, and without which he could not have en-
overnment, the covenant being the coro-
hich he hath not only broken, but made it
it fpeaks of them. And further, having
n the Mediator's chair of ftate, which is
de him of authority, even in civil matters.
aid, The land has given him that fupre-
annot take it from him again : To which
y individual perfon in the land hath not
; and therefore is free to reject him upon
n they are called to it. But O ! the fins of
at in departing away from God ; for Scot-
en back like a backfliding hiefer, for they
n like Sodom, they hide it not ; the fhew
enance do witnefs againft them. But,
ll be well with thefe that keep their gar-
or ye will find enough ado when it com-
hould live Chriftians twenty years; there-
time when ye have it ; for if death come
vill not be eafy : but well is that foul that
;ood grounds, That Chrift is all in all to
: worldly-mindednefs, and flavifh fear of
, makes their practice declare to the world,
not worthy the fuffering for, otherwife
: adventure to forfake him, who is alto-
for he will bid none go his errands upon
'ges.
the articles of my indictment, upon which
 death is paffed, is chiefly thefe. 1ft, My

owning it as lawful, my rifing in arm
bridge, which I did with great cheerful
nefs, it being felf-defence, and in defence
for my own part, the only end I had b
was, the glory of God, if I was not decei
I could not think it rebellion, or unlawfi
altho' the laws of men be againft it, who
felves in oppofition to all the commands
It was my difowning the curates to be fai
which I did very boldly; and they faid,
the curates, I difowned all authority, w
fy, that they have fet themfelves in Chri
My owning Mr. Donald Cargil, Mr. J
Mr. Richard Cameron, to be faithful mi
Chrift, which I did, and I blefs the Lo
heard them, and I fet to my feal to the
thefe mens doctrine. 4*thly*, My not prayi
in his perfon and authority, which I durf
ing a perfect owning of him in all that
Some may object, and fay, that I am ag
tures in this, becaufe in feveral places in
ment, we find, that the kings of Ifrael w
that office by the Lord, and obedience
upon enjoined. But this was only done t
and fo could not be to ours, he havir
felf in the room of God incarnate. And
fay, as the children of Ifrael faid, 1 San
we have added unto all our fins this evil, t
becaufe we follow him in things contrar
mand of God. And fhould I pray for th
ferve him in his perfon and government,
ventured upon the thick boffes of the buc]
mighty. If one fhould object, and fay, '
things : To which l anfwer, No truth i
xvi. 10. ' He that is faithful in that wh
' faithful alfo in much; and he that i
' leaft, is unjuft alfo in much.'

Now, I fhall give an account of my pr
fhall do it as in the fight of God. I am
an, truly anti-popifh, anti-prelatic, ¿
anti-fectarian, anti-eraftian, a true Pref
whatever many have faid of me, or may f
lived, and fo now I die. Now, 1*ft*, I cl
in that way of redemption, which he h

for the redemption of sinners; 1 Tim. i. 15. 'This is
'a faithful saying, and worthy of all acceptation, that
'Christ Jesus came into the world to save sinners, of
'whom I am chief.' Ver. 16. 'Howbeit, for this cause
'I obtained mercy.' 2*dly*, I give my testimony to the
followers of the holy Scriptures, for they are the rule
that men are to walk by, and they declare the revealed
will of God to men, anent man's salvation. 3*dly*, I give
my testimony to the work of reformation in the church
of Scotland; and I bless the Lord that I was born a
member of that church, but chiefly against Popery, Prelacy, and Quakerism, and Independency; and finally,
from under all the errors of the church. 4*thly*, I give
my testimony to the Confession of Faith, Larger and
Shorter Catechisms, Sum of Saving Knowledge, Directory for Worship, the order of the church of Scotland, 5*thly*, I give my testimony to the divine worship,
discipline and government of the church of Scotland,
both by kirk-sessions, presbyteries, synods, and general
assemblies. 6*thly*, I give my testimony to the Covenants,
National and Solemn League and Covenant. 7*thly*, I
give my testimony to the faithful actings of the protest-
ers, called remonstrances, against malignants and malignant interests, which is the very thing this poor church
is contending for this day. 8*tkly*, I give my testimony
to all the faithful testimonies of the people of God, that
have been given for that noble work, whether on scaffolds, or in the fields, or on the seas. 9*thly*, I give my
testimony to the faithful actings, of the last martyr; altho' this generation is calling sin a duty, and duty a sin,
because of hazard; for if this generation get leave to go
on in their pernicious ways, they will not believe that there
is a God in heaven to punish such sinners and sins as are
committed in the land. Mal. iii. 9. 'Ye are cursed
'with a curse; for ye have robbed me, even this whole
'nation.'

Now, 1*st*, I witness my testimony against the public
resolutioners, for bringing in the malignant party to
places of power and trust, for which this poor land is
smarting, and bearing the weight of their hands to this
day. 2*dly*, I leave my testimony against that Act of Supremacy, and the Act Rescissory, by which two they
have overturned the whole work of reformation, both
in kirk and state. 3*dly*, I leave my testimony against the

unfaithfulness of ministers, both indulged,
who are sheltering themselves under the win
who have declared themselves enemies to al
and I wonder how they can say, they are
for God, yet never one of them is troubled,
who will; for before my face, one of these n
(viz. Mr. Anthony Shaw by name) he praye
him from the man, that would not pray for
his person and government: To whom I said,
ought to punish evil-doers: Indeed so he do
4*thly*, I leave my testimony against the wror
lovely Lord's crown, all in general. 5*t*
my testimony against the hearers of these p
rates, throughout the land; but especially
ner of the land, to wit, Kilmarnock, for th
kirks, subscribing of bonds, paying of fines
cludeth in it the acknowledgment of a fau
deny we have done, but they have done it to
never a watchman to testify against it. 6
my testimony against paying of the cess, o
thing that may strengthen the hands of evil-
lxv. 11. *For ye are they that prepare a table fo
and that furnish a drink-offering unto that'nun*

Now, I will speak a word to three sorts c
To you that are strangers, enemies to my love
your estrangedness be done away, fly to I
break out in fury against you. O conside
you are to the destroyer, if ye fly not unt
if you fly in unto him he will abundan
Therefore I entreat, that ye would turn
evil ways, and leave off your persecutio
to him, for there is mercy with him tl
be feared; and if ye will not turn, wrath
you to all eternity. A *second* sort, are th
merly have known God, and now are faller
first love: O consider your former ways, anc
to your first husband, lest there be no spac
for all the ways that ye have taken to wir
will not hide you from him who is the great fi
God; and he will bring all your sins, and y
ance, to stand witness against you; therefo
repentance, for ye will find death have enou
itself. A *third* sort, are these who desire tc
way, and to keep themselves from the cry

nefs of thefe times. O ftand faft in the faith; for there is no other burden laid upon you, but *hold faft till he come*. O for that day when ye fhall be made one ftick in his hand, and have fervent charity among yourfelves, and *let him that ftandeth, take heed left he fall*, for ye will find enough ado with it when death comes; therefore let the main thing be your ftudy, and get once that made fure that cannot be taken from you; for ye have many enemies to fight with, if ye win through, for the way to heaven is very ftrait: for it is no wonder Satan feek to tempt poor Chriftians, when he effayed to tempt our bleffed Lord and Mafter. Let none of you think it ftrange, concerning what hath befallen me, for it is in his holy wifdom he hath carved out my lot fuch; and I have been made to blefs him for my lot. O! ftudy to wreftle againft your own corruptions, which are very heavy to me fometimes, but his love hath been great in bringing me out of the ftate of nature, and hath brought me to fee my own weaknefs, and alfo hath given me a fight of the remedy, for which my foul fhall be made to praife him throughout all eternity.

Now, my dear friends in Chrift, ftudy to walk blamelefs in all manner of converfation, as becometh the gofpel; let your light fo fhine before the world, that they may be afhamed that fhall accufe your good converfation in Chrift: for now ye need not think if ye keep the way of God, but ye will have many enemies, both within and without, therefore feek ftrength from him who is able to give it: ye need not think that all the ftock of grace that a man hath, will be fufficient when the trial comes, if there be not frefh fupply given in the time of need. O! wreftle with him, that ye may be hid in the day of his wrath, that feems to be poured out on this generation, for their great treachery and departure from God, the breach of his laws, and fubjecting to the laws of men; but my eyes fhall be clofed, that I fhall not fee it; and I am well content, feeing I get my foul for a prey, then I fhall have no lofs.

Now, as for his way with his church, it is myfterious to me; but this I think is a token for good, that he is taking fome to witnefs for his defpifed and trampled-upon truths, and he will keep fome witneffing ftill, until he return again: but indeed I think it feems it is but very few that will fee him return again in this generati-

The laſt Speech and Teſtim(
on. Now, death is called *the king of terro*
it is not ſo with me; 1 Cor. xv. 55. *O dea(*
ſting? O grave, where is thy victory? 2 Cor
know *if this earthly tabernacle were diſſolv*
building of God, an houſe not made with ha(
the heavens: For which we long earneſtl(
from the body, to be preſent with the Lord,
bet:er.

Now, I declare I am free of the bloo
and altho' men have no public ſcandal
with, yet by original and actual tranſgreſ(
chief of ſinners; but his love hath been gr
feſtations of his preſence hath been great a(
hath not been wanting to aſſault, but ye
name, who hath reſiſted him, and hath
him to get his will. Now, as my laſt wo
mend it to all, to be tender one of ano
ſinning; and be in earneſt with God, fo
death will have enough ado with itſelf; t(
not repentance, left he come when ye a
Now, as for theſe men that are unjuſtly ta
life, only for adhering to the truth, and
end; now for what they do to me, as I am of
ly forgive them and all others, and eſpecial
ed ſoldiers, that do what they do ignor
them; but as they do it to the image o
that is not mine to forgive: but I leave to
vengeance doth belong, that he may do wi
may moſt glorify himſelf.

Now, my work is finiſhed, I have fou
fight; I have finiſhed my courſe; hencefo
for me a crown of righteouſneſs: but le
condemn me read that ſcripture, Rom. viii.
lay any thing to the charge of God's elect?
juſtifieth, who is he that condemneth? For m(
me in pleaſant places; I have a goodly heritag(
not change my lot for the greateſt man
Men and angels praiſe him for this; al(
praiſe him; O! my ſoul ſhall praiſe him,
ages of eternity.

Now, farewel all true friends in Ch
Chriſtian relations; farewel ſweet and h(
farewel prayer and meditation; farewel ſ(
f:ring. Welcome heaven, welcome innum

ny of angels, and the church of the first-born, and the spirits of just men made perfect; welcome Father, Son, and Holy Ghost; welcome praises for evermore. Now, dear Father, receive my Spirit, for it is thine, even so come Lord Jesus.

Sic Subscribitur, JOHN NISBET.

The Testimony of JOHN WILSON, *writer in Lanerk, who suffered at the Grass-market of Edinburgh May* 16. 1683.

His answers before seven or eight of the council April 17*th.*

THE chancellor said, We having called James Laurie, produced to him a letter wrote by you to him, wherein you reprove him for calling Bothwel rebellion: He owned, That it had convinced his conscience, and said, That he was sorry for what he spoke, and we produced him a letter supposed to be writ in answer to yours, which he denied. Tell us, who wrote that letter? John Wilson answered, I will not tell by whom, only it was not wrote by James Laurie. *Q.* Who is the lady mentioned in the end of the letter? *A.* I dare not burden my conscience to tell. *Q.* Do you own authority? *A.* What authority? *Q.* What think you of Bothwel? Was it not unlawful to rise in arms? *A.* I dare not say that it is unlawful; for the confession contained in your test says, *Article* 15. *That it is a good work to defend the life of the harmless;* and however God hath disposed of those people, yet I suppose the Lord will own these, that hearing their neighbours had been worshipping God, (for defending themselves against those that sought their life) were in jeopardy of their lives, thought it their duty to rise for their relief. *Q.* Was Pentland rebellion? *A.* The oppression of these poor people was such, that the then rulers condemned Sir James Turner for his cruelty. Upon this, one answered, That he knew Sir James went not the length of his commission. *Q.* Was the bishop's death murder? Have me excused gentlemen, I will not answer to that. Being urged farther, he said, It being nothing concerning my salvation, I do not pry into it. Upon this they said, Did Bothwel concern your salvation? To which he replied, There are none that engage themselves in service to God, but it behoves them to be at his call, and it being for saving the life of the harmless, I durst not sit God's bidding, Q. Are you a minister? A. No. They here alledged some of his letters importing so much: and being desired to read the place, they read somewhat about a call to some ministry, nothing relating thereto. Q. Will ye not condemn the bishop's death as murder? A. I dare not, for fear God having justified some of these actors, they should rise in judgment and condemn me. Q. Is there no other way but to rise in arms against the king? A. I suppose you have read Bishop Honnyman's answer to Naphtali, wherein he says, *A king may be resisted, in case he should alienate the kingdom to strangers:* And that being granted, religion being taken away, was as dear to us as any outward interest. One replied, The bishop got little thanks for that. Q. Think you it lawful to rise against a state that are not of your opinion? Will ye go to Bothwel again? These questions they gave him not leave to answer, but ordered him to be taken away, asking, if he was a captain at Bothwel? Which he assented to.

His Answers before the council, April 17.

OMitting what he answered at his former appearance, which needs not be repeated (their questions being always the same) they asked, is Bothwel rebellion or not? A. No, It being for the defence of the harmless, who for hearing a preaching, and defending themselves; and the confession of faith contained in your test, says *It is a good work to defend the life of the harmless.* Q. Then you approve of the test; Will you take it? A. I am not speaking of the test, but of the confession of faith therein contained. Q. Think you it lawful to rise against magistracy? A. Will you condemn the reformation from Popery carried on by John Knox? We are not come here (said they) to answer questions, but to ask: But (replied he) the answering of that to me would be a full answer by me to your question. Then said the bishop, The reformation was good, but the way of carrying it on was ill. A. That is a marvellous thing, to think God would approve the actors in such actions, and yet the method be ill; and they to have a most solid peace in these actions, and to have such a mouth to defend it, as all the wits in their days could not be able to withstand, as will be clear to any that read the history of the reformation. O, said they, he has read the history of the reformation: Ay, but you will not find it in the Scripture, said they, that the people may resist the prince, for then they take the magistrates part on them, and therein declare themselves to be above their prince. *A.* The people resisted Saul, and would not let him kill Jonathan, (1 Sam. xiv. 45.) The bishop said, The people were in the wrong. *A.* The Scripture never condemns the deed. *Q.* Do you own authority? *A.* Authority may be taken several ways; 1. For the simple command of the prince. 2. For the more public command of the prince and people. 3. For a power a prince may be clothed with by a people. 4. For a prince's right to govern. In all which ways Gouldman's Dictionary, the ordinary expositor of words, takes it. And in the first two senses, since many both of the prince's edicts, and public acts of parliament, are directly against Presbyterians and Presbyterian government, to own it in these senses, I should deny myself to be a Presbyterian. In the third sense, since the people have clothed the king with the headship of the church, I cannot own that; because the eleventh article of the Confession of Faith, contained in the test, says, *That office belongs properly to Christ alone, and that it is not lawful for man, or angel, to intrude therein.* As for the last sense of authority, His right to govern, I have not seen through it. *Q.* Will you venture your life on these things? *A.* My life is in God's hand. After these questions they set down, That he was a captain at Bothwel, and an imperfect recital of his words, which they desired him to subscribe; but he refused.

F At his last appearance before the criminal court, the advocate accosted him thus, Tho', Sir, you have been a rebel, and tho' ye have studied to draw that poor man Laurie to the gallows; yet you see how merciful the king is to these men, (which were four who swore the test) and there is place left to you for mercy, if you will not obstinately persist in your opinion. He answered, I have neither done any deed, nor given you an account of any opinion, but what I have justified from the confession of faith, which you have lately sworn; from the ancient reformation, which ye cannot condemn; and from the concessions of your own doctor. What! (says Perth) Will you justify your taking arms at Bothwel? *A.* Your own test justifies the defence of the life of the harmless. The advocate says, All the indulged, yea, almost all

Presbyterians condemn it. Then says he, '
before sentence, for there is no place left f
mercy after sentence. *A.* I will not; bt
that one day, all sentences will be canvass[ed]
great judge of heaven and earth.

Follow some reasons of his answers, and re
thereupon by himself.

WHEN I was on my journey betwixt E
Lanerk, and several times before,
dered the bold testimony of Stephen, Act
Ye stiff-necked and uncircumcised in heart, &c
testimony, Acts v. 30. *Whom ye slew, and*
tree: And his desire that with all boldne[ss]
make mention of the name of Jesus: And l[a]
mise, Phil. i. 28. *In nothing terrified by you*
&c. I say, considering these, I resolved t
most of freedom with the council; but b
this town, and having considered, that th
fired to pick such quarrels with any in o
as might give the least umbrage to the wo
stice of their dealing. 2. Considering that
fessed friends we are judged imprudent; ye
demned, that they stick not to say, that w
in our own death. 3. Their own public ;
still bearing, That our design was not reli
vetousness, to possess ourselves of the gove
eviting of these, I resolved to be as cautio
without prejudice to truth. So that t[
swers for defensive arms out of the test, w
sworn; from the concessions of their gre
and from the deed of their predecessor cou
some present were members, I thought it]
diculous thing to make me condemn that w
ratified by an oath, their great doctor had
their predecessor council had approven. Bt
have God's approbation in demeaning my[
what I did therein in faith; I took that r
15. *Be ready always to give a reason of the*
you with meekness and fear. And as I thoug
son to bless God, that had guided my ton
was not a whit concerned either with sha
I came back to prison with a heart sorry
have left these two questions of the chan

'bought I it duty to rise in arms against a
pinion? In answer to which question, I
er I had occasion, I would have been
ing them, the question was wrong stat-
ght state of the question was, 'When a
the true profession of godliness sworn to
and persecutes the owners thereof.' The
; 'If I would have gone to Bothwel a-
rght if such a question came in my way,
ld them, *That I behoved to be at God's call.*
was sorry that I had not been nimble e-
taken opportunity, when the question a-
was moved, to have testified against the
leadship and sinful acts against God's
my omission, occasioned thro' their con-
ored me humiliation after I returned to

ond examination, as I desired opportuni-
ainst the headship of the church, and o-
destroying God's work, so I got opportu-
discharged my conscience: But yet there
left to exercise me with; and that was, 1.
op said, That it were a distracted act for
nate the kingdom to strangers, that I said
act of more distraction to destroy religion.
ng the words of the eleventh article of the
ist the headship, I should have said simply,
ul to presume to intrude on that office;
nfession itself calls them blasphemers, and
g his word. 3. When the bishop said, It
way to carry on reformation by the sword,
ied their present practice and violence in
onsciences; and have said, since they look-
ience as so tender a thing, to beware of
by oppression. I know I have an infirmity
f hand, anent which I hope all God's peo-
e the rule of bearing one another's infir-
I am sure that the Lord hath not suppli-
ese answers, for my further exercise. As
hy I said, I could not see thro' the denial
the last sense, (for tho' I could not see
being such an abominable stating of them-
tinual opposition unto God and godliness,
own it) the reason that moved me to say,

that I could not fee thro' it, was, I defire to tread the paths of our old reformers, who delayed the cafting off authority, till they had a probable power to back it; yet afterwards confidering his breach of covenant to us, and thefe deeds done by that authority, that in any well guided common-wealth, would annul his right; I thought I had worded authority ill in the laft fenfe, and that it had been more proper, I had faid, ' I could not ' fee thro' the denying of obedience to fuch commands ' as were indifferent, or according to God's word:' And indeed till God had furnifhed us with a probable power, I could never fee thro' this; and I am verily of that opinion, that we having lufted for a king, got him in God's wrath; and that fince we have entered into covenant with him, God will take his own way to take him away in his difpleafure, and will not let it be by our hand: tho' I grant that his breach of paction to us loofeth us, our paction being ftill conditional, to own him in defence of religion; and my earneft defire is, There may be no difference among Prefbyterians anent this, for I have a ftrong opinion, that God will take that queftion out of the way fhortly.

As for the bifhop's death, I could not call it murder, becaufe of Jael, Ehud, and Phineas, their facts; Jael ufing that expreffion, ' Turn in thither; and that there ' was peace between Heber the Kenite and Jabin;' Jael being of that family, and whatever may be alledged againft thefe as extraordinary acts, and that to do fuch deeds is to take the magiftrate's power; I am fure Phinehas was a prieft, and it was none of his office to kill any man, and yet his fact is commended. Next, Knox his preaching to, and abiding with the killers of Cardinal Beaton; and Calderwood's hiftory, which was approven by the affembly, calling them men of courage and refolution, whom God ftirred up: Next, the lord Ruthven and others killing a companion that abufed Queen Mary by his ill-counfel, and yet approven in Knox's hiftory: Therefore if the killers of the bifhop, having a zeal againft the blood-thirftinefs of that wretch, and being deeply affected therewith, and with love to the brethren, whom he like a wolf, was feeking to have devoured, and had devoured, flew him, I durft not call it murder; but if the actors were touched with any thing of particular prejudice or other by-ends, I am very con-

dent that Scripture of avenging the blood of Jezebel
pon the houſe of Jehu, would not ſuffer me to juſtify
: So not knowing the actors hearts therein, I could
either ſay, yea, nor nay; but Chriſtians ſhould judge
haritably. I forgot likewiſe to tell them, that the biſhop of Glaſgow's laying down his gown, upon making
ſhe act explanatory, might be an aggravation of my ſin,
I ſhould own the king's headſhip over the church, which
had really refolved to ſay, but forgot.

*ollow the reaſons why he refuſed at firſt to ſupplicate the
council for a reprieve, being importuned by his relations to
do it.*

UPON the 7th of May 1683, being deſired to petition, I anſwered, I could think upon no petition,
or arguments that could be acceptable with them, but
ſuch as were either directly or indirectly a receding from
that I had profeſſed: The reaſon of my petition was
moved thus, to ſeek a longer time till I was better adviſ-
ed anent my anſwers given to the council. To which I
anſwered, That would ſay to all the world, that for as
tenacious as we were of our principles, yet we might
ſeem to call them in queſtion; and it might ſay, that I
was preſſing with others to die on theſe principles, that
death put me to a ſtand anent myſelf; and ſo I ſhould
give ground of hardening to enemies. 2. It was moved,
that thro' my confuſions ſince I came to priſon, I ſhould
ſeek a reprival. To this I anſwered, I durſt not ſlander
Chriſt's croſs, wherein every ſtep to me hath been mercy and truth; and my rebellious fleſh needed no leſs
conform to my own acknowledgment to God) than what
was come to ſubdue it: and that I could not well ſee
thro' that, fearing it would be bad company ſo near my
death; that I firmly truſted all ſhould work for my well;
and to ſay that, were to contradict my conſcience and
God's goodneſs, and make me contradict my own prayer,
viz. ' Let neither fleſh nor ſpirit be moved and failed, leſt
enemies rejoice.' 3. That I ſhould petition, that I might
have a longer time, ſimply to prepare for eternity. To
which I ſaid, I could not do it in faith; for ever ſince I
came to priſon, God has made me believe, that he who
has begun a good work in me, would alſo finiſh it; and
that he would perfect that which concerned me, accord-

ing to his own word; and however little a bufinefs this may feem in the eyes of the world, yet to me it imports my going to another airth, for perfecting and finifhing of this work begun by God: Then if they refufed it, they might taunt and fay, Whatever confidence he had at his death, yet it is gotten of a very fhort fpace; and if a reprival fhould be given, they might at my fentence fay, I was their debtor for it. And befides all this, I fear, when I come back to God for prefervation, he fhould fend me to the broken ciftern I had been hewing out, Jer. ii. 13. And I know, if confcience would permit me to do it, enemies would think, either he is lying, in pretending want of preparation, and fo it is the beft time to hold to him, when he has committed fin; or otherwife they would think, I were fpeaking truth, and fo fay, the only beft way is to hold to him, when he is tottering.

Notwithftanding all thefe reafons againft petitioning, he regrets it, that his relations induced him to fupplicate twice; Firft, on account of his wife's cafe, who was then great with child, and in danger of death thro' grief: Next, on his own account; whereupon he obtained a reprival. During which time he had a conference with Sir William Paterfon; which being on the fame heads with his anfwers before the council, for brevity's fake are omitted.

The laft Speech and Teftimony of the faid JOHN WILSON.

NOW, being called to lay down my life, which I declare I do chearfully, I do declare, I adhere to the Confeffion of Faith; anent which, for exoneration of my own confcience, I am under a neceffity to leave this caution, in reference to that claufe contained in chap. xxiii. § 24. viz. That "infidelity, or difference in reli-" gion, does not make void the magiftrate's juft and le-" gal authority," &c. That the compofers having an eye to the Pope's fcurvy ufurpations, to dethrone proteftant kings, and difpofe of their kingdoms, under the notion of hereticks, did put it in: yet I could find no further proof for that in the Scripture, but what only refpects Chriftians fcattered up and down in a heathenifh empire; and that it can be no prejudice againft depofing

a proteſtant king, turning Papiſt or Pagan; ſince among
people profeſſing God, the idolater ſhould die the death;
or then it would ſeem to juſtle with Queen Mary's de-
poſition in our ancient Reformation : Deſigning offence to
none hereby, but the ſatisfying of my own conſcience.
Alſo I adhere to the work of reformation, former and
later: and I think our catechiſms well worded, for e-
rading of errors. As alſo the Solemn Acknowledgment
of Sins, in anno 1648, and Engagement to Duties; Covenants, National and ſolemn League; and particularly
to the government of the church by a parity of miniſters,
and ſubordination of preſbyteries, ſynods, and general
aſſemblies, according to the Preſbyterian way; as being
the moſt exactly according to the word of God, and as
tending moſt to the furtherance of purity and godlineſs;
and I profeſs myſelf a member thereof, as being reformed from prelacy and Eraſtianiſm, &c.

I leave my teſtimony againſt the Indulgence, as making a breach of the ſweet unity, that ſhould have been a-
mong Preſbyterians, and as depending on the magiſtrate
as to the exerciſe of their office; and for their over-ween-
ing love of eaſe; and for being bound up as to the ſhew-
ing of public duties, and reproving of public ſins; and
for refuſing the exerciſe of their office, to theſe without
their pariſh, of marrying and baptiſing, denying themſelves thereby to be miniſters of the church catholic, and
declaring plainly thereby, they will follow the injunctions laid on them by men. Yet I adviſe all the godly to
leave off hatred towards them, and to cheriſh any thing
that may look like good in them. I leave my teſtimony
againſt the paying ceſs, the payment whereof is a perfect teſt of the payer's adhering to the rooting out of conventicles, as the rendezvouſes of rebellion, and acknowledging the king's grandeur over church and ſtate, as it
is preſently eſtabliſhed by the laws of this realm; this being the very narrative and foundation of that act; and I
have found the indulged averſe to condemn it, the narrative of their licence being ſomewhat ſibb thereto. But
as to the other public burdens, ſuch as the common re-
venue of the crown, or locality (tho' I ſpeak not this to
juſtify myſelf, theſe not being my tentations) I deſire a
tenderneſs to be uſed to all ſuch as have not clearneſs
herein, in reſpect the apoſtle ſeems to difference them,

1 Cor. x. 28. ' But if any man say unto you, This is of-
' fered in sacrifice unto idols, eat not.

I leave my testimony against hearing of curates, especially by profest Presbyterians; as being contradictory to the Covenants, binding us to the uttermost of our power for the extirpating Prelacy. Our active power being stopped, our next should be to leave a testimony by suffering, and as being contrary to the rule of faith: For what Presbyterian can pray for a blessing to that ordinance, where the chief dispenser is a blasphemer, by swearing the Test; wherein the headship of the church, Christ's prerogative, is sworn by them to pertain to a man: and as being expresly contrary to that scripture, John x. 5. ' My sheep hear my voice, but a stranger they ' will not follow, but flee from him.' And here I think it not amiss to add the words of Philpot, that learned and godly martyr, of the joiners of the papistical church, seeing the reason he gives holds good here. " We can " do no greater injury to the true church of Christ, " (whereof he is the only head) nor to seem to have for- " saken her, by cleaving to her adversary; and that " God's jealousy in the day of vengeance will cry for " vengeance against such, unless they cleave inseparably " to the gospel of Christ; and that there must be no " counterfeit illusion with them in this; and there must be " no presence of the body there, we being commanded to " glorify God, as well in body as spirit." These are his words imperfectly, yet truly, as I remember; and since the prelatical church, has not Christ for her only head, the reasons hold still good.

I could heartily wish that all the serious godly would leave off their joining with the Indulgence; for in respect (to my own view) it has been attended with a coldrifeness as to public sins, a glewedness to the world, and an infatuateness as to approaching judgments; and, lastly, being a countenancing of them in that compliance with enemies. But since I have little hopes thereof, I wish all the seriously godly to be tender towards such, whose eyes are not enlightened to behold the evil of it, and to restrict their withdrawments to persons of their own number, who recede from what they profess; since the end proposed by that rule (*withdraw from every brother that walketh disorderly*) is *to make ashamed*, it cannot be supposed to attain its end any where else: and to stu-

which may be moſt edifying to all men,
done to edifying.
teſtimony againſt that abominable Teſt,
.ct of Supremacy, and all other acts over-
rk of God, and againſt all the blood ſhed
unt.
think no man coming before the council
ge the king's authority ſimply, (conſider-
oathed with one of the royal prerogatives
, viz. The headſhip of the church, where-
blaſphemy for man or angel) unleſs they
ving him that uſurped title. And this is
ny ſuffering, mainly, for affirming Chriſt's
the church, to be his prerogative alone,
caſion of the brunt of the ruler's anger.
ave a moſt ſolid peace; for Chriſt ſays,
ir witneſs to that truth, that he was a
I think that my ſufferings are merely a
; ſufferings. And tho' ſome ſay, I might
ing as to this confeſſion; I ſay, I durſt
y lips, they themſelves having that in the
Faith, in their Teſt, which I affirmed,
t is a blaſphemy for man or angel to uſurp
is the great heat of malice ſtated hereon:
) piece of my ſufferings yields me more
can any Chriſtian come before them ac-
uthority ſimply, without being guilty of
t being declared eſſential to the crown,
Cargil well notes in his teſtimony. And
ieſtion of authority being propounded, a
open door to witneſs againſt the encroach-
l's rights. I underſtand ſomewhat more
of this ſtate than I did; and conform to
eptions, you may take it up thus:
aving thro' ſtraits abroad, been comple-
robably ſupplied by Papiſts, lies under en-
introduce Popery; and for that effect,
od to overturn the hedge of church-go-
diſcipline, and turn out all honeſt-heart-
id force people to a compliance with hire-
ch men's conſciences; and, from one de-
:r, to bring in Popery; but he being a
d to pleaſures, (and whiles counteracted
) loving eaſe; wherefore Papiſts practiſe

to put him in mind of his engagements, by aiming at his life. He finding himſelf in this ſtrait, and being in ſtraits thro' his laviſhneſs to court ladies, thir ſtraits muſt be ſupplied by the king of France and the Pope; and for requital thereof, the management of the government muſt be turned over to his brother, who muſt have a cardinal, and ſome Jeſuites to contrive the myſtery of iniquity, and bring this land to Babylon. In order thereunto, ſtateſmen muſt be ſet up, who are emulators of others, and men that ſtudied to pick quarrels with others, and then comes a general mittimus from court, to act after ſuch a method of cruelty: For the Jeſuites know, where two contrary parties act this game, they will be ſure, for fear of their places, to conſent to go alongſt to the utmoſt of cruelty. The next myſtery is to conveen the whole country by circuit courts, as guilty, ſome of treaſon, ſome for one tranſgreſſion, and ſome for another (the whole country being generally guilty by their law) and force them to riſe in arms; and then gather Papiſts, and take occaſion to burn and ſlay all the country over. The Lord in his mercy take them in their own net; but I fear Popery ſhall once overſpread. And I am really of that opinion, that God ſhall root this race of kings, root and branch, away, and make them Zeba and Zalmuna-like, not only for taking God's houſe in poſſeſſion, but alſo emitting in their laſt printed proclamation or indemnity, that they reſolved to root out the ſeed of the godly, under the name of Fanatics.

My advice and humble requeſt to miniſters is, to be tender toward any this day that has zeal, tho' knowledge be not ſo great; and to be leſs fearful of outward danger, and more active where perſecution hath been hotteſt, where they may have any freedom. My advice to all profeſſors is, to lay no impoſition on miniſters conſciences; and that for the Lord's ſake, they would ſtudy to take ſome in among them, that have light and judgment to withſtand the flood of defection and Popery that is like to overſpread the land. And again, I leave another advice to miniſters and profeſſors, that where any have ſuffered for their conſciences, they would be ſparing to condemn them.

I come now to declare my firſt engagement with God, which was about ten years hence; which was thro' reading of the Fulfilling of the Scriptures, and ſcripture

ontained, and the grounds of out-making
gave a check to my atheifm, which is
in all mens hearts. The next was Gray's
ıyer; and the laft, Guthrie's Trial of an
ift: all which, God fo powerfully laid
ɔnfcience, that I then covenanted with
at that time I could not get the faith of
ret I had a refpect to all his ftatutes; fo
was a moft fweet book to me; and I took
me for near a year thereafter in ftudying
noft pleafant time that ever I had in my
it was a burden to me to turn me to my
; in the world. I found religion fharpen-
natural parts; yea, bring me, who was
ft anxious, fretting, grudging, creature,
iefs and ferenity in crofs providences, that
' there were neither hell nor heaven, re-
:ward to itfelf. And I was fo taken up
racious condefcendency, that his name
ng; yet durft I not draw a conclufion of
d perfeverance; yea, was put to queftion
, upon account of the quality of my re-
meeting with Guthrie's Trial of a Sav-
Chrift, I found fenfibly, that fwallowed
in love; but I found this, that there is
ellent piece of the armour of God, than
falvation, and which Satan is moft bufy
ın to keep it off. I found likewife, as
grace grew, that prefumption grew; that
vhat I had gotten, I could walk alone:
, ' Without me ye can do nothing,' was
fad coft. But after all this fweet time,
, moft fweet time, falling more and more
ırldly affairs, I found an impoffibility to
t in bufinefs, and fervent in fpirit; fo that
ı thefe, abated that life which I had; and
love grew to outward things, fo decreaf-
and life I had attained; yet fo as all a-
hat God has ftill been holding me by the
efire, with fubmiffion to other mens judg-
I think a perfon falling in love with god-
ting with God, to have a refpect to all
hout exception, counting the coft, and fec-
:hemfelves impreftable, and believing that

Chrift, who was the author, will be the finifher of fuch a work; I fay, I cannot think that ever God will part with fuch, who do fo covenant with him: yea, it has been a comfort to me, when I could fee no more of my intereft in him, but that I faid, 'Thou art my God.' And as I cannot conceal the loving kindnefs of God, fo upon the other hand, without complements, as the words of a dying man, I look upon myfelf as the moft worthlefs abject that ever free love has paged and waited upon thro' the world, compaffed about with fo many fins, and cloathed with fuch a perverfe nature; but it is he with whom I made the bargain, makes crooked things ftraight, and rugged places plain.

Next, I advife all fufferers to beware of propofing to themfelves, to do this and the other thing, for fafety of life, which is finful; for if fuch a falfe mind be in folk, ' God will lead them forth with the workers of iniquity;' and they will not mifs ftumbling-blocks to be laid before them. I fay this to them who have finned, and yet continue in the furnace; I fear that be their doom, Jer. xxii. 10. ' They fhall go from their native land, and return no more.' As for you that have tefted, that which has been a terror to me, may be now a terror to you; ' It is ' impoffible for thefe who were once enlightened, and ' have tafted the heavenly gift, if they fall away,' &c. by putting Chrift to open fhame, ' to renew them to repent- ' ance.' As for unconcerned folk, I fhall only fay this, Think ye nothing of mens choofing death before life. I know I have gotten Roman gallantry caft up to me, fince I came to prifon; but for my own part, I could never hear tell, that it fet up the head of it in the world, to face a gallows, fince the word of hell became fo rife in the world. But let me tell you this one thing, That tho' I have read of fome fingle ones dying for opinion, (not truth) yet could I never read of a tract of men, fuch as has been in Scotland thefe twenty-two years, laying down their lives for a naked opinion, fo calmly, fo folidly and compofedly, with fo much peace and ferenity. As for my own part, I am a man naturally moft timorous, yet the Lord has made fufferings eafy. It might do you good to enquire into the caufe of our fufferings, fo owned by God. It is a bad caufe that is defended with fwords, and beating of drums on fufferers. And befides the Lord has forced a teftimony from the mouths of several of our dying adversaries, and from the mouths of executioners and apprehenders. Yea, in this place, some Psalms they (being clear of the application thereof to themselves) would not suffer them to be sung. And as to professed Presbyterians, too many of you for your unconcernednefs, I am sure the Lord says, ye shall drink of another sort of a cup, that is brewing for you, shun it as you will, by your compliance. As for our really concerned friends, I pray the Lord to protect you, and multiply his grace towards you. I am confident, when you are beneath the rod, ye shall find it an ease to your own smart, however great a lift you have taken of others sufferings.

Next, I say to all that come under the rod, let no terrors of men, nor temptations of Satan anent eternity come into your mind; but go to God with them, acknowledging your unworthiness of his protection and counsel, and you will find him faithful, 'not to suffer 'you to be tempted above what you are able.' It is no new thing to be assaulted with 'terrors without, and 'within with fears.' The Apostle, a most experienced Christian, wanted not this. I see a Christian to be a most passive creature in his own salvation; yet there must be an All of diligence, otherways the roaring lion will soon get advantages. And you must know this, that the sufferers have a large allowance; and altho' his own want not in their sufferings the faith of adherence to him, yet ye must not think to sail that way in a bed of roses to heaven; but that ye must have fire in your trial; I mean, a deserting-God as to apprehension; yet wait patiently, and at length he will incline his ear, and you shall not want experience to say, ' For a moment lasts his wrath.'

And now, I leave my dear wife, children and sisters upon the Lord, who gave me such sweet refreshing relations, and desire all the people of God to be kind to them; and I bless the Lord he has enabled me to quit them to him: and tho' the Lord has made every one of them so sweet and so pleasing to me, that I have been forced to curb my affection with the bridle of religion; yet herein bless the Lord, he has given me heart to go thro' my cross with forgetfulness of all; yea, to be most unconcerned in the tears and weeping of my relations.

And now, I leave all God's people, and others, with

this, That his cross is beautiful; yea, t]
occasion of escaping prison since sentence
not without a check of conscience have
tho' I did petition, yet there was (to me)
ends therein: *First*, They designing to ma
that I would not seek my life; and I desirin
suffering clear to their own consciences,
And *next*, if any thing ailed my wife, I might
at their door. But I would advise all to be
for there must be frequent consulting wit
reasonable judgment to discern their sna
their main design to ensnare. I advise any
fering, never to quit with the faith of ad
they shall not want the faith of assurance;
I came to prison, I saw and believed God'
was love.: and having emptied me of all p
ferers, and of all my own righteousness,
with him, and take him for all, and beli
on him, and to have recourse to him, for g
necessity, and give me a believing (tho' to
hensible) of ' seeing him as he is, and kno
' as I am known of him.'

Now I die, commending to all the peop
duty of unity, conform to 2 Tim. ii. 22. '
' with them that call upon the Lord with
And that, 1 John i. 7. ' If we have fellov
' another, the blood of Jesus Christ his
' from all sin.' I do not say this to make
joining with these I testify against,

Sic subscribitur,   JOHN

This worthy judicious martyr being of
his testimony in several papers, and conve
cretly by parts; by reason of the strictnes
cutors, who searched the martyrs about
much severity, could not get it reduced to
fore it is hoped the candid reader will no
if he finds the method altered a little from
the manuscript, seeing there is nothing i
phrase of the author changed, but only
put in their proper place of the testimo
few things less material being left out for

The last Testimony of GEORGE MARTIN, *who suffered at the Grass-market of Edinburgh, upon the 22d of Feb.* 1684.

My dear friends,

AFTER four years, and near four months captivity and bondage, for this glorious and honourable use of Jesus Christ, for which I have been kept sometimes in bolts and fetters, night and day, without fire and other necessaries; and now at the end of the foresaid space, being sentenced to die, I thought it fit to signify to you why I was so sentenced, as the adversaries give it forth: and it is thus; I could not own nor allow of the king's authority, as it is now established, nor pray for him in a superstitious and idolatrous manner, nor call the late prelate of St. Andrews, and the late king's death murder, nor Bothwel-bridge rebellion, and abjure the Covenant: all which I refused, and could do upon no terms.

As to the first, I could not own nor allow of the present government, as it is now established, because it is derogatory to the crown and kingdom of our Lord Jesus Christ, in robbing him of his royal prerogatives; in 'their ' setting of their threshold by his threshold, and their posts by his posts, and the wall between him and them, they have even defiled his holy name, by their abominations that they have committed,' Ezek. iv. 3. 8. and, Ezek. xliv. 6. 7. 8. ' And thou shalt say to the rebellious house, even to the house of Israel, Thus saith the Lord God, O ye house of Israel, let it suffice you of all your abominations, in that ye have brought into my sanctuary strangers uncircumcised in heart, and uncircumcised in flesh, to be in my sanctuary to pollute it, even my house, when ye offer my bread, the fat and the blood, and they have broken my covenant, because of all their abominations. And ye have not kept the charge of mine holy things: but ye have set keepers of my charge in my sanctuary for yourselves. Shall even he that hateth right govern ? and wilt thou condemn him that is most just ?' Job xxxiv. 17. Who durst do it and be guiltless ? And moreover, ' Which say to the seers, see not; and to the prophets, prophesy not unto us right things, speak unto us smooth things, prophesy 'deceits. Get ye out of the way, turn aside out of the 'path, cause the holy one of Israel cease from before us,' Isa. xxx. 10. 11. And I cannot, nor dare not pray for him so superstitiously. 1*st*, Because it imports a set form of prayer, which is most superstitious, and that which is their dreadful design. 2*dly*, It imports idolatry, like unto the cry of the people made mention of Acts xix. 34. who had a cry for the space of two hours, of that idol, 'Great is Diana of the Ephesians,' which was rejected by some of their own sort, with some kind of reason, tho' Heathens, and much more ought it here. 3*dly*, Another reason why I cannot pray after such a manner, is, I find when prayer is rightly discharged, and seriously gone about, in the manner, time and place, as is warranted by the word of God; God is thereby worshipped and honoured: and if irreverently gone about, he is dishonoured, and his name profaned, and taken in vain, which is abomination to him, and which he saith, his enemies do, and for which he will not hold them guiltless. 4*thly*, I dare not pray so superstitiously for him, because I find Jeremiah three times expresly forbidden to pray for a people, not guilty of all the things that he is guilty of, though he be guilty of all their sins, and many others also. See for this Jer. vii. 16. where it is said, ' Pray 'not thou for this people, neither lift up cry nor prayer 'for them, neither make intercession to me; for I will 'not hear thee.' Jer. xi. 14. ' Therefore pray not thou 'for this people, neither lift up a cry or prayer for them; 'for I will not hear them in the time that they cry unto 'me for their trouble.' And Jer. xiv. 11, 12. ' Then said 'the Lord unto me, Pray not for this people for their 'good: When they fast, I will not hear their prayer.' Psal. xliv. 20, 21. ' If we have forgotten the name of our 'God, or stretched out our hands to a strange god; shall 'not God search this out? for he knoweth the secrets 'of the heart.' 1 John. v. 16. ' If any man see his bro-'ther sin a sin which is not unto death, he shall ask, and 'he shall give him life for them that sin not unto death. 'There is a sin unto death; I do not say, that he shall 'pray for it.' I fear some sins in this land have too near bordering with that sin. Innumerable scriptures are to this purpose, but these may suffice at present. Another thing makes me scruple, because they command no moe prayers to be prayed, ' save unto thee, O king,' Dan. vi.

dare not pray it, becaufe all the profane
is have it always in their mouth, efpeci-
are drunk; and if I do what they do, I
they go: but bleffed be the Lord, who
ed me from the paths of thefe deftroy-
his was fpoken when I was before them,
rbear to fpeak any more as to this quefti-

ftion is, in order to the prelate's death,
murder or not? Murder I dare not call
Eglon's, Sifera's, and Balaam's deaths,
;ment of God for his fearful apoftacy and
;ether with the horrid murders commit-
n the faints and fervants of God. The
)f the death of the late king; whether it
not? I am not much to meddle with it;
ioufands that were flain in England, the
:ommitted, by the Irifh, in Ireland, and
uughter of the Proteftants in Scotland,
ughts of heart, that it was a fatal ftroke.
Whether Bothwel-bridge was rebellion?
it was fo or not, may appear, if ye con-
r engagements to that effect. And 5*thly*,
ind adhering to the covenants? We an-
y before the court, That in all the Scrip-
·rantable, both to make covenants, and
:m, and that there was never a covenant
that which was punifhed by fignal judg-
ues by the Lord. Thefe were the an-
ictment, whereupon the fentence of death
ot anfwering to fome of thefe queftions;
ft lay down my life. And if this be not
iftian nations bear witnefs, if ever the like
y chriftian kingdom heretofore.
ig ftraitened for want of time and other
I cannot fay much more to you. Only
you as my laft advice, That you would
ep the way of the Lord fincerely, and not
them that are given to fuch changes,
many plead for, and are given to this day;
uld not be fo formal in many things, con-
fs, and the work and worfhip of God.
r be feared, will give many a beguile,
be mended. As firft, I befeech you, be

more obfervant in keeping the Lord's da?
times in the morning, and in fpending t
in worfhipping of God fincerely: Take
thoughts, words and actions. And whe
apart, I mean of humiliation, give God t
and notice what fuccefs ye have had, an(
found the work thrive and profper among
lefs difputings even in things feemingly r
be more in examination and edification
felves and others: And believe it, a wel!
will be helpful to fpend the week well.
bouring to have your converfation aright
will be a noble prefage to begin the fabba
ye fpare of your ordinary diet, beftow it
and needy. There is this among many,
be religious, which is odious, That they
it to be called religious, and yet they h?
fcruple to do wrong, and fpeak wrong
towards them. I befeech you fin not, t
no eye to fee you but God, either by doir
You will never perform religious duties ar
at this, that ye dare do wrong in no kind
'juftly, love mercy, and walk humbly v
Alas! it is fad to fee and hear judgmen
multiplied, and fin fo much increafing.
tendernefs one towards another! and of a
nefs and zeal for God, give yourfelves
prayer one with another, and one for an(
with him in behalf of his church, and ru:
born down, and that he may return to
pity his people; and be importunate wit
left the ruin thereof be found to be und
I fear you may expect judgments to come
this finful land; fo that ye will think, h?
that wan away before they came: Theref
you as would in any meafure efcape the d
that is coming on this finful generation, ke
and be free of the finful abominations co
in; and for witnefling againft them, we ?
our lives this day.

And now as a dying man, and a dyir
join with, and approve of all the Holy S
of the Old and New Teftament, both (
and promifes therein. As alfo I agree v

of George Martin. 299

book, called the Confeſſion of Faith,
and Shorter Catechiſms, Sum of Sav-
Directory for Worſhip; and particu-
, and allow of the two Covenants, both
lemn League and Covenant, Acknow-
s and Engagement to Duties, with all
in the forenamed book. As alſo I do
y my diſlike of the breaches and burn-
enants, and of all other horrid abomina-
ture. And likewiſe I abhor and deteſt
r joining with the enemies of our Lord
d more particularly of bonding, bargain-
ing, or putting them to do hurt, any
to any of the Lord's poor afflicted, born
g and diſtreſſed people. And in like
and deteſt all communing with, ſpeak-
f, or eating or drinking with any ſuch,
neceſſity. And in like manner, I teſti-
that dreadful, blaſphemous, and abomi-
ed teſt, and of all pretended magiſtrates
vhich have taken the ſame, and of all
join with them; or of payers of fines
ofpel, or tranſacting or colleaguing with
anner of way, upon the foreſaid account.
ate too much covetouſneſs in priſoners
capacity to maintain themſelves, and
me to other poor, mean (tho' charitable)
join heartily with the teſtimonies of our
ethren, who ſuffered either formerly or
kewife I join my teſtimony to a faithful
, by faithful Preſbyterian, lawfully cal-
ized miniſters, and lawful magiſtrates
wered, as is agreeable and warranted by
l, and none other. And notwithſtanding
th not admitting of magiſtracy and kingdo hereby declare and make it known to
t I do allow of lawful authority, agree-
mable to the will and command of God,
er, as much as any man in my ſtation in
ccounts a land happy and bleſt, in hav-
g of ſuch.
ing honoured to die for adhering to the
lie this ſame day, being the 22d. of Fe-
do hereby forgive all perſons all wrongs

The laſt Speech and Teſtimony

done to me, and wiſh them forgiveneſs, as I deſire to [
forgiven of God. And now I leave all my friends ai
chriſtian relations to the good guiding of Almighty Go
and bid you all farewel in the Lord: Farewel all worl(
ly enjoyments, and created comforts. And welcome F
ther, Son, and Holy Ghoſt, into whoſe hands I comm
my ſpirit.

GEORGE MARTI[

Together with this martyr ſuffered John Gilry wrig]
in the pariſh of Haunam in Teviotdale, whoſe indictme:
was founded upon the ſame heads, and his teſtimony
much of a piece with his. He dies admiring and prai
ing free grace, adhering to the truths of Jeſus, and firn
ly truſting in him for ſalvation.

The laſt Teſtimony of JOHN MAIN, *who lived in t,*
pariſh of Weſt Monkland, and ſuffered at the croſs of Gla
gow, March 19. 1684.

IT cannot be expected, every thing conſidered, th:
ye ſhall have ſuch a teſtimony under my hand, as]
have had from the hands of many that have gone befo:
me: but ſeeing God in his infinite wiſdom hath ſeen
fit to bring me upon the ſtage for truth, I thought m·
ſelf bound and obliged in his ſight, to teſtify before tl
world, my cloſs adherence to his written word, and wh:
is conform thereto. And firſt, I teſtify my adherence :
the Bible, the Old and New Teſtament, as the only ar.
alone rule of faith and obedience. I know, it ſtands n(
in need of my approbation; but to let the world knov
I die not as a fool, I think it my duty to aſſert my a(
herence unto it, declaring, that I take it for my onl
rule, rejecting the traditions of men as not canonical. :
I teſtify my adherence to the Confeſſion of Faith (ſayin
nothing to that 4th article of the 23d chapter, but onl
that it is miſconſtructed, and made uſe of for another en
than ever the honeſt and faithful miniſters of Jeſus Chri
had before them, when they gave their approbation (
the ſame) and Catechiſms Larger and Shorter, our Cc
venants National and Solemn League, Acknowledgmer
of Sins and Engagement to Duties, the Sum and Prac
tical Uſe of Saving Knowledge. 3. To the work of re
formation, as it was reformed from Popery, Prelacy

and malignancy; even to that work; as it is a direct opposition to every sin, and motive to every duty; and particularly to the remonstrances, protestations and testimonies against the malignant party and malignant actions, they being found out to be inconsistent with, and contrary to the written word of God, and the sworn principles of the church of Scotland, and being found to be hurtful to christian society, not only by the effects of them, but as to the nature and quality of them, even simply considered in themselves, besides the bad effects aggravating them in the sight of the truly godly, and rightly zealous ministers and professors of this church. 4. To the faithful preaching of the gospel, upon muirs and mountains, and high places of the fields, and particularly the preaching down the sins of the time, and up duty. 5. I leave my testimony to the lifting arms, for personal defence, and for defence of the gospel: For seeing that other means were failed, and an occasion offering for that, the law both of God and nature does warrant and allow the same. I need not go to quote Scripture for the probation of it, since the whole scope of it runs in this strain; and also ye may read several places of Scripture, particularly and expresly allowing, yea, commanding, the same, and many imitable Scripture examples, where the people of God lifted arms against kings, as the people's resisting of Saul. I testify to the awfulness of that hostile defence at Pentland and Both-wel-bridge, and several field meetings, where they were put to it by the violent and bloody assaults of their enemies. 6. In a word (for I study brevity, being necessitate) to all the faithful testimonies of the godly, given on scaffolds, and some other testimonies given in hostile manner, viz. The testimony given at Rutherglen, May 29. 1679. and the declarations published at Lanerk, in the years 1680. and 1682. I disown and testify against the declaration published at Hamilton, in the year 1679. particularly, because it takes in the interest of Charles Stuart; for tho' he was once a king, he is now a tyrant, by his cutting the neck of the noble government established in this land, and overturning the main and fundamental conditions, whereupon he was constitute; and it is notour to all in this kingdom, and I believe to part of our neighbour nations also, that he carries on a course contrary to the word of God, and light of nature, and

The laſt Speech and Teſtimony

deſtructive to all chriſtian and human ſociety; yea, a courſe that very Heathens would abhor, even the thing itſelf, abſtract from its aggravations.

I come now, in ſhort, (deſiring ye may pardon eſcapes) to let you know what I teſtify againſt. And 1. (not to go further back) I leave my teſtimony againſt many miniſters, for their leaving their Maſter's work, at the ſimple command of uſurpers, as if they had been only the ſervants of men; and I declare my diſapprobation, yea, my teſtimony againſt the ſinful ſilence of miniſters, after they had left the vineyard where their Maſter had placed them to labour, and their not acknowledging publicly their unfaithfulneſs; for which (together with their other grievous failings) the Lord is this day contending with them. I know not what plagues are ſo ſad as to be plagued by the hand of God, by being laid aſide from his work; I ſay, their unfaithfulneſs, in not ſtanding in the way of the people, when they were ſo generally drawn away to hear curates. Miſtake me not, thinking that I look upon the people as innocent, when I ſpeak of the ſins of the miniſters; for I ſee it my duty to teſtify againſt both, and there will not one of them excuſe another: But remember that the miniſters muſt count for the people who periſh thro' their default. 2. Againſt miniſters their tampering with that woful and hell-hatched indulgence, and more particularly, their accepting thereof. I teſtify againſt the actual accepters of it, and againſt a woful connivance in the non-accepters of the ſame; and whereas there ought to have been an open teſtifying and proteſting againſt it. I ſhall ſtudy to ſay but litle; but I die in the faith of it, That God ſhall ſend a clear diſcovery of matters, and theſe that have betrayed their truſt, and have not been as they ſhould and ought to have been, ſhall ſee and be aſhamed; but Lord grant that many may ſee the evil of their doings in time, and may mourn for the ſame, or otherwiſe it will be ſad for them; but every one ſhall ſee firſt or laſt: But remember Eſau, who found no place for repentance, tho' he ſought it carefully with tears. 3. Againſt the miniſters, their woful yielding unto and joining with the malignant party and intereſt at Bothwel-bridge, and their woful yielding unto the uſurpation made upon the prerogatives royal of our wronged Lord and prince Jeſus Chriſt, by their acceptance of liberty granted after Bothwel-bridge, and taking occasion to preach in houses according unto the liberty granted, refusing to preach without doors, notwithstanding of the great necessity sometimes requiring the same, and many of them refusing to preach when any of the people stood without doors; this was notourly known in the time, and I think it be not yet forgot, and however it may be forgot by us, yet I assure you, it is not forgot by a holy God. I testify against their sinful silence, and not jeoparding their lives for their wronged Lord and provoked Master, especially at the time when Mr. R. C. and Mr. D. C. went to the fields. I testify against their condemning of these two worthies in discourse and preaching, and also in their practice. In short against every thing in ministers and professors contrary unto, or inconsistent with the Presbyterian principles of the church of Scotland. 4. I leave my testimony against Popery, Prelacy and Erastianism, and every thing contrary to the word of God, and particularly against Quakerism, Anabaptism, Independency, and all Sectarians, and whatsoever is not warranted by the holy Scriptures. 5. Against the imposing of that cursed cess; not that I call cess-lifting in itself unlawful; but I call that cess unlawful, which was imposed by a corrupt convention of estates who met at Edinburgh, in the year 1673. For some things that are in themselves lawful, are sometimes so circumstantiated, as that they become unlawful; as sometimes the end of an action makes the action unlawful: I may give the cess for an instance of this: for the end of imposing it (as themselves declare) was mainly to bear down field meetings, and other innocent associations of the people of God, disdainfully and wickedly called by them rendezvouses of rebellion; which meetings all Scotland was bound to maintain; but they ought to been in the places constitute for worship, and would have been there, had bonds and engagements been conscientiously minded by all that were under them. O let not this perfidious generation think that they are loosed from the ties of these covenants; for as sure as God is in the heavens he will make them know another thing, even that it was not in their power to rescind these covenants, and by going about so to do, they have brought much wrath upon themselves and their posterity after them, if they repent not. But oh! do they not look like a generation of his wrath? and, not to pass the bounds of charity, I fear they will be the objects of his wrath; and it will be a dreadful day, fee it who will, when the wicked shall be as stubble and tow, and the wrath and vengeance of God shall seize upon them as fire, and burn them up, for they will not escape. And 6. Against the payers of the cess; for it was a sad thing in a people, that should have opposed all courses of that kind, instead of opposing, to contribute to the carrying on of that very course, that they ought to have opposed. O! that they would consider, and lay it to heart, and set themselves to redeem time, misspent and abused time! 7. And against locality and fines paying, seeing that it contributes to the strengthening of the adversaries hands; as for the locality, we may easily see it to be sinful, since they (the enemies) have imposed it for the maintenance of a party raised and keeped up for no other use (as their daily practice declares) but to harrass, rob and spoil the poor people of God, for their closs (O that it were closser) adhering to their sworn principles, and to kill them for not denying of these principles. And as for the paying of fines, it would be considered, that these fines are imposed upon people for their duty; and fines imposed by right and justice, ought always to be for transgression; neither can a fine be imposed by right, but for a transgression: So that by paying of these fines so imposed, we must be said either to yield active obedience to an unjust course, which we ought always to oppose, or we may be said to make ourselves transgressors, and these duties (in which we ought to venture life and fortune) to be transgressions. I say, one of these will consequently follow, if not both: But alas! those things that are grievously sinful many ways, are become so habitual, that they are never noticed nor thought any thing of, nor will be, till God come in his power and great glory, to disclose the secrets of all hearts. 8. I leave my testimony against the people their hearing of curates, basely leaving the way of truth, and following a course dishonouring to God, and destructive to themselves. Also, against the joining with the indulged and unfaithful ministers, vindicating themselves thus, *That it is good to hear the word;* not considering, that these ministers have so far gone out of the way of God, in their accepting of that indulgence, as that they ought to be testified against, and when they go on obstinately in that crooked way, ought to be withdrawn from. It may be some will say, That this is ignorantly reasoned; but I fear, if they would search things narrowly by the Spirit of God, they would find, that God is not countenancing them in it. And also, that they ought to have given far other sort of testimony against that course, than to have joined and gone alongst with it, as far as their station would have required; but now the obstinacy of this generation is so great (and we have many sad evidences of this) that I fear, there will nothing convince them but the judgments of God, which has made me the less careful to write any thing altho' I could, that might, being from the hand of a dying man, be any way convincing to them.

But as it becomes one laying down his life for his royal and princely Master Jesus Christ, I leave my testimony against joining with them; yea, against that which they call simple hearing, and this I have done to exoner my conscience in the sight of a holy and jealous God; and do declare, that if mercy in Christ prevent not (which will not be found but in mercy's gate, which is believing and repentance) they shall smart under the heavy wrath of God for their complying with such crooked and God provoking courses. And I as a man laying down my life for the interest of my sweet Lord, do warn all and every one of them, who have joined with these evil courses, to fly from the wrath to come, which will be on this generation inevitable; yea, I obtest you to flee from it, as ye tender the glory of God, and the good of your own souls. O flee from it by speedy repentance, and lay hold upon the blood and righteousness of Jesus Christ for that effect, and study to have your names scraped out of the black catalogue of these foul-destroying despisers of that precious blood and righteousness, purchased for that end, to take away the sins of all that will come, and by faith lay hold upon it, and to reconcile them to a provoked God. God's wrath is burning against the children of disobedience, and he has said, ' That such as turn aside to crooked ways, he will lead ' them forth with the workers of iniquity;' and in another place he says, ' If any man draw back, my soul shall ' have no pleasure in him.' 9. I leave my testimony against the taking of that cursed test, and the takers thereof, and I declare it to be a horrid wickedness, a God disowning, and a God daring course. 10. Against com-

pearing before their courts, and I declare it
inconsistent with a faithful testimony for
time; it being (1.) An owning of that auth
ed upon that usurped supremacy over th
royal of our Lord, which thing ought to l
tied against, as not to own or answer to a
ced in the name of Charles Stuart, because
forfeited his right to rule as king. (2.) It
demning of such as have suffered the loss o
that account, and these who have laid do
against the owning of that authority; and
me foolish in adjoining my testimony to t
of these, nor in my disowning of that au
Against the lifting of militia, and the pay
money. 12. I testify against the proceedi
bominable wretch John Gib, and these tes
by him in the name of others, as being a
cial to the interests of our Lord.

And now as to the articles of my indictm
all of them such things as cannot be made
to the first, viz. My making my escape
booth, I was doing it most innocently, do
person, neither did I ever hear that it was
to the second, viz. That I had confessed
Bothwel bridge, I cannot see how that cal
minal. If I got but the lash of their own
not abuse of language to call it law) and
for all that were on-lookers that day, cou
to be in the action. As to the third, viz.
ing with * Gavin Wotherspoon 'since Bo
they call a notorious rebel, but cannot p
neither can they shew me that law founde
of God, that makes conversing with him
since they cannot upon sufficient grounds
bel, what they say and do without ground
myself obliged to answer it; for that rebe
law strikes against, is that which can be pr
against powers acting for God, and so co
bellion against God. And sure I am whi
loweth his duty (for it is merely for follo

---

* This was a very eminent and zealous sufferer,
ed of his land and possession, for adherence to the tr
hardships of persecution: but was brought thro' withou
ing stedfast in the way of the Lord till his death, whi
years since.

that they call him a rebel) he can never be said to be in rebellion against God. As to the fourth article, That I refused to call Bothwel-bridge rebellion, I would see the law that makes a man's silence, when interrogated, criminal. And also, as to the thing itself, who knows not, that it was mere defence? And who can make it out to be rebellion against powers acting for God? For as is before said, this, and no other, is the rebellion that the law of God, and the law of our nation strikes against. And the fifth, viz. That I said, the owning of the Covenants were lawful. Who knows not that these covenants were once approven of as lawful, and solemnly sworn by the whole nation, and the Confession of Faith taken, and sworn unto as fundamentals of our religion? And I deny (altho' by an act of a pretended parliament, they may pretend to rescind the same) that it was in their power to rescind or overturn such a constitution, until they had made the unsoundness of it appear; and made it appear wherein another was better, and till they had been in case to set up a better in the room thereof. So that their so doing, was not a walking according to the will of God, but according to their own wills contrary to the will of God, for the satisfaction of their own base lusts, and no ways shewing themselves to be studying either the glory of God, or the good of his people: so that these covenants remain binding to this day, and, I hope, shall be when they are gone, who so wickedly set themselves against them. As to the sixth article, That I would not answer if it was lawful, yea or not, to obey Charles Stuart? it is only silence, which no law nor reason can make criminal. And as to my disowning his authority, as they say, they had only my silence also, which can never in law take away a man's life. As to my not asserting that the death of the late king was murder, I find they would have every one saying and attesting what they say and assert, whether they know it to be so or not. I leave my testimony, as a dying man, against all such implicite walking; and especially I testify against any laying hold implicitely upon the bare assertions or dictates of the enemies of God. And as to the prelate's death, I declare, as a dying man, that I think none can certainly judge that action, if it was murder, or not murder. And who sees not what these enemies to God, and his Son Jesus Christ are driving at,

when they would compel men to affert
their pleafures, that no human underftar
of, themfelves who were the actors only
now it is notour to all perfons of any cap
will but ufe the light of nature, that the
of juft fentence paſt againſt, or put in exe
but that we were murdered only for the
men, who are worfe than Heathens.

And now this my teftimony I feal with
ing in the faith of the proteftant religic
the Prefbyterian government of the churc
and witneffing againſt every thing that te
thereof; exhorting every one who defires
God in love, to fettle and fix here. An
to venture upon the crofs of Chriſt. for
experience, (glory be to him for it) that h
crofs and me both, or otherwife I cou
undergone it with fo fmall difficulty.
reafon of many their fainting under the cr
ing fo little weight on Jefus Chriſt, and
themfelves, and upon any bit of attainn
themfelves to have. O let every one ſtud
of independency upon all things befides h
only upon himfelf. And now I bid fare
remnant of the church of Scotland, and
God, and his good hand; I bid farewel
acquaintances; I bid farewel to my moi
mit her to God, who only can provide
neceffary both for foul and body; I bid
two fifters, and commit them to God,
ftead of all things to them, and can foo
want of a brother to them, which want
eafily born as the time now goes; farewe
believing, reading and meditating; I bi
temporal things, mercies and croffes. W
for the intereſt of my fweet Lord; welco
everlafting glory; welcome fpirits of juft
feſt; welcome angels; welcome Father,
Ghoſt, into whofe hands I commit my fp

J C

With this martyr fuffered other four,
mond, Archibald Stewart, who lived ir
Lefmahego, James Winning taylor in
James Johnſton in North Calder, all ve

udicious Chriſtians. The heads of their indictments are
all the ſame with theſe of this martyr, and their anſwers
before their examinators have been very much to the
ſame effect; all of them freely and fully owning the Covenant, avouching it before their perſecutors, and likewiſe the lawfulneſs of defenſive arms, for maintaining the
faithfully preached goſpel, and abſolutely denying the
king's eccleſiaſtic ſupremacy. Declining all of them to
anſwer the impertinent queſtions concerning the biſhop's
death, and that of King Charles I. in regard they knew
not the circumſtances of theſe facts, nor could make a
judgment upon them, and found themſelves obliged in
no law, divine or human, to give their opinion about
them; and yet upon this their prudent ſilence, was their
ſentence founded, and execute with rage; having ſcarce
forty-eight hours allowed them before their execution.
As for the heads of truth to which they leave their teſtimony, and of defection and corruption, againſt which
they leave it, they are ſo near the ſame with theſe contained in the foregoing Speech, that it would be but ſu-
perfluous to repeat them word for word as they ſtand; only
ſome few expreſſions ſhall be here inſert out of them, to ſhew
how cheerfully they underwent their ſufferings; to which
purpoſe theſe words of John Richmond are very remarkable; 'Scar not at the croſs of Chriſt; for, O! if ye
' knew what I have met with ſince I came to priſon,
' (what love! what matchleſs love from my ſweet and
' lovely Lord;) ye would long to be with him, and
' would count it nought to go thro' a ſea of blood for
' him.' To the ſame effect, ſee with what heavenly delight and complacency that ſtripling Archibald Stewart,
a youth of nineteen years accoſts a violent death, while he
ſaith, ' Now, this is the ſweeteſt and joyfuleſt day that
' ever I had ſince I was born. My ſoul bleſſeth the Lord,
' that ever he made choice of me to ſuffer for his noble
' cauſe and intereſt; that ever he ſet his love upon the
' like of me, to give a faithful teſtimony for his contro-
' verted truths, who was born an heir of hell and wrath:
' but now he hath redeemed my ſoul thro' his precious
' blood and ſuffering, from the power of ſin and Satan,
' and hath made me overcome by the blood of the imma-
' culate Lamb of God.' And thereafter; ' I die not by
' conſtraint; I am more willing to die for my lovely
' Lord Chriſt, and his truths, than ever I was to live:

'and my foul bleſſeth the Lord, that ever h
'of a teſtimony from the like of me. Scar
'way of Chriſt, becauſe of ſufferings. If ye
'of his love I have got ſince I was honoured
'ſonment for him, and what ſweet ingredie
'put into my cup, ye would not be afraid o
'He hath paved the croſs all over with love
'made all ſweet and comfortable to me, and
'all my troubles fly away, like the morning ſt
'I cannot expreſs his matchleſs love to me, n
'make mention of his goodneſs! O! it is bu
'ſpeak to the commendation of my lovely L
'croſs,' &c. At the ſame rate James Winn
bewailed his being ſo long a hearer of curat
with a ſweet and raviſhing turn, 'I bleſs th
'cauſe of his goodneſs to me, who notwit
'all my compliance with enemies, hath n
'that woful caſe, but hath brought me hith
'for his oppoſed, burdened and ruined cauſ
'O! I deſire to bleſs him for it, and call in
'ation to help me. O the wonderful power
'goodneſs of the Lord; Glory to his rich a
'name, who hath diſcovered to me the ne
'deemer, who will waſh me from my ſins, a
'pure and ſpotleſs before his throne in heav
Johnſton, among other heavenly expreſſions
concerning his lot of ſuffering; 'For this
'Lord, for I could never have ventured up
'eſpecially upon death itſelf, unleſs that he
'me to it.' They died all with a forgiving
tating their Lord and Maſter, and his hol
praying for forgiveneſs to their perſecutors
aſſuring them, that their blood would be req
hands if they did not repent, for what they
gainſt the image of God in them.

The copy of a Letter written by the fore mention
BALD STEWART, *who ſuffered*
the Croſs of Glaſgow, March 19. 1684. *T*
acquaintances.

My dear and loving friends and acquaintan
YOU and I muſt take good night of on
a while; but I hope it ſhall not be l
know that this time that we have on earth

e are but as a flower that grows up in the
t down in the morning; like the shadow
and is no more seen upon earth again;
's gourd, that grew up in a night, and
ht. Now you and I must part, and take
ι of me, and I of you, as willingly, and
tisfaction, contentment, and submission
r God, as if we were going to our sweet
: fellowship-meetings, where our souls
: been refreshed, with the fresh gales of
· God, which indeed was the life of our
ad it not been the love that we bare to
ys, he would never have made our meet-
us; so that the longer that we continu-
ener that we met, the Lord made more
n to us, in giving us new confirmations
tokens of his kindness. Now, my lov-
m going to my Father's house, to reap
hese waking nights that you and I had to-
)ne knew of it but ourselves and our hea-
ınd I die in the hope of it, we shall come
r and my Father, to your God and my
:. 17. to your Redeemer and my Redeem-
fruit of all these meetings we had toge-
hat will be a joyful harvest time: I am
:ap the fruit of all my reading, praying,
ing and meditating, and the fruits of all my
l labour. Instead of bitterness I will enjoy
ad of trouble, rest, instead of sorrow and
gladness; *For sighing and sorrow shall*
going to reap the fruit of my wounds,
oches that they have cast upon me: I am
he fruit of all my sighs and groans, espe-
e I came to prison, where I have had very
I am going to reap the fruit of my fet-
mprisonment for my lovely Lord and Ma-
l; and I am going to reap the fruit of my
nt and unjust sentence. O! but the fruits
ntioned things will be a weighty crown of
little time upon my head, up at my Fa-
when I shall go no more out, and come no
ing the name of my God written upon my
d the song of Moses and the Lamb put in
to sing through all the ages of eternity?

Now, dear friends, I cannot get him praifed, for th[e] riches of his free grace, freely beftowed on me. O! cannot get him praifed for bringing my foul out of th[e] pit of deftruction, and for reclaiming my foul from th[e] gates of hell. O my foul and heart, and all that is withi[n] me, praife the Lord for his wonderful love to me! a[nd] alfo, my foul invites all the works of creation to praif[e] him for what we hath done to my foul; for now I ca[n] fay with David, from my own experience, ' Come an[d] ' hear, all ye that fear God, and I will declare what h[e] ' hath done for my foul.' And likewife I can fay wit[h] David, Pfal. xvi. 6. ' The lines are fallen unto me i[n] ' pleafant places; yea, I have a goodly heritage.' An[d] more than all, that he hath faid to my foul, that he wi[ll] quarrel no more with me for fin, for my God hath fai[d] to me, Ifa. xliii. 1, 2. ' But now, thus faith the Lor[d] ' that created thee, O Jacob, and he that formed thee ' O Ifrael, fear not; for I have redeemed thee, I hav[e] ' called thee by thy name, thou art mine. Whe[n] ' thou paffeft thro' the waters, I will be with thee; an[d] ' thro' the rivers, they fhall not overflow thee; whe[n] ' thou walkeft thro' the fire, thou fhalt not be burnt ' neither fhall the flame kindle upon thee.' And Matth[.] ix. 2. ' Son be of good cheer, thy fins be forgiven thee. Now all is fure and well with me, I am brought nea[r] unto God, thro' the blood of his Son Jefus Chrift; an[d] I have no more to do, but to lay down this life of mine that he hath given me, and take up houfe and habitati on with my lovely Lord and Mafter Jefus Chrift, wh[o] purchafed life and falvation to me by the price of hi[s] own blood and fufferings: O! but I have got an eaf[y] caft of it; O! but I am come well and eafy to my pur[-] pofe, of redemption, peace and happinefs. But O! [I] cannot get him glorified; and I will never get him e[-] nough glorified, as long as my foul liveth, and I fhal[l] live as long as he liveth, and that is life without end.

Now, my dear and loving friends, it is but little ad-vice that I can leave to you, how to order your life an[d] converfation; yet I fhall leave you my laft advice, a[s] the Lord fhall help me. As God hath once made yo[u] to accept of him, upon his own terms and way, hol[d] faft by him, and claim a right to him, from his ow[n] promifes and former loving kindnefs, wherein he hath manifefted himfelf to you. And although you be made many times to think, that he hath left you, when you are caften down, and under defertion, yet claim a right to him; though you have deftroyed yourfelf, threep kindnefs upon him; and refolve with Job, That *though he fhould flay you, yet will ye truft in him:* For you muft not want your down-caftings and defertions; for all thefe things are given you for the trial of your faith. And you may know fomething of this from experience, that we cannot guide our Lord's prefence, when we get it, we are fo lifted up, that he muft caft us down again; for our old bottles cannot bear with the new wine of heaven, none of us can be free of defertion; for as long as we live in this earth, we are often under an Egyptian cloud of darknefs. Spend much of your time in prayer and meditation, for I think, that in thefe is the life of religion; and fpend time in Chriftian converfe with any of your own judgment, and private prayer, as you and I did when we were together: and if you can get none, do your own part, and the Lord will make up all your lofs, for he hath engaged to make up all your wants. Now, double your diligence, and make ready for the trial, for you will not get it fhifted, if ye continue faithful to the end. I am not faying that the trial will take away your life; but I am perfuaded, you will come thro' difficulties, if the Lord fee fit to fpare you, to fee the glorious days that fhall be feen in Scotland again, and to reap of the fruit of it. This will be a high honour, for they will be a happy people, that will be the remnant of the church.

Now, dear friends, hold faft, and let no man take your crown; for it is ready at the end of your race; run and never halt nor look back, till you obtain the prize. I have gotten the firft ftart of you a little; but, I hope, you will follow me, before it be long, and we fhall meet again, and O! what a joyful meeting fhall it be? Study deniednefs to your life, and die daily, that death may not furprize you.

But I muft forbear, my time is fo fhort, that I cannot get all faid here, that I have to fay; but what is wanting, himfelf make it up to you. Now I take my leave of you for a little time, hoping to meet again up above in our Father's houfe. I pray, that God's eternal blefling may reft upon you; and wifh you even as my own foul.

The last Speech and Testimony

Farewel in the Lord. Your dear and loving Christian friend, brother and soul's wellwisher,
Glasgow tolbooth,
March 15, 1684. } ARCHIBALD STEWART.

The last Testimony of Captain JOHN PATON, *who lived in the Parish of Finwick, and suffered at the Grassmarket of Edinburgh, May 9th. 1684.*

Dear friends and spectators,

YOU are come here to look upon me a dying man, and you need not expect that I shall say much, for I was never a great orator or eloquent of tongue, tho' I may say as much to the commendation of God in Christ Jesus, as ever any poor sinner had to say. I have been as great a sinner as ever lived; strong corruptions, strong lusts, strong passions, a strong body of death have prevailed against me; yea, I have been chief of sinners. I may say on every back-look of my way, tho' the world cannot charge me with any gross transgression this day, for which I bless the Lord, O! what omissions and commissions, what formality and hypocrisy, that even my duties have been my grief and fear, left thou a holy God had made them my ditties, and mayest do: My misimproven time may be heavy upon my head, and cause of desertion; and especially my supplicating the council, who has, I think, laid their snares the closer to take away my life, tho' contrary to their own professed law. I desire to mourn for my giving ear to the counsels of flesh and blood, when I should have been consulting heaven, and to reflect upon myself, tho' it lays my blood the closer to their door, and I think, the blood of my wife and bairns. I think, their supreme magistrate is not ignorant of many of their actings, but these Prelates will not be found free when our God makes an inquisition for blood. And now I am come here, desired of some indeed, who thirst for my life, tho' by others not desired. I bless the Lord, I am not come here as a thief or a murderer, and I am free of the blood of all men, but hate blood-shed directly or indirectly. And now I am a poor sinner, and could never merit any thing but wrath, and have no righteousness of my own, all is Jesus Christ's and his alone, and I have laid claim to his righteousness and his sufferings by faith in Jesus Christ, thro' imputation they are mine, for I have accepted of his offer on his own terms, and sworn away myself to him to be at his disposal, both privately and publicly many times; and now I have put it upon him to ratify in heaven all that I have essayed to do on earth, and to do away all my imperfections and failings, and to stay my heart on him. I seek mercy for all my sins, and believe to get all my challenges and sins sunk in the blood and sufferings of Jesus and his righteousness, and that he shall see of the travail of his soul on me, and the Father's pleasure shall prosper in his hand. I bless the Lord, that ever he led me out to behold any part of his power in the gospel, in kirks, or fields, or any of his actings for his people in their straits. 'The Lord is with his people while they be with him:' We may set to our seal to this, and while they be unite: And O for a day of his power in cementing of this distempered age. It is sad to see his people falling out of the way, and of such a fiery spirit, that look to be at one lodging at night, especially these who profess to keep by our glorious work of reformation and solemn engagements to God, and to hold off the sins of these times. O hold off extremities on both hands, and follow the example of our blessed Lord and the cloud of witnesses in the 11th of the Hebrews. And let your way be the good old path, the word of God and best times of the church, for if it be not according to his word, it is because there is no truth in it. Now, as to my interrogations, I was not clear to deny Pentland or Bothwel. They asked me, How long I was at them? I said, Eight days: and the assize had no more to sentence upon, for the advocate said, he would not pursue for Pentland, by reason of an indemnity, before the privy council. The council asked me, If I acknowledged authority? I said, All authority according to the word of God. They charged me with many things, as if I had been a rebel since the year 1640, and at Montrose's taking at Mauchlin muir. Lord forgive them, they know not what they do.

I adhere to the sweet Scriptures of truth of the Old and New Testament, and preached gospel by a faithful sent ministry, whereby he many times communicated himself to the souls of his people, and to me in particular, both in the kirks, and since on the fields, and in the private meetings of his people for prayer and supplication to him. I adhere to our solemn Covenants National and Solemn League, Acknowledgment of Sins and Engagement to Duties, which became national. I adhere to our Confeſſion of Faith, Larger and Shorter Catechiſms, Cauſes of Wrath, and to all the teſtimonies given by his people formerly, and of late, either on fields or ſcaffolds, theſe years bygone, in ſo far as they are agreeable to his word, and the practice of our worthy reformers, and holy true zeal, according to his rule. I adhere to all our glorious work of reformation. Now, I leave my teſtimony as a dying man againſt the horrid uſurpation of our Lord's prerogative and crown right, I mean that ſupremacy, eſtabliſhed by law in theſe lands, which is a manifeſt uſurpation of his crown, for he is given by the Father to be head of the church, Col. i. 18. 19. ' And he is the head of the body, the church: who is ' the beginning, the firſt-born from the dead; that in ' all things he might have the preheminence. For it ' pleaſed the Father, that in him all fulneſs ſhould dwell.' And againſt all Popery, Prelacy, and Eraſtianiſm, and all that depends upon that hierarchy, which is a yoke that neither we nor our fathers were able to bear, which the poor remnant is groaning under this day, by that horrid cruelty renting their conſciences by teſts and bonds; taking away their ſubſtance and livelihoods by fines and illegal exactions, plunderings and quarterings, and compelling them to ſin, by hearing, joining and complying with theſe malicious curates. Matth. xxiii. 13. ' Wo unto you Scribes and Phariſees, hypocrites; ' for ye ſhut up the kingdom of heaven againſt men; for ' ye neither go in yourſelves, neither ſuffer ye them that ' are entering to go in.' I leave my teſtimony againſt the indulgence firſt and laſt, for I ever looked on it as a ſnare, and ſo I never looked upon them as a part of the hopeful remnant of the church, and now it is ſad to ſee how ſome of them have joined by their deeds in the perſecution of the poor remnant, and almoſt all in tongue perſecution.

Now, I would ſpeak a ſhort word or two to three ſorts of folk, but I think, if one would riſe from the dead, he would not be heard by this generation, who are mad upon idols and this world. *Firſt*, Theſe who have joined deliberately with the perſecutors, in all their robberies and haling innocent ſouls to priſon, death and baniſhment. The Lord will not hold them guiltleſs; they may read what the Spirit of God hath recorded of them in Jude 11th ver. and downward, and Obadiah's prophecy. A second sort is, these who seem to be more sober and knowing, yet thro' a timorousness and fear, have joined with them in all their corrupt courses for ease and their own things: do not think that these fig-leaves will cover you in the cool of the day; it is a hazard to be mingled with the heathen, lest we learn of them their way. O Sirs, be zealous and repent; seek repentance from Christ, he purchased it with his blood; and do your first works, if ever there was any saving works on your souls; for he will come quickly, 'and who may abide the day of his coming.' O Sirs, the noble grace of repentance grows not in every field; many could not get it, tho' they sought it carefully with tears. O work while it is to day, the night draweth on, and it may be very dark. The third sort is, those who have been most tender; and O who of us can say, that we have out of love to his glory singly followed him; upon examination we fear we find it not so, but that we have come far short. We fear we find not him such as we would, nor he us such as he would. O we may say, 'From the crown of the head to the sole of the foot there is no place clean.' None can cast a stone at another; we are all wounds, bruises, and defilements. We must put this work upon him who is the fountain to wash foul souls, who 'breaks not the bruised reed, nor quenches the smoking flax.' Give him much ado, for we have much ado for him. O that there were no rest in our bones because of our sin. It is the Father's pleasure that he should see his seed, and the pleasure of the Lord prosper in his hand. O that he would make every one of us understand our errors, and seek after the good old path, followed in the most pure times of our church, and get in to our Lord Jesus Christ, by faith in his righteousness, by imputation and virtue of his sufferings for sinners, and keep by him. There is no safety but at his back; and I beseech you, improve time, it is precious when right improven; 'For ye know not when the Master cometh, at midnight, or at cock crowing. Dear friends, the work of the day is great, and calls for more nor ordinary. O be oft at the throne, and give him no rest to make sure your soul's interest. Seek pardon freely, and then he will come with peace; seek all the graces of his Spirit, the grace of love, the grace of holy fear and humility. O! but there is much need of this and the promised Spirit.

Now, I desire to salute you, dear friends in the Lord Jesus Christ, both prisoned, banished, widow and fatherless, or wandering and cast out for Christ's sake and the gospel's, even the blessing of Christ's sufferings be with you all, strengthen, establish, support and settle you, and the blessing of him who was in the bush, which while it burnt, was not consumed, and my poor blessing be with you all. Now, as to my persecutors, I forgive all of them; instigators, reproachers, soldiers, privy council, justiciaries, apprehenders, in what they have done to me; but what they have done in despite against the image of God's name in me, who am a poor thing without that, it is not mine to forgive them; but I wish they would seek forgiveness of him who hath it to give, and would do no more wickedness.

Now I leave my poor sympathising wife and six small children upon the Almighty Father, Son, and Holy Ghost, who hath promised to be ' a Father to the father- ' less, and a Husband to the widow, and the orphan's ' stay;' be thou all in all unto them, O Lord. Now, the blessing of God, and my poor blessing be with them. And my suit to thee is, that thou wouldst give them thy salvation. And now farewel wife and children; farewel all friends and relations ; farewel all worldly enjoyments; farewel sweet Scriptures, preaching, praying, reading, singing and all other duties. And welcome Father, Son, and Holy Spirit. I desire to commit my soul to thee in well-doing. Lord receive my spirit.

Sic subscribitur, JOHN PATON.

The last Testimony of JAMES NISBET, *who lived in the parish of Loudon, and suffered at the Howgate-head of Glasgow, June* 5. 1684.

NOW, I am brought hither this day, to lay down my life for the testimony of Jesus Christ, and for asserting him to be Head and King in his own house, and for no matter of fact, that they have against me. Wherefore, dear friends, and all true lovers of Zion's cause, if I could either speak or write any thing to the praise and commendation of my lovely Lord and princely Master Jesus Christ, King and Head over his own church *of James Nisbet.*

tho' the moſt part of the men of this gene-
ng it death to call him ſo, yet I as a dying
die in the faith of it, that he ſhall appear
ion, and for his own glory now trampled
g ſo low; for he has ſaid in Iſa. xlii. 8. ' I
I, that is my name, and my glory I will
nother,' &c. Now, I am to lay down my
l I do it willingly, and not by conſtraint;
, that ever he carved out my lot ſuch, as
· for him, who am ſuch a poor unworthy
I would have acknowledged a mortal man
, I might have redeemed my life, viz.
to be ſupreme over all cauſes civil and ec-
ey have now ſet him up, which belongs to
upon earth, and to have prayed for him.
ly for that man in his perſon and govern-
h broken down the work of the Lord, and
e the ſanctuary of our Lord,' who was gi-
her, as it is ſaid, Eph. i. 22. ' And hath
s under his feet, and gave him to be head
s to the church;' And in the ſecond Pſalm,
: is for the hope of Iſrael, and a witneſs
of Jeſus Chriſt, of which hope I am not
· I invite all who love his name, and the
1, to praiſe him, for I may ſet to my ſeal
is a good Maſter to all who will come to
y ſay, He hath been good to me, who has
fight of my ſins, and a fight of the reme-
s purchaſed by his blood, and thro' his
who was born an heir of hell and wrath by
lory be to his great name, who has made
ly ſin, and made me as if I had never ſin-
and praiſe be to himſelf. But what ſhall
art cannot conceive, hand cannot write,
expreſs! for ſurely, if I could ſay any thing
id commendation of my lovely Lord Jeſus
many things for which to do it. 1ſt, For
: has not letten me deny his truths and
perſecuted work; for there is nothing in
f myſelf, but I might have been amongſt
e diſplayed a banner againſt God, and
blood of his people to run in the ſtreets,
their garments with their blood. And
has carved out my lot to be in a land

where he hath set up his pure ordinances, both in doctrine, worship, discipline and government; for indeed he might have trysted it to have been among these that are worshipping Antichrist, that whore of Rome, whose sentence may be read Rev. xix. 12. And if Charles Stuart has not overturned his work, and corrupted the whole land, by overturning the whole fundamental laws, both civil and ecclesiastic, I leave it to any judicious person, that is not byassed and drawn away, by that woful Erastian supremacy, which is like to overspread the whole land. 3*dly*, That he hath given his word for a rule to walk by, which word is truth, and the true word of God. He has made me to walk by it, and it to be my rule; and by his word and Spirit bearing witness with my spirit, making me spotless and clean, and I shall be clothed with these robes of his righteousness, which are spotless and clean.

Now, I shall only give a short account of my principles, as the Lord shall assist; and the Lord help me to get it done in truth and sincerity; for there are many eyes looking on me; they eyes of an all-seeing God, ' who ' is of purer eyes than that he can behold iniquity;' and the eyes of men who are thirsting for my blood. 1*st*, I adhere and sweetly set to my testimony to the covenant of redemption, betwixt the Father and the Son, made before the foundation of the world, for the redemption of poor lost mankind, I mean of those who are elected, called, justified and sanctified; for which my soul shall bless the Lord that ever I heard tell of the same, and that ever I heard tell, ' that he came into the world to save sinners, of whom I am chief.' 2*dly*, To the sacred Scriptures, that they are the true word of God; and that there is life everlasting to be had in them, if ye will apply your hearts to search diligently, and pursue after them with a sincere and diligent seeking, with all the soul and heart; and without sincere endeavouring to make it your rule, there is no life; for says our blessed Lord, ' I came not to destroy the law, but to fulfil it.' 3*dly*, To the work of reformation as it was reformed in all the several steps thereof, from under Popery, Prelacy, and Erastianism, and all other errors whatsomever, not agreeable to the Scriptures, the written word of God. 4*thly*, To the Confession of Faith, the Sum of Saving Knowledge, Directory for Worship and Discipline, *of James Nisbet.*

nd to our Catechisms Larger and Shorter. 5thly, To the Covenants National and Solemn League, whereby these lands were engaged unto the Lord; and Scotland may bless the Lord, that ever he engaged them in a covenant with himself. I say to you that desire to own the same, make it your ground to plead with the Lord, till he come back again to these lands. 6thly, To the preaching of the gospel of our Lord Jesus Christ, as it was faithfully preached by faithful ministers, called and commissionated, and sent by himself; and also my testimony to the Acknowledgment of Sins and Engagement to Duties, and the Causes of the Lord's Wrath against this land this day: but alas! it may be said, many have gone backward, and not forward; the most part of this generation have refused to walk any more with him, ever since Bothwel, only these two, viz. Mr. Donald Cargil and Mr. Richard Cameron, which I desire to set to my seal to the faithfulness of these two mens doctrines, for my soul has been refreshed by them. And I set to my seal to all their proceedings and actings in the work they were called to, and my soul blesseth the Lord, that ever I heard them preach. 7thly, To all the appearings in arms in defence of the gospel, and self-defence, both before Bothwel and since. 8thly, To the excommunication at the Torwood, by Mr. Donald Cargil, as it is just and lawful, and will stand in force and record, ay till repentance make it null, of which there is little appearance. 9thly, To the testimony given at Rutherglen, May 29. 1679. the declaration given at Lanerk, June 11. 1682. by a party, whom the Lord raised and stirred up by his Spirit, and owned them in that work, to give a public testimony against that soul-destroying, and land-ruining thing called the test, altho' many in this generation be pleading for the lawfulness of it, and disowning the covenant which we are all bound to. O my heart trembles to think, what will come on this generation, for their dreadful apostacy and departing from the way of the Lord. 10thly, To all the fellowship meetings of the Lord's people, for reading, praying, and singing of psalms, and all the other duties proper for, and incumbent upon them. I mean these that desire to wrestle and hold up the cause of his ruined work, and his poor suffering remnant. 11thly, To the eight articles, called the New Covenant, taken at the Queensferry off worthy Henry Hall.

Now, as I have left my testimony in sh
of God; so I desire to leave my testimon
fections of the time, as the Lord shall
Therefore I, as a dying witness, leave n
Against Popery and Prelacy, which is f
nanced and set up in Scotland this day
those who seemed to be most eminent, a
6. 'I marvel that ye are so soon remove
' called you into the grace of Christ, ur
' pel,' &c. 2*dly*, Against Quakerism,
and all other errors, which are not a
word of God, and our solemn Covenant
of Faith. 3*dly*, Against the tyrant upo
Britain and Ireland, for his tyranny,
bloodshed, and for overturning the laws
ecclesiastic, and not making the law his
by, but he ruling the law, and not the l
is not according to the word of God, a
xxiii. 3. ' He that ruleth over men mus
' in the fear of God,' &c. Even against
all the upholders, aiders, assisters and
him. O what will become of this gene
apostacy and departing away from God
the oath of supremacy, for the setting u
supreme, and following and making them
not taking the word of God to be their r
gainst that bond taken in the Gray-friar
tho' there be many that denied it, unti
in his own due time made it appear, whe
to a greater length; for he has said in
' there is nothing done in secret, but he
' nifested in the light.' 6*thly*, Against the
bond of regulation, for their binding to
to the will of men, and not according to
Surely it is not according to the practice
Acts iv. 19. 'But Peter and John ans
' unto them, Whether it be right in the
' to hearken unto you more than unto C
7*thly*, Against the bond pressed by the H
the west country. O what may be said
on? It may be said, Ye have gone away
my ordinances, and ye have forsaken me
and have hewed you out broken cisterns
no water. 8*thly*, Against that land-ruini

alled the teſt. 9*thly*, Againſt all com-
ι upon bond and caution; whatever men
it is a complying with the avowed ene-
ιding themſelves to be the priſoners of
ιe priſoners of Jeſus Chriſt. 10*thly*, A-
aring at courts and paying of fines; for
we have done a fault againſt them, and
of theſe as juſt judges, that are impoſing
it ye may ſee what they are, for there is
ill get leave to plead an action there.
ɔe called judges, and owned as judges,
rs and land-judgments? 11*thly*, Againſt
ity, which is impoſed for the down-bear-
, and for maintaining bloody and avow-
ιiſh Chriſt and his goſpel out of the land,
ιnder, rob, ſpoil and perſecute the poor
for in the very narrative of the act, it
hat end, and declared to the world; ſee
inſt it. Iſa. lxv. 11. ' But ye are they
e Lord, that forget my holy mountain,
ι table for that troop, and that furniſh
ing unto that number. Therefore I will
ι the ſword,' &c. 12*thly*, Againſt hear-
ιecauſe they are wolves and boars thurſt
d's people to kill and deſtroy; and a-
ence firſt and laſt; and againſt the hear-
ιd joining with them, or pleading for
ιey are not entered in by the right door,
loctrines the commandments of men;
re in ſo far not the miniſters of Jeſus
miniſters of men, as it is ſaid, John x.
ʏ I ſay unto you, He that entereth not
to the ſheepfold, but climbeth up ſome
ſame is a thief and a robber.' And a-
rs and profeſſors, who are now lying at
is in trouble, and are ſhifting their du-
zard, and are ſheltering themſelves un-
of theſe avowed enemies, pleading in
ιd have broken the poor people of God,
ιels of the church; and eſpecially theſe
ce in the fields, to hold up a banner for
and Maſter Jeſus Chriſt, I ſhall be a
ιem if repentance prevent it not.
are the poor wreſtling remnant, weary

not of the crofs of Chrift, for he is a good Mafter, an
he fends none a warfare on their own charges, for h
will own them in all that he carves out for them. (
double your diligence, and give him no reft till he com
back again, As in Ifa. lxii. 7. 'And give him no re
' till he eftablifh, and till he make Jerufalem a praife i
' the earth.' O what will come of poor Scotland for th
horrid iniquities and abominations, perjury and blooc
fhed, and covenant-breaking? O Scotland's punifhmer
will be fad; but my eyes fhall be clofed, and I fhall nc
fee it, and I am well content, feeing I get my foul for
prey. Now I am afraid God will not know many c
this generation that have gone fuch a dreadful length i
defection and backfliding. But O what fhall I fay!
leave it to himfelf to do as he may moft glorify himfel
in preferving a feed and remnant to ferve him. Now
die in the faith of it, that he has a feed whom he wi
have preferved when he fends forth inftruments wit
flaughter weapons, that he has a party that he will fi
a mark on, as it is faid, Ezek. ix. 4. 'And the Lor
' faid unto him, Go thro' the midft of the city, thre
' the midft of Jerufalem, and fet a mark on the forehead
' of the men that figh and cry for all the abominatioi
' that be done in the midft thereof.' Now, I fay, Wea
ry not of the crofs of Chrift, altho' ye fhould fuffer pei
fecution, for he has faid, ' In the world ye fhall hav
' tribulation, but in me ye fhall have peace.' And O bu
he taketh exact notice what is done to his people. Obac
ver. 13. 'Thou fhouldft not have entered into th
' gate of my people in the day of their calamity; yei
' thou fhouldft not have looked on their affliction in th
' day of their calamity; nor have laid hands on the
' fubftance in the day of their calamity.' O but that l
a fweet word, 2 Tim. ii. 11, 12. 'It is a faithful fayinf
' for if we be dead with him, we fhall alfo live wit
' him: If we fuffer, we fhall alfo reign with him: If w
' deny him, he will alfo deny us.' O Sirs! lofe nc
heaven for mammon, and your own fouls for what j
can fuffer here. It is true, none can merit heaven b
their fufferings, but it is as true that he has faid, ' H
' that will not forfake all, and take up his crofs and fo
' low me, he cannot be my difciple.' Now I know ther
will many brand me with felf-murder, becaufe I hav
got many an offer to go to Carolina upon fuch eaf

terms. But as to that I anſwer, ſelf-preſervation muſt loop to truth's preſervation. There are indeed many of his generation who pretend to keep their preſent eaſe, and to be followers of Chriſt; but I defy any, if they be called to a public teſtimony, but they ſhall either loſe their preſent poſſeſſion, or elſe that which is of more worth, even their immortal ſouls and everlaſting ſalvation.

Now as to the heads of my indictment whereon they have ſentenced me to die, they are mainly theſe. 1ſt, My approving of Drumclog and Bothwel, and being at Glaſgow, to be lawful and in defence of the goſpel, and in ſelf-defence, which both the law of God and nature allow. And 2dly, For adhering to the National and Solemn League and Covenant; and they declared before my face, that both their king and council had diſowned the Covenant, and had taken that away by their acts of parliament; and ſaid, that they were both unjuſt and unlawful: and ſhall ſuch be owned and adhered to, who have declared themſelves againſt King Chriſt, and have broken his laws, and have ſeated themſelves in the room of Jeſus Chriſt, which belongs to no mortal man upon earth, and much leſs to him who is an uſurper and a tyrant, I mean Charles Stuart? And here I, as a dying witneſs, leave my teſtimony againſt that monſtrous beaſt, for our Saviour calls Herod a fox, and ſays, ' Go tell ' that fox, I work to-day and to-morrow, and the third ' day I ſhall be perfected. 3dly, and mainly, My ſentence was, That I diſowned their authority: For ſince they had rejected the covenant, I was the more clear to diſown them to be my judges or governors over the land; and they aſſerted it treaſonable, becauſe I ſaid, none of the people of God would ſay otherwiſe. And in plain terms and direct words, I deny them to have any power to rule either in civil or eccleſiaſtic matters. Alſo theſe avowed enemies who are thirſting for my blood, charged me with going up and down the country plundering and murdering, and ſo by their law made liable to puniſhment, even to the loſs of my life; but I declare, who am within a little to appear before the righteous Judge, that I never intended to wrong any man. And ſo it is evident they take away my life upon the account of adhering to truth, and I bleſs the Lord that ever he gave me a life to lay down for him, and that ever he counted me worthy to lay down my life for his perfecuted truth. O matchlefs free grace that is making choice of the like of me, and poor weak things to confound the ftrong, and the poor foolifh things to confound the wife.

Now, there are three forts of folk that I would fpeak a word to, The firft is, thefe that have begun in the way of the Lord, and feemingly have gone a good length, and when the ftorm of perfecution arofe, for fear of the rough fea of trouble, have drawn back. O mind that word in Heb. x. 38. 'But if any man draw back, my 'foul fhall have no pleafure in him.' And Rom. viii. 35. 'Who fhall feparate us from the love of Chrift? 'fhall tribulation, or diftrefs, or perfecution, or famine, 'or nakednefs, or peril, or fword,' &c. And many moe places of Scripture. A fecond fort are thefe who are going on in rebellion againft God openly and avowedly; as ye may fee in Pfal. ii. 'Why do the Heathen rage, 'and the people imagine a vain thing? he that fitteth 'in heaven fhall laugh, the Lord fhall have them in de- 'rifion, then fhall he fpeak to them in his wrath and 'vex them in his fore difpleafure.' O poor Scotland, that was once married away to the Lord, and now has provoked him to depart and leave it, and give a bill of divorcement, as it were! O Scotland has finned dreadfully, what by covenant-breaking, bloodfhed, lying and fwearing. Now a third fort are thefe who defire to keep their garments clean, and undefiled, with the abounding fins of this generation. Go on in the way of the Lord, and fear not what man can do, for he has faid, 'Fear 'not them that kill the body, and after that can do 'no more; but fear him who after he hath killed the 'body, hath power to caft into hell,' &c. I can fet to my feal to it, that Chrift is a good mafter, and well worthy the fuffering for. And now I can freely and heartitily forgive all men what they have done to me, as I defire to be forgiven of my father who is in heaven; but what they have done againft a holy God, and his image in me, that is not mine to forgive them, but I leave that to him to difpofe on as he fees fit, and as he may moft glorify himfelf. Now I am to take my leave of all created comforts here; and I bid farewel to the fweet Scriptures; farewel reading and praying: farewel finning and fuffering; farewel fighing and forrowing, mourning and weeping; and farewel all Chriftian friends, and relations; farewel brethren and sisters, and all things in time. And welcome Father, Son, and Holy Ghost; welcome heaven and everlasting joy and praise, and innumerable company of angels and spirits of just men made perfect. Now into thy hands I commit my spirit, for it is thine. *Sic subscribitur,*

JAMES NISBET.

This Martyr was so inhumanly treated, and constantly watched, that it was with much difficulty he got any thing written, and that only now a line and then a line, and hence some few repetitions which were in the manuscript were left out, which is hoped will be liable to no misinterpretation.

The last Testimony of ARTHUR TAKET, *taylor in Hamilton, who suffered in the Grass-market of Edinburgh, Aug.* 1. 1684.

BEing appointed to die in the Grass-market I thought it was a duty lying upon my conscience before the Lord, to leave this short word of testimony behind me, in testification of my closs adherence to all these controverted truths, as they are all agreeable and conform to the written word of God. And now I desire to bless his name with my whole heart and soul for this, that ever he made choice of the like of me, such a poor, weak, fecklefs, insignificant thing as I am, in counting me worthy to suffer for his noble cause and controverted truths, his name, interest and covenant, now controverted and brought in debate by this God-daring, Christ-dethroning, and God-contemning, adulterous and bloody generation, wherein my lot is fallen. And this I can say, that thro' his grace, I am well satisfied and heartily content with my lot, that God in his infinite wisdom has seen fit to carve out unto me; and thro' his grace I am well helped to great quietness, calmness and serenity of mind before the Lord, and a holy submission to what is his will towards me in this; that if every hair in my head, and every drop of my blood were a life, I would willingly lay them down for my lovely Lord and Master Jesus Christ. Some will possibly say, that this is an untruth, and so cannot be believed by them, notwithstanding of all this. But whether it be believed or not, it is true: for I am not

dying by conſtraint and unwillingneſs ;
ſay in his ſight (my conſcience bearing r
I am a thouſand times more willing to di(
lovely Lord and Maſter's noble cauſe, a
truths, than ever I was to live : and th
that are ſo much controverted, are bec(
ous and clearer unto me at death, that
heretofore in my life ; as David ſays, Pſa.
' I walk thro' the valley and ſhadow of (
' no evil; for thou art with me, thy r
' they comfort me.' This I have been
ſible of by my experience in all that I
that the croſs of Chriſt has been all pave(
that it has been made to become like un
unto me; and all that ever I have met
laſt, has been made ſweet and eaſy unto
ble in the leaſt ; and that he has been a l
Lord unto me, and he has been as go
This I can ſay to his commendation, anc
dation of the croſs of Chriſt, that he h
the heavy end of the croſs himſelf, that
trouble in the leaſt. O praiſe, praiſe to
free grace, for his matchleſs and unexp
I have met with ſince I was brought to p
I was foreſt put at, and threatned with
cruel and bloody tyrants, the more of h
neſs I did meet with. This I have been
ſible of, when I was hardeſt dealt with
Pſal. xxviii. 6. ' Bleſſed be the Lord,
' heard the voice of my ſupplications
' Lord is my ſtrength and my ſhield ; m
' him, and I am helped ; therefore my
' joiceth ;' for I have been well helped
Lord, and that in a very ſingular mann
fence has made my ſoul to ſing and r(
greateſt of difficulties and trials that e
with ; and this is a ſweet promiſe and
ment for me, in Iſa. xli. 10. ' Fear tho
' with thee; be not diſmayed, for I am
' ſtrengthen thee, yea, I will help thee,)
' thee with the right hand of my rigl
11. ' Behold, all they that are incenſed a
' be aſhamed, and confounded : they ſh
' and they that ſtrive with thee ſhall

of Arthur Taket.

'Thou shalt seek them, and shalt not find them, even
' them that contend with thee: and they that war against
' thee shall be as nothing, and as a thing of nought.'
Ver. 13. ' For I the Lord thy God will hold thy right
' hand, saying unto thee, Fear not, I will help thee.''
Which has been well made out unto me in all things that
I have met with. For since I was brought to prison I
have been well helped of the Lord, that the fear of hell
death and the grave, and the fear of all things is taken
away fully from me, that I am not afraid to venture upon a gibbet for my lovely Lord and Master's noble cause,
and for his controverted truths; and this I am really persuaded of, that the truths of God were never so much
controverted as now. But I am sure of it, that the
truths of God, when they are most controverted, ought
to be most zealously owned by his people. I may well
acquiesce and assent unto Psal. lxxiii. 23. 24. 25. ' Ne-
' verthelefs I am continually with thee: thou hast hol-
' den me by my right hand. Thou shalt guide me with
' thy counsel, and afterward receive me to glo-
' ry. Whom have I in heaven but thee? and there is,
' none upon earth that I desire besides thee.' This I
dare say, as in his sight, (my conscience bearing me witness) that there is nothing in heaven or in earth so desirable unto my soul as precious Christ: for I am confident and persuaded, that this is his language to me,
' Arise and depart, for this is not your rest, because it
' is polluted:' As Paul says, 2 Cor. v. 1. ' For we know,
' that if our earthly house of this tabernacle were dis-
' solved, we have a building of God, an house not made
' with hands,' &c;. And as Paul says, 1 Cor. xv. 50.
' Now this I say, brethren, that flesh and blood cannot
' inherit the kingdom of God; neither doth corruption
' inherit incorruption.' I can clearly say by experience,
that thro' Jesus Christ, whom I desire to take for my
King, Priest, and Prophet, and my only Lord and lawgiver, I have been made more than a conqueror over
death, hell and the grave, and all things in this life. '

Now, to come to shew you the only head that my sentence of death is founded upon by men, it is mainly for
my being in arms at Bothwel; which was merely in defence of ourselves, and in defence of the gospel preached,
and standing to the defence of the covenant of God,
which the whole of the land was solemnly sworn and en-

gaged to, with hands lifted up to the moſt high God, and ſo bound to ſtand to the defence thereof: for which I am unjuſtly ſentenced to death by men, of which ſentence I am not aſhamed this day, but counts it my only glory, honour and dignity, whilſt he paſſed by ſuch tall cedars, which is a matter of wonder and admiration to me. But as he has ſaid in his word, ' In nothing be ye ' terrified by your adverſaries, which is to them an evi- ' dent token of perdition; but to you of ſalvation, and ' that of God: for it is not only given you to believe, ' but alſo to ſuffer for his ſake:' ſo ſuffering is a gift not given to every one; and I deſire to bleſs his name, with my whole heart and ſoul, that he has counted ſuch a poor thing as I am worthy of the gift of ſuffering.

Now, this is to let you all know, worthy and dear Chriſtian friends, that are deſiring to keep the way of the Lord, that there was not one word, of all they interrogate me upon, in the ſentence of death that theſe bloody tyrants paſt againſt me, but only for being in arm at Bothwel-bridge. And let none think that I am ſentenced to death upon that head, that I was ſo cruelly threatned with torture by theſe bloody tyrants for, which was, for being at the Black-loch, and becauſe I would not declare who was the miniſter, and what perſons knew. And tho' men have, by a permiſſive and limited power, paſſed a ſentence of death againſt me, to take away my natural life, this I know, and am perſuaded of that there is a Judge above, who has paſſed a ſentence of life in heaven unto my ſoul this day, which ſhall never be recalled or reverſed again, which is my only encouragement: and this he has promiſed to as many as believe in him, to ' give them everlaſting life: Theſe that ſuffer ' with him, ſhall reign with him; and theſe that b ' dead with him, ſhall live with him alſo:' As Paul ſays in Rom. x. 9. ' If thou ſhalt confeſs with thy mout ' the Lord Jeſus, and ſhalt believe in thine heart, tha ' God hath raiſed him from the dead, thou ſhalt be ſav ' ed.' Ver. 10. ' For with the heart man believeth un ' to righteouſneſs, and with the mouth confeſſion is mad ' unto ſalvation.' For the Scripture ſaith, ' Whoſo ' ever believeth in him ſhall not be aſhamed;' which i my only comfort, and a noble ſweet encouragement fo me. And this he hath promiſed in his word, That ' h ' ſhall feed his flock like a ſhepherd, he ſhall gather th

lambs in his arms, and carry them in his bosom, and
shall gently lead these that are with young.' I have
und by my experience, that the Lord my God has
sweetly and gently led me thro' the greatest difficulties
that I have been trysted with since he made choice of
me to suffer for his noble cause. O if ye knew what of
his love I have met with, and what sweet ingredients of
the Lord's matchless love has been intermixed and put
in my cup, ye would not be afraid to venture upon the
sweet cross of Christ, which has been made sweet and
easy unto me.

[Because the heads of truth this martyr gives his testimony to, and the defections he witnessed against, are
such the same with the preceeding testimonies; therefore to avoid all impertinent repetition they are omitted.
He is both full and accurate, passing by nothing of the
heads of sin and duty, which at that time were controverted: Particularly (which hath not been met with in
any of the former) he gives his hearty testimony to that
faithful and called minister of Jesus Christ, Mr. James
Renwick, for his holding up the fallen down banner of
our Lord, and jeoparding his life in the open fields; altho' some are pleased to say, that he is not lawfully called and ordained to the ministry, but that he was admitted by the erastian ministers of Holland; such as Coccei-
us and Labadeans: but it is faithfully witnessed, that
he was admitted without them, and by the purest of the
ministers of the church of Holland, according to the
church of Scotland's discipline and government, Covenants and Confession of Faith. And he dies with a spirit of meekness, declaring that he forgives his enemies
all the wrongs they had done him, personally considered; tho' witnessing against the indignities which they
had done to Christ, and him as a member of that body
whereof Christ is the head. And whereas he was branded with disowning magistrates, he declares before God
and the world, that he owns and allows of all magistrates, superior or inferior, as they are conform to the
written word of God, and our solemn covenants, and
as they are ' a terror to evil doers, and a praise to them
that do well.']

The last Speech and Testimony of THOM~~~~
BERTSON, *who lived at Newcastle, and
prison there, for refusing the oath of allegiance,
ing made his escape thence to Edinburgh, wa
a public search there, Nov.* 29. 1684, *and
the Gallowlee, the* 9*th day of Dec. thereafter.*

NOW, dear friends, time seems to me
short; O now welcome long eternity.
has been the butt of my desire this considerabl
eye God's glory; and I preferred it to my c
salvation: yet when I heard my indictment,
strange effect upon me; and altho' death hath
been my desire for the cause of Christ, yet it se
a little terrible unto me, and that for the spac
seven hours; so that some times it had such a
cy, that I was afraid I should have turned ba
was so put to it, that I had nothing to hold b
mer purposes and determinations: and from
deration of Christ's faithfulness, I grappled li
more than half drowned. At last I got hold
hold of him, whom I could not see; and that
which I got, thro' his mercy, I kept till I got
that now he has discovered himself unto me, a
pleased to stay, and make with me a new co
that now thro' his grace, I am resolved not t
go, let the cost be what it will. Now, my f
say not this for the discouragement of any that
ning to follow Christ, or any that is already be
ly I do it as a warning. I would fain have po
to make sure work, and to get sure hold of him
tho' he seems to cover himself, and that when pe
think they stand in most need, yet he will ret
them in his own appointed time, and that for t
er advantage of them that are thus trysted. O
to love him! It hath been my great trouble, tha
never love him much, nor fall upon the righ
worshipping him. O to have my soul found
him! O for strength! O for strength to be carrie
and cleanly thro', so that I may loose neither
hoof of the truths of Christ! In so far as I an
understand, it hath been my great care always
what was sin, and what was duty; I think I

been out of my duty in so doing: and I think it is the duty of all persons to be concerned in that matter; for how can persons know, how to avoid the one, and cleave to the other, except they distinguish betwixt the two. Now, I shall say no more to that, but only, O that folk would make it a great part of their work, to distinguish betwixt the two.

Now, 1*st*, I adhere to the covenant of redemption betwixt the Father and the Son, before the foundation of the world, for redemption of poor things, that he has chosen out of the world. O for love to him! O for love to him! O now to be with him! that I may experience the benefit of that covenant which cost him his precious blood! And now seeing he is calling me to give a testimony, I think, if every hair of my head were a man, it is all too little to lay down for him. O for love to this non-such Jesus Christ. 2*dly*, I adhere and leave my testimony to the word of God, the Scriptures of the Old and New Testaments, by which I must be judged; for if we take any other way, we will be sure to go wrong; for the Spirit of God witnesseth with our spirits, that the word of God is the only rule, by which we ought to walk. 3*dly*, I leave my testimony to the work of reformation once glorious in our land: altho' alas! now defaced, and the hedge and government of Christ's house broken down, and the kingly office of Christ usurped, by a cruel and bloody-thirsty man, to whom I could with repentance, if it were the will of God; and to all that associate and join with him: but alas! I think it is hid from their eyes. Now, I leave my testimony to the National and Solemn League and Covenant, Confession of Faith, Larger and Shorter Catechisms, Sum of Saving Knowledge; and the several parts of reformation to this day of my death. Also, I leave my testimony to all the faithful ambassadors, and sent servants of Jesus Christ, and to the preached gospel itself; to Mr. Donald Cargil, that worthy servant of Jesus Christ, who kept up the standard and banner of Jesus Christ, when the rest fled from him and the Lord's standard. Also, I leave my testimony to Mr. James Renwick, as a faithful and lawfully ordained and called servant of Jesus Christ. And I leave my testimony to all the testimonies of the faithful martyrs and witnesses of Jesus Christ, that have laid down their lives for the cause of Christ, and are banished

to foreign lands for the name of Chrift
caufe, and alfo, I difown, difclaim and
all this evil and adulterous generation,
revolters, backflitlers and evil doers, tha
fevere punifhment, great wrath and jud
ternal death befides, except they repent.
fpecial manner, being convinced of my
adhering to Prelacy, and fpending the
time in hearing of curates, and thereb
them and their corruptions, and corrupt
withftanding that I came always awa
them, with more hardnefs of heart, tha
to hear them: but at laft I began to co:
ters were not right with me in this ca
that there was a people in the place that
Prefbyterian minifters, but not being
them, I knew not what to do to be ac
ever, I perfumed to tell my cafe to on
took me to the place where I heard a P1
fter preach; which left a conviction upc
of my former courfes, and that I was o
the Lord for falvation and eternal life:
I went no more back to follow them, t
oppofition to the way of the Lord, ou:
work of reformation; and by degrees ca
ly, that the minifters that were moft ever
and againft the defections and abominat
and this adulterous generation, were on
Lord honoured with the revealing of hi
his mind concerning the duties of the d
nald Cargil, and thefe that were faithf
and fealed the caufe with their blood. /
I love and long to be a witnefs for him,
own former ways, and the ways of that
lacy, which now I hate; and to get le
my life for Chrift and his precious trutl
has granted me my heart's defire, and I
blood, that this is the way of God, and
I now lay down my life for. Not havi
fay no more, but leaves my wife to the
the Lord, and commends him and his w:
low, and my love to her, and all my
Newcaftle. Farewel, farewel in our ble
And welcome Lord Jefus, for whom I

we I long to have in poſſeſſion; welcome heaven and
oly angels, and, the ſpirits of juſt men made perfect,
\ro' the blood of the Lamb; welcome Father, Son and
oly Ghoſt, into whoſe hands I commit my ſpirit.
  Sic ſubſcribitur,
          THOMAS ROBERTSON.

he Teſtimony of JAMES NICOL *merchant, burgeſs
of Peebles, who ſuffered at the Graſs-market of Edinburgh,
Aug.* 27. 1684.

His interrogations before the privy council, Auguſt 18.
FIRST, I was interrogate by two in a room privately thus. *Q.* Was you at Bothwel-bridge? *A.* I am
ot bound to be my own accuſer. I am not (ſaid one
f them) to deſire you, but only ſay, upon your honeſt
ord, that you were not there. *A.* I am not bound to
\tisfy you, but prove what you have to ſay againſt me,
nd eſpecially you, till I come before my accuſers. Well,
rid he, I am one of them. Then I anſwered, I was
lere. *Q.* How came you to riſe in arms againſt the
ing? *A.* Becauſe he has broken the covenant of the
,ord my God. *Q.* Was the prelate's death murder?
!. No, it was not murder. *Q.* Was Hackſtoun's death
lurder? *A.* That it was indeed. *Q.* How dare ye own
ie Covenant, ſeeing the king gave orders to burn it by
ie hand of the hangman? *A.* Yes, I dare own it; for
ltho' ye ſhould eſcape the hand of men for ſo doing, yet
e ſhall all pay for it ere all be done, and that to pur-
oſe: as for me I would not do it for the whole earth.
'hen I was interrogate by other two, who aſked ſome
ivolous queſtions, which I baffled to ſilence. Then I
as brought in before the bloody crew. What now,
ir, ſaid they, do ye own the king's authority? *A.* I
wn all things that the precious word of God owns in
:ſs or more, and all faithful magiſtrates. *Q.* But do
ou not own king Charles alſo? *A.* I dare not for a
,orld, becauſe it is perjury, for he has unkinged him-
:lf in a high degree, and that in doing all things con-
rary to the word of God, and Confeſſion of Faith, and
:atechiſms Larger and Shorter. *Q.* Know ye to whom
'e are ſpeaking? *A.* I know I am before men. But (ſaid
ne of them) ye are ſpeaking to the chancellor and mem-
ers of council, Sir. But ſaid I; I have told you al-

ready that he has unkinged himself, and
graded yourselves from being princes.
were here, what would you say, Sir? *A*
ought to speak to the king, if he were k
dinarily said to him: and so to let you l
no Quaker, or erroneous in any thing, l
byterian, and of a gospel apostolic spir
Sirs, because ye are noblemen by birth,
ye are my judges. *Q.* Will ye not say
king's majesty? A. I dare not bless them v
rejected: ' If any man bring another do
' have received, bid him not God speed,
' into your house,' 2 John 10. and Psa
beginning, says David, ' Their drink-
' not offer, nor take up their names in
them that hasten after other gods, and t
not pray for him. *Q.* And will ye not pr
If he belong to the election of grace, he
my prayers: And also if he were a king t
covenant with God I would give him a do
make mention of his name, but he is an
my friends, they looked still one to an
question and answer) *Q.* How old are
am fifty one years. *Q.* How dare ye own
seeing we have burnt them by the hand of
A. Sir, I dare own them upon all perils
the utmost of my power, all the days of
with that they smiled, and laughed one
to me, and said, my days were near an
am now in your power, but if ye take m
take innocent blood upon yourselves; as i
15. ' As for me, behold, I am in your
' me as seemeth good and meet unto yo
' ye for certain, that if ye put me to dea
' ly bring innocent blood upon yourse
' this city, and upon the inhabitants th
for me, if ye take my blood, it is as in
ever ye did take; for I did never wrong
day. *Q.* Do ye go to the church? *A.* l
church, where I could get any faithful
to: but for your prelate's kirks, and l
never heard any of them, nor never int
were to live an hundred years. But, fa
not live long now, Sir. *Q.* How do y

Scripture what ye say against the prelates? *A.* By many Scriptures; 'The kings of the Gentiles exercise lordship 'over them, and they that exercise authority upon them, 'are called benefactors; but it shall not be so among 'you; but he that is greatest among you, shall be the 'servant of all:' not like your glutton, Epicurean, belly-god prelates, who are riding in coaches, in great pomp. But they would not suffer me to speak more, nor cite moe places, but asked several questions, which I have not good memory of: only this word I said, concerning the tyrant, He was brought home by Mr. Livingston and others, and put in a nobler estate than any king in the whole world, crowned a covenanted king with the eternal God, to be for him, and to carry on his work and cause, he and all his people; which if he had continued in, he would have been the greatest king in all lands and nations in the world, and would have been a terror to all the kings in Europe; but now he hath made himself base, and a reproach to all the nations, so have all of you. And another reason why I dare not own him, or you either, is, because he and you have robbed Christ of his crown, altho' it be not in your power to do it. They bade take me away to the iron-house, and put on the irons on me, which they did on both my hands, that I could write none that day, till I got a mean to put them off the one hand.

Then on Tuesday they called me before them again, being the 19th day of this instant. *Q.* What say ye the day, do ye adhere to all you said yesterday? *A.* I adhere to all and hail upon all perils whatsomever. *Q.* Do you approve of Bothwel-bridge? *A.* Yes, I do. *Q.* Do you go to the kirk at Peebles? *A.* No, nor never intends to go there, nor no place else which pertains to the perjured Prelates. *Q.* Do you own the covenants? *A.* I adhere to every point of them, because they are in short, an obligation to the whole sum of the Scripture; and as the sum of the law is, ' to 'love the Lord our God with all our soul, and 'heart, and mind, and with our whole strength, and 'our neighbour as ourselves:' So it is the whole duty, which the Lord requires of me and all men. *Q.* And how do you reject the king, seeing the Scripture commands you to obey him? *A.* Because the coronation sermon, and the coronation itself, does openly declare, that the people makes a king, and not the king a people, and that he was received home, and crowned for no other thing or end, but to maintain that interest to the utmost of his power; and no longer to be owned as king, than he did own that wherefore he was crowned; so that we were freely loosed from him, as soon as he plaid his base pranks, in taking the malignants by the hand, and murdering a prince and a prophet. viz. Argyle, who set the crown upon his head, and Mr. Guthrie, who was a godly reformer in our land. Next I said, What thought ye of Mr. Douglas, who preached and gave him all his injunctions at Scoon? They said to me, He should have been hanged for his pains: But I said, God would be about with them all for rejecting the word of the Lord in these directions. *Q.* How do ye disown him, seeing the most part, both of ministers and professors do pray for him? *A.* Because the general assembly at the West-kirk disowned him altogether, till he made a declaration of humiliation for his own sins, and his father's: And the parliament being then sitting at Edinburgh, did ratify the assembly's act, and disowned him till he should do that, which accordingly he did, and so we are loosed freely. *Q.* Do ye own Airsmoss, Sanquhar, Rutherglen, and Lanerk declarations? *A.* Yes, I do, because they are agreable to the covenants, and work of reformation. And many moe questions they asked, which I cannot now particularly remember. But I told them in general, That I was against Popery, Prelacy, malignancy and profanity, and all that is against sound doctrine, discipline, worship and government; and all errors whatsomever, which are contrary to sound Presbyterian doctrine, be what they will; for there is none other right, but erroneous, how fair a face soever they have, which shall be found not agreeable to the apostle's doctrine. And then they read something of what I had said, and questioned, if I would subscribe what I had said. I answered, No. *Q.* Can ye write? *A.* Yes, I can write. Then do it, said they. But I said, I would not do it at all. Now, my friends, I say, these are a part of my interrogations.

Again, I was brought before the justiciary (as they call themselves) on the 19th of this instant, and interrogate thus: *Q.* What now, Sir, what think you of yourself the day? *A.* I praise my God I am the same I was.

Q. What think you of what you said yesterday before the chancellor and the council? I hold all and decline nothing; no, not one ace. *Q.* Were you at Bothwel-bridge? *A.* Yes, that I was. *Q.* Had ye arms? Yes, that I had. One of them said, God help you: And I said, I wot not if ye can pray for yourself. But, said he, I wish you better nor you do yourself. But I said, No; for ye would have me disown my great Lord, the King of Zion, and obey men, yea, base men, ' whose breath is in ' their nostrils,' who give out laws and commandments contrary to his. *Q.* How dare ye rise in arms against the king? *A.* It is better to obey God than man, and he is an enemy to God. *Q.* Would you rise yet in arms for the covenants against the king's laws, if ye had the occasion? *A.* Yes, that I would, say the contrary who will, upon all peril. *Q.* What think you of yourself in spoiling the country of horse and arms, Sir? *A.* Sir, I had not the worth of a spur whang of any man's but was mounted with horse and arms of my own. *Q.* Where have you been all this time? *A.* Sometimes here and there, in England and Scotland. *Q.* Whom have ye converted with? *A.* I was about my business, being a merchant. They said, ye have been about another business; for ye are found to be a fugitive and a vagabond. *A.* I have been a merchant from my youth. *Q.* But where had you your chamber in this town? *A.* I had none these several years. *Q.* Where quarter you in this town? *A.* I have not been much in it these seven or eight years. *Q.* But where was you the night and the last night before the execution? *A.* I was not in town, I came but in at the port just when the first was cast over. Then they looked one to another, and whispered together: But they would fain have had me wronging my landlords in all the parts of the country, and in all burghs; but glory to my Lord, I have wronged none yet, nor yet hopes to do; for it was ay my care, and prayer to God earnestly, that I might wrong no man, and that I had rather suffer before any were wronged by me, which he has keeped me from to this day. Then they read what I had said. *Q.* Will you subscribe what you have said? *A.* No, no. *Q.* Can you write, Sir? *A.* Yes, that I can. Well, said they, write down, that he can, but will not. They told me five or six times, that my time should not be long; and said to me, Will you have

The laſt Speech and Teſti

a miniſter? *A.* I will have none of your
if I could have gotten leave, I ſhould h
abominable to them, and alſo at every qu
have made them aſhamed.

After relating the occaſion of his being
which was thus; He having ſeen three of
tian brethren, condemned before the juſt
the forenoon, and going to the Weſt-por
was obliged to ſtay till his ſaddle was me
was ready to mount his horſe, he hears
men were brought to the place of execut
ternoon he went thither, and ſeeing th
the enemies in murdering his dear brethr
a ſtrong zeal againſt theſe murderers, cr
ſtile of the Prophet Amos, ' A cow of B
' ed three men to death at one puſh, cc
' own baſe laws, in an inhuman way.
Therefore ceaſe to kill me with your rep
I am dead, as ye did while I was living;
ed to kill and murder my name this many
I forgive you with all my heart, and pra
forgive you. (And having related, hov
22d day of Auguſt, one brought him his i
al telling him, that upon the 27th he w
ced, and go immediately from the bench
He adds,) Now, my dear friends, I thin
written is confuſed, becauſe I could har
write two lines, but was either put from
ers, or called from it by one confuſion
fore ye muſt excuſe me; but although it l
ly written, yet there is no error in it:
down my life for, and adhere to as th
dying man, who muſt very ſhortly ap
Lord, and give an account of all that I
written. However, my friends, miſtake
it be confuſed, and ye find ſome things
there is no more fear on me now, than t
that ever I had, as to what man can do
be ſad as to matters betwixt God and
glorious Lord and me, as good cauſe I
it as I do; but I hope, I ſhall get a g
(when his time comes, which I have alw
and not mine) for which I bleſs him thi

What further this martyr wrote in p

published as it stands, in regard that he being perpetually interrupted by the keepers, and having the irons on his hands, (as himself testifies) could not get it written with that compofure which he would. Wherefore take fome of the more remarkable heads of it, moftly in his own words, as follows : 1*st*, He declares his cheerfulnefs to lay down his life for the caufe of Chrift, and faith once delivered to the faints. Admiring the riches of the free grace of God, in Chrift's laying down his life for poor finners, and blefling them with fuch a noble, precious and excellent blefling, as to be called the fons of God, which the angels cannot take up, altho' they have been a long time prying into it; and invites others to the fame exercife of admiring and praifing God's love, in making, thro' the blood of Chrift, rebels and enemies, friends and fervants. 2*dly*, He rejoices in his lot of fuffering thus: O but it be an excellent thing to be called of the Lord, to lay down my life for him and his glorious intereft! to me it is more than all the world : I cannot prize it. It has been my defire thefe twenty four years, to die a martyr for my Lord, and to witnefs for him, if it be his will, and not elfe; I blefs my Lord for it, I have fubfcribed a blank, and put it in his hand, to do with me, whatfoever is the determinate counfel of his will and decree, and not to call myfelf. 3*dly*. He blefles God, that tho' he would have got his life for doing what others, whom he calls better than himfelf, have done; yet the Lord had made it his glory, honour and crown, to *hold faft till the Lord come*, which he hoped would be quickly to himfelf, and alfo to the land. 4*thly*, He teftifies his affurance of God's love to him, and his children, whom he heartily and cheerfully gives away to God, as he had oft devoted them to him in covenant; he exhorts them in the words of a dying father, To be for God, in their generation, to live in love and unity, leaving them to the protection and provifion of his God, charging them not to be moved for his fufferings, which he protefts he would not exchange for the whole world. 5*thly*, He charges them all to beware of wronging themfelves by reproaching him anent the manner of his being apprehended, fhewing what a hand of divine providence there was in it, and blefling God for it, and for the fweet peace he had in fuffering. 6*thly*, He owns himfelf to have been the greateft finner upon the earth, and hence

takes occasion to magnify the redeeming love
in calling him effectually, and keeping him i[n]
way, and from the national sins and corrupti[ons ...]
age. *7thly*, He refers to a list of papers writt[en]
declarative of his judgment concerning the [ ]
day, as a reason among others, why he wrote
testimony in the prison, save only that he test[ified]
Generally, against all things contrary to a[ny]
truth in the Old and New Testament, or co[ntrary]
to the covenants and work of reformation;
particularly, against the sinful silence of mini[sters in Bri-]
tain and Ireland, at the command of a bloo[dy a-]
dulterous, perjured tyrant, and his underlin[gs,]
the indulgences and indemnities; against co[mpliance]
and conforming either with a perjured tyranni[cal set of]
statesmen, or with base, vile, filthy Prela[tes,]
blind guides, and Baal's priests; against back[s-]
litters and professors, (who condemned a p[oor]
generation for adhering to truth) for slayin[g]
his members, for pleasing men, and displeasi[ng that]
enough exalted and glorious Lord. And final[ly against]
all that is contrary to a gospel and apostolic sp[irit.]
He proceeds to warn and exhort all sorts of p[ersons,]
more especially the young generation to rep[entance and]
amendment of life, enforcing his exhortatio[n by]
consideration of judgments, and strokes to [come on]
the land, upon which head he is exceeding la[rge, found-]
ing his assertions upon the threatenings pro[nounced in]
the word against these sins, whereof he d[eclares]
Scotland, England, and Ireland to have bee[n notorious-]
ly guilty. Interposing withal sweet and rav[ishing con-]
siderations of God's love to him, and his oth[er]
witnesses, which after large and pathetic eja[culations and]
praises to God, for his redeeming love, prot[ests that]
he expects salvation not by any merit, but of [free grace,]
saying, " I have been beginning to pray and [praise these]
thirty six years, weakly as I could; but yet [I shall]
begin this night, both to praise and pray: [I lay no]
more stress upon all that I have said and don[e]
and suffered, nor on a straw, God is my witn[ess,]
I must have salvation upon Wednesday at t[he ...]
of the clock, as freely as the thief on the c[ross."] He then
winds up, in imitation of David, with th[e psalm,]
" And what can poor silly James Nicol say [ ]

resuming again the consideration of God's wrath against the land, to stir up all ranks to repentance.

After he had concluded his speech with the usual formality of bidding farewel to his suffering brethren, and all sublunary things, embracing and welcoming the heavenly joys, and eternal enjoyment of God, the Father, Son, and Holy Ghost, into whose hands he commits his spirit: He adds by way of postscript:

" Now dear friends, my testimony being finished, and I being near the borders of eternity, having forgot that which I see a great necessity to leave my testimony against; I think it a most concerning and necessary duty to leave my testimony against James Russel and Mr. John Flint, because James Russel, and these in fellowship with him, have separated themselves from the persecuted suffering remnant of the church of Scotland, and Mr. John Flint has taken upon him, with their consent, to officiate the work of a minister, contrary to the word of God; he has run, altho' not sent of God, nor called, nor ordained of lawful church members: And now he and they have risen up in opposition to God, his cause and persecuted remnant in the church of Scotland, calling them all perjured, that are suffering unto death, imprisonment and banishment for precious Christ. And therefore, I as a dying witness for him, even my Lord Jesus, my only Saviour, who converted me thirty-six years since, and has these twenty-four years helped me to pray to him, to enable me to witness against all error and defection, and has keeped me right and straight to this day of my longed for desire, do leave my witness and testimony against Mr. John Flint and James Russel, and all that adhere to them."

UPon the 5th of March 1684, suffered that worthy gentleman, Mr. John Dick, student of Theology; whose elaborate and judicious Testimony had been here insert, but that it has been lately published in print by itself, and so is in a great many peoples hands already, and the reader may have recourse to the said print for it; which, upon perusal, he will find second to none, for a steady zeal and adherence to the reformation, an orderly method, pithy and pertinent defences against the cavils of the adversaries, and proper and necessary advices to fellow-sufferers, abating only his adherence to

Hamilton Declaration, wherein he seems to differ from the rest of the sufferers at that time; and owning the king's authority, which yet he does in such a limited and restricted sense, as thereby not to own the wicked laws, and exercise thereof; tho' it is true the restrictions and limitations, with which he declared his owning it, were such as did no way agree to the tyrant, and consequently it was a real, tho' not a formal denial thereof. Only in the said Printed Testimony, there are several errors of the transcriber, or the press, which the judicious reader will not impute to the Author.

The joint Testimony of THOMAS HARKNESS *in Locherbane,* ANDREW CLARK *in Leadhills, in Crawford parish, and* SAMUEL M'EUEN, *in Glencairn parish; who were sentenced, and suffered at Edinburgh, August* 15. 1684.

Dear friends and relations whatsoever,

WE think it fit to acquaint you, that we bless the Lord, that ever we were ordained to give such a public testimony, who are so great sinners. Blessed be he that ever we were born to bear witness for him. And blessed be the Lord Jesus Christ, that ordained the gospel and the truths of it, which he sealed with his own blood, and many a worthy Christian gone before us have sealed them. We were questioned for not owning the king's authority: We answered, That we owned all authority that is allowed by the written word of God, sealed by Christ's blood. Now, our dear friends, we entreat you to stand to the truth, and especially all ye that are our own relations, and all that love and wait for the coming of Christ. He will come, and will not tarry, and reward every one according to their deeds in the body.

We bless the Lord, we are not a whit discouraged, but content to lay down our life with cheerfulness, and boldness, and courage; and if we had a hundred lives, we would willingly quit with them all for the truth of Christ. Good news! Christ is no worse than he promised.

Now we take our leave of all friends and acquaintances, and declare, we are heartily content with our lot, and that he hath brought us hither to witness for him and his truth. We leave our teftimony againft Popery, and all other falfe doctrine, that is not according to the Scriptures of the Old and New Teftament, which is the only word of God.

Dear friends, Be valiant for God, for he is as good as his promife, 'He that overcometh, he will make a 'pillar in his temple.' Our time is fhort, and we have little to fpare; having got our fentence at one of the clock this afternoon, and are to die at five this day. And fo we fay no more; but farewel, all friends and relations. Welcome heaven and Chrift, and the crofs for Chrift's fake.

T. HARKNESS, A. CLARK, S. M'EUEN.

A Letter from SAMUEL M'EUEN *to a friend, after his fentence was pronounced.*

My dear friend,

I Am this day to lay down my life, for adhering to the truth of God, and I blefs his holy name that ever he honoured me, a poor country lad, having neither father nor mother to witnefs for him. And now I can fet to my feal to all the truths in the Bible, Confeffion of Faith, Catechifms Larger and Shorter, National and Solemn League and Covenants, and all the proteftations and declarations given by the poor remnant, agreeable to the fame word of God. Tho' in much weaknefs, yet I love all that is for his glory, and defire you not to be difcouraged, for I blefs the Lord, I am heartily content with my lot. It was my defire, tho' moft unworthy, to die a martyr; and I blefs the Lord, who has granted me my defire. Now, this is the moft joyful day ever I faw with my eyes. Farewel all earthly enjoyments, and friends in our fweet Lord Jefus Chrift; and farewel Glencairn my native parifh. Welcome my fweet Saviour, into thy hands I commit my fpirit, 'for thou art 'he, O Jehovah, God of truth, who haft redeemed 'me.'

SAMUEL M'EUEN.

The joint Testimony of JAMES LAWSON *and* A-LEXANDER WOOD, *who suffered at Glasgow, October* 24. 1684.

NOW this is the most joyful day that ever we had in all our life, and we join our hearty testimony to the written word of God, as it is contained in the Old and New Testament, and to the Confession of Faith, the Larger and Shorter Catechisms, the Engagement to Duties; and solemn Acknowledgment of Sins, and to the Covenants both National and Solemn League, and to the Causes of God's Wrath; and we also join our hearty testimony to the true and faithful preached gospel, by his true and faithful sent ministers, both formerly and of late, commissioned and cloathed with his message to declare the whole counsel of God, as it was reformed from Popery, Prelacy, Erastianism and supremacy. We also join our hearty testimony to the testimonies of those that have gone before us, both formerly and of late, who suffered for the cause and interest of Jesus Christ. And likewise to all the appearances of the Lord's people, and their being in arms, for the defence of the gospel, and self defence, viz. Pentland, Drumclog, Bothwelbridge, and the declarations given at Rutherglen, the 29th of May, 1679, and Sanquhar, and to the papers found upon Henry Hall at the Queensferry, and to that declaration put forth at Lanerk, by the suffering remnant. We also join our hearty testimony to the Christian fellowship meetings, whereby our souls have sometimes been refreshed.

Now, likewise, we shall shew you what we disown: 1st, We disown and leave our testimony against Popery and Prelacy, Quakerism, Erastianism, and all other errors, that are contrary to the word of God. Likewise we leave our testimony against all the indulgences, both first and last; because they have disowned Christ from being head of the church, and have taken their liberty from a mortal man. Likewise we leave our testimony against all these that have left the standard of Christ, and taken themselves to a sinful quietness, to shun suffering; and also their condemning of the faithful practices and preaching of these two worthies, who sealed the truth with their blood, viz. Mr. Donald Cargil, and Mr. Rich-

of James Lawson and Alexander Wood.

ard Cameron, who declared the whole counsel of God faithfully. We desire to bless the Lord, that ever we heard them preach. Likewise we leave our testimony against the declaration at Hamilton, because of the taking in of that tyrant's interest. Likewise against Charles Stuart, because he hath seated himself in Christ's room, and has taken to himself the prerogative of our Lord, to be head of the church, which belongs to no mortal man on earth, but Christ only. Likewise we leave our testimony against that hell-hatched Test, and against that oath, called the oath of allegiance; against compearing at courts, coming out of prison upon bond and caution. Ye will find the unlawfulness of it in John viii. 34. 'Verily, verily I say unto you, whosoever committeth sin, is 'the servant of sin.' And in Rom. vi. 20. 'For when ye 'were the servants of sin, ye were free from righteous-'ness. What fruit had ye in these things, whereof ye 'are now ashamed? for the end of these things is death.' And 2 Pet. ii. 19. 'While they promise you liberty, 'themselves are the servants of corruption: for of whom 'a man is overcome, of the same is he brought in bon-'dage.' And against the cess and locality, or any paying of militia money, or any other thing, which may strengthen the hands of those open and avowed enemies of Jesus Christ. Likewise we leave our testimony against these wicked men called judges, which ought not to be called judges, but rather tyrants, because they are thirsting for blood; for they charge us in one of the articles of our indictment, with murder, and shaking off all the fear of God: but we bless the Lord we are free of all such crimes as murder.

Now, dear friends, we exhort you to cleave close to Christ, keep his way, and do not fear at it because of suffering: for we can assure you, that the cross has not been troublesome to us, but easy; for he paves the cross all over with roses, and never lays a grain weight of affliction more upon his people, than he gives sufficient strength to bear: and this we can say by experience, *He finds none a warfare upon their own charges,* but he gives still sufficient strength to carry them thro'. Therefore it is our earnest desire and request, that ye will follow on to know the Lord, for if ye follow on to know him, he has promised, *that ye shall know him.* Therefore we desire you to follow his way, and fear not man, whose

breath is in his noftrils, but fear God and keep his ways
Keep at a diftance from the leaft of fin; for the leaft fi
deferveth death: but his love hath been great and con
defcending to us, for he hath taken us, who were th
vileft of finners, for we have deftroyed ourfelves by ori
ginal fin, and corrupt nature; but now he hath redeem
ed us, and plucked us out like fire-brands out of th
midft of the burning. Now we may fay, he hath lette
out fuch a gale of his condefcending love, that he hat
gained our fecklefs love; fo that we dare fay, that
every hair of our head were a man, and every drop o
our blood a life, we would willingly lay them all dow
for Chrift and his caufe, if he called for them at ou
hand; ' for he is altogether lovely, the chief among te
' thoufands;' he is without compare, he is incompre
henfible, glorious and mighty: Therefore it is our de
fire to all friends, that ye would ware your love on him
and credit him; and labour to get the inheritance mac
fure, that Jefus Chrift hath purchafed. Now clear
clofe to him, and clofe with him, and then lofe wh;
ye will in this world, ye fhall be noble gainers, and r
lofers.

Now, we heartily forgive all men any wrong they ha
done us, or can do to us, as we defire to be forgiven
the Lord; but what they have done againft God and h
caufe, we leave that to himfelf, to do in it as may mo
glorify himfelf. Now, we bid farewel to all earth
comforts and enjoyments; farewel all Chriftian frien
and acquaintances in the Lord; farewel fweet focietie
and Chriftian fellowfhip-meetings; farewel hearing
the precious gofpel; farewel reading, finging, prayir
and believing; farewel fweet prifon and irons for o
lovely Lord; farewel holy Scriptures; farewel fun, moo
and ftars, and all created comforts in time. Welcor
heaven; welcome finging of praifes; welcome fpirits
juft men made perfect; welcome Father, Son, and Ho
Ghoft, into whofe hands we commit our fpirits.

    Sic fubfcribitur,
      JA. LAWSON, A. WOOl

The Interrogations of GEORGE JACKSON, *tenant to Pollock, who was apprehended at Glasgow, and suffered at the Gallowlee, December 9th, 1684.*

AT Glasgow after he was taken, and had been asked some few questions by them who apprehended him, he was brought before the bishop of Glasgow, who interrogate him thus. *Quest.* What now, Mr. Jackson? *Ans.* I was never a scholar. *Q.* Can you read the Bible? *A.* Yes. *Q.* Was you at Bothwel-bridge? *A.* Yes. *Q.* What arms had ye? *A.* A halbert-staff. *Q.* Was you an officer? *A.* No, I was but sixteen years of age. *Q.* Who was your captain? *A.* A young man. *Q.* How called they him? *A.* I am not bound to give an account to you. *Q.* Was you at Bothwel rebellion, or not? *A.* I allow myself in no rebellion against God. *Q.* Whether was it rebellion against the king, or not? *A.* I have answered that question already. *Q.* Would you go to it again? *A.* The question is like yourself; I know not. *Q.* Will ye say, *God save the king?* *A.* It is not in my power to save or condemn. *Q.* Will you pray for him? *A.* I will pray for all within the election of free grace. *Q.* Whether is the king within the election or not? *A.* If you were the man you profess to be, you would not ask such a question at me: it belongs only to God. *Q.* Do you own the authority as it is now established? *A.* No; but I own all authority, so far as it is according to the written word of God. *Q.* Do you own the king, and inferior magistrates? *A.* In so far as they are *a terror to evil doers, and a praise to them that do well.* *Q.* Are they not that? *A.* When the Lord Jesus Christ shall sit Judge, they and you, and the like of you, will count for it whether ye be or not. *Q.* Is the bishop's death murder, or not? *A.* If your questions be upon these matters that I am not concerned with, I will keep silence. Then the bishop asked him concerning some papers that were found in the room where he was apprehended; he refused to answer any further anent them, having answered the same question in the guard to these who took him. Whereat the bishop enraged said, Sir, the boots will make you free. To which the said George replied, If my Master think me worthy of them, I will get them; and if not, it is in his power to preserve me. *Q.* Will ye sub-

scribe what ye have said? *A.* No. *Q.* Whe
ye not? *A.* Becauſe it is an acknowledgme
unjuſt laws. After this he was tranſported f
gow to Evandale on the Lord's day. He rel
letters, what ſweet joy and conſolation he h
way. After his having gone about the worſh
in preſence of the ſoldiers, who at firſt kept on
but afterwards ere he had done, diſcovered.
one Bonſay their commander, and ſaid, Prepa
a bare horſe back to morrow, and your hea
ſhall be bound hard and faſt together. Geor
ed, It is not in your power to do it. Bonſay
let you know, it ſhall be in my power, and o
the king's health: he refuſed, ſaying, I am
drink healths, eſpecially on the Lord's night.
row when they were ſet on horſe back, Bon
found a trumpet, holding it to George's ear,
Sound him to hell: at which the martyr ſn
they came to Edinburgh upon the 13th of M
Being called before a committee of the council
with his Bible in his hand. The advocate jeer
There's him and his Bible: come away, let u
the text is. George anſwered, I was never a ſe
texts; that is the proper work of a miniſter.
advocate ſaid, Put up your Bible, for we a
preaching at this time. He anſwered, I am n
preach, for I never could; but, Sir, this is tl
God, whereby I am come here to be judged, an
you, and not only you, but all of you, that
anſwer in one day before our Lord Jeſus Ch
he ſhall ſit and judge betwixt the juſt and unju
judge me by what is written in this holy Bib
ways remember ye, and the reſt of you, f
account for it in that day, when our Lord
Judge, and ye ſhall ſtand naked and bare be
and if ye do it not, I ſhall be a witneſs againſ
this they returned, That he was come to be jud
judge: And after a while's ſilence, when he
who were his accuſers, the advocate replied,
accuſer; and interrogate him thus: *Q.* W
Bothwel? *A.* I have anſwered that in my firſ
tion. *Q.* But, ſaid the advocate, you muſt
now. *A.* It being criminal by your law, you
it. *Q.* Do you hold theſe that were there

A. I allow myſelf to be among no rebels; but whom call you rebels? The advocate ſaid, Theſe that were rebels to the king. George anſwered, If they be not rebels to God, the matter is the leſs. *Q.* Do you approve of them? *A.* Yes, in as far as they were for Chriſt and his cauſe. *Q.* Do you allow yourſelf to riſe in arms againſt the king? *A.* No. *Q.* Wherefore then did ye riſe in arms? *A.* I have warrant in the word of God to riſe in arms in defence of the goſpel and work of reformation, according to our ſolemn engagements, wherein we are ſworn to uphold and defend to the utmoſt of our power the work of reformation. *Q.* What, are ye engaged to be againſt your king? *A.* You heard not me ſay that, but I ſaid, I am for the king and all authority, as far as they are for the work of God, but no further. *Q.* Do you own the preſent authority? *A.* I own no unlawful authority. *Q.* Will you take the bond of regulation, and you ſhall win your way. *A.* I will have nothing to do with you, or your bonds either. Being deſired to ſubſcribe what they had wrote down as his confeſſion, he refuſed.

At his ſecond compearance before the council, after they had read to him and ſeveral other priſoners, the declaration emitted at Sanquhar, they aſked, if he approved of that paper, which caſts off the king, and all his authority and laws, and declares open war againſt him, and approves to murder his ſoldiers, militia, gentlemen or intelligencers, wherever they can have the occaſion? He anſwered, I diſown all murder. *Q.* But do you approve of that paper? *A.* As far as it owns truth. *Q.* Knew ye of it before? *Q.* I knew not of it this morning when I aroſe, no more than the child unborn. *Q.* Who ſet it out? *A.* You have it there, perhaps it has been yourſelves for ought I know. *Q.* Was you never in theſe meetings called *ſocieties* or *general correſpondencies?* *A.* Since ever the Lord made me to hate ſin and follow duty, it was my deſire to be in the company of the godly, and to go where I might have edification to my ſoul. *Q.* Would you think it lawful to kill the ſoldiers, if they were going to take you? *A.* Yes, in ſelf-defence.

This account is abſtracted out of his own letters. As for his large teſtimony, it hath not been thought neceſſary to publiſh it? for theſe anſwers, which he gave, were his teſtimony before the enemies; theſe were the

grounds of his indictment and sentence
are the chief points of truth upon which
testimony: and moreover, it appears fro[m]
petitions of the same matter, that the sev[eral]
secutors has occasioned his large testim[ony]
with less accuracy than he would. He
praising God, for calling him to, and str[engthening]
under his sufferings: professes a great [deal]
laying down his life for the cause of Ch[rist]
thers to forsake the love of the world, a[nd]
cross of Christ, and undergo the hatred
he is full in enumerating the heads of tru[th]
adheres, and national sins against whic[h]
ness; so that he passes scarce any point o[f]
in the former testimonies, tho' they are
disposed as in some others. He forewar[ns]
zard of approaching judgments, encour[ages]
with a prospect of Christ's return to the l[and]
them to take hold of him, wrestle with
turn; withal deploring the case of the
count of such wrestlers and mourners;
lemn farewel to earthly relations, friends
and enjoyments, with a welcome of hea[ven]
concludes his dying testimony: in the w[hole]
vidences of one near and dear to Christ,
and strengthened by him.

Together with the foresaid martyr, W[att]
in Kilkeagow received his indictment,
same causes, viz. Being at Bothwel, unde[r]
of Robert Hamilton, brother to the laird
suing out treasonable proclamations, a[nd]
which he owned as his duty in defence o[f]
covenanted work of reformation, and ref[using]
death of the arch-bishop of St. Andrew[s]
not being free to pay cess to the king, &[c]
he left any testimony or not, it has not co[me]
of the publishers.

Upon the 14 day of November, 1684
Watt in the parish of Kilbride, and Joh[n]
parish of Glassart; Whose testimonies (if [they])
came not to the hands of the publishers o[f]
only it is certain from their indictments th[at]

their adherence to the same truths, at the Gallowlee, which was in the twilight of the evening. While they were singing the 11. section of the cxix. Psalm, particularly these words in the 84. ver. 'How many are thy 'servant's days? when wilt thou execute just judgment 'on these wicked men that do me persecute?' The soldiers made such a hellish noise, and turned back so upon the people that were spectators of the action, that the people verily conceived they should have been trodden down and massacred in the spot, which occasioned all to flee, so that none of their christian friends durst stay to do the last duty to them, in dressing their dead bodies, but they were left to the insolent soldiers disposal.

A copy of a Letter, written by JOHN SEMPLE *in Craigthorn, while in prison. Directed to his mother and sister, who were then in prison.*

Loving Mother and Sister,

THIS is to let you know, That that day which I was brought to the tolbooth of the Cannongate, and we were put into the irons, and the shackles put upon our arms, and to morrow about eleven o'clock, I was brought before the council, and they shewed me the paper which was found upon the crosses and kirk-doors, and they asked, If I knew it? I answered, What know I what is in that paper? The duke having it in his hand, and the rest of the council bade him read it to me; he read some lines of it, and then said to the rest, It would take a long time to read. They offered to give it to me to read, and promised me time to consider it, if I would give my judgment of it. *A.* I will not have it, neither will I be judge of papers. *Q.* Own ye the king's authority, as it is now established? *A.* I own all authority, as is agreeable to the word of God. *Q.* Will ye own this paper or not? *A.* What know I what is in that paper. Then they said, to be short with you, Own ye the covenants and Presbyterian principles? *A.* I own the covenants and Presbyterian principles with my whole heart. Then said they, So, that is a frank and free fellow. Then they caused to take me away for a while; and I was brought before them again; and then they said, Come and declare the truth, and give your oath, what you know concerning the contrivers and publishers of

these papers. *A.* I am not bound to wr
bours, neither will I give an oath. Aft
ons and answers, the chancellor said, F
me do it; for he said, he would make
snuff. I answered, Sometimes the perfec
ed the saints to blaspheme. The bishop
I was a liar, for the Scripture says no
said, That it says the same thing, and I
it was. Then they caused take me awa
little after they brought me before them
time, and pressed upon me again to de
refused. Then they caused the executi
a little back, and made me sit down with
bar, and threw on the thumbkins upon
til I fell into a swoon; and when I overc
were standing about, looking upon me,
rise; and then I rose. Then some of tl
will ye say now to the chancellor? I sai
thing to him. Then they took me to the
to the iron-house.

Now, I desire that I could bless the
That he keeped me, for in the time of the
not a word good or bad, but got it born
to a swoon. All their countenances dash
for I did not fear their faces, nor the fa
who were gazing upon me, from about
till seven o'clock in the afternoon. And
that was a sign of God's presence: but t
countenance was not with my spirit. E
to believe and hold fast: For I knew no
to-morrow might have been my last day

The next morning I was brought bef
into a chamber: He said, How are ye
I said, As I was. *Q.* What is the rea
not tell the truth to the chancellor? for
do it. *A.* Doeg told the truth, when h
he saw David come to Ahimelech, and
gave him bread, and did enquire of Gc
yet the Scripture calls it lying, Psal. lii.
fore there is a sinful pernicious speakir
which is a great sin, and accounted as
him also, That I, knowing the terror
thought that the terror of men was tl
borne, and that I would say no more t

tho' they should torture all the fingers and toes that I had, till they should be cut off; but as the Lord should give me strength, I would stand.

After this, he never opened his mouth more, but humbred and rose up, and went his way, and the keeper brought me back to the iron-house, where I remain. One thing is come to my mind, which he said more; That it was for rebellion against the king that they were pursuing for. I answered, so did the persecutors of the Son of God say, That it was for rebellion; for they called him an enemy to Cæsar. Moreover they threatned me with the boots. Now what the Lord will permit them to do, I know not; but there are hard things determined against me; and I am very weak, for flesh and blood is but weak; therefore forget not my case. I am well contented with my lot, blessed be the Lord, only I am afraid of my own weaknesses, lest I wrong the truth.

No more at present, but wisheth that the Lord's presence may be with you, my dear mother and sister. Give my love to my dear brother and sisters. I am in good health, blessed be God; my thumbs, they are not very sore, only they are something feelless; I and others thought, they should scarcely have ever served me, at least for a long time.

JOHN SEMPLE.

The Last Testimony of JAMES GRAHAM, *Taylor in Corsmichael, in the Stewarty of Galloway, who suffered at the Gallowlee, betwixt Leith and Edinburgh, December* 9. 1684.

Men and brethren,

I Am come here this day to lay down my life for the cause of Christ, and I bless the Lord, that ever he gave me a life to lay down for such a noble cause; and now I wish this day that every hair of my head, and every drop of my blood were a life, I would willingly lay them down for him, for it is all too little I can do for him. O it is a wonder, that ever he should have chosen me, or the like of me, to witness or die for him in such a cause! for he hath no need of me, or any of the lost sons of Adam, but he hath testified in his word, that he will make the poor things of the earth, to confound the prudent. And now I bless the Lord, that

I die not as a murderer or a thief, or as an evil doer, or as a busy body in other men's matters. The heads whereupon I am indicted, are, Because I refused to disown that paper, which is most agreeable to the word of God, and to our sworn covenants and work of reformation; and because I would not swear to that which I durst not for my soul do. Now, I giving a short account of what I am indicted for, I shall likewise give an hint of what I adhere to. *First*, I adhere to the holy Scriptures of the Old and New Testament, Confession of Faith, Catechisms Larger and Shorter, and to the whole work of reformation, as it was once established in our land, altho' now, alas! defaced, and denied by the most part of this generation. 2*dly*, To the Covenants National and Solemn League, to which we are sworn with hands uplifted to the most high God, and bound to maintain it. 3*dly*, To the Sum of Saving Knowledge, the Acknowledgment of Sins and Engagement to Duties. 4*thly*, To the preached gospel, as it was faithfully preached in our land, by the sent messengers of Jesus Christ; especially by Messrs. John Kid, John King, Donald Cargil, and Richard Cameron, who took their lives in their hands, and went forth upon all hazards, when the rest of their brethren turned their back upon the cause. 5*thly*, To Mr. James Renwick, as a faithful sent servant of Jesus Christ, who has lifted up the standard where Messrs. Donald Cargil and Richard Cameron left it, who sealed the cause with their blood. 6*thly*, To all the appearances in arms in defence of the gospel, and our sworn covenants, and the whole work of reformation. 7*thly*, To the excommunication at the Torwood by Mr. Donald Cargil. 8*thly*, To the Sanquhar declaration, as a thing most agreeable to the word. 9*thly*, To the declaration at Rutherglen. 10*thly*, To the paper that was taken off worthy Henry Hall, at the Queensferry. 11*thly*, To the burning of that hell-hatched thing, called the Test, at Lanerk. 12*thly*, To the fellowships of the Lord's people, for reading, singing and praying; according to the Scripture in Mal. iii. 16. and Heb. x. 25. and several other Scriptures which warrant this. 13*thly*, To all the testimonies of the faithful witnesses of Jesus Christ, from the appearance in arms at Pentland-hills to this day. 14*thly*, To that paper upon which I was indicted, in so-

of James Graham.

far as it is agreeable to the word of God, and our sworn covenants, and work of reformation.

And now, on the other hand, I shall desire to let you see what I shall witness and testify against, so far as I am enabled by his holy Spirit. *1st*, I leave my testimony against all breach of covenant, which is a sin that hath overspread the whole land. *2dly*, Against the accepters of the indulgence, first and last, because they have fled from their first engagements, which engagement was to be faithful ministers to the church of Christ, which they have broken and rent. *3dly*, Against the hearers of curates, because they have broken our sworn covenants and work of reformation. *4thly*, Against Popery, Prelacy, Quakerism, and all heresy, and whatsoever is contrary to the word of God. *5thly*, Against paying of the cess and locality, and against paying of fines, because it is a bearing up of these foul-murderers, and an acknowledgment that we have done a fault in following our duty. *6thly*, Against Charles Stuart, in regard he hath broken the covenant that he was once sworn to, and put forth his hand against the people of God. *7thly*, Against that perjuring and abominable thing called the Test, and the oath of allegiance, which is an oath against our covenant. *8thly*, Against Gib, and all his followers, and all their pernicious ways. *9thly*, Against the overthrowing of our work of reformation, which we had for our Lord and Master, and his faithful servants, to be comforts to our souls. Now, the time being short, I shall say no more, but farewel mother, brethren, and sisters; farewel all Christian friends and acquaintances in the Lord; farewel holy Scriptures which have been my comfort many a day; farewel meat and drink, sun, moon, and stars. Welcome eternity; welcome heaven; welcome holy angels; welcome God in Christ, into thy hands I commit my spirit.

Sic subscribitur,

JAMES GRAHAM.

The laſt Speech and Teſtimony of ROBERT POLLOCK *cordiner in Kilbride, who was taken at Glaſgow, and ſuffered at the Gallowlee, January* 23. 1685. *betwixt eight and nine of the clock in the morning.*

[The body of this teſtimony being much of a piece with ſeveral of the foregoing, as declaring his adherence to the ſame truths, and abhorrence of the ſame errors and abominations; the reader will find here only the preamble and poſtſcript, as follows.]

Dear friends,

I Being ſentenced to die by men, thought it fit to leave this ſhort word of teſtimony behind me. Now, if I could ſay any thing to the commendation of Chriſt, I have as much to ſay to his commendation, as any poor ſinner ever had to ſay. For he has done more for me than heart can think, or tongue can ſpeak, or hand can write, for he has made good his promiſe to me, Iſa. xliii 2. ' When thou paſſeſt thro' the waters, I will be with ' thee, and thro' the rivers they ſhall not overflow thee ' When thou walkeſt thro' the fire thou ſhalt not be burn' ' ed, neither ſhall the flames kindle upon thee.' This promiſe I can ſay upon good ground has been made out to me. And I can ſay with the ſpouſe in Song ii. 6. ' His ' left hand is under my head, and his right hand doth ' embrace me. A bundle of myrrh is my beloved unto ' me,' Song i. 13. And now I cannot ſtudy to ſave my life without prejudice to his glory, and vindicating of evil doers. For I deſire to fear and ſerve him, and alſo to confeſs him, that hath ſaid in his word, Matth. x. 23 ' Whoſoever therefore ſhall confeſs me before men, him ' will I confeſs alſo before my Father which is in heaven. Ver. 33. ' But whoſoever ſhall deny me before men, him ' will I alſo deny before my Father which is in heaven. And he has ſaid in Luke ix. 62. ' No man having put ' his hand to the plough, and looking back, is fit for the ' kingdom of God.' And alſo he hath ſaid Heb. x. 38 ' If any man draw back, my ſoul ſhall have no pleaſure ' in him. But he that ſhall endure unto the end, the ' ſame ſhall be ſaved,' Matth. xxiv. 13. Now, I ſay death and life, heaven and hell, even Chriſt being on the one hand, and the world on the other hand, and

Chrift holding forth an offer of himfelf to me, and making me welcome to come to him, I defire rather to fuffer any thing he is pleafed, than to run after the multitude: and now truth being fo much controverted, I think I cannot refufe to be at his difpofing in fuffering for it.

And now, I being fome what confufed in the time of my writing, and therefore could not keep order; wherefore I take leave to leave my teftimony to feveral things that I forgot before. And now as a dying man I leave my teftimony to the Sanquhar declaration, and to the late declaration, November, 1684. And now I have two particulars to leave my teftimony againft, viz. The duke of York, and the duke of Monmouth. Againft the duke of York for marrying a ftrange woman, and as he is a Papift himfelf. And againft the duke of Monmouth for coming down to Scotland, to help the enemies of God to kill the Lord's people, for hazarding their lives in defence of the gofpel. And now I am come here this day to lay down my life for the hope of Ifrael, of the which hope I am not afhamed this day; for I defire to blefs his holy name, that thefe twelve years and more, my foul has loved him; and many times my foul has been refrefhed when I thought upon fuffering for him. Now, I do not fay I am free of fin, but I am at peace with God thro' a flain Mediator, and he fhall make my foul as clean of fin, as I had never finned. And now I am to ftep out of time into eternity, where I fhall be as full of him as my foul defires to be. And now again, I take my farewel of all created comforts in time; and let none fay that thefe are not my words, for they are even my laft words. And now, I being never loofed out of the fhackles on my hands I cannot write myfelf, but I do fubfcribe myfelf; and whether any think it right or not, I have peace in doing of it. But it may be fome will fay, that I have not been right principled, and have been in error: and it may be fome will fay, that they would not have ventured their life on fuch grounds. But I can fay, the leaft of the controverted truths is fufficient ground to lay down my life for. And the main thing is authority, that now is cried up, and Charles Stuart to be fupreme: if any join with that, and approve of his deeds, it will never be afked whether they fear God or not; altho' they were the greateft blafphemers that ever lived, if they will ap-

The Last Speech and Testi[

prove of the acts and laws made by thef[
rulers, tho' they rule wrong, there is no
them: they never ask whether they fear [
that says that they fear him not thems[
they study no further than to please [
which will be their ruin in the end. A
this to say to the commendation of Ch[
without parallel or comparison; he is alt[
and in the greatest of straits he is most co[
tenance is refreshful to me, and has been
of straits and difficulties, his countenan[
me, and it is delightsome to a weary sou[
any comfort like unto him, ' His yoke i[
' burden light.' Yea, he has been so ki[
I have not gone one hairs-breadth on m[
He spares not expences; he gives enou[
that are about his work; for ay when I [
it, I got enough from my lovely Master t[
ges with. Now, my advice is to all the[
be upright for Christ, Walk on, and do[
for ye will not want enough to do you[
does not stand to ware any thing upon h[

And now, I as a dying man, intrea[
fear imprisonment; fear nothing; for i[
him, there is no fear you shall be left[
yourself. I can say no more to make yo[
only this I can say, That he has ay mad[
since I was his prisoner. And now I ca[
afraid to venture upon a gibbet for him,[
dication of his cause. And now let none[
matter that my life should be taken a[
cause; for I say unto you, that I would[
ten such an offer to quit my life for; [
sorry, that I am taken away out of th[
wrath; for there are many in Scotland th[
where to fly from his wrath pursuing tl[
many that are not much concerned w[
now. And therefore, I say, fly unto[
would study not to be trampled down[
these that would not have the wrath of [
out upon them; my advice is, to make[
the Prince of peace: For sad will the c[
are coming on this land. O! prepare f[
he will come and make inquisition for the[

been shed in Scotland, before the controversy end, and the calamity overpass. It looks very like that the fowls of the air will eat the bodies of the dead men and women not being buried. I shall say no more, but study to fly out of the way of God's wrath; only fly unto him, and forsake your evil ways. And now it is not, I declare, upon the account of suffering, that I expect to be saved; nor any righteousness of mine own, but only thro' the imputed righteousness of Jesus Christ, thro' his merits and intercession; for I have no righteousness of my own, neither can I merit any thing by my suffering: But it is as sure that he has said, 'He that denies 'me before men, him will I deny before my Father who 'is in heaven, and before the holy angels.' And now I am brought here this day, to lay down my life for the cause and interest of Jesus Christ, and for no other thing: And I desire to bless the Lord, that I am not suffering as an evil-doer, and that I die not as a fool. And I desire to bless the Lord that ever he honoured me with suffering for him, for many times my soul has been refreshed, when I saw any thing like that, that I would be a sufferer for him. Now, I desire to take my farewel of all things in time: Farewel sweet Scriptures, reading, singing, praying, and believing; farewel sun, moon, and stars, and all created comforts in time. Welcome heaven and happiness; welcome innumerable company of angels; welcome spirits of just men made perfect; welcome praising without ceasing, or wearying in the least; welcome Father, Son, and Holy Ghost, into thy hands I commit my spirit.

ROBERT POLLOCK.

The last Testimony of ROBERT MILLAR, *mason, who lived in the parish of Rutherglen, and suffered for the truth at the Gallowlee of Edinburgh, upon the 23d of January, betwixt six and seven in the morning,* 1685.

Loving and dear friends,

I Being sentenced to die by men, have thought it fit to leave behind me this mite of a testimony; and to let you know upon what ground I suffer: and it is only because I would not acknowledge the present authority, which is in a direct opposition to the word of God; and also because I would not take that oath against the Apo-

logetical declaration, and fwear myfelf a
covenant and work of reformation ; wh
do, no not for my foul.

Now, I confefs, I have been a great finr
but I never acted any thing againſt man, v
bonds, or impriſonment. Now, glory
hath not been wanting to me; I have
meaſure, his hand of providence, ay i:
from my very infancy, guiding me to
now it is about fifteen years ſince he enɡ
derfully to him, altho' I have many ti
back on him, and alſo though I followed
many failings, yet he never ſuffered me
kept me with a long reſpect to him, and
truths; and ay when I was like to be ſnaı
temptations from Satan, the world, and
ed heart, then ' he broke the ſnare, and
' bird out of the hand of the fowler.'
to that word, he hath, in a wonderful m
' all things work together for my good.'
times have I turned back, and provoked
face, and to defert me, and to plague m(
of heart! but ay when I was ready to finl
nifeſted his power, and brought me up o
depth; and alſo made out that word,
' When my father and my mother forſak
' Lord will take me up.' Now, I ſay, (
him, who hath plucked me as a brand oı
ing, and hath made a priſon, and irons,
to me. O! what an honour is it, to trea(
that my loving Lord hath gone before m
is become ' altogether lovely, and the cl
' thouſands.' I can now ſay from my expe
' my beloved is mine, and I am his.'

Firſt, Now, I heartily adhere, and leav
to that covenant of free grace, agreed up(
Father and the Son, that noble work o
and defire to take him in all his offices, a
and Prophet. 2*dly*, I heartily adhere tc
ſacred word of God, with which my ſou
hath been refreſhed. 3*dly*, And alſo to
of Faith, Larger and Shorter Catechiſms
alſo to the National and Solemn League ;
5*thly*, And alſo to that glorious work of r

it was reformed from Popery and Prelacy, and all other errors. 6thly, And likewise I leave my testimony to all the fellowship-meetings of the Lord's people, for keeping up of the fallen down standard of our Lord. 7thly, And likewise I leave my testimony to these worthy mens doctrine, viz. Mr. Donald Cargil, and the rest who jeoparded their lives upon the high places of the earth, for the bearing up of the fallen down standard of our Lord, when the rest most shamefully left it at the command of men. 8thly, And likewise I heartily adhere, and leave my testimony to that worthy man's doctrine, called Mr. James Renwick, who is now carrying on that great work, when there is so few to own it; and I desire to bless the Lord, that ever I heard him preach. 9thly, And likewise I leave my testimony to the excommunication at the Torwood, passed by Mr. Donald Cargil, against these enemies of God. 10thly, And likewise I leave my testimony to all protestations and declarations given by the Lord's people, against his enemies. 11thly, And also, to the making use of defensive arms. 12thly, And likewise I desire to tell you what I disown, and leave my testimony against.

And in the *first* place, I leave my testimony against Popery, and Prelacy; and Erastianism, and all other errors not agreeable to the word of God, and against all these that adhere to, and own these abominable practices, and principles. 2dly, I leave my testimony against that tyrant that is now upon the throne, viz. Charles Stuart, who hath not only broken the covenant, but burned it, and overturned the whole work of reformation, which he was sworn and engaged unto; and is yet going on with uplifted hands, in his perjury, and making to do the like, according to that of Jeroboam who made Israel to sin; and also for his supremacy over the prerogatives of our Lord. 3dly, And also, I leave my testimony against those called the council of Scotland, who at this day sleep not, except they have done mischief, and they are now taking away my life, not having any matter of fact against me, either worthy of death or bonds, but only because I would not perjure myself, and state myself an open enemy to God, and his truth, which I durst not do, no not for my soul. 4thly, And likewise I leave my testimony against that wicked thing called the Test, invented by Satan. 5thly, And also against all

bonds and declarations sent forth by the
led the council of Scotland. 6*thly*, And
my testimony against cess and locality p:
for no other use; but to bear down th
Lord Jesus. 7*thly*, And also against militi
is for that same use. 8*thly*, And also ag
gencers and apprehenders of the Lord's
ver. 10. 9*thly*, And likewise against all
courts, or coming out of prison upon bo
or paying of jaylor's fees; for it says, the
them wrong, whereas we have done then
tho' they be forced to it, yet that will n
for there is not a liberty in all the word
a confederacy with his open and avowed e
And also I leave my testimony against
these tested curates, who are these that a
God's word, viz. Wolves and bears, wl
vour the Lord's flock. 11*thly*, And agair
shed, before and since Pentland, in the fiel
folds, and also in the seas. 12*thly*, And ag
dulgences first and last, who lay down tl
Lord at the command of men, and have
selves in that wo, that is pronounced agair
ease, when Zion is in trouble: For since I
ledge I never had any clearness for minister
ledged any to be the head of the church, t
13*thly*, And against all sort of complianc
there is few that ever complies with them
leave to look behind them, till they be the f
now, I must tell you, I have not been free
of it this many a day, That the church of
land shall be upon the borders of Babylo
get a delivery.

 Now, dear friends, study to be diligen
and also make good use of your Bibles,
gotten the thoughts of it off my spirits th
that ere long it shall come to that, That
to the person with whom a Bible is fou
must tell you, That there was nothing n
to me, that they were enemies to truth,
carriage when I was before them. Now,
upon me to prophesy, but they are blin
there are sad days abiding these poor lands
study holiness and labour to follow your d

neft, for there is a black cloud of judgment ready to break upon thefe lands. And now I dare not doubt, but Chrift is upon his way to return again to thefe lands, and O be earneft with him, that he would fpare a remnant, and that he would not pafs that fad fentence mentioned in Ezek. ix. 6. Where he hath given a commiffion to ' flay ' utterly old and young;' and alfo ver. 10. Where he hath faid, ' His eye fhall not fpare, neither will he have ' pity.' Now, I fay likewife, be earneft with him, that ye may be marked by the man with the writer's inkhorn by his fide, that ye may be keeped in the hollow of his hand, in the day of Scotland's fad calamity.

Now, forfake not the affembling of yourfelves together, and employ your ftrength, in the holding up of the fallen-down ftandard of our Lord, and if ye be found real in this duty, ye fhall either be members of the church militant, and fee that glory of the fecond temple, which fhall be a glorious fight, or elfe ye fhall be tranfported, and be members of the church triumphant; fo ye fhall be no lofers, but noble gainers either of the ways, for I dare not doubt, but that Chrift is upon his way, and that he will keep a remnant even of holy feed, which fhall yet be the fubftance of poor covenanted Scotland. Now I defire to die a Prefbyterian, altho' one of the meaneft and pooreft finful things that ever followed him and his way. But O praife! praife and glory to him, who hath taken this way of dealing with me, as to honour me with fuffering for him, and his controverted truths, and royal prerogatives, kingdom and fceptre. And now, in a word, I am fully perfuaded that it is his truth I am fuffering for, and in this cafe, have both his word and Spirit on my fide, and fo I fhall not be difappointed of my expectation.

Now, I defire heartily to forgive all men, what they have done to me, as I am of myfelf; but what they have done againft the image of God in me, that is not mine to forgive, but I muft leave it before the great Judge to be decided, in his own time, when he fhall arife and plead Zion's quarrel. Altho' men have buried his work, and fworn it fhall not rife again, yet the commiffion fhall go forth, ' Arife and fing, ye that dwell in the duft. But I muft leave it, becaufe my time is but fhort; but I have one word more to fay to the poor remnant, Fear not to venture upon the crofs of Chrift, for altho' ye fee but

the black side of it at the beginning, yet
to a trial upon his truth's account, then
and be a present help in time of trouble,
his word; and the more sharp your trial b
will be seen perfecting strength in your wea
ing to that, Isa. xl. 29. 'He giveth powe
'and to them that have no might he incre
Ver. 31. 'But they that wait upon the L
'their strength,' &c.

Now, I say, fear not to contend for the
hour to be as free of self in it as ye can;
you, Christ and your idols will not lodge i
gether, but if ye can say upon good gro
pure love and zeal to his glory upon wh
fering, then I say, Come away, for ye sha
perience to the full. Many Scriptures I
for your encouragement in this, but I ca
perience, that he is a Prince of his word,
not to mean who are in the furnace, if t
be with them. For I may now say with
therford, " He hath paid me many hun
" one to the hundred." O! who would
who hath carried thro' a poor dwarf mo
wings of omnipotency.

Now, my time is but short, but I giv
great name of my God, for my interest is
and I have had much of his sweet preser
prisoner for him, and his persecuted tru
times before: And now, I bless his great
perfected his work in me, and I shall have
ment of him thro' all eternity; for I ha
away myself to be at his disposal, and ha
be my King, Priest, and Prophet; and
may say with Job, Job xix. 25. 'I kno
'deemer liveth, and that he shall stand a
'upon the earth.' Ver. 26. 'And the
'worms destroy this body, yet in my
'God:' Ver. 27. 'Whom I shall see
'mine eyes shall behold, and not anothe
'be consumed within me.'

Now, my dear friends, I must bid fare
leave you to him who hath promised to
tuary to his own, to be kept by his m
salvation, and also I bid farewel to sun,

And I muft bid farewel to all the fweet focieties of the Lord's people; farewel reading and finging, and praying; farewel holy and fweet Scriptures, with which many a time my foul hath been refrefhed; and to conclude, farewel all created comforts in time. And welcome the fweet fellowfhip of angels, and the fouls of juft men now made perfect, and the fweet fellowfhip of the firft-born; welcome Father, Son, and Holy Ghoft, into whofe hands I commit my fpirit, for it is thine. *Sic fubfcribitur*.

ROBERT MILLAR.

UPON the 11th of May 1684, Margaret Lauchlane in the parifh of Kirkkinner, and Margaret Wilfon in Glenvernock, in the fhire of Galloway, being fentenced to death for their noncompliance with Prelacy, and refufing to fwear the oath of abjuration, by the laird of Lagg, Captain Strachan, Colonel David Graham, and Provoft Cultron, who commanded them to receive their fentence upon their knees, which they refufing, were preffed down by force, till they received it: And fo were by their order tied to a ftake within the fea mark, in the water of Blednoch, near Wigton; where, after they had made them wreftle long with the waves; which flowing fwelled on them by degrees; and had fometimes thurft them under water, and then pulled them out again, to fee if they would recant; they enduring death with undaunted courage, yielded up their fpirits to God. The former was a widow woman of about fixty-three years, of a moft chriftian and blamelefs converfation, a pattern of piety and virtue, who having conftantly refufed to hear the curates, was much purfued and vexed, and at length taken by the foldiers, while fhe was devoutly worfhipping God in her family; and being indicted of being at Bothwel-bridge, Airfmofs, and twenty field conventicles, and as many houfe conventicles, after fore and long imprifonment, without neceffary refrefhments of fire, bed or diet, at length fuffered this cruel death. The other (Margaret Wilfon) a young woman of fcarce twenty-three years of age, after fhe with her brother, who was about nineteen, and her fifter fifteen years old, had been long driven from their father's houfe, and expofed to ly in dens and caverns of the earth, wandering thro' the moffes and mountains of Carrick, Nithfdale, and Galloway; going to Wigton fecretly to vifit the forefaid

Margaret Lauchlane, was taken by the fraud of one Patrick Stuart, who under colour of friendship, having invited her and her sister to drink with him, offered them the king's health, and upon their refusal of it, as not warranted in God's word, and contrary to christian moderation, went presently out and informed against them; her sister was dismissed, as being but fifteen years of age, upon her father's paying 100 l. Sterling for her ransom; she being detained and examined, whether she owned the king as head of the church? and would take the abjuration oath? Not answering to their pleasure, but adhering to the truths of Christ, was in like manner condemned; and after great severities of imprisonment, suffered the foresaid death. Being put oft into the water, and when half dead, taken up again, to see if she would take the oath, which she refused to her last breath; while her fellow-sufferer was wrestling with the waves, as being put first in to discourage her; the persecutors asked her, What she thought of that sight? She answered, What do I see but Christ (mystical) wrestling there? One of the times that she was taken out of the water they said, Say, God save the king. She returning with christian meekness, I wish the salvation of all men, but the damnation of none. Upon which one of her friends, alledging she had said what they demanded, desired them to let her go; but they would not, seeing she refused to take the oath. During her imprisonment, she wrote a large letter to her friends, wherein, besides the lively and feeling expression of her sense of God's love, she doth, with a judgment not usual for her age and education, disclose the unlawful nature of the abjuration oath, hearing of curates, owning the king's supremacy, which was the thing the persecutors meant by his authority; and proves the necessity of her suffering upon these heads.

The last Testimony of THOMAS STODDART, *who suffered at the Grass-market of Edinburgh, August* 12. 1685.

Men, brethren and fathers, hearken,

I being to take my farewel of the world, I leave this my dying Testimony, according to the form of the Christians of old. I having like the same ground for it, that he had, who used that word, that was Stephen,

who was condemned, because he spoke blasphemous words against the law and the temple. So because I will not adhere to, or approve of their laws, which now have power in their hands, they condemned me to die, tho' they could not witness so much against me for speaking against them, and they never essayed to prove the sentence upon me: which now I shall study in a word to give you an account of. And first, I received my sentence of banishment, and then notwithstanding of that, I was committed to the justices to abide the assize, and they past upon me the sentence of death, for no other cause, as I can give, but because I could not give such an answer to their questions about the government and the king's authority (as they called it) as could satisfy their lusts, and that I durst not disown the Apologetic Declaration; and so I humbly conceive it will come to this as the ground of my suffering, that I could not own Christ's enemies, nor the power that they have taken to themselves against him, nor disown Christ's friends and their actings, as they required, and therefore I am sentenced, albeit I owned as much of the authority as any Christian can be obliged to, that is to say, lawful authority according to word of God; but I desire to be submissive to his will, who hath called me to this, and to have high thoughts of him. I cannot get words to set him out, but I find something to say to the commendation of Christ, as it is said in Cant. ii. 1. ' He is the rose of Sharon, and the lily of the valleys;' the sweetest rose that ever I smelled, and never sweeter than when under the cross, and suffering upon his account. Now, I shall not be long, I have told you upon what account I suffer, it is out of love to Christ, and by faith in his mercy, that I venture upon it. I shall end it with a word, I thought it my duty to adhere to the word of God, and to every thing agreeable thereto: And I would suffer for every thing as a ground, which I think is right, and taken out of the word of God, having encouragement from his blessed promises Isa. xliii. 1. ' But now, thus saith the
' Lord that created thee, O Jacob, and he that form-
' ed thee, O Israel, Fear not; for I have redeemed thee
' I have called thee by thy name, thou art mine. When
' thou passest thro' the waters, I will be with thee.'
And I have this to say also, that in all my imprisonments he was wonderfully seen in owning me, and carrying me

through all the temptations that I was tryſted
would tell you them all, they would take up
per and time; and time being very ſhort, I ca
done; but I think I muſt ſpeak ſomething to the
dation of free grace, that hath made me to
chearfully. I have read in the Apoſtle, 2 Tim.
' is a faithful ſaying, For if we be dead with
' ſhall alſo live with him: If we ſuffer, we
' reign with him.' It is good at all times,
ally now. O but the people of this generation
involved in ſin by reaſon they are ſo greatly a
involved in the breach of covenant; which th
not be owned by the laws of the land, yet I d
own it. I would fain ſay as it is ſaid, 1 King
' And Eliſha ſaid, as the Lord of hoſts live
' whom I ſtand, I will ſurely ſhew myſelf to hi
I own it before all, and I own myſelf to ha
and do allow it heartily, in joining with that
ſecuted party ſo much diſowned; the thing th
that caſe, I thought it my duty, I leave my te
my owning of it; and that I have joined myſ
which was moſt agreeable to the word of Go
my teſtimony in behalf of theſe that I joined
little handful in their ſocieties and fellowſhi
have been very refreſhful to my ſoul, and I
much delighted in theſe; for I thought it was t
of God.

And therefore, I leave my teſtimony againſt
ſtition and error, contrary to that way I recei
Lord there; and every thing contrary to the
God. I leave my teſtimony againſt all unlaw
and all murdering acts and actings whatſoeve
I leave my teſtimony againſt Popery and Pre
whatſoever plant is not of my heavenly Father's
and every thing contrary to ſound doctrine, and
er of godlineſs. I leave my teſtimony alſo ag
that hear the curates, and againſt all them
ſaid in effect, The word is a lie; that is, bec
will not take it to be their rule; for that is
thing we ſhould take to be our rule, in all t
our ſojourning here.

Now, I think I muſt take my farewel of a
comforts, and all the things of the world; w
been ſo great a mean to make many of this

fear at the cross of Christ, which is much mistaken by the world. He was so condescending, that he paved the way for poor sinners himself, and made it straight and easy and wonderful it is to think upon. The way that leads to heaven is very straight, and very easy also to these that believe. He is that universal king that lives and reigns for ever; and all who subject themselves and obey him, and consent to his terms, shall even know peace, and shall enjoy his presence, which is the chief of all things. It is peace with God, that is the matter of the believers rejoicing, and makes them all to flighter with joy in following him, who is ' the way, the truth, ' and the life;' and ' whom to know is life everlasting;' that doth and may give great courage to these who love this way of his, that is so greatly reproached by the people of this generation. I think ye may conceive what I mean by the saying of this. And now, my dear friends and fellow sufferers, and brethren in the Lord, O but the counsel of the Lord be wise in bringing me hitherto! And I shall say no more, but touch at one thing, and that is, That here I join my hearty testimony with all that ever the people of God did in his way, and for his cause in his gospel terms; to all the blood that has been shed for the gospel, in all fields and scaffolds whatsoever. So I take my farewel of all things under heaven. Farewel to the world, the flesh, and sin; and also to all friends and relations, and kinsmen and brethren; and also I take my farewel of mother and brethren, and sisters; and also I bid farewel to all my wonted privileges and enjoyments; as also, I take my farewel of all the sweet societies, that have been so refreshful to my soul several times; farewel friends in Christ; farewel sun, moon, and stars. Welcome heaven; welcome my God, and angels, and glorified spirits; and so come Lord Jesus.

THOMAS STODDART.

Together with the foregoing martyr, two others received the sentence of death, viz. Matthew Brice and James Wilkie, who suffered at Edinburgh, July 27. 1685. The former whereof declares in his testimony, That they were interrogate only on these two questions. 1. Will ye take the oath of allegiance? To which they answered, No, we will not take it. 2. Will ye own the authority? They answered, we will own all authority according to the word of God. Upon which they were immediately all three sentenced to be hanged. Whence the said martyr very justly infers, That they had nothing else to charge upon him as the cause of his death, but that he spoke of the word of God. His testimony, as to all the material heads, is consonant with that of Thomas Stoddart's.

The last Testimony of EDWARD MARSHAL *of Kaemuir, in the parish of Morvenside, who suffered at the Grass-market of Edinburgh, December* 4. 1685.

FIRST, I leave my testimony against all that have joined with the malignant party, either in rising in arms, or in paying of cess, or any manner of way contrary to our covenants, and work of reformation, once famous, and maintained by the whole ministry, noblemen, gentlemen, and commons of all sorts, but now opposed and borne down by the generality of this kingdom. And particularly against such as once owned the covenant, and avowed the cause of Christ, and are now employing their strength for the overturning the same; as it is in Psalm lxxiv. 6. Now, the things upon which I was accused and sentenced were, My joining in arms with that party at Bothwel, and owning of the truth and covenants, and for adhering thereunto: For they questioned me, If I would call it rebellion? But I would not, but accounted it my duty. Then they asked me If I would own James VII. as king of Britain? And told them, I owned him as far as he owned God, his cause and people. Then some of them said, That was not all. Then they asked, If I would pray for the king of Britain? I answered, This is not a place appointed for prayer, Then they laughed, and said, Remov you.

Now, dear friends, be not discouraged altho' the threaten you with imprisonment, or death for the caus of Christ; for he that calls you to suffering, is able to support and bear you up under it; for I found more o his presence since I came to prison than I did heretofore For Christ suffered imprisonment and death for us, an ought not we to suffer for him? As concerning this, tha my enemies and carnal friends, reproach me with self murder, I am conscious to myself, that it is not so, bu out of love to Christ and his covenanted work. Now, I recommend my wife and seven children to the good guiding of my God, who hath hitherto protected me; for he has promised, to be ' a husband to the widow, and a ' father to the fatherless,' providing they will ' walk in ' his ways, and keep his commandments.' Now, I recommend my soul to God, who hath preserved me hitherto, and who unexpectedly has singled me out to suffer for him, who am the unworthiest of all sinners; and I never thought that he should have so highly privileged me, as to account me worthy to give a testimony for him; tho' sometimes it entered into my thoughts, O if I would be called to it. Now, farewel dear wife and sweet children; farewel all friends and relations, especially such of you as have given up your names to Christ; farewel sun, moon, and all worldly enjoyments. Welcome Father, Son, and holy Ghost, into whose hands I commit my spirit.

Sic subscribitur,
EDWARD MARSHAL.

ON the 4th of December, 1685, suffered John Nisbet of Hardhill, in the parish of Loudon, whose testimony, altho' omitted in some of the former editions of this book, is now inserted immediately after this short relation concerning him, wrote by one of his near relations, who had full knowledge of the whole matter.

About the year 1664, he having received the sacrament of baptism to his child, from one of the outed ministers, came to be troubled by the enemies on that account; and the curate declared out of the pulpit, his purpose to excommunicate him the next Lord's day, but was prevented by sudden death. When that handful of the Lord's people renewed the covenant at Lanerk, and appeared in arms at Pentland-hills, he engaged in the covenant with them, and was sore wounded in the fight, insomuch that he was left for dead: but by God's goodness he recovered. And all alongst testified against the abominations of Prelacy, supremacy, arbitrary government, and indulgence. till the rising in arms at Bothwel, where he did good service, being not only a zealous Christian, but a couragious soldier. After this the enemies seized all his goods, expelled his wife and four small children from house and hold; offered a large sum of

money for himself, but the Lord preserv[ed]
he had work for him.

He was a clofs follower of the gofpel, fa[vour]
ed in the fields, was kept ftedfaft in the
tremes on right or left hand; and was a[pub]
lifhing the declarations for truth, emitt[ed in his]
time. At length, in November, 1685, [at one]
man's houfe in the parifh of Finnick, wi[th others,]
after being fore wounded, he was taken [by]
Nifbet's party, the other three being fh[ot on the]
fpot. The Lieutenant, having caufed t[o ask him]
What he thought of himfelf now? He an[fwered]
as much of Chrift and his caufe, for wh[ich I fear]
ever; but I judge myfelf at a lofs, being i[n with my]
dear brethren in eternity, whom you hav[e mur-]
dered. The bloody wretch fwore, That [he reserv-]
ed him for further judgment. He anfwer[ed, Lord]
ftand by me, and help me to be faithful [to the end, I]
care not what piece of fuffering I be put [to. He]
was carried firft to Kilmarnock, from the[nce next]
morning; and being brought back to Kil[marnock,]
was thence tranfported to Edinburgh; [and being]
brought before the council by the forego[ing Philip]
Nifbet, who demanded his money for h[im, did in-]
terrogate him to this effect. Q. Was y[e at a]
venticle? (naming time and place.) A. [Yes. Q. How]
many men and arms were there? A. I [went to]
hear the gofpel preached, and not to tak[e notice]
what men and arms were there. Q. W[here went]
ye when the preaching was done? A. [Where I]
could beft think of to efcape your cruelt[y. Q. Do ye]
keep you your general meetings? and [who are at]
them? While he was about to anfwer, o[ne of the coun-]
fellors interrupted him telling, in his fa[ce, what was]
done at fuch general meetings, and that [there was one]
of them kept at Edinburgh; and afked [him, whether]
he was there? Who anfwered, No. Th[ey then asked]
him, We hope you are fo much of a Chri[ftian as to pray]
for the king. He anfwered, Prayer bei[ng an ordi-]
nance of God, we ought to pray for ki[ngs and all]
others; but not when every profligate bi[ds us. Q. Do]
you own the king as fole fovereign? A[nfwered in this]
pith, and that from his youth, and I a P[resbyterian, of the]
Prefbyterian covenanted perfuafion, I neit[her]

own him, while he remains such. Whereupon incontinent, without further process they passed sentence upon him; which he received, not only with Christian submission, but with much thankfulness; blessing and praising God, who had counted him worthy to suffer for his name. And during the time of his imprisonment he was wonderfully assisted, and graciously supported of the Lord under his cross; having both assurance of the pardon of all his sins, and his peace with God, and also a firm persuasion of the justness of the cause and work to which he adhered, and for which he was put to such sufferings. Besides the seven wounds which he received when he was apprehended, he had a merciless weight of irons upon him during the whole time of his imprisonment.

The last and dying Testimony of JOHN NISBET, *of Hardhill, which he delivered to a friend in the Iron-house, when he was taken out to the scaffold in the Grass-market of Edinburgh, where he died, Friday, December 4. 1685.*

I Have always thought, that to live for Christ, and die for Christ, is a sufficient testimony for truth; yet now when I am within a few hours of eternity, to prevent mistakes, to satisfy my dear friends, and let them know how it is with me, and to let the world know what I die witnessing for, and testifying against, I judge it proper to leave a few lines behind me.

As for myself, it hath pleased the Lord Jehovah, of his super-abundant goodness, and infinite mercy, powerfully to determine my heart to close with, and embrace the Lord Jesus Christ, as he is made offer of in the everlasting gospel, for my King, Priest and Prophet. And that conquest captivating of me to his obedience, who was an heir of wrath, and a mass of sin and sinful corruption, is the fruit of electing love, according as it is manifested in the covenant of free, free, free grace, will evidently appear from these Scriptures following; which he, by the power and concurrence of his holy Spirit, hath made effectual to the convincing, converting, strengthening and enabling of me to be his, and to be for him thro' weal, and thro' woe, thro' good report, and thro' bad report;

and they are so many sweet cordials to
stepping out of time into eternity.

Psal. cx. 3. 'Thy people shall be will
' of thy power.' Rom. ix. 11. 'For th
' ing not yet born; neither having don
' evil, that the purpose of God accord
' might stand, not of works, but of hin
Ver. 15. 'For he saith to Moses, (See Ex
' I will have mercy on whom I will have
' will have compassion on whom I will ha
Ver. 16. 'So then it is not of him that will
' that runneth, but of God that sheweth m
ii. 13.—'God hath from the beginning ch
' vation, through sanctification of the Spir
' the truth.' Prov. viii. 30. 'Then was I
' brought up with him: and I was daily
' joicing always before him.' Ver. 31.
' the habitable part of his earth, and my
' with the sons of men.' Ver. 32. 'Now
to verse 36. Rom. viii. 29. 'For whor
' know, he also did predestinate to be co
' image of his Son, that he might be th
' mong many brethren.' Ver. 30. 'Mor
' did predestinate, them he also called;
' called, them he also justified; and who
' them he also glorified.' Ver. 35. 'Wh
' us from the love of Christ? shall tribu
' tress, or persecution, or famine, or nak
' il, or sword?' Ver. 37. 'Nay, in all t
' are more than conquerors, through him
Eph. i. 13. 'In whom ye also trusted,
' heard the word of truth, the gospel of y
' in whom also after that ye believed, y
' with that holy spirit of promise,' Ver.
' the earnest of our inheritance, until the
' the purchased possession, unto the prais
2 Tim. i. 9. 'Who hath saved us, and
' an holy calling: not according to our
' cording to his own purposes and grac
' given us in Christ Jesus, before the world
iii. 5. 'Not by works of righteousness v
' done, but according to his mercy he sa
' washing of regeneration, and renewin
' Ghost.' Ver. 6. 'Which he shed on

'thro' Jesus Christ our Saviour.' 1 Cor. i. 9. 'God is
' faithful, by whom ye were called into the fellowship
' of his Son Jesus Christ our Lord.' Rom. iii. 24. 'Be-
' ing justified freely by his grace, thro' the redemption
' that is in Jesus Christ.' Ver. 25. 'Whom he hath set
' forth to be a propitiation thro' faith in his blood, to
' declare his righteousness for the remission of sins that
' are past, thro' the forbearance of God.' And chap.
iv. 6. 'Even as David also describeth the blessedness
' of the man unto whom God imputeth righteousness
' without works.' Heb. ix. 14. 'How much more shall
' the blood of Christ, who thro' the eternal Spirit, offer-
' ed himself without spot to God, purge your conscience
' from dead works to serve the living God.' 2 Cor. v.
19. 'To wit, That God was in Christ, reconciling the
' world unto himself, not imputing their trespasses unto
' them.' Eph. iii. 17. 'That Christ may dwell in your
' hearts by faith, that ye being rooted and grounded in
' love,' &c. Gal. ii. 16. 'Knowing that a man is not
' justified by the works of the law, but by the faith of
' Jesus Christ; even we have believed in Jesus, that we
' might be justified by the faith of Christ, and not by
' the works of the law; for by the works of the law shall
' no flesh be justified.' Rom. v. 17. 'For by one man's
' offence, death reigned by one, much more they which
' receive abundance of grace, and of the gift of righte-
' ousness, shall reign in life by one Jesus Christ.' John
vi. 37. 'All that the Father giveth me, shall come to
' me; and him that cometh to me, I will in no wife cast
' out.' Ver. 39. 'And this is the Father's will which
' hath sent me, that of all which he hath given me, I
' should lose nothing, but should raise it up again at the
' last day.' Rom. xiv. 17. 'For the kingdom of heaven
' is not meat and drink, but righteousness and peace,
' and joy in the Holy Ghost.' Chap. viii. 1. 'There is
' therefore now no condemnation to them which are in
' Christ Jesus, who walk not after the flesh, but after
' the spirit.' 1 John v. 13. 'These things have I writ-
' ten unto you that believe on the name of the Son of
' God, that ye may know that ye have eternal life, and
' that ye may believe on the name of the Son of God.'
Eph. iv. 23. 'And be renewed in the spirit of your mind.'
Philip. iii. 9. 'And be found in him, not having mine
' own righteousness which is of the law, but that which

' is through the faith of Chrift, the
' which is of God by faith.' Ver.
' I may know him, and the powe
' furrection, and the fellowfhip of his fu
' made conformable unto his death.'
' Therefore we are buried with him by
' death, that like as Chrift was raifed up fr
' the glory of the Father: even fo we al
' in newnefs of life.' Prov. iv. 18. ' But
' juft is as the fhining light, that fhineth
' unto the perfect day.' Philip. i. 6. ' B
' this very thing, that he which hath begu
' in you will perform it until the day of
Pfalm lxxxix. 33. ' Neverthelefs, my lovin
' I not utterly take from him, nor fuffer
' to fail.' Ver. 34. ' My covenant wil
' nor alter the thing that is gone out of n
v. 1. ' Therefore being juftified by faith,
' with God thro' our Lord Jefus Chrift.'
' whom alfo we have accefs by faith i
' wherein we ftand, and rejoice in the ho
' of God.' 1 Pet. i. 5. ' Who are kept
' of God, thro' faith unto falvation, read
' ed in the laft time.' Rom. viii. 17. ' A
' then heirs, heirs of God, and joint hei
' if fo be that we fuffer with him, that v
' glorified together.' Chap. i. 16. ' Fc
' fhamed of the gofpel of Chrift; for it i
' God unto falvation, to every one that
' the Jew firft, and alfo to the Greek.
' To whom God would make known wh
' of the glory of this myftery among the C
' is Chrift in you, the hope of glory.'
' Take my yoke upon you, and learn of
' meek and lowly in heart; and ye fhall
' your fouls.' Pfal. lv. 22. ' Caft thy bu
' Lord, and he fhall fuftain thee; he w
' the righteous to be moved.' 2 Cor. x
' weapons of our warefare are not carna
' thro' God, to the pulling down of ftron
lvii. 2. ' I will cry unto God moft high;
' performeth all things for me.' Prov.
' that covereth his fins, fhall not profpe
' confeffeth and forfaketh them, fhall hav

Kr. 16. 'But I will sing of thy power; yea, I will sing
'aloud of thy mercy in the morning; for thou haſt been
'my defence and refuge in the day of my trouble.' Ver.
17. 'Unto thee, O my ſtrength, will I sing: for God
'is my defence, and the God of my mercy.' Pſal. lxviii.
18. 'Thou haſt aſcended on high, thou haſt led capti-
'vity captive; thou haſt received gifts for men; yea,
'for the rebellious alſo, that the Lord God might dwell
'among them.' Ver. 19. 'Bleſſed be the Lord who
'daily loadeth us with benefits, even the God of our
'ſalvation, Selah.' Ver. 20. 'He that is our God, is
'the God of ſalvation; and unto God the Lord belong
'the iſſues from death.' 2 Cor. v. i. 'For we know,
'that if our earthly houſe of this tabernacle were diſ-
'ſolved, we have a building of God, an houſe not made
'with hands, eternal in the heavens.' Heb. xii. 23.
'To the general aſſembly and church of the firſt born,
'which are written in heaven, and to God the judge of
'all, and to the ſpirits of juſt men made perfect, and to
'Jeſus the Mediator,' &c. Pſalm xlv. 1. to 9. John i.
r. to 15. and chap. xviii. throughout. Iſa. liii. to the
end, with many more.

Let none reflect upon me for citing ſo much? for the
Scripture hath been to me from my youth the living ora-
cles of his divine and ſacred lips. When I was crying,
'What ſhall I do to be ſaved?' And when I was ſaying,
'How ſhall I know the way of the Lord that I may walk
'therein?' Then his word was 'a light to my feet, and
'a lamp to my path,' exhorting me as it is in Iſa. lv. 1.
'Ho every one that thirſteth, come ye to the waters;
'and he that hath no money, come ye buy and eat; yea,
'come buy wine and milk without money and without
'price.' Ver. 2. 'Wherefore do ye ſpend your money
'for that which is not bread, and your labour for that
'which ſatisfieth not? hearken diligently unto me, and
'eat ye that which is good; and let your ſoul delight
'itſelf in fatneſs.' Ver. 3. 'Incline your ear and come
'unto me, hear and your ſoul ſhall live: And I will
'make an everlaſting covenant with you, even the ſure
'mercies of David.' Ver. 4. 'Behold I have given
'him for a witneſs to the people, a leader and command-
'er to the people.' Ver. 5. 'Behold thou ſhalt call a
'nation that thou knoweſt not, and nations that knew
'not thee ſhall run unto thee, becauſe of the Lord thy

'God, and for the holy One of Israel; for he hath glorified thee.' Ver. 6. 'Seek ye the Lord while he may be found, call ye upon him while he is near.' Ver. 7. 'Let the wicked forsake his way, and the unrighteous man his thoughts; and let him return unto the Lord, and he will have mercy upon him, and to our God, for he will abundantly pardon.' Ver. 8. 'For my thoughts are not your thoughts, neither are your ways my ways, saith the Lord.' John vi. 35. 'And Jesus said unto them, I am the bread of life; he that cometh to me shall never hunger; and he that believeth on me shall never thirst.' Rev. iii. 20. 'Behold I stand at the door, and knock: If any man hear my voice, and open the door, I will come in to him, and sup with him, and he with me.' Jer. iii. 13. 'Only acknowledge thine iniquity, that thou hast transgressed against the Lord thy God, and hast scattered thy ways to the strangers under every green tree, and ye have not obeyed my voice, saith the Lord.' Ver. 14. 'Turn, O backsliding children, saith the Lord, for I am married unto you: and I will take you, one of a city, and two of a family; and I will bring you to Zion.' Ver. 22. 'Return ye backsliding children, and I will heal your backslidings: Behold, we come unto thee, for thou art the Lord our God.' Ver. 23. 'Truly in vain is salvation hoped for from the hills, and from the multitude of mountains; truly in the Lord our God is the salvation of Israel.' Hosea xiv. 1. 'O Israel, return unto the Lord thy God, for thou hast fallen by thine iniquity.' Ver. 2. 'Take with you words, and turn unto the Lord, say unto him, Take away all iniquity, and receive us graciously, so we will render the calves of our lips.' Jer. xxxi. 18. 'I have surely heard Ephraim bemoaning himself thus, Thou hast chastised me, and I was chastised, as a bullock unaccustomed to the yoke: Turn thou me, and I shall be turned; for thou art the Lord my God.' John xiv. 6. 'Jesus saith unto him, I am the way, and the truth, and the life: no man cometh unto the Father, but by me.' Rev. xxii. 17. 'And the Spirit and the bride say, Come. And let him that heareth, say, Come. And let him that is athirst, come. And whosoever will, let him take of the water of life freely.'

When I was grapling with sin, Satan and the world,

and my own wicked and deceitful heart, the enemies of my falvation, his words were as props and pillars to me: fo that tho' I got my wounds, and was oft forely beat; yet at the laſt I came off victorious, by the help of him who is God all-fufficient to all who, thro' grace, lay hold on him for help. It is by him, that I have fought the good fight, that I have finifhed my courfe, and that I have kept the faith; henceforth there is laid up for me a crown of righteoufnefs, which the Lord the righteous Judge fhall give me at that day. It is by him fhining in his word, that I know all my manifold fins and tranf-greffions are freely pardoned, and that I have a juſt right and title to what is expreſſed. 1 Cor. i. 30. So that now the guilt and condemning power of fin being fully pardoned by a judicial act of God's free and fove-reign grace, thro' the merits of the Lord Jefus Chriſt, efpecially applied and witneffed unto by the Holy Spirit, upon, and to my fpirit, there is no room left me to doubt any more of my being freely juſtified by him, or my being in union with him, and in a ſtate of grace; or the power, dominion and filth of fin, original and actual, being fubdued, taken off, and wafhed away by the virtue of the fpirit of fanctification, being created anew in Chriſt Jefus unto good works, and being fanctified throughout in foul, body and fpirit, and made meet to be a partaker of the inheritance of the faints in light, by him who loved me, and gave himfelf to the death for me, and redeemed me by power and price.

Now, being in fuch a cafe of communion with him, I am pained till I be freed of the remains of a body of fin and death, till I be freed of the world and all things therein, and alfo of this natural life, and be poffeffed of himfelf, and with himfelf in his eternal inheritance, which is incorruptible, undefiled, and that fadeth not away; a place which he hath provided for all whom he hath chofen, for all whom he hath called, for all whom he hath juſtified, for all whom he hath fanctified: O to be there, where I fhall fin no more, where I fhall be tempted no more, neither feel any more of the withdraw-ings of his Spirit's prefence, and light of his glorious countenance; but fhall be ever with him, fee him as he is, and ferve him for ever and ever.

Now, my dear friends in Chriſt, I have always, fince the public refolutioners were for bringing in the malig-

nants and their interest, thought it m[ight]
with the Lord's people, in witnessing aga[inst]
courses; and now we see clearly that it h[as]
thing less than making captains that we [may return to]
Egypt, by the open doors, that are mad[e]
in Popery, and set up idolatry in the Lor[d's]
land, to defile it, and thereby to provo[ke]
down fierce wrath upon it, and the inha[bitants.]
Wherefore it is the unquestionable and in[cumbent duty]
of all who have any love to God, to his [Son]
Jesus Christ, to the thriving of his kingdo[m,]
soul's salvation, and to the following ge[nerations,]
a close, constant, and needy dependance [on Je-]
hovah's all sufficiency, for light, for cou[nsel, for direc-]
tion, for strength and ability, to make con[science of bear-]
ing testimony for him, for his persecute[d cause]
and interest in these lands, which was sw[orn to with]
lifted hands to God the searcher of heart[s, that]
herein all could act a faithful part for [him who hath]
done so much for poor wretched us! wh[en he was sweat-]
ing, dying and rotting in our blood-red [woundings, pas-]
sing by us with his love and life-giving v[oice, and said]
to us, Live, live. And on the other ha[nd, to witness]
faithfully, constantly and conscientiously [against all that]
the enemies have done, or are doing to t[hrow down]
the glorious work of reformation; and b[anish Christ]
out of these lands, by robbing him of hi[s headship,]
(for he, and he alone, is head of his ow[n church)]
by burning the covenants, which are the [marriage-contract]
betwixt him and these lands; and by pers[ecuting his gos-]
pel-ministers and members, who are lab[ouring to keep]
their garments clean, and their hands fre[e from the cor-]
ruptions and compliances in these evil tim[es. And how-]
ever it be, that many, both ministers an[d professors, are]
turning their backs upon Christ and his c[ause, and mock-]
ing and casting dirt upon you and the testim[ony of Jesus,]
yet let not this weaken your hands, stumb[le or discourage]
you from going on in the strength of the L[ord,]
to contend earnestly for the faith once d[elivered to the]
saints, and witness a good confession for hi[m, even unto]
resisting unto blood, striving against sin;
your souls possess themselves with patien[ce, for I assure]
you, it will not be long to the fourth wat[ch, when Christ]
will come with garments dyed in blood,

ours upon the mount of Zion, to judge the mount of Esau; and then the houſe of Jacob and Joſeph ſhall be for fire, and the malignants, Prelates and Papiſts ſhall be ſtubble, the flame whereof ſhall be great.

But my generation work being done with my time, I go to him who loved me, and waſhed me from all my ſins; to him who has counted me worthy to ſuffer for his name: And O that I had many lives to lay down for him, and much blood to ſeal his noble and honourable cauſe with, even he who gracioufly pitied, and hath now given me the full aſſurance of being a member of his church triumphant, which is the new Jeruſalem, and the city of the living God!

I die adhering to the Scriptures of the Old and New Teſtament as the undoubted word of God, an unerring rule of faith and manners, and a firm foundation for principle and practice in the ways of godlineſs and true holineſs. 2 Tim. iii. 16. ' All Scripture is given by infpira' tion of God: and is profitable for doctrine, for reproof, ' for correction, for inſtruction in righteouſneſs.' And the Confeſſion of Faith, Catechiſms Larger and Shorter, as agreeable thereunto, and ſafely founded thereupon. 2 Tim. i. 13. ' Hold faſt the form of found words, which ' thou haſt heard of me in faith and love which is in ' Chriſt Jeſus,' Heb. vi. 1. ' Therefore leaving the prin' ciples of the doctrine of Chriſt, let us go on unto per' fection, not laying again the foundation of repentance ' from dead works, and of faith towards God.' The Sum of Saving Knowledge, the Directory for Church government in her doctrine, worſhip and diſcipline. I own all the attained unto pieces of reformation in the church of Scotland, particularly betwixt the years 1638, and 1649. The Covenants National and Solemn League; the Acknowledgment of Sins and Engagement to Duties. I own the proteſtation given by the remonſtrators againſt the Public Reſolutions, the Apologetical Declaration, and all declarations hitherto emitted at Rutherglen, Sanquhar, and Lanerk; with all dying ſpeeches and teſtimonies of theſe who have ſealed the truth with their blood, ſo far as they agree with God's holy word.

I own all the appearances in arms that have been at Pentland, Drumclog, Bothwel, Airſmoſs, and elſewhere, againſt God's ſtated enemies, and the enemies of th. goſpel, as it hath been preached by all Chrift's faithful ambaffadors in Scotland, fince the reformation; and not by that faithful fervant of Chrift, Mr. James Renwick; and the teftimony of the day, as it is ftated and carried on by him and his adherents at home and abroad; and kingly government, as appointed and emited in the word of God, and entring covenant ways, and with covenant qualifications. But I am perfuaded, Scotland's covenanted God will cut off the name of the Stuarts, becaufe they have ftated themfelves againft religion, reformation, and the thriving of Chrift's kingdom and kingly government in thefe lands. And altho' men idolize them much now, yet ere long there fhall none of them be to tyrannize in covenanted Britain any more.

On the other hand, I die protefting againft, and difowning Popery in all its fuperftitious bigotry and bloody cruelty; and Prelacy the mother of Popery; and all that depends upon that hierarchy; and the unhinging and overthrowing of the glorious work of reformation, by their woful Act Refciffory: burning the Covenant, turning out gofpel minifters, filling their rooms with profane, erronious curates, and fetting up Charles Stuart to be head of the church; and fo robbing Chrift of his royal and incommunicable prerogatives, by their curfed act of fupremacy.

I proteft againft the putting malignants in places of power and truft in church, ftate, and armies; and all declarations * any where publifhed tending thereunto; and againft all paying of ftent, cefs, and locality, to ftrengthen the enemies hands to perfecute Chrift's people in fields, prifons or any other ways; and robbing, plundering, or fpoiling them of their goods; and all raifing of the hue and cry after them; and all finful oaths fuch as the oath of fupremacy, the bond of peace, the teft, the oath of conformity, the abjuration oath, and the oath *fuper inquirendis*.

I die teftifying againft the woful indulgences, the fruits and confequences of which have fo much ftrengthened the enemy, increafed our divifions, widened our breaches, and deadned the fpirits, and cooled the zeal of the Lord's people, ftumbled and offended the weak, and in a great meafure retarded the carrying on of a teftimony for truth,

---

* See the fhort relation before this teftimony.

of John Nisbet of Hardhill.

by condemning the things contended for, and reproaching thefe that contend for truth.

Wherefore I leave my teftimony againft all the accepters thereof, and all minifters and profeffors, who are any way guilty of any of the woful defections, and finful compliances with the enemies of truth, or any way guilty of condemning, reproaching and ridiculing Mr. James Renwick, and his correfpondents, or the teftimony which they are carrying on. And let all fuch minifters and profeffors know, that this their practice at the beft is a denying of Chrift, and a fhifting of his crofs: therefore let them take warning, and ponder thefe fcriptures. Matth. x. 32. 'Whofoever therefore fhall con-
' fefs me before men, him will I alfo confefs before my
' Father who is in heaven.' Ver. 33. 'But whofoever
' fhall deny me before men, him will I alfo deny before
' my Father who is in heaven.' (See Luke xii. 8, 9.)
Ver. 37. 'He that loveth father and mother more than
' me, is not worthy of me; and he that loveth fon
' or daughter more than me, is not worthy of me.' Ver.
38. 'And he that taketh not his crofs, and followeth
' after me, is not worthy of me.' Matth. xvi. 24.
' Then faid Jefus unto his difciples, If any man will
' come after me, let him deny himfelf, and take up his
' crofs, and follow me.' (See Mark viii. 34.) Mark viii.
35. 'For whofoever will fave his life, fhall lofe it; but
' whofoever fhall lofe his life, for my fake and the gof-
' pel's, the fame fhall fave it.' (See Matth. x. 49. alfo
chap. xvi. 25.) Matth. xvi. 26. 'For what is a man pro-
' fited if he fhall gain the whole world, and lofe his
' own foul? or what fhall a man give in exchange for his
' foul?' (See Mark viii. 36, 37.) Mark viii. 38. 'Who-
' foever therefore fhall be afhamed of me and my words,
' of him alfo fhall the Son of man be afhamed, when he
' cometh in the glory of his Father, with the holy angels.'
Ifa. viii. 11. 'For the Lord fpake thus to me with a
' ftrong hand, and inftructed me, that I fhould not walk
' in the way of this people, faying,' Ver. 12. 'Say ye
' not, A confederacy, to all them to whom this people
' fhall fay, A confederacy; neither fear ye their fear,
' nor be afraid.' Ver. 13. 'Sanctify the Lord of hofts
' himfelf, and let him be your fear, and let him be your
' dread.' Ver. 14. 'And he fhall be for a fanctuary:
' but for a ftone of ftumbling, and for a rock of offence

K k

'to both the houses of Israel, and for a snare to the in-
'habitants of Jerusalem.' Ver. 15. 'And many among
'them shall stumble and fall, and be broken, and be snar-
'ed, and be taken,' (as it is expressed ver. 9, 10.) Prov.
i. 10. 'My son, if sinners entice thee, consent thou not.'
Ver. 11. 'If they say, Come with us, let us lay wait
'for blood, let us lurk privily for the innocent without
'cause.' Ver. 12. 'Let us swallow them up alive as the
'grave, and whole as those that go down into the pit.'
Ver. 13. 'We shall find all precious substance, we shall
'fill our houses with spoil.' Ver. 14. 'Cast in thy lot
'among us, let us all have one purse.' Ver. 15. 'My son,
'walk not thou in the way with them, refrain thy foot
'from their path.' Ver. 16. 'For their feet run to e-
'vil, and make haste to shed blood.' Isa. v. 20. 'Wo
'unto them that call evil good, and good evil; that put
'darkness for light, and light for darkness; that put
'bitter for sweet, and sweet for bitter.' Ver. 21. 'Wo
'unto them that are wise in their own eyes, and pru-
'dent in their own sight.' Ver. 23. 'Which justify the
'wicked for reward, and take away the righteousness of
'the righteous from him.' Ver. 24. 'Therefore as the
'fire devoureth the stubble, and the flame consumeth the
'chaff; so their root shall be rottenness, and their blos-
'som shall go up as dust, because they have cast away
'the law of the Lord of hosts, and despised the word of
'the holy One of Israel.' Prov. xvii. 15. 'He that
'justifieth the wicked, and he that condemneth the just,
'even they both are abomination to the Lord.' Amos
v. 10. 'They hate him that rebuketh in the gate, and
'they abhor him that speaketh uprightly.' Gal. ii.
18. 'For if I build again the things which I destroyed,
'I make myself a transgressor.' Psal. l. 16. 'But un-
'to the wicked, God saith, What hast thou to do to
'declare my statutes, or that thou shouldst take my co-
'venant in thy mouth?' Ver. 17. 'Seeing thou hatest
'instruction, and castest my words behind thee.' Ver.
18. 'When thou sawest a thief, then thou consentedst
'with him, and hast been partaker with adulterers.'
Ver. 19. 'Thou givest thy mouth to evil, and thy
'tongue frameth deceit.' Ver. 20. 'Thou sittest and
'speakest against thy brother, thou slanderest thy own
'mother's son.' Ver. 21. 'These things hast thou done,
'and I kept silence; thou thoughtest that I was altoge-

'ther such an one as thyself; but I will reprove thee,
'and set them in order before thine eyes.' The prophecy of Obadiah throughout, the first and last chapters of Isaiah to the end, with many more.

Now, it is my last request and soul's desire that all who have made Moses's choice, 'to suffer affliction with the peo-
'ple of God, rather than enjoy the pleasures of sin for a
'season;' and are true lovers of Zion's righteous cause;'
that you set much time apart, and mourn, and afflict your souls, for your original sin, heart-plagues, sins of persons and families, sins of kings and kingdoms; and for all the dreadful apostasies, hateful compliances, and sinful sidings of ministers and people, with the enemies of God and godliness, and mourn that there is not more faithfulness and zeal for the cause of God amongst his people. Read Psalm 1. Ezra ix. Neh. ix. Jer. ix. Lam. iii. and Ezek. ix. to the end.

My dear friends, forbear your contentions and censuring one of another; sympathize with and love one another, for this is his commandment; keep up your sweet fellowship meetings, and desirable general meetings, with which my soul has been often refreshed; and what is agitate in them, for carrying on of a testimony for truth, and against defections, let it be managed with scripture light for direction, and with zeal temperate with knowledge, and with the spirit of meekness accompanied with patience and humility. Be always ready to give a reason of your faith, and be much denied to the world, to yourselves, and to your natural life; and when God in his providence calls you to lay it down for him, do it cheerfully, and embrace the cross of your sweet Lord Jesus with open arms; for he will not send any a warfare on their own charges.

Take for your rule and encouragement these Scriptures, with others, that I leave to your own search. Gal. v. 19. 'Now the works of the flesh are manifest,
'which are these, adultery, fornication, uncleanness,
'lasciviousness.' Ver. 20. 'Idolatry, witchcraft, ha-
'tred, variance, emulation, wrath, strife, seditions,
'heresies,' Ver. 21. 'Envying, murders, drunkenness,
'revellings, and such like, of the which I tell you be-
'fore, as I have also told you in time past, that they
'which do such things shall not inherit the kingdom of
'God.' Ver. 22. 'But the fruit of the Spirit is love,

'joy, peace, long-suffering, gentleness, goodness, faith,' Ver. 23. 'Meekness, temperance; against such there is 'no law.' Ver. 24. 'And they that are Christ's have 'crucified the flesh, with the affections and lusts.' Ver. 25. 'If we live in the Spirit, let us also walk in the Spi-'rit.' Ver. 26. 'Let us not be desirous of vain glory, 'provoking one another, envying one another.' Chap. vi. ver. 7. 'Be not deceived, God is not mocked: for 'whatsoever a man soweth, that shall he also reap.' Ver. 8. 'For he that soweth to his flesh, shall of the 'flesh reap corruption; but he that soweth to the Spi-'rit, shall of the Spirit reap life everlasting.' Ver. 9. 'And let us not be weary in well doing; for in due sea-'son we shall reap, if we faint not.' Ver. 10. 'As we 'have therefore opportunity, let us do good unto all 'men, especially unto them that are of the houshold of 'faith.' Mal. iii. 16. 'Then they that feared the Lord, 'spake often one to another, and the Lord hearkened 'and heard it, and a book of remembrance was written 'before him, for them that feared the Lord, and that 'thought upon his name.' Ver. 17. 'And they shall 'be mine, saith the Lord of hosts, in that day when I 'make up my jewels, and I will spare them as a man 'spareth his own son that serveth him. Ver. 18. 'Then 'shall ye return and discern between the righteous and 'the wicked; between him that serveth God, and him 'that serveth him not.' Isa. iii. 10. 'Say ye to the 'righteous, that it shall be well with him; for they shall 'eat the fruit of their doings.' Ver. 11. 'Wo unto the 'wicked, it shall be ill with him; for the reward of his 'hands shall be given him.' Ver. 9. 'The shew of their 'countenance doth witness against them, and they de-'clare their sin as Sodom, they hide it not: Wo unto 'their soul, for they have rewarded evil unto themselves.' And chap. viii ver. 20. 'To the law and to the testi-'mony, if they speak not according to this word, it is 'because there is no truth in them.' Mal. iv. 2. 'But 'unto you that fear my name, shall the Son of righte-'ousness arise with healing in his wings; and ye shall 'go forth and grow up as calves of the stall.' Isa viii. 17. 'And I will wait upon the Lord, that hideth his 'face from the house of Jacob, and I will look for him.' Phil. i. 27. 'Only let your conversation be as it becom-'eth the gospel of Christ, that whether I come and see

'you, or else be absent, I may hear of your affairs,
'that ye stand fast in one spirit, with one mind, striving
'for the faith of the gospel.' Ver. 28. 'And in nothing
'terrified by your adversaries; which is to them an e-
'vident token of perdition, but to you of salvation, and
'that of God.' Ver. 29. 'For unto you it is given in
'the behalf of Christ, not only to believe on him, but
'also to suffer for his sake.' Rev. x. 11. 'And he said
'unto me, Thou must prophesy again before many peo-
'ples, and nations, and tongues, and kings.' Heb. x.
from the 11. verse to the end; and chap. xii. 11. 'Now
'no chastening for the present seemeth to be joyous, but
'grievous: nevertheless afterward it yieldeth the peace-
'able fruit of righteousness unto them which are exercis-
'ed thereby.' Ver. 12. 'Wherefore lift up the hands
'which hang down, and the feeble knees.' Ver. 13.
'And make straight paths for your feet, lest that which
'is lame be turned out of the way, but let it rather be
'healed.' Ver. 14. 'Follow peace with all men, and
'holiness, without which no man shall see the Lord.'
Ver. 15. 'Looking diligently, lest any man fail of the
'grace of God; lest any root of bitterness springing up,
'trouble you, and thereby many be defiled.' Rev. xiv.
1. 'And I looked, and lo, a Lamb stood on the mount
'Sion, and with him an hundred forty and four thou-
'sand, having his Father's name written in their fore-
'heads.' Ver. 2. 'And I heard a voice from heaven,
'as the voice of many waters, and as the voice of great
'thunder; and I heard the voice of harpers harping with
'their harps.' Ver. 3. 'And they sung as it were a
'new song before the throne, and before the four beasts,
'and the elders, and no man could learn that song, but
'the hundred and forty and four thousand, which were
'redeemed from the earth.' Ver. 4. 'These were they
'which were not defiled with women, for they are vir-
'gins; these are they which follow the Lamb whither-
'soever he goeth, these were redeemed from among men,
'being the first fruits unto God, and to the Lamb.'
Ver. 5. 'And in their mouth was found no guile; for
'they are without fault before the throne of God.' Jude
ver. 3. 'Beloved, when I gave all diligence to write un-
'to you of the common salvation; it was needful for
'me to write unto you, and exhort you, that ye should
'earnestly contend for the faith which was once deli-

'vered to the saints.' Eph. vi. 10. 'Finally, my breth-
'ren, be strong in the Lord, and in the power of his
'might.' Ver. 11. 'Put on the whole armour of God,
'that ye may be able to stand against the wiles of the
'devil.' Ver. 12. 'For we wrestle not against flesh and
'blood, but against principalities, against powers, a-
'gainst the rulers of the darkness of this world, against
'spiritual wickedness in high places.' Ver. 13. 'Where-
'fore take unto you the whole armour of God, that ye
'may be able to withstand in the evil day, and having
'done all to stand.' Ver. 14. 'Stand therefore, having
'your loins girt about with truth, and having on the
'breast-plate of righteousness.' Ver. 15. 'And your
'feet shod with the preparation of the gospel of peace.'
Ver. 16. 'Above all, taking the shield of faith, where-
'with ye shall be able to quench all the fiery darts of the
'wicked.' Ver. 17. 'And take the helmet of salvati-
'on, and the sword of the Spirit, which is the word of
'God.'

And fear not at his sweet, lovely and desirable cross; for altho' I have not been able, because of my wounds, (that I received at my taking) to lift up or lay down my head, but as I was helped, yet I was never in better case all my life; he has not given me one challenge since I came to prison, for any thing less or more; but on the contrary, he has so wonderfully shined on me with the sense of his redeeming, strengthening, assisting, supporting, through-bearing, pardoning and reconciling love, grace and mercy, that my soul doth long to be freed of bodily infirmities and earthly organs, that so I may flee to his royal palace, even the heavenly habitation of my God, where I am sure of a crown put on my head, and a palm put in my hand, and a new song put in my mouth, even the song of Moses and the Lamb, that so I may bless, praise, magnify and extol him for what he hath done to me, and for me. Wherefore I bid farewel to all my dear fellow-sufferers for the testimony of Jesus, who are wandering in dens and caves. Farewel my children, study holiness in all your ways, and praise the Lord for what he hath done for me, and tell all my christian friends to praise him on that account. Farewel sweet Bible, and wanderings and contendings for truth. Welcome death; welcome the city of my God, where I shall see him, and be enabled to serve him eternally with full freedom; welcome blessed company, and angels, and spirits of just men made perfect. But above all, Welcome, welcome, welcome our glorious and alone God, Father, Son, and Holy Ghost, into thy hands I commit my spirit, for thou art worthy. Amen.

JOHN NISBET.

The last Speech and Testimony of the Rev. Mr. JAMES RENWICK, *Minister of the gospel, who suffered in the Grass-market of Edinburgh, February* 17*th* 1688. *Emitted from his own hand, the day before his suffering.*

My dear friends in Christ,

IT hath pleased the Lord to deliver me into the hands of men; and I think fit to send you this salutation, which I expect will be the last. When I pose my heart upon it, before God, I dare not desire to have escaped this lot; for no less could have been for his glory and the vindication of his cause on my behalf: And as I am free before him of the profanity, which some, either naughty, wicked, or strangers to me, have reported, that I have been sometimes guilty of; so he hath kept me from the womb, free of the ordinary pollutions of children, as these that have been acquainted with me thro' the tract of my life, do know. And now my blood shall either more silence reproaches, or more ripen them for judgment: But I hope, it shall make some more sparing to speak of those who shall come after me; and so I am the more willing to pay this cost for their instruction, and my succeeders ease. Since I came to prison, the Lord has been wonderfully kind to me, he hath made his word to give me light, life, joy, courage and strength; yea, it hath dropped with sweet smelling myrrh unto me, particularly these passages and promises, Gen. xxii. 12. latter part of the verse, ' For now I know that thou fearest ' God, seeing thou hast not witheld thy son, thine only ' son.' Neh. viii. 10. latter part of the verse, ' Neither ' be you sorry, for the joy of the Lord is your strength.' Job. iii. 17. ' There the wicked cease from troubling; ' and there the weary be at rest.' Ver. 18. ' There the ' prisoners rest together, they hear not the voice of the ' oppressor.' Job. xxiii. 10. ' But he knoweth the way ' that I take: when he hath tried me, I shall come forth ' as gold,' Ver. 11. ' My foot hath held his steps, his 'way have I kept, and not declined.' Ver. 12. 'Neither have I gone back from the commandment of his lips, I have esteemed the words of his mouth, more than my necessary food.' Ver. 13. 'But he is in one mind, and who can turn him? and what his soul desireth, even that he doth.' Ver. 14. 'For he performeth the thing that is appointed for me: and many such things are with him.' Psal. cv. 19.--'The word of the Lord tried him.' Luke xxi. 12. 'But before all these they shall lay their hands on you, and persecute you, delivering you up to the synagogues, and into prisons, being brought before kings for my name's sake.' Ver. 13. 'And it shall turn to you for a testimony.' Ver. 19. 'In your patience possess ye your souls.' Heb. xii. 23. 'To the general assembly and church of the first born, which are written in heaven, and to God the judge of all, and to the spirits of just men made perfect.' James. i. 12. 'Blessed is the man that endureth temptation: for when he is tried, he shall receive the crown of life, which the Lord hath promised to them that love him.' 1 Pet. v. 7. 'Casting all your care upon him, for he careth for you.'. Ver. 8. 'Be sober, be vigilant; because your adversary the devil, as a roaring lion, walketh about seeking whom he may devour.' Rev. iii. 8. 'I know thy works: behold I have set before thee an open door, and no man can shut it; for thou hast a little strength, and hast kept my word, and hast not denied my name.' Ver. 10. 'Because thou hast kept the word of my patience, I also will keep thee from the hour of temptation, which shall come upon all the world, to try them that dwell upon the earth.' Ver. 11. 'Behold, I come quickly: hold that fast which thou hast, that no man take thy crown.' Ver. 12. 'Him that overcometh, will I make a pillar in the temple of my God, and he shall go no more out: and I will write upon him the name of my God, and the name of the city of my God, which is new Jerusalem, which cometh down out of heaven from my God; and I will write upon him my new name.' Rev. xix. 20. 'And the beast was taken, and with him the false prophet that wrought miracles before him, with which he deceived them that received the mark of the beast, and them that worshipped his image. These both were cast alive into a lake of fire

'burning with brimstone.' Ver. 21. 'And the rem-
'nant were slain with the sword of him that sat upon the
'horse, which sword proceedeth out of his mouth: and
'all the fowls were filled with their flesh.' And many
other scriptures.

O what can I say to the Lord's praise! It was but little that I knew of him before I came to prison; I have found sensibly much of his divine strength, much of the joy of his Spirit, and much assurance from his word and Spirit concerning my salvation; my sufferings are stated upon the matters of my doctrine, for there was found with me the sum of my last two sermons at Braid's-craigs, which I wrote after I preached them: the former whereof was upon Psal. lxvi. 10. ' Be still and know that I
' am God; I will be exalted among the heathen, I will
' be exalted in the earth.' And the latter upon Heb. x. 38. ' Now the just shall live by faith: but if any man
' draw back, my soul shall have no pleasure in him.'
And so I was examined upon the application made therein unto the sins of the time; all which I owned once and again, as it is to be seen in my indictment: and I being tried, and an assize set, I adhered to my former confession explicitely; so my sentence of death was drawn forth, upon these heads.

First, Because I could not own James VII. to be my lawful sovereign.

Secondly, Because I taught the unlawfulness of paying the cess, expresly exacted for the suppressing the faithful and free preaching of the gospel.

Thirdly, Because that I taught that it was the peoples duty to carry arms at the preaching of the gospel, now when it is persecuted, for defending themselves, and resisting of unjust violence.

I think such a testimony is worth many lives, and I praise the Lord, for his enabling me to be plain and positive in all my confessions: for therein I found peace, joy, strength, and boldness. I have met with many assaults in prison, some from some of the indulged party, and others from some of the prelatic; but by the strength of God, I was enabled to stand, that they could neither bow me, nor break me. I was also assaulted by some of the popish party, (I suppose they were some of the ecclesiastic creatures) but they found none of their own stuff in me. I told them, after sundry debatings, That I had lived, and should die an enemy to their way. However some that knew me not, reproached me with Jesuitism. I was pressed by sundry to seek a reprieve, and my answer was always, That I adhered to my former confession, and if they pleased to let that appointed time of my death stand, let it stand; and if they pleased to protract it, let them protract it; for I was ready and willing both to live and die; howbeit there came a reprieve for eight days, but I had no hand in it. They still urged, would I but say, that I desired time for conference with some persons anent my principles: I answered, That my time was in the Lord's hand, and I was in no hesitation, or doubt about my principles myself; I would not be so rude as to decline conference with any, so far as it might not be inconvenient for me in my present circumstances, but I will seek it with none. I have no more to say on this head, but my heart doth not smite me for any thing in the matters of my God, since I came to prison. And I can further say to his praise, with conscioufness of integrity, that I have walked in his way, and kept his charge tho' with much weakness, and many infirmities, whereof ye have been witnesses.

Now, my dear friends in precious Christ, I think I need not tell you, that as I have lived, so I die in the same persuasion with the true reformed and covenanted, Presbyterian church of Scotland; that I adhere to the testimony of the day, as it is held forth in our Informatory Vindication, and in the Testimony against the present toleration; and that I own, and seal with my blood all the precious truths, even the controverted truths, that I have taught. So I would exhort every one of you, to make sure your personal reconciliation with God in Christ: for I fear many of you have that yet to do; and when ye come where I am, to look pale death in the face, ye will not be a little shaken and terrified, if ye have not laid hold on eternal life. I would exhort you to much diligence in the use of means, to be careful in keeping up your societies, to be frequent and fervent in secret prayer, to read much the written word of God, and to examine yourselves by it. Do not weary to maintain, in your places and stations, the present testimony; for when Christ goes forth to defeat Antichrist, with that name written on his thigh and on his vesture, KING OF KINGS, AND LORD OF LORDS, he will make it glorious in the earth: And if ye can but tranfmit it to the pofterity, ye may count it a great generation-work. But beware of the minifters, that have accepted of this toleration, and all others that bend that way; and follow them not, for the fun hath gone down upon them. Do not fear, that the Lord will caft off Scotland; for he will certainly return again, and fhew himfelf glorious in our land. But watch and pray, for he is bringing on a fad overthrowing ftroke, which fhall make many fay, That they have eafily got thro', that have got a fcaffold for Chrift; and do not regard the prefent fufferings of this world, for ' they are not worthy to be compared to ' the glory that fhall be revealed.'

I may fay to his praife, that I have found his crofs fweet and lovely unto me, for I have had many joyful hours, and not a fearful thought fince I came to prifon; he hath ftrengthened me to outbrave man, and outface death, and I am now longing for the joyful hour of my diffolution; and there is nothing in the world that I am forry to leave but you: but I go to better company, and fo I muft take my leave of you all. Farewel beloved fufferers, and followers of the Lamb; farewel chriftian intimates: farewel chriftian and comfortable mother and fifters; farewel fweet focieties; farewel defirable general meetings; farewel night-wanderings in cold and wearinefs for Chrift; farewel fweet Bible, and preaching of the gofpel; farewel fun, moon, and ftars, and all fublunary things; farewel conflicts with a body of fin and death. Welcome fcaffold for precious Chrift; welcome heavenly Jerufalem; welcome innumerable company of angels; welcome general affembly, and church of the firft-born; welcome crown of g'ory, white robes, and fongs of Mofes and the Lamb; and above all, welcome, O thou bleffed Trinity, and one God! O eternal One! I commit my foul into thy eternal reft.

JAMES RENWICK.

A Letter to his Chriftian friends, writ in the time of his reprival.

My dear friends in Chrift,

I See now what hath been the language of my reprieve, it hath been, that I might be further tempted and tried; and I praife the Lord, he hath affifted me to give

further proofs of stedfastness; I have bee
ed by some Popish priests; but the last tin
told them, I would debate no more wit
were, and that I had lived and would di
and testify against the idolatries, heresies
and errors of that Antichristian way.]
was cast into a deep exercise, and made
an impression of the dreadfulness of ev
might grieve the Spirit of God. I found
bitter than death, and one hour's hiding
more insupportable. And then at night,
fore a part of the council, and the chanc
the Informatory Vindication, and asked
I answered, I know it. And being inte:
fessed that I had a great hand in writir
pressed me to tell my assistants: I told th
those whom they persecuted; but would
further. They also urged me upon pair
tell, Where our societies were! Who ke
correspondencies? And where they were k
ed, Tho' they should torture me, which
all law, after sentence of death, I woul(
further notice than the books gave. I
threatened to tell my haunts and quarter:
to make known to them any such thing
turned to prison. Such exercise as I had
ful for such a trial; and I would rathe
they could do unto me, than have disho
offended you, and brought you unto tro
hope, within less than three days, to
reach of all temptations. Now I have r
Farewel again in our blessed Lord Jesus.

A short account of his last Words upon

Before he went out of the tolbooth, h
with his mother and sisters, and
friends, when the drum beat the first war
cution; which so soon as he heard, he lea
ment of heavenly joy, saying, 'Let us be g
' for the marriage of the Lamb is come:'
some measure, 'The bride, the Lamb's v
' herself ready.' And till dinner was ov
upon the parallel of a marriage, and inv
to come to the wedding, meaning his execv

of Mr. James Renwick.

was come to the scaffold, the drums being beat all the while, none of the distant spectators could hear any thing that he said; only some very few, that were closs by him did hear it, whereof one has collected the following account: He delivered himself to this effect;

Spectators, or (if there be any of you) auditors, I must tell you, I am come here this day to lay down my life for adhering to the truths of Christ, for which I am neither afraid nor ashamed to suffer; nay, I bless the Lord, that ever he counted me worthy, or enabled me to suffer any thing for him; and I desire to praise his grace, that he hath not only kept me free from the gross pollutions of the time, but also from many ordinary pollutions of children; and such as I have been stained with he hath washed me from them in his own blood. I am this day to lay down my life for these three things. 1. For disowning the usurpations and tyranny of James duke of York. 2. For preaching, That it was unlawful to pay the cess, expresly exacted for bearing down the gospel. 3. For preaching, That it was lawful for people to carry arms, for defending themselves in their meetings for the persecuted gospel-ordinances. I think a testimony for these is worth many lives, and if I had ten hundred, I would think it little enough to lay them all down for the same.

Dear friends, spectators, and (if any of you be) auditors, I must tell you, That I die a Presbyterian Protestant. I own the Word of God as the rule of faith and manners. I own the Confession of Faith, Larger and Shorter Catechisms, Sum of Saving Knowledge, Directory for Worship, &c. Covenants National and Solemn League, acts of general assemblies, and all the faithful contendings that have been for the work of reformation. I leave my testimony approving the preaching of the gospel in the fields, and the defending of the same by arms. I adjoin my testimony to all that hath been sealed by blood, shed either on scaffolds, fields or seas, for the cause of Christ. I leave my testimony against Popery, Prelacy, Erastianism, &c. Against all profanity, and every thing contrary to found doctrine; particularly against all usurpations made on Christ's right, who is the PRINCE OF THE KINGS OF THE EARTH, who alone must bear the glory of ruling his own kingdom, the church: And in particular, against the absolute power usurped by this usurper, that belongs to no mortal, but is the incommunicable prerogative of JEHOVAH; and against this toleration flowing from that absolute power.

Upon this, he was bid have done. He answered, I have near done. Then he said, Ye that are the people of God, do not weary in maintaining the testimony of the day, in your stations and places; and whatever ye do, make sure an interest in Christ; for there is a storm coming that shall try your foundations. Scotland must be rid of Scotland, before the delivery come. And you that are strangers to God, break off your sins by repentance, else I will be a witness against you in the day of the Lord. Here they caused him desist. Upon the scaffold, he sung a part of the ciii. Psalm from the beginning, and read the xix. chap. of the Revelation. And having thus finished his course, served his generation, and witnessed a good confession for his Lord and Master, before many witnesses, by the will of God, he yielded up his spirit into the hands of God who gave it.

He was the last that sealed the Testimony of this suffering period in a public way upon a scaffold.

An APPENDIX;

Containing some particulars relating to the foregoing Testimonies, and other sufferings of that time.

A short relation concerning the Reverend Mr. RICHARD CAMERON, *Minister of the gospel, who was killed in a rencounter at Airsmoss, July 22d,* 1680.

BEcause in the foregoing Speeches, there is frequent mention made of the Reverend Mr. Richard Cameron, and testimony given to the faithfulness of his ministry; it will not be (perhaps) ungrateful to some, to insert the following relation of some remarkable things anent his call to the ministry, which was rehearsed by himself a little before his death; where he told some christian friends, That, after his having gone through the ordinary course of university learning, he was a schoolmaster and a precentor to a curate at Falkland, for some time, and at some occasions used to attend the sermons of the indulged ministers, as he had opportunity. At length it pleased the Lord to incline him to go out to the field-meetings; which when the curates understood, they set upon him, partly by flatteries, partly by menacing threats, and at length, by more direct persecution, to cause him forbear attending these meetings. But such was the powerful and wonderful working of the Lord by his Spirit upon him, that he intirely deserted these prelatic curates, having got a lively discovery of the sin and hazard of that abominable Prelacy. And no sooner was he enlightned anent the evil of Prelacy, but beginning more narrowly to search into the state of things, that he might know what was his proper and necessary duty, the Lord was pleased to discover to him the sinfulness of the indulgence, as flowing from that ecclesiastical supremacy, usurped by the king; and being zealously affected for the honour of Christ, wronged by that Erastian acknowledgment of the magistrate's usurped power over the church, he longed for an opportunity to give a testimony against it: And accordingly being in the family of Sir William Scot of Harden, who attended the indulged meetings, he took opportunity (notwithstanding many strong temptations from Satan to the contrary) to witness in his station against the indulgence: Particularly, one Sabbath, after he was called to attend the lady to the church, he returned from the entry, refusing to go that day, and spent the day in his chamber, where he met with much of the Lord's presence (as he testified) and very evident discoveries of the nature of these temptations and suggestions of Satan, which had like to have prevailed with him before. And upon the Monday, giving a reason to the said Sir William Scot and his lady, why he went not to church with them, he took occasion to be plain, and express in testifying against the sinfulness of the indulgence, in its complex nature, and original rise and spring from whence it flowed; and thereupon leaving that service, being no further acceptable to them, because of his faithfulness, he came to the south, and having met with the Reverend Mr. John Welch, he stayed in his company a considerable time; who finding him a man qualified for the ministry, pressed upon him to receive a licence to preach, which he refused for some time, chiefly upon this reason, That he having such clear discoveries of the sinfulness of the indulgence, could not but testify against it explicitely, so soon as he should have opportunity to preach in public; and considering, that none of the outed ministers, who had been of standing and experience in the ministry, had yet expresly declared the sinfulness thereof in public, he was afraid that his being singular in it, considering his youth, and his being but new entered upon the work of the ministry, might perhaps make his doctrine the less useful and weighty to the people. But the force of his objection being removed, by Mr. Welch's serious solicitations he was prevailed with to accept a licence from some of the outed ministers, who had not complied with the indulgence, and were as yet preaching the gospel in the fields. And having preached occasionally with Mr. Welch and others, in several places of the western shires, and finding the people warmed and affected with his doctrine, by the good hand of God blessing the word; he adventured some times, as the Lord assisted him, to be express and clear in declaring the sinfulness of the indulgence, and of joining with the accepters thereof; whereupon the ministers, who had licensed him to preach, conceiving it prudence not to be so explicite anent that step of compliance, began to prosecute him with censure for his freedom in preaching against it; and called three several meetings upon that account, one at Dunscore in Nithsdale, another at Dendough in Galloway, and a third at Edinburgh.

After his return from Holland, where he received ordination to the exercise of the ministry, he went to some of these outed ministers, inviting and pressing them much to come out and preach in the fields, as they had done before the overthrow at Bothwel: But the persecution being then very hot against all such as had not accepted the indulgence and indemnity, they refused to adventure upon that hazard. Wherefore, notwithstanding such sad discouragements from the professed friends, and violent persecutions by the declared enemies of the reformation, he adventured, upon all hazard, to preach publicly in the fields, in order to discharge the dispensation of the gospel, which the Lord had entrusted him with: And he continued so doing, till he sealed that cause and testimony with his blood; being, after some valiant resistance in his own defence, killed by a party of soldiers, under the command of Eaflthal, and his head and hand cut off by one Robert Murray, were brought and laid before the council, who ordered them to be placed upon the Netherbow-port of Edinburgh.

The following bond of mutual defence, was found upon him when he was killed; subscribed by him, his brother Michael Cameron, Archibald Stewart, John Potter, and about thirty others; which justly deserveth to be insert here in its proper room, being most agreeable to the true state of the testimony which these renowned martyrs sealed with their blood.

WE under subscribers bind and oblige ourselves to be faithful to God, and true to one another, and to all others who shall join with us, in adhering to Rutherglen testimony, and disclaiming the Hamilton declaration, chiefly, because it takes in the king's interest, which we are loosed from by reason of his perfidy and covenant-breaking, both to the most high God, and the people over whom he was set, under the terms of his propagating the main ends of the covenants, to wit, The reformation of religion; and instead of that, usurping to himself the royal prerogatives of Jesus Christ, and encroaching upon the liberties of the church; and so stating himself, both in opposition to Jesus Christ the Mediator, and the free government of his house.

And also, in disowning and protesting against the reception of the duke of York, a professed Papist, and whatever else hath been done in this land (given to the Lord) in prejudice to our covenanted, and universally sworn to reformation. And altho', as the Lord who searcheth the heart knows, we be for government and governors, both civil and ecclesiastic, such as the word of God, and our covenants allow; yet by this, we disown the present magistrates, who openly and avowedly are doing what in them lies, for destroying utterly our work of reformation from Popery, Prelacy, Erastianism, and other heresies and errors. And by this we declare also, That we are not any more to own ministers indulged, and such as drive a sinful union with them: nor are we to join any more in this public cause with ministers or professors of any rank, that are guilty of the defections of this time, until they give satisfaction proportioned to the scandal and offence they have given.

     RIC. CAMERON, M. CAMERON,
     A. STEWART, J. POTTER, &c.

An ACROSTICK

Upon the Name of that godly, faithful and zealous Minister and Martyr of Jesus Christ, Mr. RICHARD CAMERON. *Done by a true lover of his memory, and owner of the honourable cause which he sealed with his blood.*

M OST noble Cameron of renown,
A Fame of thee should ne'er go down;
S ince truth with zeal thou didst pursue,
T o Zion's King loyal and true.
E v'n when the dragon spew'd his flood,
R esist thou didst unto the blood;

R an swiftly in thy christian race,
I n faith and patience to that place,
C hrist did prepare to such as thee,
H e knew would not his standard flee.
A pattern of valour and zeal,
R ather to suffer than to fail;
D idst shew thyself with might and main,

C ounting that dross, others thought gain,
A faithful witness 'gainst all those,
M en of all sorts did truth oppose;
E v'n thou with Moses did esteem,
R eproaches for the God of heav'n;
O n him alone thou didst rely,
N ot sparing for his cause to die.

 Torfoot, November 28th, 1749. *W. W.*

A Relation of some remarkable passages in the life of Mr. DONALD CARGIL.

THese foregoing Testimonies every where speaking so honourably of the Rev. Mr. Donald Cargil, as a faithful minister of Jesus Christ; a true and full relation of his life, and more especially of his ministry, would be very necessary to a right understanding of the state of

Appendix. 403

their testimony: but by reason that there are not in the hands of the publishers such well attested narrations thereof, as might furnish them with an exact and full history thereof, let it suffice at present to set down these following accounts, collected by that worthy and religious gentleman, Sir Robert Hamilton of Preston; who ushers them in with this personal character of Mr. Cargil. " First, saith he, as he was of a most holy, strict, tender and composed practice and conversation, so he was affectionate, affable, and tender-hearted, to all he judged had any thing of the image of God in them: sober and temperate in his diet, saying commonly, " It was well won that was won off the flesh:" Generous, liberal and most charitable to the poor, a great hater of covetousness, a frequent visiter of the sick, much alone, loving to be retired, but when about his Master's public work; laying hold of every opportunity to edify; in converse still dropping what might minister grace to the hearers; his very countenance was edifying to beholders; often sighing with deep groans: preaching in season and out of season, upon all hazards, ever the same in judgment and practice."

There were several things remarkable in the manner of his calling to the ministry; for after he had perfected his philosophy course, at the university of St. Andrews, his father, a godly and religious gentleman pressed much upon him, to study divinity, in order to fit him for the ministry; but he, thro' his great tenderness of spirit, constantly refused, telling his father, " That the work of the ministry was too great a weight for his weak shoulders;" and requesting him to command him to any other employment he pleased. But his father still urging, he resolved to seek the mind of the Lord therein, and for that end set apart a day of private fasting, and after long and earnest wrestling with the Lord by prayer the third chapter of Ezekiel's prophesy, and chiefly these words in the first verse, ' Son of man, eat this roll, and ' go speak unto the house of Israel,' made a strong impression upon his mind, so that he durst never after refuse his father's desire, to betake himself to that study, and dedicate himself wholly to that office. And having got a call to the barony parish of Glasgow, divine providence ordered it so that the first text upon which the presbytery ordered him to preach, was in these very words of the third of Ezekiel, which he had got clearness from before; whence he was the more confirmed, that he had God's call to that parish. The parish had been long vacant, by reason that two ministers of the public resolution party, viz. Mr. George Young, and Mr. Hugh Blair, had still opposed the settlement of such godly men as had been called by the people, and had practised secretly with the council of Glasgow, not to suffer any to be settled there, that might be against the public resolutions: But in reference to Mr. Cargil's call, they were by God's good providence much bound up from their wonted opposition. Mr. Cargil perceiving the lightness of the people, and their unconcernedness under the word, was much discouraged thereat, and resolved to return home, and not to accept the call; and when urged by the godly ministers not to do it, and his reason asked, he answered, *They are a rebellious people.* The ministers solicited him much to stay, but could not prevail. At last when his horse was drawn, and he just about to take journey, being in Mr. James Durham's house, when he had saluted several of the christian friends that came to see him take horse, as he was bidding farewel to a certain godly woman, she said to him, "Sir, you have promised to preach on Thursday, and have you appointed a meal to poor starving people, and will ye go away, and not give it? If you do, the curse of God will go with you." This so commoved him, that he durst not go away as he intended; but sitting down, desired her and others to pray for him. So he remained, and was settled in that parish, where he continued to exercise his ministry with great success, to the unspeakable satisfaction of his own parish, and of all the godly who heard and knew him, till after the introduction of Prelacy, he was first put from the exercise thereof in public, and likewise chased and pursued for exercising it privately, by the bloody violence of persecutors.

For upon the 29th of May, which was then consecrated to King Charles, in commemoration of his happy (unhappy) restoration, he had occasion to preach in his own church, it falling upon the ordinary week day, wherein he used to preach, he saw an unusual throng of people come to hear him, as thinking he had preached in compliance with that solemnity; upon his entering the pulpit he said, "We are not come here to keep this day

int for which others keep it. We thought
leſſed the day wherein the king came home
w we think, we ſhall have reaſon to curſe
y of you be come here in order to the
this day, we deſire you to remove."
d upon the unlawfulneſs of ſolemnizing it,
ighty arguments. This did extremely in-
gnant party againſt him, ſo that being
and ſearched for, he was forced to ab-
ng ſometimes in private houſes of his pa-
lying without all night among broom,
y, yet never omitting any proper occaſi-
reaching, exerciſing, catechiſing, viſiting
ther miniſterial duties. And after a while
his church, and preached publickly, and
union, not without great fear among the
ſhould have been taken out of the pulpit
ors. At length, when the churches were
Preſbyterians, by an act of council, com-
by the name of *the Act of Glaſgow;* Mid-
band of ſoldiers to apprehend him, who
church found him not, he having provi-
epped out of the one door a minute before
at the other; whereupon they took the
hurch door with them, and departed.
council paſt an act of confinement, ba-
the North; but he did not regard it;
t length apprehended at Edinburgh, was
the council, and ſtrictly examined; be-
engthened to bear faithful teſtimony to
nour, and his perſecuted cauſe and truths.
erpoſition of ſome perſons of quality, his
ife's relations, he was liberated. And he
ntly to Glaſgow, and there performed all
duties as when he was in his own church,
g the diligence of perſecutors in ſearching

time, partly the great grief he conceived
the work of God in the land, partly the
irs of his calling, and inconveniences of
ation, did ſo break his voice, that he could
y many people together, which was a ſore
n, and a diſcouragement to come and
ields. But one day, Mr. Blackadder com-

ing to preach at Glasgow, he essayed to preach with him, and standing on a chair, as his ordinary was, he lectured on Isa. xliv. 3. ' I will pour water on him that ' is thirsty, and floods on the dry ground,' &c. The people knowing that his voice was sore broken, were very much discouraged left they should not have heard, by reason of the great confluence; but it pleased the Lord so to loose his tongue, and restore his voice to that distinctness and clearness that none could readily exceed him in that respect ever after: and not only his voice, but his spirit was so enlarged, and such a door of utterance given him, that Mr. Blackadder succeding him, said to the people, " Ye that have such preaching as this, have no need to invite strangers to preach to you. Make good use of your mercy." After this he continued to preach within a very little of the city, a great multitude still attending upon and profiting by his ministry, being wonderfully preserved in the midst of dangers; the enemies several times sending out some to watch him, and catch something from his mouth, whereof they might accuse him. Particularly one day the archbishop of Glasgow, sent one of his domestic servants to take notice what he would say concerning the prelates; he knowing nothing thereof, was directed of the Lord to have these words in prayer, while he was bewailing the overthrow of the work of God; " What shall we say of the prelates, the good Lord make us quite of them; for we will never have a day to do well, till once the Lord remove that abominable party, that has destroyed the vineyard of the Lord:" Which was all that the spy had to return to his master with.

To relate all the surprising deliverances that he met with, in escaping very narrowly from his enemies, would take much time; take only a few instances. In the month of October 1665, they made a public search for him in the city; he being informed of it, took his horse and rode out of the town, and at a narrow pass of the way, he met a good number of musketeers, and as he passed by them, turning into another way upon the right hand, one of them asked him, *Sir, what of the clock is it?* He answered, *It is six*. Another of them, knowing his voice, says to his fellows, *There is the man we are seeking;* which he hearing, put the spurs to the horse, and escaped. He most usually resided for the space of three years and up-

Appendix. 407

wards, in a chamber in the houfe of one Margaret Craig, a godly and honeft woman, lecturing evening and morning to fuch as came to hear him; where, tho' they fearched frequently for him, yet divine providence fo ordered it, that all the times he was either cafually or purpofely abfent, tho' they managed their fearches with much clofenefs: but the Lord was fo gracioufly kind to him, that he left him not without fome peculiar notices of approaching hazards. (Our atheiftical wits perhaps will call them enthufiafms: but *the fecret of the Lord is with them that fear him*.) As for inftance, on a certain Sabbath, when he was going to Woodfide to preach, as he was about to mount his horfe, the one foot being in the ftirrup, he turned about to his man, and faid, *I muft not go yonder to-day;* and within a little a party of horfe and foot, came in queft of him, and not finding the mark they aimed at, fell upon the people, apprehending and imprifoning many of them. Another remarkable efcape was, at a fearch purpofely made for taking him in the city, they came to his chamber, and found him not, for he was providentially in another houfe that night. The fearch was fo ftrict, that feveral other minifters were taken, but they were not permitted to come near the houfe where he was. But the following is yet more remarkable. One day while he was preaching privately in one Mr. Callender's houfe, they came and befet the houfe; the people within put him and a friend with him out at a window, clofing the window up with books; and they two ftood at the outfide of the window all the while of the fearch, which was fo ftrict that they fearched the very ceiling of the houfe, till one of them fell thro' to the lower loft. Had the fearchers removed but one of the books, they had infallibly apprehended him, but the Lord fo ordered it, that they did it not; for when one of the foldiers was about to take up one of them, a maid cried to the commander, that he was going to take her mafter's books; fo he was ordered to let them alone. Thus narrowly he efcaped this danger. Another not imparallel was, that one day hotly purfued upon the ftreet, being obliged to flee into the firft houfe he could come at, which happened to be a foldier's houfe; yet the foldier's wife was fo far from difcovering him, that fhe kept him fafe till the fearch was over.

A little before the fight at Bothwel, he was purfued

from his own chamber out of the town, being forced to go thro' several thorn-hedges; and no sooner is he out, but he sees a troop of dragoons in rank, right opposite to him: Back he could not go, soldiers being every where posted to catch him; wherefore he went forward near by the troop, who looked to him, and he to them, till he was gone by them; but coming to the place of the water where he intended to go over, he saw another troop standing upon the opposite bank of the water, who called to him; he made them no answer: but going a mile farther up the water, escaped to Langside, and preached there next Sabbath, without interruption. At another time, being in a house beset with soldiers; he escaped thro' the throng of them, they taking him to have been the good-man of the house. So much anent his remarkable deliveries.

After Bothwel, he fell into deep exercise anent his call to the ministry, but by God's grace he happily emerged out of that, and had also much light anent the duty of the day, being a faithful contender against the enemies usurped power in granting, and ministers and professors lukewarmness, and sinful compliance in accepting indulgences and indemnities, oaths and bonds, and other corruptions and abominations of the time, till at length he suffered for his testimony.

Among other parts of his contendings against the enemies of truth and godliness, that which exasperate the enemies most was the Torwood Excommunication; wherein he, moved with zeal against the indignities done to the Son of God, by overturning his work, and destroying his people, delivered up to Satan some of the most scandalous, and principal promoters and abettors of this conspiracy against Christ, as formally as he could, in his circumstances; who having earnestly sought the concurrence of his brethren, could not obtain it; and therefore was left to do the work alone, or leave it undone, which he could by no means think of; considering that all other sorts of weapons had been used against them, save that of ecclesiastic censure, and the neglect of it might bring upon this church that severe reproof given to Pergamus, Rev. ii. 14. 15. for having in her communion the Nicolaitans, and them that held the doctrine of Balaam: And that sore animadversion made upon the church of Thyatira, for suffering that woman Je-

Appendix. 409

zebel, &c. And left the Lord might come and fight against his church with the sword of his mouth, on account that such were not expresly cast out of her communion. Wherefore in September 1680, after sermon upon Ezek. xxi. 25. 26. 27. *And thou profane wicked prince of Israel, whose day is come,* &c. Having made a short and pertinent discourse on the nature, subject, causes, and ends of excommunication, and declared his motives leading him to it, not to be any private spirit of passion, but conscience of duty and zeal to God, he pronounced the sentence as follows.

We have spoken of excommunication, of the causes, subject and ends thereof, we shall now proceed to the action, being constrained by the conscience of our duty and zeal for God, to excommunicate some of these who have been the committers of so great crimes, and authors of the great mischiefs of Britain and Ireland, but especially these of Scotland: and in doing of this, we shall keep the names by which they are ordinarily called, that they may be the better known.

I being a minister of Jesus Christ, and having authority and power from him, do in his name, and by his Spirit, excommunicate Charles II. king, &c.—and that upon the account of these wickednesses. 1*st*, For his high mocking of God, in that after he had acknowledged his own sins, his father's sins, his mother's idolatry, and had solemnly engaged against them, in a declaration at Dunfermline the 16th of August 1650, he hath, notwithstanding of all this, gone on more avowedly in these sins, than all that went before him. 2*dly*, For his great perjury, after he had twice, at least, solemnly subscribed that covenant, did so presumptuously renounce, disown, and command it to be burned by the hand of the hangman. 3*dly*, Because he hath rescinded all laws for establishing of that religion and reformation engaged to in that covenant, and enacted laws for establishing its contrary: and is still working for the introducing of Popery into thir lands. 4*thly*, For commanding of armies to destroy the Lord's people, who were standing in their own just defence, and for their privileges and rights, against tyrannies, oppressions, and injuries of men; and for the blood he hath shed, in fields, on scaffolds, and in the seas, of the people of God, upon account of religion and righteousness, (they being most willing in all other things to render him obedience, if he had reigned and ruled them according to his covenant and oath) more than all the kings that have been before him in Scotland. *5thly*, That he hath been ſtill an enemy to, a perſecutor of the true Proteſtants, a favourer and helper of the Papiſts, both at home and abroad, and hath hindered, to the utmoſt of his power, the due execution of juſt laws againſt them. *6thly*, For his relaxing of the kingdom, by his frequent grant of remiſſions and pardons for murderers, (which is in the power of no king to do, being expreſly contrary to the law of God) which was the ready way to embolden men in committing of murders, to the defiling of the land with blood. *Laſtly*, To paſs by all other things, his great and dreadful uncleanneſs of adultery and inceſt, his drunkenneſs, his diſſembling with God and man; and performing his promiſes where his engagements were ſinful, &c.

Next, By the ſame authority, and in the ſame name, I excommunicate, caſt out of the true church, and deliver up to Satan, James duke of York, &c. and that for his idolatry, (for I ſhall not ſpeak of any other ſins but what have been perpetrated by him in Scotland) and for ſetting up idolatry in Scotland, to defile the Lord's land; and his enticing and encouraging others to do ſo, &c.

Next, In the ſame name, and by the ſame authority, I excommunicate, and caſt out of the true church, and deliver up to Satan, James duke of Monmouth, &c. for coming into Scotland, upon his father's unjuſt command, and leading armies againſt the Lord's people, who were conſtrained to riſe, being killed in, and for the right worſhipping of the true God; and for his refuſing that morning at Bothwel-bridge a ceſſation of arms, for hearing and redreſſing their injuries, wrongs and oppreſſions, &c.

Next, I do, by virtue of the ſame authority, and in the ſame name, excommunicate, caſt out of the true church, and deliver up to Satan, John duke of Lauderdale, &c. for his dreadful blaſphemy, eſpecially that word to the Prelate of St. Andrews, *Sit thou at my right hand, until I make thine enemies thy footſtool.* His atheiſtical drolling on the Scriptures of God, ſcoffing at religion, and religious perſons. His apoſtacy from the covenant and work of reformation; and his perſecuting thereof, after he had been a profeſſor, pleader and preſſer thereof: For his perjury in the bufinefs of Mr. James Mitchel, who being in council, gave public faith, that he fhould be indemnified, and that to life and limb, if he fhould confefs his attempt upon the prelate; and notwithftanding of this, before the jufticiary court, did give oath that there was no fuch act in council: For his adulteries and uncleannefs: For his counfelling and affifting the king in all his tyrannies, overturning and plotting againft the true religion: For his gaming on the Lord's day. And Laftly, for his ufual and ordinary curfing.

Next, I do, by virtue of the fame authority, and in the fame name, caft out of the true church, and deliver up to Satan, John duke of Rothes, &c. for his perjury in the matter of Mr. James Mitchel; and for his adulteries and uncleannefs; for alloting the Lord's day for his drunkennefs: For his profeffing and avowing his readinefs and willingnefs to fet up Popery in this land at the king's command: And for the heathenifh, barbarous, and unheard of cruelty, (whereof he was the chief author, contriver and commander, notwithftanding that he had otherwife engaged lately) to that worthy gentleman David Hackftoun of Rathillet. And laftly, for his ordinary curfing, fwearing, and drunkennefs.

Next, I do, by virtue of the fame authority, and in the fame name, excommunicate, caft out of the true church, and deliver up to Satan, Sir George M'Kenzie, the king's advocate, for his apoftacy, in turning into a profligatenefs of converfation, after he had begun a profeffion of holinefs: For his conftant pleading againft, and perfecuting to death the people of God, and alledging and laying to their charge things which in his confcience he knew to be againft the word of God, truth, reafon, and the ancient laws of this kingdom: And his pleading for forcerers, murderers, and other criminals, that before God, and by the laws of the land, ought to die: For his ungodly, erroneous, fantaftic and blafphemous tenets, printed to the world, in his pamphlets and pafquills.

And laftly, I do, by virtue of the fame authority, and in the fame name, excommunicate, caft out of the true church, and deliver up to Satan, Thomas Dalziel of Bins, &c. For his leading armies, and commanding the killing, robbing, pillaging and oppreffing of the Lord's people, and free fubjects of this kingdom: And for executing of lawless tyrannies, and lustful laws: For his commanding to shoot at a post one Finlay at New-milns, without any form of law, civil or military, he not being guilty of any thing that they themselves counted a crime: For his lewd and impious life, led in adultery and uncleanness from his youth, with a contempt of marriage, which is the ordinance of God: For all his other atheistical and irreligious conversation. And lastly, For his unjust usurping and retaining of the estate of that worthy gentleman William Muir of Caldwel; and his other injurious deeds in the exercise of his power.

I think, none that acknowledge the word, can judge thir sentences to be unjust; yet some, it may be, to flatter the powers, will call them unorderly and unformal, there not being warning given, nor probation led. But for answer, There has been warning given, if not of all these things, at least of a great part of them: And for probation, there needs none, the deeds being notour and public, and the most of them such as they themselves do avow and boast of. And as the causes are just, so being done by a minister of the gospel, and in such a way as the present persecution would admit of, the sentence is just: And there are no kings nor ministers on earth, without repentance of the persons, can reverse these sentences upon any (such) accounts: God who is the author of that ordinance is the more engaged to the ratifying of them; and all that acknowledge the Scriptures ought to acknowledge them. Yet some, perchance, will think, that tho' they be not unjust, yet that they are foolishly rigorous. We shall answer nothing to this, but that word which we may speak with much more reason than they did who used it, 'Should he deal with our sister 'as with an harlot?' Should they deal with our God as with an idol? Should they deal with his people as murderers and malefactors, and we not draw out his sword against them.

A brief relation of the persecutions and death of that worthy gentleman HENRY HALL *of Haughhead, who suffered martyrdom at Queensferry, June 3d,* 1680.

HENRY HALL of Haughhead, having had religious education, began early to mind a life of holiness; and was of a pious conversation from his youth;

He was a zealous oppofer of the public refolutions, infomuch that when the minifter of the parifh where he lived complied with that courfe, he refufed to hear him, and went to Ancrum, to hear Mr. John Livingfton. Being oppreffed with the malitious profecutions of the curates and other malignants for his nonconformity with the profane courfes of abomination that commenced at the unhappy reftoration of that moft wicked tyrant Charles the fecond, was obliged to depart his native country, and go over the border into England in the year 1665, where he was fo much renowned for his fingular zeal in propagating the gofpel among that people, who before his coming among them were very rude and barbarous; but many of them became famous for piety after. In the year 1666, he was taken in his way to Pentland, coming to the affiftance of his covenanted brethren and was imprifoned with fome others in Selsford caftle, but by the divine goodnefs he foon efcaped thence thro' the favour of the earl of Roxburgh, to whom the caftle pertained, the faid earl being his friend and relation; from which time, till about the year 1679, he lived peaceably in England, much beloved of all that knew him, for his concern in propagating the knowledge of Chrift in that country; infomuch that his blamelefs and fhining chriftian converfation, drew reverence and efteem from his very enemies. But about the year 1678, the heat of the perfecution in Scotland obliging many to wander up and down thro' Northumberland and other places; one colonel Struthers intended to feize any Scotfman he could find in thofe parts; and meeting with Thomas Ker of Hayhope, one of Henry Hall's neareft intimates, he was engaged in that encounter upon the account of the faid Thomas Ker, who was killed there: Upon which account, he was forced to return to Scotland, and wandered up and down during the hotteft time of the perfecution, moftly with Mr. Richard Cameron and Mr. Donald Cargil, during which time, befides his many other chriftian virtues, he fignalized himfelf for a real zeal in defence of the perfecuted gofpel preached in the fields, and gave feveral proofs of his valour and courage, particularly at Rutherglen, Drumclog, Glafgow, and Bothwel-bridge; whereupon being forfaulted and violently purfued, to efchew the violent hands of his indefatigable perfecutors, he was forced to go over to Holland; where he had not stayed long, when his zeal for the persecuted interest of Christ, and his tender sympathy with the afflicted remnant of his covenanted brethren in Scotland, then wandering thro' the desolate caverns and dens of the earth, drew him home, chusing rather to undergo the utmost efforts of persecuting fury, than to live at ease when Joseph was in affliction, making Moses's generous choice, rather to suffer affliction with the people of God, that he might be a partaker of the fellowship of Christ's sufferings, than to enjoy that momentary pleasure the ease of the world could afford; nor was he much concerned with the riches of the world, for he stood not to give his ground to hold the prohibited field-preachings upon, when none else would do it: He was a lover and follower of the faithfully preached gospel, and was always against the indulgence; he was with Mr. Richard Cameron at these meetings where he was censured.

About a quarter of a year after his return from Holland, being in company with the Rev. Mr. Donald Cargil, they were taken notice of by two blood-hounds the curates of Borrowstounness and Carridden, who went to Middleton governor of Blackness-castle, and informed him of them; who having consulted with these bloodthirsty ruffians, ordered his soldiers to follow him at a distance by two or three together, with convenient intervals for avoiding suspicion; and he (the said Middleton) and his man riding up, observed where they alighted and stabled their horses; and coming to them, pretended a great deal of kindness and civilites to Mr. Donald Cargil and him, desiring that they might have a glass of wine together. When they were set, and had taken each a glass, Middleton laid hands on them, and told them they were his prisoners, commanding in the king's name all the people of the house to assist, which they all refused save a certain waiter, thro' whose means the governor got the gates shut till the soldiers came up; and when the women of the town, rising to the rescue of the prisoners, had broke up the outer gate, Henry Hall after some scuffle with the governor in the house, making his escape by the gate, received his mortal blow upon his head with a carabine by Thomas George waiter, and being conveyed out of the town by the assistance of the women, walked some pretty space of way upon his foot, but unable to speak much, save only that he made some

Appendix. 415

short reflection upon a woman that interposed between him and the governor, hindered him to kill the governor, and so to make his escape timeously. So soon as he fainted, the woman carried him to a house in the country, and notwithstanding the care of surgeons, he never recovered the power of speaking more. General Dalziel being advertised, came with a party of the guards, and carried him to Edinburgh; he died by the way: His corps they carried to the Cannongate tolbooth, and kept them there three days without burial, tho' a number of friends conveened for that effect, and thereafter they caused bury him clandestinely in the night. Such was the fury of these limbs of antichrist, that having killed the witnesses, they would not suffer their dead bodies to be decently put in graves.

There was found upon him the rude draught of a paper, containing a mutual engagement to stand to the necessary duty of the day, against its stated enemies; which was called by the persecutors, Mr. Cargil's Covenant, and frequently in the foregoing testimonies, The Queensferry paper, because there it was seized by the enemies. This paper divine providence seems to have made as it were the dying words and testimony of that worthy gentleman; and the enemies made it one of the captious and ensnaring questions they constantly put to the sufferers, and therefore it will not be impertinent here to insert the heads of it, as they are compendized by the learned author of the Hind let Loose, Page 133. For it was still owned by Mr. Donald Cargil, that the draught was not digested and polished, as it was intended, and therefore it will be so far from being a wrong to recite the heads of it only, that it is really a piece of justice done him, who never intended it should see the world as it was when the enemies found it. I shall not pretend to justify every expression in it, but rather submit it intirely to better judgments, nor did the sufferers for most part adhere to it, without the limitation (so far as it was agreeable to the word of God, and our national covenants) and in so far as it seems to import a purpose of assuming to themselves a magistratical authority, their practice declares all along, that they did not understand it in that sense.

The tenor of it was an engagement.

1. To avouch the only true and living God to be their

God, and to close with his way of redemption by his Son Jesus Christ, whose righteousness is only to be relied upon for justification: and to take the Scriptures of the Old and New Testament to be the only object of faith, and rule of conversation in all things. 2. To establish in the land righteousness and religion, in the truth of its doctrine, purity and power of its worship, discipline and government; and to free the church of God of the corruption of Prelacy on the one hand, and the thraldom of Erastianism on the other. 3. To persevere in the doctrine of the reformed churches, especially that of Scotland, and in the worship prescribed in the Scriptures, without the inventions, adornings and corruptions of men; and in the Presbyterian government, exercised in sessions, presbyteries, synods, and general assemblies, as a distinct government from the civil, and distinctly to be exercised, not after a carnal manner, by plurality of votes, or authority of a single person, but according to the word of God, making and carrying the sentence. 4. To endeavour the overthrow of the kingdom of darkness, and whatsoever is contrary to the kingdom of Christ, especially idolatry and Popery in all its articles, and the overthrow of that power that hath established and upheld it.——And to execute righteousness and judgment impartially, according to the word of God, and degree of offences, upon the committers of these things especially, to wit, blasphemy, idolatry, atheism, buggary, sorcery, perjury, uncleanness, profanation of the Lord's day, oppression and malignancy.——5. Seriously considering,—there is no more speedy way of relaxation from the wrath of God, that hath ever lyen upon the lands since it engaged with these rulers, but of rejecting them, who hath so manifestly rejected God,—disclaiming his covenant—governing contrary to all right laws, divine and human—and contrary to all the ends of government, by enacting and commanding impieties, injuries and robberies to the denying of God his due, and the subjects theirs; so that instead of government, godliness and peace, there is nothing but rapine, tumult and blood, which cannot be called a government, but a lustful rage —— and they cannot be called governors, but public grassators and land judgments, which all ought to set themselves against, as they would do against pestilence, sword, and famine, raging amongst them—— Seeing they have stopped the course of the law and justice against blasphemers, idolaters, atheists, buggerers, murderers, inceftuous and adulterous persons—and have made butcheries on the Lord's people, sold them as slaves, imprisoned, forfeited, &c. and that upon no other account, but their maintaining Christ's right of ruling over their consciences, against the usurpations of men. Therefore, easily solving the objections: 1. Of our ancestors obliging the nation to this race and line; that they did not buy their liberty with our thraldom, nor could they bind their children to any thing so much to their prejudice, and against natural liberty, (being a benefit next to life, if not in some regard above it) which is not an engagement to moral things: they could only bind to that government, which they esteemed the best for common good; which reason ceasing, we are free to choose another, if we find it more conducible for that end. 2. Of the covenant binding to defend the king; that that obligation is only in his maintenance of the true covenanted reformation,—which homage they cannot now require upon the account of the covenant which they have renounced and disclaimed; and upon no other ground we are bound to them,—the crown not being an inheritance, that passeth from father to son, without the consent of tenants.— 3. Of the hope of their returning from these courses, whereof there is none; seeing they have so often declared their purposes of persevering in them. And suppose they should dissemble a repentance,—supposing also they might be pardoned for that which is done—from whose guiltiness the land cannot be cleansed, but by executing God's righteous judgments upon them,—yet they cannot now be believed after they have violated all that human wisdom could devise to bind them.

Upon these accounts they reject that king, and those associate with him in the government,—and declare them henceforth no lawful rulers, as they had declared them to be no lawful subjects,—they having destroyed the established religion, overturned the fundamental laws of the kingdom, taken away Christ's church-government, and changed the civil into tyranny, where none are associate in partaking of the government, but only those who will be found by justice guilty as criminals.—And declare they shall, God giving them power, set up government and governors according to the word of God, and the qualifications required, Exodus xviii. 20.—And shall not commit the government to any single person or lineal succession, being not tyed as the Jews were to one single family,—and that kind being liable to most inconveniencies, and aptest to degenerate into tyranny.—And moreover, that these men set over them, shall be engaged to govern, principally by that civil and judicial law, (not that which is any way typical) given by God to his people Israel—as the best, so far as it goes, being given by God—especially in matters of life and death, and other things so far as they reach, and are consistent with christian liberty—exempting divorces and polygamy, &c.—6. Seeing the greatest part of ministers not only were defective in preaching against the rulers for overthrowing religion—but hindred others also who were willing, and censured some that did it—and have voted for acceptation of that liberty, founded upon, and given by virtue of that blasphemously arrogate and usurped power—and appeared before their courts to accept of it, and to be enacted and authorized their ministers—whereby they have become ministers of men, and bound to be answerable to them as they will.—And have preached for the lawfulness of paying that tribute, declared to be imposed for the bearing down of the true worship of God.—And advised poor prisoners to subscribe that bond,—which if it were universally subscribed,—they should close that door, which the Lord hath made use of in all the churches of Europe, for casting off the yoke of the whore,—and stop all regress of men, when once brought under tyranny, to recover their liberty again.——They declare they neither can nor will hear them, &c. nor any who encouraged and strengthned their hands, and pleaded for them, and trafficked for union with them. 7. That they are for a standing gospel ministry, rightly chosen, and rightly ordained,—and that none shall take upon them the preaching of the word, &c. unless called and ordained thereunto.

And whereas separation might be imputed to them, they refel both the malice, and the ignorance of that calumny.—For if there be a separation, it must be where the change is; and that was not to be found in them, who were not separating from the communion of the true church; nor setting up a new ministry, but cleaving to the same ministers and ordinances that formerly they followed, when others have fled to new ways, and a new authority, which is like the old piece in the new garment. 8. That they shall defend themselves in their civil, natural and divine rights and liberties.--And if any affault them, they shall look on it as a declaring a war, and take all advantages that one enemy does of another —But trouble and injure none, but those that injure them.

A Lift of the Banifhed.

TO fpeak nothing of thofe whom the cruelty of the perfecutors forced to a voluntary exile, of whom there can be no particular account had, befides the fix or feven minifters that were banifhed and went to Holland, and feven or eight country people to France, feveral others to Barbadoes, before the year 1666; after the year 1678, there were banifhed to be fold for flaves, for the fame caufe for which others fuffered death at home, of men and women about 1700, viz. anno 1678, to Virginia 60, whereof three or four were minifters, who were all by the mercy of God delivered at London. *Item*, anno 1679, of the prifoners taken at Bothwel, were banifhed to America 250; who were taken away by —— Paterfon merchant at Leith, who tranfacted for them with Provoft Milns, laird of Barnton, the man that firft burnt the covenant; whereof 200 were drowned by fhipwreck at a place called the Mule-head of Darnefs near Orkney, being fhut up by the faid Paterfon's order beneath the hatchets, 50 efcaped; whereof the names, fo many of them as could be had, follow; thefe who efcaped are printed in Italic characters, for diftinction's fake. Out of the fhire of Clydefdale and city of Glafgow, Francis Wodrow, Walter M'Kechnie, Alexander Pirie, William Miller. Out of the parifh of Govan, Andrew Snadgrafs. Out of the parifh of Kilbride, Robert Auld, John Struthers, James Clark, John Clark, William Rodger. Out of the parifh of Shots, Peter Lermont, Robert Ruffel, John Aitkih, Robert Chalmers, *John Thomfon*, John Killen, Alexander Walker. Out of the parifh of Cambufnethen, *William Scular*. Out of the Monklands, *William Waddel*, William Grinlaw, Thomas Mathie, William Miller, John Wynet, James Waddel, *John Gardner*, Thomas Barton. Out of the parifh of

Bothwel,—— *More*, William Breakenrig. Out of the parish of Evandale, John Cairnduff, John Cochran, Robert Alifon, Andrew Torrence, Thomas Brownlee, John Watfon, William Alifon, Andrew Aiton. Out of the parish of Calder, *William Fram*. Out of the parish of Glasfoord, John Miller, John Craig. Out of the parish of Carnwath, Thomas Crichton, James Couper. Out of the parish of Quathquan, *James Penman*, James Thomfon, Thomas Wilfon. Out of the parish of Carftairs, *Thomas Swan*. Out of the parish of Biggar, John Rankin. Out of the parish of Lefmahego, George Wier, Robert Wier, *George Drafin*. Out of the shire of Air and parish of Finnick, James Gray, Andrew Buckle, David Currie, David Bitchet, Robert Tod, John White, *Robert Wallace*, John Wylie, William Bitchet. Out of the parish of Loudon, Thomas Wylie. Out of the parish of Damellington, Hugh Simpfon, Walter Humper, *Walter Humper* younger, *Hugh Cameron*, *Quintin MacAdam*. Out of the parish of Cumluck, John Gemil, James Mirrie. Out of the parish of Ochiltree, Andrew Welsh. Out of the parish of Auchinleck, Andrew Richmond. Out of Dindonald, *Andrew Thomfon*. Out of Mauchlin, William Reid, William Drips. Out of the parish of Moorkirk, John Campbel, Alexander Paterfon. Out of the parish of Digen, James Boufton. Out of the parish of Gaufton, James Young, George Campbel. Out of the parish of Kilmarnock, Thomas Finlay, John Cuthbertfon, William Brown, *Patrick Watt*. Robert Anderfon, James Anderfon. Out of the parish of Stewarton, Thomas Wylie, Andrew Wylie, Robert Wylie. Out of the parish of Bar, Alexander Burden. Out of the parish of Colmonel, Thomas M'Lurg, John M'Cronock, John M'Clellen. Out of the parish of Girvan, William Caldwel. Out of the parish of Dalry, David M'Cubin, William M'Culloch. Out of the parish of Maybole, William Rodger, Mungo Eccles, John M'Whirter, Thomas Horn, Robert M'Garron, John M'Harie. Out of the parish of Craigie, *George Dunbar*. Out of the parish of Straiton, James M'Murrie, Alexander Lamb, George Hutchefon. Out of the parish of Kirkmichael, John Brice, Robert Ramfay, John Douglafs, John M'Tire, James M'Connell. Out of the parish of Kirkofel, John White, Thomas Germont. Out of the shire of Fife and parish of Newburn, James Beal. Out of the parish of Largo and Kilconquhar, Andrew Prie, James Kirk. Out of the parish of Ceres, John Kirk, *Thomas Miller.* Out of the parish of Stramiglo, Robert Bog. Out of the town of Kinrofs, James Lilburn. Out of the parish of Orwel, *Robert Kirk, Robert Sands.* Out of the shire of Perth and parish of Kilmadock, John Chriftifon. Out of the parish of Kincardine, Patrick Keir, John Donaldson. Out of the parish of Glendovan, John Murie, Andrew Murie. Out of the shire of Renfrew, and parish of Eastwood, James Cunningham. Out of the parish of Neilston, John Govan. Out of Paisley, William Buchan, William Auchinclofe. Out of the shire of Lennox and parish of New-Kilpatrick, James Finlayfon. Out of the shire of Stirling and parish of Drummond, Daniel Cunningham. Out of the parish of Kippen, James Galbraith. Out of Gargunnock, Thomas Miller, Patrick Gilchrist, *James Sands,* Thomas Brown, James Buchanan. Out of the parish of St. Ninians, *Thomas Thomfon, Andrew Thomfon,* John Neilfon, John M'Nure. Out of the parish of Denny, James M'Kie. Out of the parish of Airth, Andrew Young, John Morifon, Robert Hendrie. Out of the parish of Falkirk, *Hugh Montgomerie.* Out of Morrenfide, Thomas Phalp. Out of the shire of West-Lothian, in the parish of Torphican, John Allan, John Thomfon, *John Pender,* James Easton, *John Eafton,* Andrew Easton, John Addie, Alexander Bishop. Out of Dalmannie, John Thomfon. Out of Livingftoun, Thomas Ingles, Patrick Hamilton, John Bell, Patrick Wilfon, William Younger, William Henderfon, John Steven   Out of the parish of Kirkliftoun, John Govan. Out of Bathgate, David Ralton. Out of the parish of Abercorn, John Gib, James Gib. Out of the parish of Linlithgow, Thomas Barthwick, Out of the parish of Kinneill, Andrew Murdoch. Out of the shire of Mid-Lothian and parish of Calder, James Steel, Thomas Gilchrist, James Graze, John Ruffel. Out of Mid Calder, John Brown, Alexander Mutray. East Calder, *David Samuel,* Alexander Biffit. Out of the parish of Stow, Thomas Pringle. Out of the parish of Temple, James Tinto. Out of the parish of Liberton, *Thomas M'Kenzie.* Out of the parish of Crichtoun, James Fork. Out of the parish of Cranstoun, Thomas Williamfon. Out of the town of Muffelburgh, William Reid.

Out of the shire of East-Lothian, and parish of Dunbar, James Tod. Out of the shire of Nithsdale, and parish of Glencairn, David Mackervail, John Fergufon, Robert Milligan, *John Milligan, John Murdoch, John Smith, William Fergufon*, James Colvil, Thomas Rofper. Out of the parish of Clofeburn, Thomas Milligan, John Kennedy. Out of the shire of Galloway, and parish of Kirkcudbright, James Corfan, *Andrew Macquhan, John Machratney, John Macgie.* Out of the parish of Balmaghie, *Robert Caldow*, James Houftoun. Out of the parish of Kelton, James Donaldfon. Out of the parish of Kilmackbrick, Robert Brown, Samuel Beck, Samuel Hannay. Out of the parish of Penningham, John Mactagart, *Alexander Murray.* Out of the parish of Borgue, Andrew Sprot, Robert Bryce, *John Richardfon, John Martin*, John Bryce, William Thomfon. Out of the parish of Girthon, Andrew Donaldfon. Out of the parish of Dalry, *John Smith, John Malcolm.* Out of Irongray, Andrew Wallet. Out of Balmaclellen, *John Edgar.* Out of Lochrutan, *Andrew Clark.* Out of Etrick or Forreft, John Scot. Out of the parish of Gallafhiells, *Robert Macgill*, Robert Young. Out of the shires of Merfe and Teviotdale, and parish of Nethen, Samuel Nifbet, John Deans, *James Atchifon.* Out of the parish of Cavers, *James Leidon, John Glafgow, William Glafgow*, John Greenfhields, Richard Young, Samuel Douglas, *James Young*, James Hobkirk. Out of the town of Kelfo, William Hardie. Out of the town of Jedburgh, John Mather. Out of the parish of Ancrum, George Rutherford. Out of the parish of Sproufton, Walter Waddel, and Thomas Cairns. Out of the parish of Melrofs, John Young and Andrew Cook. Out of the parish of Caftletoun, William Scot, John Pringle, Alexander Waddel, and John Unnes. Out of the parish of Afkirk, William Herd. Out of the parish of Bandon, Andrew Newbigging. Out of the parish of Sudon, James Coufton, *William Swanfton*, John Elliot. Out of the parish of Hobkirk, John Oliver.

Thefe feven following were fentenced and banifhed to Weft Flanders, who departed the kingdom, March 4th, 1684. Thomas Jackfon, George Jackfon, James Forreft elder, James Forreft younger, John Coline, James Gourlay,—— Gillies.

Afterwards were banifhed to Carolina thirty, who

Appendix. 423

were tranfported in James Gibfon's fhip, called fometime Bailie Gibfon in Glafgow, of whom it is obfervable, that in God's righteous judgment he was caft away in Carolina bay, when he commanded in the Rifing Sun. They received their fentence, June 17. 1684. The names of fuch as fubfcribed the joint teftimony, are thefe, Matthew Machan, James M'Clintock, John Gibfon, Gavin Black John Paton, William Ingles, John Young, John Galt, John Edwards, Thomas Marfhal, George Smith, William Smith, Robert Urie, John Buchanan, Thomas Bryce, John Symon, Hugh Symon, William Symon, Archibald Cunningham, John Alexander, John Marfhal.

Thereafter in July 19. 1684. John Mathifon, John Crichton, James M'Gachen, John M'Chefnie, James Baird, were banifhed to New Jerfey in America. Thereafter were taken away in banifhment by one Robert Malloch, fourteen men, whofe names are not recorded. Anno 1685. In the time of Queenfberry's parliament, of men and women were fent to Jamaica two hundred. And the fame year, one Pitlochie tranfported to New Jerfey one hundred, whereof twenty-four were women. And in the fame year, thirteen more were fent to Barbadoes: Their names are not in the hands of the publifhers, if they be at all recorded. Anno 1687. one and twenty men and women were fent to Barbadoes, whofe names that fubfcribed the joint teftimony, are as follows, John Ford, Walter MacMin, Adam Hood, John MacGhie, Peter Ruffel, Thomas Jackfon, Charles Dougal, James Grifton, John Harvie, James Forfyth, George Johnfton, John Steven, Robert Young, John Gilfillan, Andrew Paterfon, John Kincaid, Robert Main, James Muirhead, George Muir, John Henderfon, Anaple Jackfon, Anaple Gordon, Jean Moffat. Anno 1687, March 30. were banifhed to Barbadoes, John Stewart, James Douglas, John Ruffel, James Hamilton, William Hannay, George White, Gilbert M'Culloch, Thomas Brown, John Brown, William Hay, John Wright, John Richard, Alexander Bailie, Marion Weir, Betty Weir, Ifabel Steel, Ifabel Caffils, Agnes Keir.

A short account of those who were killed in the open fields, without trial, conviction, or any process of law, by the executioners of the council's murdering EDICT, whose names are here specified.

TO give an account of the many hundreds, who either died or contracted their deaths in prison, by the severities they met with of cold, hunger, thirst, want of room and air, fetters, tortures, stigmatizing, whipping, &c. would be a work of immense labour, nor can any full account thereof be had, considering both the vast numbers of such, and the neglect of writing memoirs of these things, or their being seized by the persecutors, who were industrious to supprefs such accounts of their own villanies from the view of posterity. The number of such as suffered under colour of law, and judicial trial, from Mr. James Guthrie the first, to Mr. James Renwick the last, has been computed to amount to about 140. But the councellors, willing to ease themselves of that lingering way of doing business, not content with Popery's gradual advancement, were for doing their work all at once; and accordingly authorised captains, lieutenants, serjeants, and single soldiers to shoot all suspected persons where-ever they could catch them, without further trial of their pretended crimes. And accordingly betwixt the years 1682. and 1688. when a revolution of affairs put a stop to their carreer of blood-shed, there were murdered in the open fields, the following persons besides others that no certain list has been got of, as they are enumerated in a print, intitled, *A short memorial of the sufferings and grievances of the presbyterians in Scotland.* Printed in the year 1690. Which is as follows.

John Graham of Claverhouse, viscount of Dundee, in the year 1682. with a party of his troop, pursued William Graham in the parish of —— in Galloway, making his escape from his mother's house, and overtaking him, instantly shot him dead. *Item*, The said Claverhouse, together with the earl of Dumbarton, and lieutenant-general Douglas, caused Peter Gillies, John Bryce, Thomas Young, (who was taken by the laird of Lee) William Fiddison, and John Buiening to be put to death upon a gibbet, without legal trial or sentence, suffering them neither to have a Bible, nor to pray before they died, at Mauchlin, 1684. *Item*, The said Claverhouse coming to Galloway, in answer to the viscount of Kenmure's letter, with a small party, surprised Robert Stewart, John Grier, Robert Ferguson and James MacMichael, and instantly shot them dead at the water of Dee in Galloway, December, 1683. Their corps being buried, were at his command raised again. *Item*, The said Claverhouse, in May 1685, apprehended John Brown in Priesthill, in the parish of Moorkirk, in the shire of Air, being at his work, about his own house, and shot him dead before his own door in presence of his wife. *Item*, The said Claverhouse authorised his troops to kill Matthew Micklewrath, without any examination, in the parish of Colmonel in Carrick, Anno 1685. Colonel James Douglas, brother to the duke of Queensberry, together with lieutenant John Livingston, and a party with them, surprises five men in a cave at Ingleston in the parish of Glencairn, being betrayed by Andrew Watson: Their names were, John Gibson, Robert Grierson, Robert Mitchel, James Bennoch and John Edgar, all which were at the command of the said colonel Douglas brought forth, and immediately shot dead, without giving them so much time as to recommend their souls to God. One John Ferguson, sometimes a professed friend, thrust one of them through, supposing he was not dead: This was done in the year 1685. *Item*, the said colonel James Douglas and his party shot to death John Hunter, for no other alledged cause, but the running out from the house at Corehead, the same year 1685. *Item*, The said colonel or lieutenant-general James Douglas, with lieutenant Livingston and coronet James Douglas, surprised six men at prayer at the Calduns in the parish of Minigaf; viz. James Dun, Robert Dun, Andrew Mackale, Thomas Stevenson, John MacCloud and John Stevenson, in January, 1685. *Item*, The said colonel or lieutenant-general James Douglas caused take Andrew Macquhan out of his bed, sick of a fever, and carry him to Newtown of Galloway, and the next day shot him dead, the foresaid year 1685. *Item*, The said colonel or lieutenant-general Douglas commanded Thomas Richard an old man of seventy years, to be shot in time of prayer; (he was betrayed and taken by Peter Ingles) Anno 1685, at Cumnock in Kyle. Captain Douglas finding one —— Mowat a taylor, merely because he had some pieces of lead belonging to his trade, took him, and without any further trial shot him dead, between Fleet and Dee in Galloway. *Item*, The said captain Douglas and his men, finding one —— Achenleck, a deaf man, for not making answer, thro' defect of his hearing, instantly shot him dead off horseback, near Carlin-work, Anno 1685. Sir Robert Dalziel and lieutenant Straton, having apprehended Daniel M'Michael, not able to flee, by reason of his being sick, and detained him twenty four hours prisoner, took him out and shot him at Dalveen, in the parish of Durisdeer in Nithsdale, January, 1685. *Item*, The said captain Dalziel, and lieutenant Straton, with their men, found William Adam hiding in a bush, and instantly killed him, at the Welwood in Kyle, February, 1685. Captain Bruce, captain of dragoons, apprehended James Kirko, at the intelligence of one James Wright, carried him to Dumfries, detained him prisoner one night, next day brought him forth to the water sands, and without any process shot him dead. The dying man desired a little time to make his peace with God: The captain answered, oftener than once or twice, *Devil a peace ye get more made up.* Some gentlewomen coming to beg his life, were hindred by one John Craig of Stewarton: The foresaid Dalziel's second son was one of them that shot him, tho' without command, June 1685. *Item*, The said captain Bruce surprised at Lochenkithil, in the parish of Kirkpatrick in Galloway, six men, and instantly killed dead four of them, viz. John Gordon, William Stewart, William Heron, and John Wallace; and carried the other two Edward Gordon and Alexander MacUbine, prisoners, and the next day he and monstrous Lagg, without any trial caused hang upon a growing tree, near the Kirk of Irongray, and left them there hanging, February 1685. *Item*, The said captain Bruce and his men took out of his bed William MacHaffie, sick of a fever, and shot him instantly, in the parish of Straton in Carrick, January, 1685. *Item*, James Douglas coronet of dragoons, commanded to shoot John Semple, essaying to escape out of a window, in the parish of Dellie, Anno 1685. Kilkerron shot him. *Item*, The said coronet Douglas apprehended Edward Mackeen and by search, finding a flint stone upon him, presently shot him without any further trial, February 1685. Lieutenant general Drummond commanded, without any procefs of trial, John Murchie and Donald Miklewrock to be inftantly fhot after they were taken, in the parifh of Colmonel in Carrick, Anno 1685. At the fame time his foldiers did fhoot dead Alexander Lin. Captain Ingles and his dragoons purfued and killed James Smith at the burn of Ann in Kyle, 1684. Peter Ingles his fon, killed one John Smith in Cunningham, 1685. *Item*, The faid Peter, or Patrick Ingles, killed one James White, ftruck off his head with an ax, brought it to Newmilns, and plaid at the foot-ball with it, he killed him at Little-blackwood, the forefaid year 1685. *Item,* The faid Peter Ingles fhot John Burrie, with his pafs in his hand, in Evandale, April 1685. Major Balfour, together with captain Maitland and their party, apprehended at their work, Robert Tom, John Urie and Thomas Cook, and inftantly fhot them, at Pomadee, near Glafgow, May 1685. Colonel Buchan, with the laird of Lee and their men, fhot John Smith in the parifh of Lefmahego, February, 1685. Lieutenant Lauder fhot to death William Shillilaw, at the Woodhead on the water of Air, Anno 1685. Lieutenant Nifbet and his party, fhot to death John Fergufon, George Whiteburn and Patrick Gemmil in the parifh of Finnick, in the faid year. Lieutenant Murray and his party fhot one John Brown after quarters given at Blackwood in Clydfdale, March 1685. Lieutenant Crichton did moft barbaroufly after quarter, fhoot David Steel, in the parifh of Lefmahego, December 1686.

The laird of Stenhoufe, Sir Robert Laurie of Maxwelton, and John Craig of Stewartoun, did inftigate and urge Cornet Bailie's party of dragoons to fhoot William Smith in Hill, after he had been prifoner one night, (it was the day of Maxwelton's daughter's marriage) who alfo refufed to let him be buried in the church-yard. This Douglas of Stenhoufe, being a laird of mean eftate, was advanced for fuch fervices as this, and his exceflive haraffing, fpoiling and fining of the people of God, and becaufe he was a Papift, to the honour of being fecretary for Scotland to James VII. But the wicked's honour is fhort lived; his name is extinct, having neither root nor branch, male or female, nor any remembrance left unto him. The faid Laurie of Maxwelton's fteward reported, that a cup of wine delivered that day into his hand, turned into congealed blood: But be that as it will, himself died by a fall from his horse, some years after. Sir James Johnston of Westerhall, caused apprehend Andrew Hyslop in the parish of Hutton in Anandale, and delivered him up to Claverhouse, and never rested until he got him shot by Claverhouse's troops: Claverhouse would have delayed it, but Westerhall was so urgent, that Claverhouse was heard say, *This man's blood shall be upon Westerhall.* At length, upon his urgency, Claverhouse ordered a Highland captain, who was there, to do it, but he refused; and drawing off his Highlanders to a convenient distance, swore, *That her nain-sell would fight Claverhouse and all his dragoons first.* Whereupon he caused three of his own dragoons do it, May 1685. It is observeable of this Westerhall, that he was once a great professor, and one who had sworn the Covenant; and when the Test was framed, he bragged, that he was an actual covenanter, and scorned the Test; but when he had the trial, he embraced it, and became a bitter enemy to the work and people of God: and this man having been taken in his ground, he would have him shot, to give proof of his loyalty. He died about the revolution, in great torture of body by the gravel, and horror and anguish of conscience, insomuch that his cries were heard at a great distance from the house, as a warning to all such apostates. Sir Robert Grierson of Lagg, having the command of a part of Claverhouse's troop, and Strachan's dragoons, surprised John Bell of Whiteside, David Halliday portioner of Mayfield, Andrew M'Crabit, James Clement, and Robert Lenox of Irlintoun, and barbarously killed them after quarter, without time allowed to pray. When John Bell of Whiteside begged a little time to pray, Lagg answered, *What devil have ye been doing? Have ye not prayed enough these many years in the hills?* and so shot him presently in the parish of Tongland in Galloway, February 1685. *Item,* The said laird of Lagg, with the earl of Anandale, having command of some troops of heritors, pursued another David Halliday, and George Short, and apprehended and shot them, under cloud of night, in the parish of Twynhame in Galloway, anno 1680. The laird of Lagg, who was so wicked an oppressor and destroyer of the people of God in Galloway and Nithsdale, is now a justice of the peace, notwithstanding his being excommunicate for his adultery and impenitent obstinacy.

Appendix. 429

The laird of Colzean, for that time captain of a troop of militia and heritors, killed William M'Kergue at Blairquhan miln, anno 1685. *Item*, The laird of Colzean, with the laird of Ballochmiln, shot Gilbert MacAdam in the parish of Kirkmichal, July 1685. A party of Highlanders killed Joseph Wilson, David Dun, Simeon Paterson, and other two, near the water of Kyle, in a moss in Kyle, anno 1685. The laird of Ardenkeple commanding a party of Highlandmen, killed Robert Lockart and Gabriel Thomson, about that time also. Likewise William Paterson was shot at Strevan, uncertain by whom, 1685. Also John M'Clorgan was killed at Drummellian's house in the night time, not known by whom. John Reid, belonging sometimes to Craigie's troop, did, under cloud of night, kill by a shot, one George Wood, about sixteen years old, without asking one question at him, in Tinkhorn-hill, in Kyle, June 1688. In sum, their number amounts to seventy eight.

Besides these cold blood-murders, there were many killed at several skirmishes at Pentland, Bothwel, Airsmoss, &c. while fighting in their own defence, and the defence of the field meetings, the number whereof amounts to about 400, and some odds.

A short account of the oppressive exactions.

Expecting that others, who have the particular informations of matters of fact by them, will be concerned to publish a more full account of these illegal fines and robberies, it shall suffice at present to transcribe only the general account of some of them, out of the forementioned *Memorial of Grievances*. Which run thus:

For fines, and other exorbitant and illegal exactions of money, the particular sums cannot be here enumerated; but their vastness, when together calculate, may be easily collected by the scraps already gathered off some poor families of farmers, cottars, servants, &c. and many of these omitted, or not known (which would very considerably augment the sum) in some few shires, *viz.* Clydsdale, Renfrew, Air, Galloway, Nithsdale and Anandale, only but for a few years, *viz.* since Bothwelbridge insurrection, amounting to above 288000 l. Scots. Besides the many honest families, which have been casten out of their houses, harrassed and spoiled of their All; some of their houses being thrown down, some burnt, some shut up, their goods and moveables seized upon, their crop and cattle also disposed of, at the will of their persecutors, in the forementioned shires, amounting to above 200.

The immediate authors, actors and instruments of these oppressions, were principally the curates, instigating the privy council, which impowered the forces, and noblemen and gentlemen of the country to prey upon the poor people. All cannot be here expressed, but some of the most noted in the western shires shall be named, who were the greatest persecutors and oppressors, by fining and other exactions. Of officers of the forces, Colonel Douglas, brother to the duke of Queensberry, exacted above 2000 l. Scots money, in Galloway, Nithsdale, shire of Air, and other places. Lieutenant General Drummond, besides the forfaultures of gentlemen, did also exact monies of the poor in the shire of Air. The earl of Linlithgow, and his soldiers spoiled much in Galloway. The earl of Airly and his troop, in the same shire. The Lord Balcarras, a great oppressor in Galloway, besides all the robberies he committed in Fife. ——⋯ Graham of Claverhouse, afterwards viscount of Dundee, with his brother, and subaltern officers in Galloway, Nithsdale, and Anandale, exacted by fines and otherways, above 13500 l. Scots money. Colonel Buchan a most violent persecutor in Galloway and shire of Air, by robberies took from the people upwards of 4000 l. Scots. Major Cockburn a great oppressor in Galloway, Major White in Clydsdale, and shire of Air, exacted, by fines and otherways, above 2508 l. Scots. Major Balfour a great oppressor and persecutor in Clydsdale, Captain Strachan in Galloway, Inglis in Galloway, Air and Clydsdale; Douglas in Galloway, Dalziel in Anandale, and Bruce in Nithsdale, oppressed and spoiled the people much. —— Meldrum in Clydsdale, took from poor families upwards of 2800 l. and vast sums in Merse and Teviotdale, with the earl of Hume, and Ker of Grandoun, with the laird of Hayning and Blindle, and in Tweedale, with the Laird of Possa. Lieutenant Winram and Barns, were very vigilant persecutors in Galloway, and took much spoil. Lieutenant Lauder in Air, Bonshaw a highwayman, and Duncan Grant, a cripple with a tree leg in Clydsdale, oppressed the people excessively; this last exacted in Clydsdale, 1500 l.

Appendix. 431

The chief of the oppreffors among noblemen and gentlemen, were in Clydfdale, Summervail of Spittel, who exacted from the poor people above 1200 l. Haljards more than 5800 l. Bonytoun and Symme were alfo great and violent exactors. In the city of Glafgow, Provoft Johnftoun and Barns; Bailies Anderfon, Zuil, Graham, and Stirling, exacted above 20,000 l. In Renfrew, the earl of Glencairn exacted above 2400 l. Likewife Semple a Papift, Alexander Hume in Egleſhome, and Ezekiel Montgomery, were all great exactors. In the fhire of Air, the Earl of Dumfries exacted above 1000 l. Likewife the Lord Craigie, William Crichton fheriff-depute, Crawford of Ardmillan, Montgomery of Bozland, the laird of Broyche, and clerk Oglivie, were all great and wicked perfecutors. In Galloway, Grierfon of Lagg, who exacted there, and in Nithfdale, above 1200 l. Liddefdale, Ifle and Canon of Merdograte, were alfo great oppreffors. In Nithfdale, Queenſberry and his fons, and John Alifon his chamberlain, who when dying faid, *He had damned his foul for the duke his mafter;* and George Charter, another of his factors, who vaunted, *He had made twenty-fix journeys in a year, in purfuit of the Whigs.* John Douglas of Stenhoufe a Papift, exacted 15,000 l. The laird of Clofeburn above 700 l. Sir Robert Dalziel 400 l. from a few families. Sir Robert Laurie of Maxweltoun was alfo a great oppreffor and perfecutor. In Anandale the earl of Anandale perfecuted much; and likewife in Galloway the laird of Wefterhall exacted above 11,000 l. Sir Patrick Maxwel of Sprinkel was alfo a very active and violent perfecutor. The lairds of Powdeen and Caftlemilk, Robert Carruthers of Rennarfal, Thomas Kennedy of Heybeiths, were moft violent perfecutors of the poor people.

Form thefe fhort accounts of the oppreffions, bloodfhed and illegal tyranny exercifed in this land, it may be conjectured what the total would amount to, if a hiftory thereof were publifhed: But all thefe, however great perfecutions, are but little in comparifon of what the mother of harlots and her children intended againft us; which that the Lord may prevent, ought to be the ferious prayer and ftrenuous endeavour of all them that have a regard to the greateft interefts of themfelves and pofterity.

F I N I S.

THE
EPITAPHS or INSCRIPTIONS

Upon the TOMBS or GRAVE STONES of the MARTYRS, in several church-yards, and other places where they ly buried *.

The Inscription and Epitaph upon the monument in the Grayfriars church-yard at Edinburgh.

Upon the head of the tomb there is the effigies of an open Bible drawn with these scripture citations, Rev. vi. 9, 10, 11. 'And when he had opened the first seal, I saw
' under the altar the souls of them that had been slain for
' the word of God, and for the testimony which they
' held. And they cried with a loud voice, saying, How
' long, O Lord, holy and true, dost thou not judge and
' avenge our blood on them that dwell on the earth?
' And white robes were given unto every one of them,
' and it was said unto them, that they should rest yet
' for a little season, until their fellow servants also, and
' their brethren, that should be killed as they were,
' should be fulfilled. Rev. vii. 14. These are they which
' came out of great tribulation, and have washed their
' robes and made them white in the blood of the Lamb.'

Follows the verse.

HALT passenger, take head what you do see,
This tomb doth shew, for what some men did die.
Here lies interr'd the dust of those who stood,
'Gainst perjury, resisting unto blood;
Adhering to the covenants, and laws
Establishing the same; which was the cause
Their lives were sacrific'd unto the lust
Of Prelatists abjur'd. Though here their dust
Lies mixt with murderers, and other crew,
Whom justice did justly to death pursue:

* The reader is desired to remember, that these Epitaphs being mostly composed by illiterate country people, one cannot reasonably expect neatness and elegant poetry in them, and therefore will readily pardon any harshness in the phrase or metre which he may meet with.

But as for thir, no caufe in them was found
Worthy of death, but only they were found,
Conftant and ftedfaft, zealous, witneffing,
For the prerogatives of Chrift their King.
Which truths were feal'd by famous Guthrie's head,
And all along to Mr. Renwick's blood.
They did endure the wrath of enemies,
Reproaches, torments, deaths and injuries.
But yet they're thefe who from fuch trouble came,
And now triumph in glory with the Lamb.

Thereafter follows this profe.

From May 27, 1661, that the noble marquifs of Argyle fuffered, to the 17th of February, 1688, that Mr. James Renwick fuffered, were execute at Edinburgh, about an hundred of noblemen, gentlemen, minifters, and others, noble martyrs for Jefus Chrift. The moft part of them ly here.

Upon the foot of the monument ftands a crown, with this infcription; ' Be thou faithful unto the death, and ' I will give thee a crown of life.'

Infcription upon a grave ftone in the church-yard of Hamilton, lying on the heads of John Parker, Gavin Hamilton, James Hamilton, and Chriftopher Strang, who fuffered at Edinburgh, Dec. 7th, 1666. Their teftimony is extant in Naphtali, p. 306.

STAY paffenger, take notice what thou reads,
At Edinburgh ly our bodies, here our heads;
Our right-hands ftood at Lanerk, thefe we want,
Becaufe with them we fware the-covenant.

Infcription upon a ftone in the high church-yard of Glafgow.

Here lies the corps of Robert Bunton, John Hart, Robert Scot, Matthew Patoun, John Richmond, James Johnfton, Archibald Stewart, James Winning, John Main, who fuffered at the crofs of Glafgow, for their teftimony to the covenants and work of reformation, becaufe they durft not own the authority of the then tyrants, deftroying the fame, betwixt 1666, and 1688.

YEARS fixty-fix, and eighty-four,
Did fend their fouls home into glore,

Whofe bodies here interred ly,
Then facrific'd to tyranny;
To covenants and reformation
'Caufe they adhered in their ftation.
Thefe nine, with others in this yard,
Whofe heads and bodies were not fpar'd,
Their teftimonies, foes, to bury,
Caus'd beat the drums then in great fury,
They'll know at refurrection day,
To murder faints was no fweet play.

Infcription on the ftone lying on John Wharry and James Smith, who are buried at Inchbelly-bridge.

HALT, paffenger, read here upon this ftone
A tragedy, our bodies done upon.
At Glafgow crofs we loft both our right hands,
To fright beholders, th' en'my fo commands:
Then put to death, and that moft cruelly,
Yet where we're flain, even there we muft not ly;
From Glafgow town we're brought unto this place,
On gallow-tree hung up for certain fpace:
Yet thence ta'en down interred here we ly
Beneath this ftone: our blood to heaven doth cry.
Had foreign foes, Turks, or Mahometans,
Had Scythian Tartars, Arabian Caravans,
Had cruel Spaniards, the pope's bloody feed,
Commenc'd the fame, had been lefs ftrange their deed;
But Proteftants, once Covenanters too,
Our countrymen, this cruel deed could do:
Yet notwithftanding this their hellifh rage,
The noble Wharry leapt upon the ftage,
With courage bold, he faid, and heart not faint,
This blood fhall now feal up our covenant.
Ending, *They who would follow Chrift, fhould take
Their crofs upon their back, the world forfake.*

Infcription on James Nisbet, James Lawfon, and Alexander Wood, buried at the gallows foot at Glafgow.

HERE ly martyrs three,
Of memory,
Who for the covenants did die;
And witnefs is
'Gainft all thefe nations perjury.

Inscription on a stone in Eastwood parish, lying upon the corps of James Eagle, and John Park, who suffered at the cross of Paisley, for refusing the Oath of abjuration, in the year 1685.

STAY, passenger, as thou goes by,
And take a look where these do ly:
Who for the love they bare to truth
Were depriv'd of their life and youth.
Tho' laws made then, caus'd many die,
Judges and 'sizers were not free;
He that to them did these delate,
The greater count he hath to make;
Yet no excuse to them can be:
At ten condemn'd, at two to die.
So cruel did their rage become,
To stop their speech caus'd beat the drum.
This may a standing witness be
'Twixt Presbytry and Prelacy.

Inscription on the grave stone at Cathcart, lying on the bodies of Robert Tam, Thomas Cook and John Urie, who were shot at Pomadie, May 11*th,* 1685.

THE bloody murderers of these men
Were Major Balfour and captain Maitland.
And with them others were not free,
Caus'd them to search in Pomadie.
As soon as they had them out found,
They murder'd them with shot of gun,
Scarce time to them did they allow
Before their Maker their knees to bow.
Many like in this land have been,
Whose blood for vengeance cries to heav'n.
This horrid wickedness you see
Was done in lane of Pomadie;
Which may a standing witness be
'Twixt Presbytry and Prelacy.

Inscription on a stone in the church-yard of Eglesham, upon the bodies of Gabriel Thomson and Robert Lockhart, shot by a party of Highlandmen and dragoons, under the command of Ardencaple, May 1st, 1685.

THESE men did search through moor and moss
    To find out all that had no pass.
These faithful witnesses were found,
And murdered upon the ground.
Their bodies in this grave do ly,
Their blood for vengeance yet doth cry:
This may a standing witness be
For *Presbytry* 'gainst *Prelacy*.

Inscription on the monument at Airsmoss, lying upon the bodies of them that fell there, July 20. 1680. Namely the reverend and faithful Mr. Richard Cameron minister of the gospel, Michael Cameron, John Hamilton, John Gemmil, James Gray, Robert Dick, John Fuller, Robert Paterson, Thomas Watson, &c.

HALT, curious passenger, come here and read;
    Our souls triumph with Christ our glorious head,
In self-defence, we murder'd here do ly,
To witness 'gainst this nation's perjury.

Inscription on a grave stone in the church yard of Strevan, on the corpse of William Paterson, who lived in the parish of Cambusnethan, and John Barrie in Evandale, anno 1685.

HERE ly two martyrs; severally who fell
    By Captain Inglis, and by bloody Bell.
Posterity shall know they're shot to death,
As sacrifices unto Popish wrath.

Inscription on the stone lying at Blackwood in the parish of Lesmahego, upon the corpse of John Brown, who was shot by —— Murray, without sentence of law, anno 1685, and buried there in the open fields.

MURRAY might murder such a godly Brown,
    But could not rob him of that glorious crown
He now enjoys. His credit, not his crime,
Was non-compliance with a wicked time.

Inscription upon a stone lying on the corps of John Brown, who lived in the parish of Moorkirk, who was shot dead by Graham of Claverhouse, at his own door, May 1st, 1685. and lies buried there in the open fields.

I N death's cold bed the dusty part here lies
O f one who did the earth as dust despise,
H ere in this place from earth he took departure;
N ow he has got the garland of the martyr.
B utcher'd by *Clavers* and his bloody band,
R aging most rav'nously o'er all the land.
O nly for owning Christ's supremacy,
W ickedly wrong'd by encroaching tyranny.
N othing, how near soever, he too good
 Esteem'd, nor dear for any truth his blood.

Upon the grave stone of David Steel, in the church yard of Lesmahego, is this motto.

DAVID, a shepherd first, and then
 Advanced to be king of men,
Had of his graces in this quarter,
This heir a wand'rer, now a martyr.
Who for his constancy and zeal,
Still to the back did prove good STEEL.
Who for Christ's royal truths and laws,
And for the covenanted cause
Of Scotland's famous reformation;
Declining tyrants usurpation;
By cruel Crichton murder'd lies,
Whose blood to heav'n for vengeance cries.

Upon the grave stone of Andrew Hislop, lying in Craickhaugh in Eskdale moor, being the place where he was shot by Claverhouse and Sir James Johnstoun of Westerhall.

HALT, passenger, a word with thee or two,
 Why I ly here wouldst thou truly know?
By wicked hands, hands cruel and unjust,
Without all law, my life from me they thrust,
And being dead they left me on the spot,
For burial this same place I got:
Truth's friends in Eskdale, now rejoice their lot,
To wit, The faithful, for truth my seal thus got.

In the church-yard of Dumfries, upon the grave stone of John Grierson, who lived in the parish of Irongray, and suffered January 2d, 1667, is this inscription.

UNderneath this stone doth ly
  Dust, sacrific'd to tyranny:
Yet precious in Emmanuel's sight,
Since martyr'd for his kingly right.
When he condemns these hellish drudges,
By suff'rage, saints shall be their judges.

Upon the grave stone of William Welch, in the same church-yard, who lived in the same parish, and suffered at the same time with the former, there is this epitaph.

HALT passenger, read, here interr'd doth ly
  A witness 'gainst poor Scotland's perjury,
Whose head once fixt, upon the Bridge port stood,
Proclaiming vengeance for his guiltless blood.

In the same church-yard, on the grave stone of James Kirko, who lived in the parish of Kier, and was shot dead on the sands of Dumfries, by Captain Bruce, June 1685. is this motto.

BY bloody Bruce and wretched Wright,
  I lost my life in great despight;
Shot dead without due time to try,
And fit me for eternity;
A witness of Prelatic rage,
As ever was in any age.

On the grave stone lying on Edward Gordon and Alexander M'Ubine, execute at the church of Irongray, at the command of the laird of Lagg and captain Bruce.

AS Lagg and bloody Bruce command,
  We were hung up by hellish hand;
And thus their furious rage to stay,
We died at Kirk of Irongray:
Here now in peace sweet rest we take,
Once murder'd for religion's sake.

Upon a stone lying in a muir near Lochenkilhil, on the grave of John Gordon, William Stewart, William Heron and John Wallace, shot by captain Bruce.

BEHOLD here in this wilderness we ly,
Four witnesses of hellish cruelty.
Our lives and blood could not their ire asswage,
But when we're dead, they did against us rage;
That match the like, we think, ye scarcely can,
Except the Turk's, or duke de Alva's men.

Upon three several grave stones, lying on John Gibson, James Bennoch, Robert Edgar and Robert Mitchel, who were shot at Inglistoun in the parish of Glencairn, by colonel Douglas and lieutenant Livingstoun, anno 1685, are these verses.

1. On John Gibson.

MY soul's in heaven, here's my dust,
By wicked sentence and unjust
Shot dead, convicted of no crime,
But non-compliance with the time,
When Babel's bastards had command,
And monstrous tyrants rul'd the land.

2. On James Bennoch.

HERE lies a monument of Popish wrath;
Because I'm not perjur'd, I'm shot to death
By cruel hands; men godless and unjust
Did sacrifice my blood to Babel's lust.

3. On Robert Edgar and Robert Mitchel, both under one stone.

HALT passenger, tell if thou ever saw
Men shot to death without process of law.
We two, of four who in this church yard ly,
Thus felt the rage of Popish tyranny.

Upon a stone in Tynron church-yard, lying on William Smith, who being a youth of eighteen years of age, was shot at the bridge end of Minni-ive, by the command of Sir Robert Lawrie laird of Maxwelton, and John Douglas of Stenhouse, May 1685.

I WILLIAM SMITH now here do ly,
Once martyr'd for Christ's verity.

EPITAPHS.

Douglas of Stenhouse, Lawrie of Maxwelton
Caus'd coronet Baillie give me martyrdom;
What cruelty they to my corps then us'd,
Living may judge; me burial they refus'd.

Upon Daniel MacMichael, who was shot by Dalziel of Kirkmichael, January 1685. lying in the church-yard of Durisdeer.

AS Daniel cast was into lion's den,
For praying unto God, and not to men;
Thus lions cruelly devoured me,
For bearing unto truth my test'mony.
I rest in peace, till Jesus rend the cloud,
And judge 'twixt me and those who shed my blood.

Upon the grave stone in the church-yard of Balmaghie, upon the corps of David Halliday, portioner of Mayfield, shot by the laird of Lagg, February 1685. and of David Halliday in Glenap, shot by the laird of Lagg and the earl of Annandale, in the same year 1685, is this epitaph.

BENEATH this stone two David Hallidays
Do ly, whose souls now sing their Master's praise.
To know if curious passengers desire
For what, by whom, and how they did expire?
They did oppose this nation's perjury,
Nor could they join with lordly Prelacy.
Indulgence-favours from Christ's enemies
Quench not their zeal: This monument then cries,
These are the causes not to be forgot,
Why they by Lagg so wickedly were shot.
One name, one cause, one grave, one heaven do tye
Their souls to that one God eternally.

Upon the grave stone in the church-yard of Anwith, lying on the corps of John Bell of Whiteside, who was most barbarously shot to death at the command of Douglas of Morton and Grierson of Lagg, in the parish of Tongland in Galloway, anno 1685.

THIS monument shall tell posterity,
That blessed Bell of Whiteside here doth ly;
Who at command of bloody Lagg was shot;
A murder strange, which should not be forgot.

Douglas of Morton did him quarters give;
Yet cruel Lagg would not let him survive.
This martyr sought some time to recommend
His soul to God, before his days did end,
The tyrant said, *What devil! ye've pray'd enough*
These long seven years, on mountain and in cleugh.
So instantly caus'd him with other four,
Be shot to death upon Kirkconnel muir.
So thus did end the lives of these brave saints,
For their adhering to the covenants.

Upon the grave stone lying on the corps of Robert Stewart,
son to Major Robert Stewart of Ardoch, and John Gri-
erson, who were murdered by Graham of Claverhouse, at
the water of Dee, in Galloway, anno 1684.

BEHOLD! behold! A stone here's fore'd to cry,
Come see two martyrs, under me that ly,
At water of Dee, who slain were by the hand
Of cruel Claverhouse and's bloody band.
No sooner had he done this horrid thing,
But's forc'd to say, *Stewart's soul in heaven doth sing.*
Yet strange, his rage pursu'd ev'n such when dead,
And in the tombs of their ancestors laid;
Causing their corps be rais'd out of the same,
Discharging in Church-yard to bury them.
All this they did, because they would not abjure,
Our covenants and reformation pure;
Because like faithful martyrs for to die
They rather chus'd than treacherously comply
With cursed Prelacy, the nation's bane,
And with indulgency, our church's stain.
Perjur'd intelligencers were so rife,
Show'd their curs'd loyalty, to take their life.

Upon a grave stone lying on the corps of William Hunter
and Robert Smith, who were sentenced and hanged at
Kirkcudbright, anno 1684, by captain Douglas, Graham
of Claverhouse, and captain Bruce.

THIS monument shall show posterity,
Two headless martyrs under it do ly,
By bloody Graham were taken and surpriz'd,
Brought to this town, and afterwards were 'fix'd;

By unjust law were sentenced to die,
Them first they hang'd, then headed cruelly.
Captain Douglas, Bruce, Graham of Claverhouse,
Were these that caused them be handled thus:
And when they were unto the gibbet come,
To stop their speech, they did beat up the drum,
And all because that they would not comply
With indulgence and bloody Prelacy.
In face of cruel Bruce, Douglas and Graham,
They did maintain, *That Christ was Lord supreme;*
And boldly owned both the covenants:
At Kirkcudbright thus ended these two saints.

Upon a stone in the church yard of Balmaclellan, on the body of Robert Grierson, who was slain by command of colonel James Douglas at Inglistoun in the parish of Glencairn, 1685.

THIS monument to passengers shall cry,
   That godly Grierson under it doth ly,
Betray'd by knavish Watson to his foes,
Which made this martyr's days by murder close.
If ye would know the nature of his crime,
Then read the story of that killing time,
When Babel's brats with hellish plot conceal'd,
Design'd to make our south their hunting-field.
Here one of five at once were laid in dust,
To gratify Rome's execrable lust.
If carabins with molten bullets could
Have reach'd their souls, these mighty Nimrods would
Them have cut off; for there could no request
Three minutes get, to pray for future rest.

BESIDES these mottos in verse, there are in the stewarty of Kirkcudbright in Galloway, several other monuments both in church yards and open fields, the mottos whereof are in prose, intimating, That they died for their adherence to the covenants and work of reformation. Namely, in the churchyard of Kircudbright, upon the corps of John Hallum, who was wounded in taking, and sentenced by Captain Douglas to be hanged, in the year 1685. In the church-yard of Borgue, upon the body of Robert Macquhae shot to death in that parish by the said captain Douglas Anno 1685. In the church-

EPITAPHS.

yard of Girthon, upon the body of Robert Lenox sometime in Irlintoun, shot by the laird of Lagg, Anno 1685. In the same parish, in the muir of Auchencloy, upon the body of Robert Ferguson, shot by Graham of Claverhouse in that place, Anno 1684. In the parish of Tongland in Kirkonnel hill, upon the body of James Clement, shot to death there by the laird of Lagg, Anno 1685. In the church-yard of Balmaghie, upon the body of George Short, shot by the same laird of Lagg, Anno 1685. In the church-yard of Kells, upon the corps of Adam Mac-Quham, who being sick of a fever, was brought from his own house to Newtoun of Galloway, and next day shot dead by comand of lieutenant general Douglas, brother to the duke of Queensberry, 1685. Item, upon the corps of William Graham, who was shot while making his escape from his mother's house, by a party of Claverhouse's troop, Anno 1682.

Upon a stone in the church-yard of Air, lying on the bodies of James Smith, Alexander MacMillan, James MacMillan, George MacCartney, John Short, John Graham and John Muirhead, who suffered martyrdom at Air, December 27. 1666.

HERE ly seven martyrs for our covenants,
A sacred number of triumphant saints.
Pontius MacAdam th' unjust sentence past;
What is his own the world shall know at last.
And Herod Drummond caus'd their heads affix;
Heav'n keeps a record of the sixty-six.
Boots, thumbkins, gibbets, were in fashion then;
Lord, let us never see such days again.

Upon a stone lying beside the gallows of Air, upon the body of Andrew MacGill, who was apprehended by the information of Andrew Tom, and suffered there, November 1684.

NEAR this abhorred tree a sufferer lies,
Who chus'd to fall, that falling truth might rise.
His station could advance no costly deed,
Save giving of a life the Lord did need.
When Christ shall vindicate his way, he'll cast
The doom which was pronounc'd in such a haste,
And incorruption shall forget disgrace,
Design'd by the interment in this place.

Upon the stone at Machline, lying on the bodies of Peter Gillies, John Bryce, Thomas Young, William Fiddison, and John Bruning, who were apprehended and hanged up there without trial, Anno 1685.

BLOODY Dumbarton, Douglas and Dundee,
Mov'd by the devil and the laird of Lee,
Dragg'd thefe five men to death with gun and fword,
Not fuffering them to pray, nor read God's word.
Owning the work of God was all their crime,
The eighty five was a faint killing time.

Upon the tomb stone at Irvine, lying on the bodies of James Blackwood and John M'Coul, who fuffered there December 31. 1666.

THESE honeft countrymen, whofe bones here ly,
A victim fell to Prelates cruelty;
Condemn'd by bloody and unrighteous laws,
They died martyrs for the good old caufe,
Which Balaam's wicked race in vain affail;
For no inchantments 'gainft Ifrael prevail.
Life and this evil world they did contemn,
And dy'd for Chrift, who died firft for them.

Upon a stone at Kilmarnock, lying on the heads of John Rofs and John Shields, who fuffered at Edinburgh, the 27th of December, 1666, and had their heads fet up at Kilmarnock.

OUR perfecutors mad with wrath and ire;
In Edinburgh members fome do ly, fome here;
Yet inftantly united they fhall be,
And witnefs 'gainft this nation's perjury.

Upon another stone at Kilmarnock, lying upon the corps of John Nisbet, who fuffered there the 14th of April, 1683.

COME, reader, fee, here pleafant Nifbet lies,
His blood doth pierce the high and lofty fkies;
Kilmarnock did his latter hour perceive,
And Chrift his foul to heaven did receive.
Yet bloody Torrence did his body raife,
And buried it into another place;
Saying, *Shall rebels ly in graves with me?*
We'll bury him where evil-doers be.

Upon a grave stone at Fixnick, lying on the dust of John Fergushill and George Woodburn, who were shot to death by Nisbet and his party, Anno 1685.

WHEN bloody Prelates, once this nation's pest,
Contriv'd that curs'd self-contradicting test;
These men for Christ did suffer martyrdom,
And here their blood lies waiting till he come.

Upon another grave stone there, lying on the corps of Peter Gemmel, who was shot to death by the same Nisbet and his party, Anno 1685.

THIS man, like holy Anchorites of old,
For conscience sake, was thurst from house and hold,
Blood-thirsty red coats cut his prayers short,
And ev'n his dying groans were made their sport.
Ah Scotland! breach of solemn vows repent;
Or bloody crimes will bring thy punishment.

Upon a third stone, lying on the body of James White, shot by Peter Ingles and his party, 1685.

THIS martyr was by Peter Ingles shot,
By birth a tyger rather than a Scot;
Who, that his monstrous extract might be seen,
Cut off his head, and kick'd it o'er the green.
Thus was that head, which was to wear a crown,
A foot ball made by a profane dragoon.

Upon a stone in the church-yard of Wigtoun, on the body of Margaret Wilson, who was drowned in the water of Blednoch, upon the 11th *of May* 1684, *by the laird of Lagg,* &c.

LET earth and stone still witness bear,
There lies a virgin martyr here,
Murder'd for owning Christ supreme,
Head of his church, and no more crime,
But her not owning Prelacy,
And not abjuring Presbytery.
Within the sea, ty'd to a stake,
She suffered for Christ Jesus' sake,
The actors of this cruel crime
Was Lagg, Winram, Strachan and Graham,

Neither young years, nor yet old age,
Could quench the fury of their rage.

Upon a stone in the church-yard of Colmonel, on the body of Matthew Meiklewrath, who was killed in that parish by Claverhouse.

IN this parish of Colmonel,
  By bloody Claverhouse I fell,
Who did command that I should die,
For owning covenanted Presbytery.
My blood a witness still doth stand,
'Gainst all defections in this land.

Upon a stone in the church-yard of Stratoun, on the body of Thomas M'Haffie, who was taken out of his bed, being sick of a fever, and shot by Captain Bruce in that parish, 1685.

THOUGH I was sick and like to die,
  Yet bloody Bruce did murder me;
Because I adhered in my station
To our covenanted reformation.
My blood for vengeance yet doth call,
Upon Zion's haters all.

Upon a stone in the church-yard of Tweed's-muir, lying on the body of John Hunter, who was shot at Corehead, by Colonel James Douglas, 1675.

WHEN Zion's King was robbed of his right,
  His witnesses in Scotland put to flight,
When Papists, Prelates, and indulgency,
Combin'd 'gainst Christ to ruin Presbytry,
All who would not unto these idols bow,
They sought them out, and whom they found they slew.
For owning of Christ's cause I then did die,
My blood for vengeance on his enemies doth cry.

Upon the grave stone of Thomas Burn, James Wood, Andrew Sword, John Waddel, and John Clyd, who suffered martyrdom at Magus-muir, November 25th, 1689, and ly buried in a corn field near Magus-muir, is this inscription.

'CAUSE we at Bothwel did appear,
  Perjurious oaths refus'd to swear;

EPITAPHS.

'Cause we Christ's cause would not condemn,
We were sentenc'd to death by men,
Who rag'd against us in such fury,
Our dead bodies they did not bury;
But up on poles, did hing us high,
Triumphs of Babel's victory.
Our lives we fear'd not to the death,
But constant prov'd to the last breath.

When the grave-stone was set up in October 1728, the chains were taken out of their graves, and some of their bones and cloaths were found unconsumed, now 47 years after their death.

Upon the grave stone of Andrew Gulline, who suffered at the Gallowlee of Edinburgh, July 20, 1683, and afterwards was hung upon a pole in Magus-muir, and lieth buried in the Long-cross of Clermont, near Magus-muir, is this inscription.

A Faithful martyr here doth ly,
A Witness against perjury;
Who cruelly was put to death,
To gratify proud Prelates wrath;
They cut his hands ere he was dead,
And after that struck off his head.
To Magus-muir then did him bring,
His body on a pole did hing.
His blood under the altar cries,
For vengeance on Christ's enemies.

Monumental Inscription on a grave stone at Rullion Green, Pentland-hills.

Here, and near to this place, lies the reverend Mr. John Crookshanks, and Mr. Andrew M'Cormock, ministers of the gospel, and about fifty other true covenanted Presbyterians, who were killed in this place, in their own innocent self-defence, and defence of the covenanted work of reformation, by Thomas Dalziel of Binns, upon the 28th of November 1666. Rev. xii. 11. Erected September 28, 1738.

On the opposite side of the stone is the following verse.

A CLOUD of witnesses ly here,
  Who for Christ's interest did appear,
For to restore true liberty,
O'erturned then by tyranny;
And by proud Prelates, who did rage
Against the Lord's own heritage;
They sacrific'd were for the laws
Of Christ their King, his noble cause.
These heroes fought with great renown,
By falling got the martyrs crown.

Upon the grave-stone of John Murchie, and Daniel Meiklewrath, near the Cross-water of Dusk, in Colmonel parish.

HERE in this place two martyrs ly,
  Whose blood to heav'n hath a loud cry;
Murder'd contrary to divine laws,
For owning of King Jesus' cause,
By bloody Drummond they were shot,
Without any trial, near this spot.

Upon the grave-stone of James Smith, in Muir-kirk church-yard.

WHEN proud apostates did abjure,
  Scotland's reformation pure,
And fill'd this land with perjury,
And all sorts of iniquity.
Such as would not with them comply,
They persecute with hue and cry.
I in the chase was overta'en,
And for the truth by them was slain.

Upon the grave-stone of John Law, in a kail-yard of New-milns.

'CAUSE I Christ's prisoners reliev'd,
  I of my life was soon bereav'd,
By cruel enemies with rage,
In that rencounter did engage,
The martyr's honour and his crown,
Bestow'd on me, O high renown!

That I should not only believe,
But for Christ's cause my life should give.

Upon the grave-stone of William Dingwal, in the church-yard of Straven.

THIS hero brave who here doth ly
Was persecute by tyranny,
Yet to the truth he firmly stood,
'Gainst foes, resisting unto blood.
Himself and th' gospel did defend,
Till for Christ's cause his life did end.

Upon the grave-stone of James Thomson, in Stenhouse church-yard.

THIS hero brave who doth ly here,
In truth's defence he did appear,
And to Christ's cause he firmly stood,
Until he seal'd it with his blood.
With sword in hand upon the field,
He lost his life, yet did not yield.
His days did end in great renown,
And he obtain'd the martyr's crown.

The famous Mr. Samuel Rutherford, who was cited before that parliament, who rescinded the covenanted work of reformation, to appear before them, when he was in a dying condition; being soon after that called to answer at that tribunal, where his Judge was his friend: tho' he did not actually suffer martyrdom, being called home to the joy of his Lord, before his persecutors got their wicked devices put in execution against him; yet since he was a martyr both in his enemies design and his own resolution, the epitaph upon his grave-stone, done above 74 years after he died, by a true lover of his memory, and owner of the honourable covenanted cause, which he faithfully contended and suffered for, deserveth room here among martyrs epitaphs.

An epitaph upon the grave-stone of the reverend, godly and learned Mr. Samuel Rutherford, minister of the gospel, and professor of divinity in St. Andrews, who died February 20. 1661. and lies buried in the church-yard of St. Andrews.

WHAT tongue, what pen, or skill of men,
 Can famous Rutherford commend?
His learning justly rais'd his fame;
True godliness adorn'd his name.
He did converse with things above,
Acquainted with Emmanuel's love.
Most orthodox he was and found,
And many errors did confound.
For Zion's King and Zion's cause,
And Scotland's covenanted laws;
Most constantly he did contend,
Until his time was at an end,
That he wan to the full fruition
Of that which he had seen in vision.

October 9th, 1735. By W. W.

An epitaph upon the grave stone of the reverend and pious Mr. John Welwood, who (after he had endured a great fight of affliction and persecution) died at Perth, April 1679, and lies buried in the church-yard of Avon.

HERE lies a follower of the Lamb,
 Thro' many tribulations came;
For long time of his christian race,
Was persecute from place to place.
A Scottish prophet here behold,
Judgment and mercy who foretold:
The gospel banner did display,
Condemn'd the sins of that sad day,
And valiantly for truth contended,
Until by death his days were ended.

THE END.

AN INDEX

To the foregoing

SPEECHES.

	Page
THE laſt ſpeech and teſtimony of Mr. Donald Cargil	34
A letter of his to Mr. James Skeen	39
A letter of his to ſome friends before he went abroad	41
A letter of his to John Malcolm and Archibald Aliſon	42
A letter of his to the priſoners in the correction-houſe	46
The teſtimony of Mr. Walter Smith	53
His laſt words on the ſcaffold	56
The laſt teſtimony of Mr. James Boig	59
David Hackſtoun of Rathillet his interrogations	61
A letter of his to a chriſtian friend	64
A letter to a gentlewoman of his acquaintance	73
A third letter, and a letter to his ſiſter	76 and 78
The teſtimony of Archibald Aliſon	78
The teſtimony of John Malcolm	85
The teſtimony of Mr. James Skeen	96 and 106
His letter to the profeſſors in the ſhire of Aberdeen	100
Two letters to his fellow priſoner N.	104
The teſtimony of Archibald Stewart	112
The teſtimony of John Potter	117
The interrogations of Iſabel Aliſon	129
Her dying teſtimony	134
The teſtimony of Marion Harvie	138
The teſtimony of William Gouger, Robert Sangſter, and Chriſtopher Miller	149
The teſtimony of Laurence Hay	161
The teſtimony of Andrew Pittilloch	167
The teſtimony of William Thomſon	174
The teſtimony of William Cuthil	179
The teſtimony of Robert Garnock	189

	Page
The testimony of Patrick Forman	195
The testimony of David Farrie	201
The testimony of James Stewart	209
A relation concerning Alexander Russel	217
The interrogations with a letter of Robert Gray's	ib.
His testimony and his last words on the scaffold	219 and 226
The interrogations of James Robertson	228
His testimony	229
The testimony of John Finlay	246
The testimony of William Cochran	255
The testimony of Andrew Guiline	259
The testimony of John Cochran	262
A relation concerning Arthur Bruce and John Whitelaw	263
A letter from John Wharry	264
A letter from James Smith	266
Interrogations of John Nisbet younger	268
The testimony of John Nisbet younger	269
Answers by John Wilson writer in Lanerk, before seven or eight of the council, with his answers before the council	269
Reasons of his answers, and reflections thereupon	282
His reasons against supplicating the council for a reprieve	285
His testimony	286
The testimony of George Martin	295
The testimony of John Main	300
A relation concerning John Gilry	ib.
A relation concerning John Richmond, Archbald Stewart, James Winning and James Johnstoun	308
A letter of Archibald Stewart's	310
The testimony of Captain John Patoun	314
The testimony of James Nisbet	318
The testimony of Arthur Taket	327
The testimony of Thomas Robertson	332
Interrogations of James Nicol	335
A relation concerning Mr. John Dick	343
The joint testimony of Thomas Harkness, Andrew Clark, Samuel M'Euen	344
The joint testimony of James Lawson and Alexander Wood	346
The interrogations of George Jackson	349

A relation concerning William Keagow, John
   Semple and John Wat   352
A letter of John Semple's   353
The teſtimony of James Graham   355
The teſtimony of Robert Pollock   358
The teſtimony of Robert Millar   361
A relation concerning Margaret Lauchlane and
   Margaret Wilſon   367
The teſtimony of Thomas Stoddart   368
A relation concerning Matthew Brice and James
   Wilkie   371
The teſtimony of Edward Marſhall   372
A relation concerning John Niſbet of Hardhill   373
His teſtimony   375
The laſt teſtimony and dying words of Mr. James
   Renwick   391
A ſhort relation concerning Mr. Richard Cameron   398
The paper at Airſmoſs   401
A relation of ſome remarkable paſſages in the life
   of Mr. Donald Cargil   402
Form of the excommunication at Torwood   409
A relation of the perſecution and death of Henry
   Hall   412
An abſtract of the Queens-ferry Paper   415
A liſt of the baniſhed   419
Account of thoſe who were murdered without pro-
   ceſs of law   424
A ſhort hint of the oppreſſive fines and exactions   429
The epitaphs upon the tomb-ſtones of the martyrs   432

www.ingramcontent.com/pod-product-compliance
Lightning Source LLC
Chambersburg PA
CBHW032007300426
44117CB00008B/936